Professors, Politics and Pop

THE HAYMARKET SERIES

Editors: Mike Davis and Michael Sprinker

The Haymarket Series offers original studies in politics, history and culture, with a focus on North America. Representing views across the American left on a wide range of subjects, the series will be of interest to socialists both in the USA and throughout the world. A century after the first May Day, the American left remains in the shadow of those martyrs whom the Haymarket Series honours and commemorates. These studies testify to the living legacy of political activism and commitment for which they gave their lives.

Professors, Politics and Pop

JON WIENER

VERSO

London · New York

First published by Verso 1991
© Jon Wiener 1991
All right reserved

Verso
UK: 6 Meard Street, London W1V 3HR
USA: 29 West 35th Street, New York, NY 10001–2291

Verso is the imprint of New Left Books

British Library Cataloguing in Publication Data
Wiener, Jon
Professors, politics and pop. –
(The Haymarket series)
I. Title   II. Series
306

ISBN 0-86091-356-2

Library of Congress Cataloging-in-Publication Data
Wiener, Jon.
Professors, politics, and pop / Jon Wiener.
p.   cm. — (The Haymarket series)
Includes index.
ISBN 0-86091-356-2
1. United States—Intellectual life—20th century. 2. Politics
and culture—United States—History—20th century. 3. Education,
Higher—United States—1965–   I. Title.   II. Series.
E169.12.W49   1991
973.92—dc20

Typeset in Baskerville by Leaper & Gard Ltd, Bristol
Printed in USA by Courier Companies Inc.

for my parents,
Gladys Spratt
and
Daniel Wiener

Contents

CONTENTS

Acknowledgments

Grateful acknowledgement is made to the following publications for permission to reprint previously published material, some of which appears in this book in a slightly different form: "Rockin' with Ron: Springsteen and Regan" (originally titled "Rockin' with Ron"), "A Soft Rain: *Dylan*" (originally titled "A Soft Rain"), © *The Nation* magazine/ The Nation Company, Inc., 1984; "The Sears Case: Women's History on Trial," "Footnotes to History: the David Abraham Case," © *The Nation* magazine/The Nation Company, Inc., 1985; "Accuracy in Academia: Reed Irvine Rides the Paper Tiger," "History Wars: Why the Right is Losing in Academe," "Tom Hayden's New Workout," "Divestment Report Card: Students, Stocks and Shanties," © *The Nation* magazine/The Nation Company, Inc., 1986; "School for Spooks: Yale and the CIA," "The Odyssey of Daniel Boorstin," "Poles, Jews, and Historians: the Case of Norman Davies," (originally titled "The Case of Norman Davies: When Historians Judge Their Own"), "The CIA Goes Back to College," "The Other Nancy Davis: Not Necessarily the First Lady," © *The Nation* magazine/The Nation Company, Inc., 1987; "Deconstructing de Man," "Campus Voices, Right and Left," "Looking Back, Moving Ahead: Students Today and the Sixties," © *The Nation* magazine/The Nation Company, Inc., 1988; "Debating de Man," "Campus Capitalism: Harvard Chases Biotech Bucks," "Bringing Nazi Sympathizers to the US: Talcott Parsons' Role," "Law Profs Fight the Power," "Racial Hatred on Campus," © *The Nation* magazine/The Nation Company, Inc., 1989; "Free Speech for Campus Bigots?", "Freshman Activists," "Dollars for Neocon Scholars: the Olin Money Tree," "Inside the Nixon Liebrary,"

Preface

For a long time I wanted to write for *The Nation*. I first met Victor Navasky in 1980 when I interviewed him for KPFK radio in Los Angeles about *Naming Names*. But it wasn't until 1984, when I pitched a story to him about Ronald Reagan quoting Bruce Springsteen, that I got into print: "Rockin' with Ron" ran that October. Since then I have learned what a smart and generous person Victor is—a great writer and historian, an inspired story-teller, a gifted editor, and the best lunch partner a writer could want.

The earliest of these pieces appeared in *Dissent* in the mid seventies and were edited by Michael Walzer, who provided my first example of a professor who thrived while writing a lot for political journals. Careful readers will note that three pieces here were published originally in *The New Republic*, which is—shall we say—unusual these days for those on the masthead of *The Nation*. The strange thing is that each of these pieces was first rejected by *The Nation* ("John Lennon versus the FBI," "Beatles Buy-out," and "When Old Blue Eyes was 'Red'.") Maybe *The Nation* editors were right, but these three are among my favorites, and I thank *The New Republic* editors who put so much work into them: Rick Hertzberg, Dorothy Wickenden, and Michael Kinsley. Marty Peretz and I disagree about the obvious things, but he urged me to write "John Lennon versus the FBI," and then put it on the cover, for which I am immensely grateful.

Some wonderful editors worked hard to make these pieces better: at the *Village Voice*, Ellen Willis and Maria Margaronis; at *The Nation*, Elsa Dixler, a good friend with flawless judgment; Elizabeth Pochoda, who asked me to write about de Man, thus getting me into lots of trouble; Richard Pollak, Richard Lingeman, Micah Sifrey, and of course Victor Navasky. David Thelen put immense effort into editing "Radical Historians"—he solicited comments from more than a dozen pre-publication readers, which must make this the most rewritten article in history.

Special thanks to Chris Stansell, who first told me about the Sears case; to Jean-Christophe Agnew, who through a bizarre series of events caught a lot of the flak directed at me for my David Abraham article; and to Mark Poster, for his advice on the de Man pieces, not all of which I took. For good talk and good arguments about various issues raised in these pieces, thanks to Perry Anderson, Bob Brenner, Willie Forbath, Eric Foner, Barbara Herman, Mike Johnson, Mickey Morgan, Spence Olin, Bob Scheer, Ron Steel, and Sean Wilentz.

This book was Mike Davis's idea; I'm especially grateful to him for his enthusiasm and commitment, and to Michael Sprinker and Colin Robinson for all their help with the editing. Bill Billingsley and Kathleen Kennedy provided immense help as research assistants.

My best editor is Judy Fiskin, who worked on virtually every one of these pieces: tough and fearless, clear-eyed and fair-minded, smart and funny, with a keen eye for the awkward sentence and the vague argument. I rely on her completely.

PART I

The Academic Battleground

1

Deconstructing de Man

Scandal erupted in 1988 in the school of literary criticism known as deconstruction, centering on revelations that Paul de Man, the Yale professor who initiated the school in America, wrote more than one hundred articles for anti-Semitic, pro-Nazi newspapers in Belgium during Word War Two. The controversy generated a great deal of comment about both the author and the politics of deconstruction. De Man, a distinguished professor who died in 1983 at the age of sixty-four, had concealed his political past from colleagues and students, who were shocked and dismayed at the revelations. After his past was brought to light de Man became something of an academic Waldheim.

In one of the articles in question, "Jews in Contemporary Literature," which appeared in March 1941, de Man examined the argument that "the Jews" had "polluted" modern literature. The article argued that "our civilization" had remained healthy by resisting "the Semitic infiltration of all aspects of European life." It endorsed sending the Jews of Europe to a colony "isolated from Europe" as "a solution to the Jewish problem."[1]

De Man's defenders acknowledged the seriousness of the revelations, but argued that the content of his collaborationist articles has been distorted. Neil Hertz, a teacher of literature at Johns Hopkins

---

1. See Paul de Man, *Wartime Journalism, 1939–1943*, edited by Werner Hamacher, Neil Hertz, and Thomas Keenan (Lincoln: University of Nebraska Press, 1988), for a complete edition of de Man's collaborationist writings. "Les Juifs dans la littérature actuelle" appears on p. 45.

University, pointed out that, of the ninety-two articles de Man is known to have published in the collaborationist Belgian newspaper *Le Soir*, only two were explicitly anti-Semitic. However, Jeffrey Mehlman of Boston University, a practitioner of deconstruction as well as the author of an influential book on anti-Semitism in French literature, explained that the rest included explicit calls for collaboration and numerous book reviews that "plugged the Nazi hit parade." An article of de Man's titled "Testimony on the War in France," published in March 1941, concluded that "no abyss separates the two peoples (French and German). When a common task is presented, their agreement has been perfect. That is the principal teaching to be drawn from this beautiful book." The author of the book in question, Benoist-Méchin, later proposed that the French take up arms against the British and Americans. De Man's other wartime articles included references to Hitler's war as "the current revolution" and a statement that "the necessity of immediate collaboration should be obvious to every objective mind."

De Man, who came to the United States in 1947, successfully concealed his pro-Nazi past except for one or two incidents. In 1953, when he was a member of the prestigious Society of Fellows at Harvard, he was denounced, anonymously, perhaps by his ex-wife, as a former collaborator; Harvard asked him for a response. De Man then told a few friends, and apparently Harvard as well, that the charge was false and that he had in fact been a member of the Belgian resistance. The friends, who have asked not to be identified, accepted his response; at least one of them subsequenty described that response as "a lie." De Man clearly told other people different things about his past. Juliet MacCannell was a student of his at Cornell in the mid 1960s; she now teaches comparative literature at the University of California, Irvine: "I asked him what he did during the war. He said, 'I went to England and worked as a translator.'" There was also the matter of de Man's relationship to the German literary critic Hans Robert Jauss. He wrote about Jauss in *Blindness and Insight* and brought Jauss to Yale as a guest lecturer in the mid 1970s; Jauss is now known to have served in the SS.

The debate over the collaborationist writings has become part of a wider questioning of the politics of deconstruction. J. Hillis Miller of the University of California, Irvine, the leading deconstructionist in the

United States and a friend of de Man, complained that journalists have defined deconstruction incorrectly, but he balked at providing a definition. He has referred those who want to know what he thinks deconstruction is to his book, *The Ethics of Reading*. Edward Said, professor of English and comparative literature at Columbia University, author of *The World, the Text, and the Critic* and a critic of deconstruction, provided a definition: Deconstruction is "a form of commentary that shows the connection between the stated content of a piece of writing and the rhetorical system which controls it. The connection establishes a discrepancy between the content and the rhetorical system. The deconstructive reading establishes the range of possible meanings that are thereby generated. In the range of decidable meanings, the deconstructed meaning locates itself." "The deconstructionists won't accept that," he adds. "Their whole point is that their positions are not paraphrasable."

Deconstruction claims that not only are books "texts," but that everything is at some level a text and thus "undecidable." De Man wrote that this is true even of the texts that "masquerade in the guise of wars or revolutions." ("Tell that to the veterans of foreign texts," a Yale historian remarked.) Critics on the left have argued that the presuppositions of deconstruction—that literature is not part of a knowable social and political reality, that one must be resigned to the impossibility of truth—make it at worst nihilistic or implicitly authoritarian and at best an academic self-indulgence.

Whatever the current reservations about it, de Man's work had a tremendous appeal, especially for students in the 1960s and 1970s. Even more than the New Criticism had, it freed literature from context and history, opening it to complex new meanings in a way that was fertile, inventive and playful. His work engaged the best of twentieth-century philosophy. At the same time he made criticism *the* creative activity of the period; the novel might have been dead, but criticism had become the inheritor of the ambitions of art. The critic could create meaning. And de Man's writing was brilliant. Deborah Esch, an English teacher at the University of Toronto, who was a student of de Man's from 1979 to 1983, said, "de Man provided his students with a set of tools for reading, the most important function of which may be the unmasking of ideology. What we call ideology, he showed, entails taking a linguistic construct for a natural reality. This questioning of the authority of language yielded the most subversive pedagogy I know."

To those who would read de Man's mature work with an eye to his youthful publications, Hillis Miller responded, "I see no connection between de Man's collaborationist writings and deconstruction." But not everyone agrees. Mehlman has pointed to de Man's chapter on Rousseau's *Confessions* in *Allegories of Reading*. There de Man writes that "it is always possible" to "excuse any guilt" because "the experience always exists simultaneously as fictional discourse and as empirical event and it is never possible to decide which one of the two possibilities is the right one. The indecision makes it possible to excuse the bleakest of crimes." Is it possible to read this now without thinking of de Man's collaboration?

De Man's discussion of forgetting in his classic essay "Literary History and Literary Modernity" from *Blindness and Insight* is full of references to a hidden past. He discusses Nietzsche's conception of "a past that ... is so threatening that it had to be forgotten." He quotes Nietzsche's observation that we undertake "the destruction and dissolution of the past in order to be able to live," we "try to give ourselves a new past from which we should have liked to descend." But for Nietzsche, de Man writes, "the rejection of the past is not so much an act of forgetting as an act of critical judgment directed against himself." Frank Lentricchia, a teacher at Duke University, argued in his book *Criticism and Social Change* that this chapter of de Man's "shades into political allegory." That was a prescient argument. De Man persistently emphasized the significance of allegory. He argued that what makes allegories interesting is that they are haunted by a meaning that has come before.

De Man's critique of history is also relevant. He goes beyond the useful post-structuralist point that facts about the past are structured like texts; Lentricchia wrote that de Man "is saying that history is an imitation of what he has defined as the literary," a "projection ... of all those paralytic feelings of the literary onto the terrain of society and history." This argument leads to passivity, which, according to Lentricchia, is "the most genuine meaning of political conservatism," and that is the message of de Manian deconstruction in the United States. According to Anson Rabinbach, an intellectual historian at Cooper Union, the young de Man became a Fascist the way many intellectuals did in Europe in 1940: "They had a sense of malaise, of having been defeated by history." They turned to Fascism, hoping that it would provide a route to cultural renewal, but eventually abandoned it. The connection between de Man's early and mature writings, Rabinbach argued, "is not in their content, which is quite different; it is in the attitude of exhaustion in the face of politics, the feeling of despair at the possibilities that history offers."

However, Gerald Graff, of Northwestern University, author of *Literature Against Itself* and *Professing Literature*, has been much more cautious in his approach to the connection between de Man's early writing and deconstruction. He observed that "people who adopt deconstructionist positions have various sorts of politics—including radical feminism and other progressive commitments—so an attempt to smear all de Manian deconstruction with de Man's past in unfair." But, Graff went on, "there is an irony here, since deconstructionists have a problem appealing to what politicians call 'deniability.' One of the themes of deconstruction is that the position you try to separate yourself from tends to reappear as a repressed motif in your own text." Graff suggested that an episode like this one "may make some theorists think twice about claiming that the reality of historical events is indeterminate, and that insisting on this indeterminacy is politically subversive." Graff also thought it important to emphasize that the overall effect of the trend toward theory, including deconstruction, "has been an overwhelmingly democratic and progressive force which has raised central questions about the politics of language and culture which orthodox literary study still resists."

Whatever one makes of the politics of deconstruction, both followers and critics of Paul de Man will have to examine his past more thoroughly. In particular they will have to ask: what could de Man have known about the fate of European Jews, and when could he have known it? De Man's collaborationist articles appeared in 1941 and 1942. Raoul Hilberg, a Holocaust historian at the University of Vermont, was quoted in the *New York Times* as saying that educated Belgians like de Man "knew by 1941 or at the latest, 1942, that Jews were being sent eastward to be exterminated." That is wrong, according to Arno Mayer, a Princeton historian and author of a book on the "final solution." "'Auschwitz' is not likely to have had any concrete meaning in Belgium in 1942. No one had a clear picture of the fate of even Poland's Jews before Germany's attack on Russia in June 1941."

The first train of Belgian Jews left Malines, near Brussels, on August 4, 1942, and arrived at Auschwitz the next day. It contained 998 people, of whom 428 were women, 80 were young boys and 60 girls. According to Maxime Steinberg's book *Dossier Bruxelles-Auschwitz*, 254 were gassed on arrival. These deportations were pubic information; the collaborationist Belgian newspaper *Défense du Peuple* wrote on August 8, 1942, "The Jews are being forced to work the way we do. They are charging others with assassinating them because they are being asked to work. Reserve your pity for the members of your own race suffering from this Jewish war." De Man must have been aware of this.

But "at that time it wasn't clear what it meant for Jews to be sent to the east," Mayer said. The Nazis demanded that all the occupied countries provide manpower for compulsory labor service in Germany. As a result, Mayer said, the deportation of Jews, especially in 1942, "seemed less aberrant; it desensitized the population to the Jews' fate." The last of the de Man pieces which have been discovered is dated October 20, 1942. If he stopped his pro-Nazi writings at this point— which is not yet certain—his last collaborationist article appeared before he could have known of the extermination of the Jews. Nevertheless, one can assume that the young journalist who endorsed sending Europe's Jews to a colony "isolated from Europe" as "a solution to the Jewish problem" did not find the deportations of 1942 objectionable.

And there was plenty going on that de Man did know about: Belgium's first anti-Jewish law was passed in October 1940; it required that Jews register with the government and expelled them from the professions of law, teaching, journalism and government service. De Man's article on whether Jews "pollute" modern fiction appeared five months later. On May 31, 1941, Belgian Jews were forced to sell their businesses; in August 1941 they were restricted to four cities and subjected to a curfew. De Man certainly knew all that. Yet in December 1941, he published an article praising Drieu la Rochelle, a leading collaborator, for "the elan and conviction with which [he] has thrown himself into the creation of a radically new type of human being." As of June 1, 1942, Belgian Jews were required to wear the yellow star. Hendrik de Man, Paul's uncle, a former Socialist leader who had joined the collaborationist government, changed his mind about his affiliation and fled from Belgium in 1941; yet Paul remained and he continued to publish, at least until October 1942.

"Anyone who thinks that he left this all behind him, that it did not motivate the life and career that followed, is crazy," Lentricchia said. "He came here in 1947 at age twenty-eight with a Belgian wife and son; he divorced his wife when he got here, and didn't speak to his son ever again. The man tried very hard to separate himself from his Belgian collaborationist past, to cut that thing out of himself. I think he suffered, he wished he never did it. He didn't start graduate school until 1952, when he was thirty-three. What was he doing before that? Working in a book-store, working for a publisher—a brilliant man, prepared for a literary career, who does nothing for several years. Why?

"Then you come to deconstruction: a philosophy that says you can never trust language to anchor you into anything; that every linguistic act is duplicitous; that every insight you have is beset by blindness you can't predict. In an attempt to undercut politically engaged critics, de Man writes that whatever you thought about political events is not the case. His mature work is not just ahistorical; it is a principled, intentional, passionate antihistoricism. He didn't just say 'forget history'; he wanted to paralyze the move to history. And the work is beautifully rigorous. There's not a better example in the world."

Colleagues and students admired de Man not only for his scholarship but because he "was exemplary in his relations with people," Hertz said. "You used him as a standard for your own conduct. He was something special." Lentricchia disagreed: "The real problem of the de Manians is hero worship—the spectacle of grown men and women idolizing another person. That is O.K. for fourteen-year-olds, but not for adults. And it's very bad to communicate this hero worship to students. It's politically ugly. Students need independence, scrutiny, self-reliance."

De Man's defenders argue that they should get credit for making his pro-Nazi writings public. The collaborationist articles were discovered in the summer of 1987 by a Belgian graduate student, Ortwin de Graef. In late October 1987, Jacques Derrida, the renowned French philosopher and literary theorist who founded deconstruction, brought copies to the United States to a meeting of deconstructionists. At this conference—held in Tuscaloosa, Alabama, in late October and attended by some twenty persons—they discussed how to handle the material. Critics of the school describe this meeting as an exercise in "damage control."

The deconstructionists decided to publish de Man's pro-Nazi articles in a special issue of the *Oxford Literary Review* in April 1988, eight months after their discovery. The dozen articles of de Man's originally published in Flemish will appear in English, but the ninety-two articles in French will not be translated. "We feel that anyone interested in these materials ought to read them in the original," Hertz said. In fact, that will discourage anyone but experts from examining the documents or taking part in the debate. De Man's defenders were surprised when the *New York Times* published an article on the controversy in early December 1987, and were angered by the press coverage, which they regard as premature, misleading and inaccurate. "I don't think this is a matter for journalists and newspapers," said Werner Hamacher of Johns Hopkins University, an organizer of the special issue.

Although it has become routine to refer to de Man's "hundred collaborationist articles," neither the complete contents nor the total number of de Man's wartime writings are known at this time. De Graef found ninety-two appearing in *Le Soir* between February 1941 and June 1942; of those, only eighteen are being distributed by the deconstructionists. De Graef's list ends with a handwritten parenthetical note, "probably another twenty to thirty in the period July–December 1942." However, he now reports that June 1942 is the date of the last of the *Le Soir* articles. Other scholars working backward from October 1941 have found articles de Man published in *Le Soir* between January and July 1941; they have not yet examined 1940. (The Nazis conquered Belgium in May 1940.) The last of de Man's articles in the Flemish collaborationist journal *Het Vlaamsche Land* is dated October 20, 1942. The date at which de Man stopped writing pro-Nazi articles is extremely significant; all we know now is that he was writing in October 1942, and perhaps later.[2]

---

2. *Wartime Journalism* contains 170 articles from *Le Soir*, the last of which appeared in November 1942.

The publication of de Man's pro-Nazi articles will be accompanied by comments from critics; fifty have been invited to contribute, including both those who have previously supported his work and those who have criticized it. Some have refused to contribute; one critic who was very close to de Man but asked not to be identified, commented, "I am shocked that there is a symposium. Paul must have known the Jews of Belgium were being carted away. We are discussing the butchery of the Belgian Jewish community, down to the babies. To treat this as one more item about which to have a symposium is outrageous. The people who are organizing this have lost all moral perspective; they are so much under the sway of the man they cannot bear to consider what they are doing."

The de Man materials came to light not long after revelations about Martin Heidegger, the German philosopher acknowledged by Derrida as the intellectual progenitor of deconstruction. Heidegger's commitment to Nazism was much stronger than has previously been realized, according to a new book by Victor Farrias published in France. A reevaluation of the politics of deconstruction and the writings of de Man is now at the top of the agenda of both the deconstructionists and their critics.

The Nation, January 9, 1988

2

Debating de Man

The eagerly anticipated volume *Responses: On Paul de Man's Wartime Journalism* contains thirty-five essays by the late critic's defenders and critics.[1] The contributors fall into two groups: the textualists, who limit themselves to close readings of de Man's articles, and typically find ambiguities and arguments that they interpret as resisting the Nazis; and the historicists, who place de Man's work in its political context and conclude that his collaboration was deeper and more extensive than it initially appeared.

De Man's defenders could have limited themselves to a straightforward acknowledgment that his collaborationist articles were bad, but things could have been worse: He did not fight for the Nazis, few of his articles were explicitly anti-Semitic, and he stopped writing for the collaborationist press at the end of 1942 and never again expressed anything like a pro-Nazi sentiment. They could have argued that, since de Man's mature works are immensely valuable and significant, they outweigh the unacceptable things he did during World War Two. Unfortunately, virtually all the defenders go considerably beyond this line of reasoning.

The longest and most spectacular defense of de Man comes from Jacques Derrida, the French literary theorist whose name is synonymous with deconstruction. Derrida devotes his most energetic interpretive efforts to de Man's anti-Semitic article "The Jews in

---

1. *Responses: On Paul de Man's Wartime Journalism*, edited by Werner Hamacher, Neil Hertz, and Thomas Keenan (Lincoln: University of Nebraska Press, 1989).

Contemporary Literature," which begins with a critical remark about "vulgar anti-Semitism." Derrida declares that "to condemn 'vulgar anti-Semitism,' *especially if one makes no mention of the other kind,* is to condemn anti-Semitism itself." (Emphasis in original.) Other de Man defenders, including J. Hillis Miller of the University of California, Irvine, offer similar textualist interpretations of de Man's reference to "vulgar anti-Semitism."

The historicist interpretation of this phrase is presented by Alice Yaeger Kaplan of Duke University. De Man's rejection of "vulgar anti-Semitism," she argues, was part of the "micro-polemics among anti-Semites, polemics that divide anti-Semitic texts along class lines or 'taste' lines." *Le Soir*'s Léon van Huffel argued against what he called "social" anti-Semitism; the French anti-Semitic writer Brasillach argued against what he called "irrational" anti-Semitism, as exemplified by Céline. De Man's contribution to this debate, Kaplan says, was the argument that Jews haven't ruined Western literature "simply because they are mediocre.... [and] with the Jews gone, nothing will be lost." For Peggy Kamuf of the University of Southern California, the heart of "The Jews in Contemporary Literature" is not the reference to "vulgar anti-Semitism" but rather de Man's phrase "a solution to the Jewish problem." "The seeming equanimity with which this possibility is envisioned ... cannot be excused," she writes, because de Man's phrase contains "a terrible omen of the equanimity with which most of Europe's population would witness the racial 'purification' of the land." Although Kamuf is Derrida's translator, here she reads de Man's article by referring to its historical context.

John Brenkman of Northwestern University presents the strongest example of the historicist position. De Man, he argues, was "a fascist and an anti-Semite as well as an active collaborator with the Nazi occupation of Belgium." De Man did not confine himself to literary topics, as his defenders argue; instead he supported political initiatives of the Nazi occupation. For example, in an August 1941 review, de Man criticized those "who remain blinded by nationalist passions." Those who confine themselves to textual analysis might interpret that as a subtle criticism of German nationalism. In fact, Brenkman shows, it had the opposite meaning: the occupation government had recently condemned anti-German demonstrations after crowds in Brussels had jeered German officers and soldiers, and townspeople wearing the

Belgian national colors on their lapels had attacked members of the Flemish collaborationist "black brigades." De Man, in criticizing Belgians for their "nationalist passions," was using his literary column to criticize acts of protest and resistance.

Although the textualists emphasize their commitment to close reading, most of them somehow missed de Man's other anti-Semitic articles. Richard Klein, for instance, writes that "The Jews in Contemporary Literature" is "the only one, among hundreds, that is devoted to the Jewish question and that reiterates Nazi 'conceptions.'" That's wrong, according to S. Heidi Kruger of the New School for Social Research, who describes a de Man piece called "A View of Contemporary German Fiction," which appeared in *Het Vlaamsche Land* late in August 1942. That periodical was, according to Els de Bens of the University of Ghent, "the unofficial spokesman of Devlag," a group "backed by the SS" that "repeatedly took part in Gestapo raids against Jews and resistance fighters." In that essay de Man "promotes the new 'cleansed' version of German literary history," which excluded the work of expressionists, who were "mainly non-Germans, and in specific Jews."

Kruger emphasizes the context in which each essay was written: "The Jews in Contemporary Literature" appeared in March 1941, when "a solution to the Jewish problem," as de Man called it, remained only a subject of discussion; by the time "A View of Contemporary German Fiction" appeared, neighborhoods of Jews in de Man's city had been rounded up and deported to Auschwitz in a most visible way. Kruger emphasizes that the August 1942 article, far from rejecting "vulgar anti-Semitism," represents "capitulation" to Nazi ideology on the question of the Jews. Derrida did not submit this article of de Man's to textualist analysis; he ignored it.

The challenge to the textualists included a critique of the editors' letter soliciting articles for this volume. Stanley Corngold of Princeton University begins his essay by challenging the editors' characterization of de Man's articles as "texts ... [that] at times take up the themes and idioms of the discourse promulgated during the Occupation by the Nazis." Texts, Corngold writes, do not by themselves "take up ... themes and idioms." These texts "were written by an actual person, Paul de Man, and flow from a moral choice."

Several of the articles in this volume defend de Man by attacking those who have written about his collaborationist articles, especially journalists and "journalist professors." Thus Samuel Weber of the University of Massachusetts, Amherst, criticizes Walter Kendrick for his article in the *Voice Literary Supplement*, J. Hillis Miller criticizes my article in *The Nation* and Andrzej Warminski of Northwestern University describes the articles on de Man in *The Nation* and *Newsweek* as "the slime that has passed for 'journalism.'" Lindsay Waters of Harvard University Press, who is editing a volume of de Man's essays from the 1950s, counters that "It will not do ... to attack journalism." De Man himself wrote during the 1960s for the *New York Review of Books*, Waters points out: "For him it was part of the intellectual's job to try to convey complex ideas for as general an audience as would receive them, despite the risks of distortion [and] the need to make deadline."

Miller defends the value of the mature de Man's textualist approach, arguing that it provides the tools necessary to read de Man's early work. Allan Stoekl of Yale rejects that argument. De Man's later writings, he argues, are "extremely elaborate devices" that "preclude the possibility of any moral or political critique or analysis of his early work." If we adopt de Man's approach, Stoekl writes, "we cannot justify even asking about the motives, desires, and responsibility of the (un)committed intellectual." The de Man case, he concludes, exposes the limitations of de Man's theory.

Reponses provides an opportunity to reconsider Derrida's maxim that "there is nothing outside the text." Gerald Graff, of Northwestern University, defends Derrida's statement as meaning that "all social phenomena can be usefully viewed as 'texts.'" He's right that this premise "has proved immensely useful to Marxists, feminists, new historicists, and other socially-oriented scholars who have been challenging the established conceptions of the disciplines and their boundaries." But some contributors to this volume seem to take Derrida's maxim literally; they seldom consider social phenomena of any kind. The historicist interpretations, by contextualizing de Man's writings, provide the most persuasive readings of them, and reveal what the textualists failed to see—the variety of ways the young Paul de Man contributed to the Nazi project.

The Nation, February 13, 1989

3

The Responsibilities of Friendship:

Jacques Derrida on Paul de Man's

Collaboration

In his article "Like the Sound of the Sea Deep within a Shell: Paul de Man's War,"[1] Jacques Derrida indicates that his purpose is not to provide what he calls a "general judgment" of Paul de Man's writings for the collaborationist Belgian newspaper *Le Soir* between 1940 and 1942; instead, he seeks to fulfill what he describes as his "responsibilities" to a "friend" (pp. 631, 595).

In this project Derrida has adopted some familiar strategies, including turning the tables on de Man's critics and accusing them of committing even more serious offenses than de Man's. "To judge, to condemn the work or the man," Derrida writes, ". . . is to reproduce the exterminating gesture which one accuses de Man of not having armed himself against sooner" (p. 651). Derrida thus draws a rhetorical connection between criticism of de Man and extermination of the Jews—an offensive argument that hardly helps de Man's case.

Derrida's argument is objectionable in other ways. De Man's problem was not that he failed to "arm himself" against Nazism, but that he collaborated with it and made explicitly anti-Semitic statements. To review briefly: de Man wrote 170 articles for the Brussels newspaper *Le Soir*, at a time when that publication, in the words of its editors today, " 'was stolen and controlled by the occupiers, the directors and the editorial board of our newspaper having, on the contrary, decided not to collaborate' " (p. 604 n. 11). *Le Soir* in those years was thus a Nazi publication, and the official postwar tribunal—

---

1. *Critical Inquiry* 14 (spring 1988), pp. 590–652.

the Conseil de Guerre—considered those who published in its pages to be collaborators. Even if de Man had published nothing but sports scores or recipes in *Le Soir* he would properly be defined as a collaborator. But de Man went well beyond that, publishing praise for leading collaborators and in one article adopting an explicitly anti-Semitic position.[2]

Nevertheless, Derrida refuses to use the term "collaborator" to characterize de Man and displays great ingenuity in finding euphemisms for it. De Man's writing "conforms to official rhetoric" and makes "concessions to the occupier" (pp. 607, 599). Derrida refers to "the fund of coded and stereotyped arguments from which Paul de Man had to draw" (pp. 599–600)—but of course de Man "had to" draw on those arguments only because he had committed himself to collaboration. Derrida goes even further, concluding with a quote that de Man " 'was anything but a collaborator' " (p. 652). This refusal to admit that de Man collaborated does not provide a persuasive defense of him.

The best of Derrida's varied arguments is the appeal to context. De Man made his initial decision to begin writing for *Le Soir* in a political context whose uniqueness deserves emphasis: in 1940, no power on the European continent challenged Nazism, no resistance movement had yet been formed, Stalin was an ally of Hitler, England stood alone, the United States was neutral, the war seemed to be over; moreover, the genocidal intention of the Nazis had not yet been institutionalized, the decision for the "final solution" lay in the future. At this moment, it made sense to address the issue of German hegemony over European culture, which was indeed de Man's intention in many of his *Le Soir* pieces. But of course Derrida's appeal to context and to authorial intention constitutes an abandonment of the deconstructive method. As Christopher Norris had written of de Man, "we read in defiance of his own repeated counsel" if we read his work "by asking what might have been the motives, political or otherwise, that led to his adopting the stand they exhibit."[3]

---

2. De Man was questioned by the Auditeur Général in 1945 but not formally charged, while twenty-eight staff members of *Le Soir* were charged (Jonathan Culler, letter to author, August 12, 1988).

3. Christopher Norris, "Paul de Man's Past," *London Review of Books*, February 4, 1988, p. 9.

Derrida emphasizes repeatedly that de Man's objectionable acts were committed almost half a century ago, when he was twenty-one and twenty-two years old. That's an important argument. But the moral problems de Man poses do not end in 1942 when he stopped writing for *Le Soir*; a second and in some ways more serious moral problem recurs throughout his adult life, during which de Man kept his youthful pro-Nazi and anti-Semitic writings a secret. Should de Man have told the truth about his past to his students and colleagues? Derrida answers that telling the truth would have been a "pretentious, ridiculous" gesture for de Man, one that was "indiscreet and indecent," a "pointlessly painful theatricalization" (p. 638). Moreover, telling the truth "would have deprived us of a part of his work" because it "would have consumed his time and energy." Thus de Man "did the right thing" when he hid the truth about his past (p. 639). Telling the truth should be avoided because it is time-consuming: that is a morally bankrupt argument.

Derrida might have asked how de Man could have acknowledged his wartime writing if he had wanted to. What could he have done— call a press conference? But in fact we do have appropriate examples of acknowledgments by intellectuals of past offenses—offered by former Stalinists who came to regret their previous writings and to want to explain what had led them to adopt such a position and then to reject it. Many examples from this genre are unappealing; they display some of the problems Derrida raises—pretentiousness, self-dramatization, and so on. But others are serious intellectual works: that of Arthur Koestler, for example. If Paul de Man had wanted to, he could have found a way during his adult life to explain what he had done and what he thought about it. In this case as in others, Derrida minimizes the extent of the problem de Man's actions pose. De Man did more than "hide the thing" (p. 636). One of his students has reported that when asked about his past, de Man lied. Derrida was aware of this evidence when he wrote his essay: Juliet MacCannell, a comparative literature teacher at the University of California, Irvine, was a student of de Man at Cornell in the mid sixties. "'I asked him what he did during the war. He said "I went to England and worked as a translator." ' [4]

---

4. See p.4 above.

Among the information revealed for the first time in Derrida's article is de Man's 1955 explanation of his wartime collaboration, written in response to a denunciation Harvard received: "'In 1940 and 1941 I wrote some literary articles in the newspaper "Le Soir" and, I like most of the other contributors, stopped doing so when Nazi thought-control did no longer allow freedom of statement. During the rest of the occupation I did what was the duty of any decent person'" (p. 636 n. 45). Derrida declares that with this letter de Man "explained himself" in "a public act" (p. 636). But it was not public, it was private—a private letter to a Harvard official, a letter de Man concealed from the public at that time and subsequently. The letter, moreover, is misleading: he wrote not only "'in 1940 and 1941,'" but also in 1942—the year that the "final solution" was initiated, the year that Jews in Belgium were first sent to Auschwitz. And de Man's statement that his writings were limited to "'some literary articles'" conceals the fact that he wrote 170 articles, which, in the words of one authority, "'plugged the Nazi hit parade'"[5] and included an explicitly anti-Semitic article. Thus de Man's 1955 statement to Harvard does not provide a truthful explanation of his actions. Some acknowledgment by Derrida of these problems would have been better than denying them.

Derrida writes that de Man, in collaborating with the Nazis, was "accepting what we know today to be unacceptable" (p. 599). The fact is that "we" knew Nazism was unacceptable then. Only a small number of French and Belgian intellectuals cast their lot with the Nazis as de Man did.[6] De Man himself seems to have known Nazism was unacceptable before the war began, as Derrida indicates elsewhere in his piece: when Germany invaded Belgium and France, de Man was editor of a journal, *Les Cahiers du Libre Examen*, that defined itself as "democratic" and "antifascist." De Man wrote in its pages in February 1940, at the beginning of the war and before the defeat of France, "*against* Germany and *for* democracy, for 'the victory of the democracies' in a war defined as a 'struggle ... against barbarity'" (pp. 600–601).

Is there a connection between de Man's youthful collaborationist

5. Jeffrey Mehlman, quoted in ibid.
6. See James D. Wilkinson, *The Intellectual Resistance in Europe* (Cambridge, Mass., 1981), especially chapter 1.

writings and his mature criticism? J. Hillis Miller has said there is " 'no connection' "[7]—a position that is consistent with the post-structuralist critique of the unified subject. Derrida could have argued that those who see a continuity between the collaborationist and the mature writings are committed to an untenable assumption—the unity of the subject. One of the achievements of post-structuralism has been to question this assumption. But Derrida apparently doesn't believe the critique of the unified subject applies to Paul de Man. Derrida writes that de Man's youthful work "has to have marked his public gestures, his teaching and writing" (p. 594). With this argument, Derrida centers de Man as a subject, and thereby abandons what Derrida elsewhere in his essay calls "the lessons of Paul de Man" (p. 591). Yet Derrida goes on to attack critics who have made this kind of argument. Their view, Derrida declares, is that "everything [in de Man's mature work] is already there in the 'early writings,' everything derives from them or comes down to them," that de Man's mature writing was "the pursuit of the same war by other means" (pp. 640–41). This is dishonest; no one has said *Blindness and Insight* or any of de Man's other mature works pursue Nazi goals. The critics to whom Derrida is referring have made an argument similar to his own: de Man's early writing "has to have marked" his mature work.

Derrida also adopts the strategy of denouncing the messenger for bringing bad news about his friend. Thus Derrida attacks what he calls "the sensationalist flurry full of hatred" displayed by the *New York Times*, which first carried the story (p. 591). The article in question, however, was hardly "full of hatred"; it began, "In a finding that has stunned scholars, a Yale professor revered as one of the most brilliant intellectuals of his generation wrote for an anti-Semitic, pro-Nazi newspaper in Belgium during World War II."[8] "Full of hatred" is a description that applies more to Derrida, responding to those who have reported the news about his friend.

De Man's anti-Semitic article, "Les Juifs dans la littérature actuelle," receives Derrida's most energetic efforts. In that article de Man addressed the issue of whether Jews had "polluted" modern literature

---

7. See p.6 above.

8. "Yale Scholar's Articles Found in Pro-Nazi Paper," *New York Times*, December 1, 1987.

and concluded that "a solution to the Jewish problem that aimed at the creation of a Jewish colony isolated from Europe would entail no deplorable consequences for the literary life of the West."[9] Derrida points out, correctly, that the article begins with a "critique of 'vulgar antisemitism'" (p. 625). He then declares that "to condemn 'vulgar antisemitism,' *especially if one makes no mention of the other kind*, is to condemn antisemitism itself *inasmuch as* it is vulgar" (p. 625). This argument is lacking in logic. If you condemn vulgar art and make no mention of the other kind, have you condemned all art? Derrida goes on to argue that since de Man's article is surrounded on the page by other vicious anti-Semitic articles, which "*coincide in a literal fashion, in their vocabulary and logic, with the very thing that de Man accuses*," it is "as if his article were denouncing the neighboring articles" (pp. 625–6). In writing about "a solution to the Jewish problem" in 1941, de Man was not "denouncing" anti-Semitism; he was endorsing it. Derrida's preposterous effort cannot erase this simple fact.

Derrida's least persuasive strategy is to read de Man's collaborationist articles for their literary quality. He declares he found in them "an extraordinary culture," "an exceptional sense of historical, philosophical, political responsibilities" (p. 599). Wolfgang Holdheim, de Man's successor at Cornell, who spent the years of the German occupation in the Low Countries, describes de Man's *Le Soir* articles as "excruciatingly dull and totally unoriginal, embarrassing to read in their mediocrity," as "common Nazi hack work."[10] Derrida argues that deconstruction is a tool for "the analysis of the conditions of totalitarianism" (p. 648). But the only totalitarianism he criticizes in this article is that which he claims to find in the critics of de Man. Derrida says that de Man's critics put into practice the principles of "the worst totalitarian police" (p. 641). Totalitarian acts, he writes, are "more numerous and more serious on the part of those who accuse de Man than in the latter's books or teaching" (p. 648). But no one has said de Man's "books or teaching" were pro-Fascist; they said his articles in *Le Soir* were. The articles on de Man in the *New York Times* and *The*

---

9. Paul de Man, "Les Juifs dans la littérature actuelle," *Le Soir*, March 4, 1941 (my translation).

10. Wolfgang Holdheim, "Letter to the Editor," *London Review of Books*, March 17, 1988, p. 4.

Nation—the only publications Derrida criticizes—contain nothing that qualifies as "totalitarian."

Derrida writes that "Paul de Man's war is ... the one that this man must have lived and endured *in himself.*" He declares de Man suffered "torment," that he must have been "torn apart" by his "internal conflicts" (p. 594). Deconstruction is ill-suited to make such judgments about character and psychology. Derrida presents no evidence that de Man ever wrote or said he was tormented, or torn apart, or at war with himself over what he had done; he presents no evidence that de Man had any regrets at all, or felt any shame. Defending de Man's character, Derrida quotes Georges Goriely, a "former Belgian resist-ant" who "knew de Man well," as saying that de Man was not "'ideologically ... antisemitic'" (p. 651). Goriely, who today is professor emeritus of sociology at the Free University of Brussels, subsequently described de Man as "'completely, almost pathologicaly, dishonest,'" declaring that "'swindling, forging, lying were, at least at the time, second nature to him.'"[11] That suggests de Man did not suffer "torment" about collaborating with the Nazis.

Derrida suggests "rules" for "rereading de Man," the first of which is "respect for the right to error" (p. 644). That's a reasonable suggestion, but for Derrida it applies only to de Man, not to his critics. The con-clusion one is left with is that what de Man did—collaborate with the Nazi occupiers of Belgium—should be understood and forgiven, but what de Man's critics have done—commit "reading mistakes" (p. 647 n. 50)—should be condemned as unforgivable. Outside the circle of de Man's most committed defenders, few readers will find this argument persuasive.

Critical Inquiry, Summer 1989

---

11. Georges Goriely, quoted in James Atlas, "The Case of Paul de Man," *New York Times Magazine*, August 28, 1988, p. 37.

4

The Sears Case:

Women's History on Trial

At its trial in June 1985 for sex discrimination, Sears, Roebuck & Company offered a novel defense. Attorneys for the nation's largest retailer presented a prizewinning scholar in women's history, Rosalind Rosenberg, as an expert witness. She told the court that history shows women don't want the better-paying jobs at Sears—selling big-ticket goods on commission—because those positions conflict with deeply held values centering on home and family. To rebut Rosenberg's testimony, the Equal Employment Opportunity Commission enlisted another prizewinning expert on women's history, Alice Kessler-Harris, who argued that despite the existence of an ideology of domesticity, women have consistently taken better-paying jobs when those have been available.

The suit, filed in 1979, was the last of the major antidiscrimination actions brought by the pre-Reagan EEOC. Other big firms charged during the Carter years with sex bias—notably, AT&T, General Motors and General Electric—settled out of court, awarding back pay to those discriminated against and pledging to do better. Sears decided to fight.

The complaint covered the years 1973 through 1980. During that period, 60 per cent of the applicants for all sales jobs at Sears and 40 per cent of those qualified for commission sales posts were women. Only 27 per cent of those hired for commission jobs were women, however. Although 72 per cent of Sears noncommission salespeople were women, they received only 40 per cent of the promotions. The source of this pattern of discrimination, the commission charged, lay in the company's subjective hiring practices. Sears had no written guide-

23

lines, and its training of interviewers was minimal. Thus there were no checks on interviewer bias, conscious or unconscious, which courts in other discrimination cases have taken into account. Tests were administered to applicants, and Yes answers to a few key questions were used to identify promising commission salespeople: Did the applicants like boxing, swear often, enjoy an event more when they bet on it, and speak with a low voice? The EEOC argued that not only were the questions biased against women but Sears had offered no evidence that they predicted sales ability.

Sears attorneys, led by Charles Morgan Jr, former civil rights activist and former head of the Washington office of the American Civil Liberties Union, responded that the company had done its best to hire women for the better-paying jobs. An affirmative action program established with great fanfare in 1973 required that half of all new employees be women or minority men. The EEOC said it is satisfied that the program reached its goals for minority groups but contended that it has failed for women. Between 1973 and 1980, the proportion of female commission salespeople rose from 20 per cent to 29 per cent; Sears's goal had been 38 per cent. Sears argued that it had been unable to hire more women for commission sales because so many of them didn't want those jobs. Women are afraid of competition with other salespeople and rejection by customers, Sears attorneys told the court; they are unfamiliar with most product lines sold on commission (which include fencing and auto parts, but also washing machines and draperies), and they didn't want additional responsibilities.

The evidence for this argument consisted mainly of Sears managers' anecdotes and opinions. The corporate director of equal opportunity testified that women were unwilling to take jobs selling tires because they didn't like going outside when "it's snowing or raining or whatever." Managers testified that they "continually tried to persuade reluctant women—even those only marginally qualified—to consider commission selling," that in many places they had "interviewed every woman in the store and found not one who was willing to sell big-ticket merchandise." In these efforts managers "purposely deviated from sound personnel practices," company attorneys told the judge, and "Sears stores lost sales because they retained poorly performing commission saleswomen in order to meet affirmative action requirements." Sears also presented evidence from surveys of its employees, which the EEOC claimed were biased and unreliable.

Sears attorneys counted on Rosenberg, an associate professor at Barnard College and the author of *Beyond Separate Spheres: Intellectual Roots of Modern Feminism*, to provide historical evidence for their argument that women don't want commission sales jobs. "Women have goals and values other than realizing maximum economic gain," she told the court, values centering on their roles as wives and mothers. Citing more than fifty works in women's history and women's studies, she described the development of a women's culture that emphasized nurturance and selflessness and that disavowed competition. These "traditional values ... continue to be the ideal," Rosenberg reported; as a result, women's relative absence from high-paying jobs is the consequence not of employer discrimination but of the choices women make.

Kessler-Harris, a professor then at Hofstra University, the author of *Out to Work: A History of Wage-Earning Women in the US* and *Women Have Always Worked: A Historical Overview* and chair of the American Historical Association's committee on women historians, responded in her brief that "choice can be understood only within the framework of available opportunity." Where opportunities have been denied women, they have rationalized their situation in terms of domesticity. But when opportunities for better-paying jobs have been present, women have taken them. In the past two hundred years, American women have worked at a variety of jobs, many of them "nontraditional." Kessler-Harris provided dozens of examples, from the 175 industries in which women were employed in 1850 to the experiences of "Rosie the Riveter" during World War Two. The main reason women work outside the home, she argued, and the main reason they want better-paying jobs, is that their families need the money. (A Sears witness, appropriately named Rex Rambo, had testified that women work "to get away from children.") Sears's own data showed that 28 per cent of the full-time noncommission saleswomen had husbands who were unemployed; 27 per cent had husbands earning less than $15,000 a year; and 75 per cent had husbands with incomes below $25,000. The notion that work and family obligations are in conflict is less applicable to these women than it might be to women seeking self-fulfillment in demanding careers.

In an interview, Rosenberg said she agreed with Kessler-Harris's argument that working women want to make more money. "But Sears found that men were much more likely to want commission sales jobs," she maintained, the reason being that those jobs "involve risk of reduced income as well as an opportunity for greater income." Kessler-Harris replied: "There is no such risk at Sears. Sears guaranteed a salary against commissions. The guaranteed salary for commission salespeople was considerably higher than for noncommission salespeople."

Rosenberg offered other reasons why women turn down commission sales positions. "Working women who are married are likely to put family and children first," she said, "and therefore, as the survey evidence of the Sears work force shows, are less willing to work evenings and weekends than men—evenings and weekends which are required of commission salespeople." Kessler-Harris replied: "The argument that women are not willing to work evenings and weekends doesn't hold up. Evenings and weekends are required of all salespeople, whether or not they work on commission. They all rotate their schedules. Moreover, many women choose jobs with evening and weekend hours because those are the hours husbands can babysit." Husbands and relatives provide most child care for working women, according to surveys. "And there are predominantly female occupations that require extensive evening and weekend work, especially nursing and heath care."

Rosenberg cited still other evidence against Kessler-Harris's argument that when good jobs are available, women take them. "Kessler-Harris may have been unaware that Sears presented Exhibit 25, identifying 680 women in only one district who had been offered promotions to commission sales jobs as part of Sears's affirmative action program and who had refused those offers." Rosenberg's characterization of Exhibit 25 is incorrect, however. According to company attorneys, only some of the 680 were offered promotions; the rest did not receive offers but rather "indicated a lack of interest." Sears did not say how many women received genuine offers of promotion; the EEOC estimates that at most there were one hundred. "The EEOC tried to find out more about these offers," Kessler-Harris said. "What conditions were attached? Were the women required to move to distant locations? Were part-time workers required to take full-time jobs? How many men turn down the same kind of offers? Sears refused to identify any of the women who supposedly had turned down offers of better jobs."

In our interview, Rosenberg justified her testimony in defense of Sears as part of the "fight against the oppression of women," saying she told the truth about "the sources of women's oppression." Ellen DuBois, a historian at the State University of New York at Buffalo and author of *Feminism and Suffrage*, commented:

> The EEOC lawsuit is part of a political battle that has been altering the cultural configuration Rosenberg says she laments. She argues that history shows the situation is "too complicated" for an affirmative action program to remedy. This argument is the essence of conservatism and must be read as an attack on working and sexual equality, an attack on the whole concept of affirmative action.

Rosenberg asserted that "Sears was not discriminating against women" in the period covered by the suit. Why didn't the Reagan Administration drop the case? She said:

> They've let this case go on, for their own cynical reasons. Because it's such a weak one, it actually damages the cause of affirmative action.
>
> Sears was the first major retailer to establish an affirmative action program. It spent millions on this program.... [Other retailers] will say Sears spent all this money, and look where it got them; we might as well save the money. Sears's winning would show that their commitment to affirmative action was worth it—that if you've made a good faith effort you can survive this kind of legal attack.

To that, Kessler-Harris said, "There's no evidence that Sears had a *good* affirmative action program for women. To say the Reagan Administration is supporting this suit as a way of attacking a good affirmative action program makes little sense." Indeed, Administration officials have made it clear they'd like to lose the case to discourage EEOC officials from bringing similar suits. EEOC chair Clarence Thomas repeatedly criticized the suit because of its reliance on statistical evidence. When his opposition to it made page one of the *New York Times* in December, Sears attorneys sought a deposition from him; the judge ruled that his testimony would be irrelevant. Democratic Representative Augustus F. Hawkins summoned Thomas before the House

Subcommittee on Employment Opportunities to complain that it was not "appropriate for you, as chairman of the commission . . . to criticize the commission's own case while the case [was] still before the court."

Rosenberg said the biggest factor influencing her to testify for Sears was the EEOC's failure to produce women who had been denied good jobs by Sears: "I do not believe statistical disparities alone constitute proof of employer discrimination." But given the immense size of the Sears work force, statistical evidence is the only good indication of a pattern of discrimination. Such evidence was accepted by the courts as the basis for the AT&T settlement, the biggest in the history of sex discrimination litigation. It is difficult to find complainants in sex discrimination suits. Women looking for jobs at Sears between 1973 and 1980 filled out applications, had five-minute interviews and later were notified that they did or didn't get the job. Those who weren't hired had no way of knowing if they had been the victims of sex discrimination. Even if they had known, most lacked the resources to pursue a complaint and needed a job right away. Rather than file charges, they would have kept looking. Two women who had been turned down did appear at the end of the trial. Sears picked three applications out of a pool of one hundred as examples of women who were not interested in selling on commission, and the EEOC managed to locate two of them. Each said she was indeed interested and showed she was qualified; one had considerable experience in commission sales.

Sears asked a number of experts in women's history to testify in its behalf, but Rosenberg was the only one who accepted the invitation. Kathryn Kish Sklar, a professor then at the University of California, Los Angeles, and the author of *Catherine Beecher: A Study in American Domesticity*, said, "Sears asked me. I said they were wasting their time. There was no way I was going to be a witness against the EEOC." Although Rosenberg cited Sklar's book in her brief, Sklar told me, "I'm profoundly troubled by the use of scholarship about women in the past as a justification for discrimination against women in the present. It ignores the basic tenet of historical study: change over time. Evidence about the nineteenth century simply doesn't explain women's labor force participation today." Carl Degler of Stanford University, the author of *At Odds: Women and the Family in America* (which Rosenberg also quoted) and president of the American Historical Association, also declined Sears's invitation to testify. "I don't like the idea of using historical evidence as a justification for limiting opportunities," he commented. "Of course it's true that few women in the past have taken these jobs; nevertheless, it's likely that more will in the future, with changed opportunities and more willingness on the part of employers to consider women for nontraditional jobs."

Other historians cited by Rosenberg objected to her use of their scholarship. William Chafe, a professor at Duke University and the author of *The American Woman: Her Changing Social, Economic, and Political Roles, 1920–1970*, said, "All of the examples Rosenberg cited from my work emphasize the institutional, cultural and political *obstacles* to the achievement of sex equality in the United States. None of them suggest women wanted to be unequal or chose to have inferior jobs."

Asked to identify historians who would approve of her use of their scholarship in this case, Rosenberg cited only one, Regina Morantz-Sanchez, then of the University of Kansas, author of *Sympathy and Science: Women Physicians in American Medicine*. When she was asked to comment, Morantz-Sanchez's endorsement was qualified: "Is it possible for women to have chosen not to take those jobs at Sears? My work on women physicians suggests that theoretically it is. That does not mean institutions don't discriminate against women. Sears may be discriminating in this case."

On June 28, when closing statements were presented, Morgan, once a hero of the civil rights movement, summed up for the company in demagogic style. He called on the judge to reject the EEOC's statistics and the testimony of "these Ph.D.s" called by the government, and instead use "common sense ... walking-around sense." Common sense suggested sex discrimination didn't exist at all: "Strange, isn't it, that we live in a world where there is supposed to be a monopsony of white men who somehow get up every morning trying to find a way to discriminate against their wives, their daughters, their mothers, their sisters." He linked the EEOC case against Sears to the antiwar protests at the 1968 Democratic National Convention in Chicago:

What was Sears in 1968? Sears was God, motherhood and country.... In those years God, motherhood and country became controversial, [opposed by] that new generation coming alive in the streets of Chicago with values

29

quite different from mine and from some others'.... My heavens, what did the pill do? Said to women, ... You don't have to have children at all. You can devote and dedicate yourself to a career.

In her summation, EEOC attorney Karen Baker told the court that the company's witnesses had "said women aren't interested in these jobs; they are afraid of the products; they are afraid of going to people's homes; they are afraid of competition; they are afraid of risk in income; they are afraid of going out in the rain. When you listen to [the] Sears store witnesses, you get the idea that women are really a very weak lot." Those opinions, the basis of Sears managers' decisions about hiring and promotion, constitute "the essence of discrimination."

There is little reason to fear that the Sears case represents the beginnings of a trend among historians of women: Sears's expert witness has virtually no support in the field. Nevertheless, the historical testimony in the case reflected in an exaggerated way the divisions in the feminist movement. Betty Friedan, in her book *The Second Stage,* and others have called for a return to the family in the name of preserving female values. Feminists on the left reply that all arguments about distinctive female values play into the hands of conservatives. The Sears case exposes the political implications of the "female values" position. If something in women leads them to reject higher-paying jobs, why should the government press any employer to establish an affirmative action program?

The Nation, September 7, 1985

5

The Sears Case: What Happened?

When Judge John A. Nordberg ruled in January 1986 that Sears, Roebuck & Co. had not discriminated against women employees, as the Equal Employment Opportunity Commission had charged, he gave judicial sanction to the politics of post-feminism. Nordberg justified the argument that women faced with equal opportunity don't really want the burdens of male occupations. Nordberg, a Reagan appointee with his first big case, agreed with Sears attorneys that the company was unable to hire more women for its high-paying commission sales jobs because women had a "relative lack of interest" in them, because they "feared or disliked" competition, feared "being unable to compete, being unsuccessful and losing their jobs."

Sears struck back at the EEOC in February 1986, suing the commission to recover the $20 million in legal fees billed by its attorney Charles Morgan, one-time Alabama civil rights lawyer and former head of the American Civil Liberties Union Washington office. Sears argued that the sex discrimination charge was "frivolous, groundless and without merit." They also sued the EEOC attorneys as individuals, asking the judge to require that they pay Sears's legal fees, on the grounds that their participation in the suit was based on "bad faith."

The EEOC announced it would appeal the ruling, arguing that Judge Nordberg's decision contained "serious legal flaws and errors." The judge found that women were "uncomfortable or unfamiliar with the products sold on commission," listing "furnaces, fencing and roofing" as typical jobs at issue. In fact, 56 per cent of the part-time jobs at issue in 1973 were in footwear, including shoes. The judge accepted Sears's claim that it could not find women to do traditionally male jobs, yet during the years at issue AT&T hired ten times as many women to climb up poles and go down manholes as Sears hired women to sell home improvements. Although women who went from noncommission to commission sales jobs at Sears typically doubled their income the first year, few women employees made that move. But Sears's argument that women preferred not to work in male-oriented product lines is contradicted by their own surveys, which came to light during the trial. When women applicants at Sears filled out interview guides in 1979, 40 per cent said they had the highest level of interest in selling home improvements, yet women were awarded only 9 per cent of those jobs.

The EEOC appeal also pointed to the striking transformation in Sears's hiring of women following EEOC's filing of the suit in August 1973. From the period before the suit to the year after it was filed, the proportion of women Sears hired to sell furniture increased from 8 to 33 per cent, while in floor coverings the number increased from 4 to 16 per cent. Judge Nordberg's decision suggests that women suddenly became less fearful of competition in 1973, but the EEOC has a better explanation: Sears started hiring more women when it learned the EEOC was about to file suit. Judge Nordberg's failure to find that Sears discriminated against women is especially egregious for the years 1973–74 and provided the appeals panel with the simplest grounds for a reversal.

The judge complained that the EEOC had failed to present individual victims of discrimination. The EEOC appeal argued that presenting 20 or 30 women who had been turned down for the 47,000 jobs Sears filled during the years under consideration would have been meaningless. The question at issue, as defined by the Supreme Court in a case involving the Teamsters Union, is whether discrimination against women is the "company's standard operating procedure, the regular rather than the unusual practice." Other courts have ruled that testimony by individual victims of discrimination is unnecessary in this kind of case. Judge J. Skelly Wright of the District of Columbia circuit ruled in 1984 that when the statistical evidence of discrimination is significant, requiring anecdotal evidence "would reflect little more than a superstitious hostility to statistical proof, a preference for the intuitionistic and individualistic over the scientific and systemic.... Discrimination might exist even when the affected individuals can point to no specific instances of an employer's discriminatory conduct."

Sears's fierce counterattack on the EEOC since the ruling may be part of a strategy in which the company would give up its claim for attorney's fees in exchange for the EEOC abandoning its appeal. EEOC chairman Clarence Thomas's oft-expressed opposition to the suit suggested that such a settlement was possible, but EEOC spokesperson Renee Divine said, "We appealed on the basis of 'serious legal flaws'—that says it all."

Judge Nordberg declared in his decision that he found Sears expert witness Rosalind Rosenberg "well informed ... highly credible" and "convincing"; the EEOC's Kessler-Harris, he said, made generalizations that "were not supported by credible evidence." The case was debated at a session of the Organization of American Historians convention in New York in April 1986. Historian Morgan Kousser of the California Institute of Technology, who has testified as an expert witness in federal district court in six voting rights cases, told the audience of three hundred that he found Judge Nordberg "overwhelmingly biased against the EEOC." If it had produced a sign from a Sears personnel office that read "no women need apply," Kousser said, "Judge Nordberg would have asked for proof that females were interested in and qualified for the jobs from which they were excluded, produced Sears surveys to show they were neither ... [and] praised a Sears manager who said he ignored all such signs anyway." Kessler-Harris's testimony "was sure to be rejected," Kousser said, "however solid it seemed to anyone except the judge," while Rosenberg's was "treated patronizingly as window-dressing by a man who already knew what he was going to buy."

In These Times, July 9–22, 1986

Postscript: The Court of Appeals affirmed Judge Nordberg's ruling in January, 1988. Charles Morgan's lawsuit to recover $20 million in fees from the EEOC is still pending.

6

Dealing with Deadwood:

the Arizona Approach

They are called "unproductive" or "professionally inactive." Their research "fails to meet normal expectations" and does not "merit advancement." They constitute "cases of less than desirable excellence." Henry Rosovsky, former dean of the faculty of arts and sciences at Harvard, reports that a Stanford dean once tried to deal with one of "them" by suggesting that he take a well-earned early retirement at half salary; "the professor declined, pointing out that, after all, he was already retired on full salary." We are speaking, of course, about that dark side of academic life: the delicate matter of faculty deadwood.

The over-the-hill professor has always been good for a ritual swipe or two but not much serious attention. This may be about to change, however. Several schools across the country are taking a hard look at proposals to deal with this problem—ranging from imposing sanctions to providing professional counselling. In particular, the University of Arizona is considering one of the most controversial and provocative policies, one that would bar unproductive faculty members from participating in promotion and tenure-decisions. The new proposal, authored by Annette Kolodny, dean of the university's humanities faculty, states that "faculty entrusted to membership on all promotion and tenure committees shall be composed only of those faculty who have met, and continue to meet, the criteria stipulated by rank in the university, college, and departmental guidelines." The key phrase here is "continue to meet." The criteria in question require a high level of scholarly productivity; if the proposal is adopted by the university, faculty members who no longer publish will not be allowed to sit on tenure and promotion committees or vote on tenure and promotion cases in department meetings, even if they have tenure themselves.

Why the University of Arizona, located in a state never known to be in the social vanguard (the state that may have lost the 1993 Super Bowl because voters in November 1990 refused to establish a paid state holiday in honour of the Rev. Dr Martin Luther King Jr)? For Kolodny, a feminist literary scholar, the issue is one of fairness: "I do affirmative action workshops around the country," she explains, "and one of the most frequent complaints one hears is that 'the people making decisions about me don't understand my work and are incapable of understanding it because they are not keeping up with the field.' It became increasingly clear to me that bright, innovative young scholars more often than not were hampered in the tenure process by people who were unfamiliar with where their own professions had gone. This is a problem especially for women and minorities trying new approaches at the cutting edge of their discipline."

There's another element: Arizona is one of the many schools that have transformed themselves since the sixties from quiet teaching institutions into ambitious research universities, competing nationally for grants and new faculty. At such institutions, a great divide separates older faculty members, hired at a time when steady scholarly productivity was not a requirement, from the more recent appointments—a generation gap in scholarship and theory, a divide between what might uncharitably be called the achievers and the deadwood. The problem is especially acute in literature, according to Holly M. Smith, Arizona's acting vice-provost, "where there is a lot of recent scholarship—multicultural and feminist work—that doesn't fit the traditional mold. Departments are divided about how seriously to take this work. People trained in earlier eras and traditions sometimes see this work as a passing fad; they don't understand it very well and don't give it much weight. Active scholars are more likely to have a fairly high level of exposure to the cutting edge of their discipline; they will thus have ample opportunity to come to appreciate it."

Kolodny's proposal augments the university's existing promotion and tenure guidelines. Like similar documents at other ambitious institutions, Arizona's guidelines declare that the university wishes to inform "the Arizona public" that "the University is absolutely serious in holding itself to the highest standards, commensurate with its ranking as a top twenty Research I public university." (That will come as a surprise to those aware only of its reputation as a Sun Belt party school.) According to the guidelines, the university's "research function requires faculty members devoted to and actively engaged in the expansion of humanity's intellectual and creative frontiers"—a daunting goal for any scholar. Kolodny is proposing that her school take seriously this exalted boiler-plate and bar those faculty members no longer going where no one has gone before from evaluating the work of those who seem to be.

How do you decide which faculty members are not pushing the envelope of intellectual inquiry? Arizona's criteria are familiar: "the quality of the specific media of publication or presentation, the opinion of peers from prestigious institutions (who rank the candidate in reference to his or her cohorts), the winning of grants, awards, and fellowships"; among full professors, "the regular publication of scholarly or interpretive articles in refereed journals," articles "of such quantity and quality as to have made a major impact on the field." An "international reputation" is preferred, "as attested by letters, citations, and reviews from abroad." Kolodny has pointed out that her proposal requires excellence in teaching as well as publication: "We must assure that those teaching in the classroom keep up with the field, know what the latest debates and theoretical problems may be, and teach their students about that—not what was happening twenty years ago. Students will tell you that the most exciting teachers are the ones offering new and innovative ideas. It's an argument that needs to be made loud and clear in the humanities. In the sciences, nobody argues that physics should be taught in 1990 the way it was in 1950. The same is equally true in language and literature. We owe it to our students to keep up with the fields and bring into the classroom people at the cutting edge."

Implementing the proposed guidelines would not be easy. Arizona reviews every faculty member every year; a departmental peer-review committee's recommendation is used in determining whether merit increases are due. Some departments use grades of "unsatisfactory," "satisfactory," and "outstanding," while others evaluate colleagues in terms of whether their work "meets normal expectations." To implement the guidelines, those judged "unsatisfactory" or whose work fails to "meet normal expectations" most likely would be barred from participating in decisions regarding tenure and promotion to full professor. In some schools at the University of Arizona, members of schoolwide review committees are elected. To implement the proposed guidelines, candidates for election would have to be evaluated in terms of their productivity. Either a nominating committee would have to verify candidates' compliance with the productivity guidelines or candidates would compete with one another on the basis of their lists of publications.

Kolodny's proposed change in Arizona's school of humanities policy guidelines was defeated in the spring of 1990 by four votes. It will be revived in 1991, as a procedural rather than a policy statement, and the faculty will vote again, but probably not until spring. Kolodny is optimistic that this time it will pass. "The split here is between people of the old school and the more recent hires," said Thomas Rehm, chairman of the university's faculty and professor of chemical engineering. "I think you can guess who is on which side." Rehm opposed Kolodny's proposal: "The duties of faculty members have to do with teaching, service, and research—all three. Concentrating on the first two but not the last does not make that individual a less valuable member of the department. That member should not be excluded just because he is not doing research. To do so flies in the face of equal participation on the part of all faculty in departmental decisions."

Keith Lehrer, Regents' Professor of Philosophy at Arizona, disagreed. "I don't think Annette's proposal would be very controversial in the social sciences," he said. (At Arizona the philosophy department is in the school of social sciences.) "The fairness argument is a real one. Research is what universities are all about. Tenure and promotion depend on research; people actively engaged in research should make those decisions. I'm an editor, and I know that people who haven't written a book have very unrealistic expectations about what a good manuscript looks like. It's a matter of knowing the difficulties and the agonies of doing research and writing."

Proposals to do something about deadwood have aroused passionate opposition on other campuses. Joyce Appleby, president of the Organization of American Historians, former chair of the history department at UCLA, and Harmsworth Professor of American History at Oxford University for 1990–91, said, "I hate the term 'deadwood.' It's part of an absorption with academic stardom that has made a good many fine people feel marginal. I don't like the ideal of the person who is constantly producing. Sometimes we have fallow periods, sometimes we are more involved in teaching. There are different rhythms to being a professor." Appleby objects as well to Kolodny's definition of fairness. "The fairness argument makes these fields into fiefdoms and undermines the whole conception of an educated person," she says. "It's offensive to argue that only those educated narrowly in a specialty can appreciate that scholarship. We are competent to evaluate scholarship across a broad range of topics and subjects. The problem is an intractable one: There are bastards out there who make life miserable for others. But creating new procedural rules and new levels of bureaucracy will not solve that problem"—especially when some of those bastards publish a lot.

In this regard, Christine Stansell, director of women's studies at Princeton University, noted that it has become increasingly difficult to judge the significance of a colleague's publishing record. "A speedup in scholarly publishing occurred during the eighties. We've had a proliferation of arcane debates in conference papers and anthologies; articles are being churned out, especially by young people launching their careers. I'm not persuaded that everything being published needs to be published or that this kind of publishing is the best sign of an active intellectual life. Experimentation in different styles of intellectual work never got a chance. The result has been the loss of a more reflective and meditative kind of work. I think it's a mistake for an institution to put all its eggs in the basket of academic productivity."

"The problem is how to assess 'scholarly activity,'" said Nancy Schrom Dye, dean of the faculty at Vassar College. "There are people who aren't active as publishing scholars who are still active intellectually. I would have a great deal of difficulty establishing guidelines for making those determinations." Kolodny replies that "you would not want to exclude from the decision loop teachers who in the classroom present materials at the cutting edge of the discipline but who don't publish regularly." That argument, however, contradicts the guidelines she herself has proposed, which require regular publications by those participating in tenure decisions—publications that make "a major impact on the field." Liberal arts colleges define their mission differently from research universities, Dye pointed out, which makes the deadwood problem less pressing for them: "We do not require the same relentless effort at research productivity. [At Vassar] we have faculty members I would call active and effective who probably would not live up to some productivity norms. They don't trouble me, they don't trouble this institution, and I don't think they should."

What about Kolodny's belief that an undergraduate's education should be based on something as inherently unstable as the "cutting edge"? Rosovsky, for one, rejects that idea. He argues, instead, that older professors make the best undergraduate teachers, because there "the latest specialist wrinkles are less important than wisdom." Undergraduates need a liberal education, says Rosovsky, and older faculty members can provide the necessary "context and broad perspective." Rather, it is graduate teaching, he argues, that should be the turf of newly minted Ph.Ds, the younger faculty whose recent graduate education has put them at the "technical and theoretical frontiers of a subject."

Doing something about deadwood is difficult at most institutions, because they have no formal means of assessing productivity after tenure. Faculty members are evaluated for promotion to full professor, but aside from that, salary increases at most institutions are negotiated with the department chair and dean, who control the budget for salaries. Little or no documentation of scholarly productivity is required. The alternative, which Kolodny recommends as "a relatively sane process," can be found at the nine-campus University of California system, which requires regular scheduled post-tenure merit reviews of all regular faculty. Every three years professors are required to submit newly published work for evaluation and to list work in progress, along with teaching and administrative service. (Associate professors are reviewed every two years.) The review can have two outcomes: a merit increase to a higher step, or what the system calls "no action." Some campuses are now debating what they call "the repeated 'no action' problem"—those faculty members who receive more than one "no action," who can be identified as deadwood and made the target of sanctions.

Few institutions have gone further in developing sanctions for unproductive faculty than the University of California, Irvine; even in the academic pressure cooker of the California system "Irvine is in the forefront on this issue," said Ellen Switkes, director of academic personnel policy in the University of California president's office. In 1985 the Irvine Academic Senate adopted a proposal under which faculty members who receive two "no actions" over a six-year period are required to submit "a written plan for resumption of a sound and productive program of scholarly work with a specified time frame for its execution." Deans and department chairs are instructed to "aid in the formulation of such plans" by, among other things, suggesting "redirections in research focus." A faculty senate committee commented that this procedure "should not involve counterproductive confrontations."

Under the policy, three years later another regularly scheduled review would be conducted. A third "no action"—nine years without publications justifying a merit increase—constitutes "persuasive evidence of professional negligence or research 'burnout'." At this point faculty members who are good teachers can be asked to take on an increased teaching load. The guidelines state that, in cases of "flagrant or persistent refusal or inability to meet the teaching and research obligations of a University of California professor," the administration may seek to shift the offending professor to part-time status at a reduced salary or encourage early retirement. Joyce Appleby favors increasing the teaching loads of professors who don't publish. "At the University of California, half our time is presumed to be spent in research," she pointed out. "For this reason, we have lightened teaching loads. For people who don't devote that time to research, we need to find alternate routes of work."

There is one glaring exception to California's "no action" situation: the university requires reviews of full professors every three years but not forever; those who have reached Professor Step V ($69,400), normally twelve years after promotion, are not subject to review again, unless they request it. Step V is defined as a "terminal step" or "barrier step," a barrier akin to the one that separates associate from full professor; to cross the barrier into the stratosphere of Step VI and beyond (above $75,000), professors must present evidence of "great scholarly distinction" (along with "highly meritorious service" and excellent teaching). If you move up the scale on schedule, you reach Step V when you are around fifty years old. That means the University of California does not expect professors to remain active scholars after they reach their early fifties.

This practice, which has existed for decades, is itself being reconsidered: A proposed systemwide policy would require reviews of Step V professors every five years. However, " 'no action' is not intended to be a negative comment on performance at Step V and above; it's perfectly acceptable to remain at that level," Switkes said. The astonishing fact is that although Step V professors have published steadily for twenty-five years and still have twenty more years until retirement, they are expected, or at least allowed, to become deadwood.

The problem of unproductive older professors will become only more widespread in the future, because there will be more of them. Employers may now make retirement mandatory at age seventy, but on December 31, 1993, mandatory retirement will be eliminated (unless Congress changes the law). This "uncapping" of retirement has been the subject of administrative anxiety and conferences. Advocates of older professors argue that faculty members do not necessarily become nonproductive at a certain age: K. Warner Schaie, professor of human development and psychology at Pennsylvania State University, pointed out that faculty members "can become deadwood at any time."

Doing something about deadwood requires understanding its development. That isn't hard: a young scholar gets tenure in his or her mid thirties; after that come another thirty years of doing more or less the same thing—writing and teaching about Shakespeare, or slavery, or macroeconomics. Thos who do not become academic superstars have to find ways to remain active and interested despite the absence of major rewards and major challenges. You spend five years on a second book; it sells a few thousand copies; a year after publication it gets a handful of mildly positive reviews in scholarly journals; then you start on the third. In the meantime new schools of interpretation have arisen; you discover you have invested an entire decade in an approach that is now regarded as routine and uninteresting by the brighter and more energetic graduate students. It's hardly surprising that, facing this situation, some academics lose enthusiasm for their work or become pessimistic about the possibility of making intellectual progress. The problem is hardly unique to professors; the *Wall Street Journal* reports that "boredom and burnout are the biggest reasons business owners cite for selling their firms." Academics have some opportunities that other professionals don't: they can shift their interests. But only a few follow this course. A handful of literary critics become novelists, but, for the most part, experts on the modern American novel do not become Chaucer scholars in their declining years.

Part of the deadwood mentality stems as well from the grandiose claim that all university faculty members are, or ought to be, "actively engaged in the expansion of humanity's intellectual and creative frontiers." We need a more workable and reasonable conception of intellectual life in the university. Such a conception ought to recognize that those who don't publish should do more teaching—especially at institutions like the University of California, where the expectation of research justifies light teaching loads. Deciding who should do more teaching requires judgments about what constitutes adequate publishing, but academics make those kind of judgments all the time.

Finally, how serious is the deadwood problem? Rosovsky estimated that fewer than 2 per cent of major university faculty are genuine dead-wood. "That seems accurate to me," Kolodny said. How, then, could her proposal to exclude that tiny number from promotion and tenure decisions make those decisions more fair? Under Kolodny's proposal, in a department with fifty tenured people—a very large department— one person would not be allowed to vote on tenure decisions. In two departments of twenty-five people, a total of one person would be excluded, on the average. Kolodny seems to think that one person is the source of unfairness in the tenure review process. But when young scholars in gender and multicultural studies complain that the people making decisions about them don't understand what's happening in their fields, they are not talking about only that one case of deadwood; they're talking about many of the others who do publish. Allan Bloom, like it or not, is not deadwood.

Doubtlessly, there are colleges and universities where an old guard unjustly denies tenure and promotion to women and minorities. Perhaps Arizona is such a place, although Kolodny has denied it. Departments that have established a pattern of discrimination can and should be sued. But there's no good evidence that the problem in those cases stems from unproductive or professionally inactive professors. And universities have many ways of supporting controversial new work: they provide grants and extra time off to assistant professors to enable them to complete the books that will get them tenure; they

42

establish procedures requiring that assistant professors be treated fairly when they are considered for tenure; they appoint deans and administrators who are committed to protecting faculty members from unfair treatment. Where there is an issue of fairness in the evaluation of work in gender and multicultural studies, lopping off deadwood is not a solution but rather a bureaucratic red herring: an evasion of a problem, not an answer to it.

Lingua Franca, December 1990

PART II

Right-wing Professors

7

Capitalist Shock Therapy:

the Sachs Plan in Poland

In January 1990, Poland's Solidarity government adopted the capitalist shock treatment prescribed by Harvard economist Jeffrey Sachs—the 36-year-old professor the *Los Angeles Times* called "the Indiana Jones of economics." Sachs, like other privatizers and marketeers, has called for eliminating all subsidies and controls and opening Poland's economic doors to unfettered capitalism. What makes his plan distinctive is the ferocious speed, indeed the ruthless abandon, with which the "reforms" have been put into effect. Sachs persuaded Poland's leaders to gamble their country's future on one gigantic dose of free-market medicine. Everyone agrees that Poland's economic health will be affected; the question is, for better or for worse? Sachs has said his goal is to create a thriving Slavic Sweden, but others foresee a bleak Baltic Bolivia. At this point, the Swedish future looks extremely unlikely.

The first requirement of the Sachs plan, its author explained in the *Economist* in January 1990, is the rejection of "any lingering ideas about a 'third way'" between Soviet-style command economies and American-style capitalism; Poland must not experiment with democratic controls, public ownership, market socialism, cooperatives or worker self-management. The country is to establish a market economy in a single year, 1990, by abolishing price controls and subsidies, ending all restrictions on private enterprise, privatizing state-run firms, balancing the budget, making the currency fully convertible and introducing tough limits on wages—in short, freedom for the capitalists and "direct controls" on the workers.

So far, the Sachs plan has succeeded in slashing the Poles' standard of living. In the plan's first six months, according to *Business Week*, Poles suffered a 40 per cent drop in real wages. The London *Financial Times* said smallholders "may have seen their standards of living halved." This devastating decline is not an unfortunate byproduct or unintended effect of the Sachs plan; Sachs and Solidarity had hoped for a 20 per cent reduction in real wages when they ended government subsidies on basic commodities. Food prices doubled in January; the price of bread rose from the equivalent of a penny a loaf to 25 cents. Families are now spending 60 per cent of their income on food. Before Sachs, Poland had a problem of shortages. As soon as food and other basic goods showed up in the stores, people bought them at low, subsidized prices, so the shelves were usually empty. Now the shelves are full, which would seem to be evidence of prosperity. But, said Marta Petrusewicz, a Polish historian teaching at Princeton University, "shortages don't exist anymore because prices are so outrageous people can't buy anything."

Slashing Poles' real wages is only the first part of the Sachs plan. The next objective is to fire "unproductive" workers and increase unemployment. The Sachs prescription calls for closing down many of the biggest factories and mines, some of which employ tens of thousands of workers. 1 million workers may be laid off, raising the unemployment rate from less than 1 per cent to 7.5 per cent by the year's end. The government's chief economic adviser, according to the *Washington Post*, estimated that as many as one-third of all Polish workers will lose their jobs. Sachs hopes workers will see their hardship as unavoidable because their own government tells them there is no alternative. "People are being patient with the shock therapy," Petrusewicz said. "But they won't be patient forever." Sweeping layoffs and declining real wages make a new strike wave possible later in 1990 or in 1991. The first big strike challenging the shock treatment began May 24 and was led by railroad workers. It lasted a week and paralyzed Poland's Baltic ports. It will not be the last.

Even if Polish workers don't strike again, the Sachs plan is unlikely to move the country into economic high gear. Economists on the left as well as the right agree that if prices are raised to the extent that few can afford to buy goods, inflation and shortages will be licked and price stability will return. The problem is that such a policy also causes a depression. Sachs seems to have forgotten the simple Keynesian notion that stimulating demand is the key to economic growth; investment is not automatic but requires inducements. And Poland is now experiencing "a far deeper-than-expected recession," according to the *Economist*; industrial sales for the first quarter of 1990 were 27 per cent lower than for the same period in 1989. "You don't need Jeffrey Sachs to prove that a depression cures inflation," said UCLA historian Robert Brenner; "that was proved by Herbert Hoover."

The news media, nevertheless, love Sachs with a passion seldom directed toward economists. His picture has appeared in the *New York Times*, the *Washington Post*, the *Economist* and *Time*; he's been featured in the *Wall Street Journal*, *Fortune*, *Newsweek* and the *New Yorker*. The *Economist* called him "one of the world's leading young economists." As evidence of his genius, the press regularly reminds us that Harvard promoted him to full professor when he was only twenty-nine. In fact, his economic plan for Poland represents familiar Reagan–Thatcher thinking about the virtues of opening countries to uncontrolled foreign investment and the need for disciplining unruly workers.

If it's not hard to see why the American press idolizes Sachs, it's more difficult to understand how he convinced the Solidarity government to adopt his unremarkable ideas. Before the Poles took him on, Sachs was a specialist on international debt and Latin American hyperinflation; he had no experience with Eastern bloc economies. The Poles first became interested in him after he advised Latin American countries not to pay their debts; since Poland had immense debts, that sounded good to them. Then Sachs came up with his shock-treatment plan. Jacek Kuron, once the embodiment of Solidarity's egalitarian ethos, became his champion, along with the editorial board of *Gazeta Wyborcza*, the Solidarity newspaper. In 1989 Sachs delivered a passionate speech to Solidarity's Parliamentary Club, in which he told the Poles he had ended Bolivia's 24,000 per cent inflation rate, and did it, he said, overnight. Poland, he said, needed the same kind of shock therapy. Since Poland's inflation in 1989 was only one-twentieth of what Bolivia's had been in 1986, the prospects for success seemed excellent. Sachs was bursting with brash American self-confidence and Harvard know-how; the Solidarity government pledged to take the Sachs cure.

The Poles didn't seem to realize that Sach's program for Bolivia had resulted in unmitigated disaster for the great majority of Bolivians. Thirty thousand tin miners were fired as part of Bolivia's effort to control hyperinflation. Sachs assumed the "free market" would direct those workers, and tens of thousands of others who were newly unemployed, into what was supposed to be a more dynamic and efficient private sector. It didn't work. In November 1989 the Bolivian government imposed a state of siege in response to a wave of strikes and sentenced almost 150 trade union activists to internal exile in a remote region of the Amazon—the Bolivian Siberia. But the Sachs plan for Bolivia did stimulate economic growth in one area of the private sector: coca farming. Thousands of tin miners, "after searching in vain for alternative employment (the kind promised by free market doctrine) invested their indemnification funds into land and began to cultivate coca," Latin America scholar James Petras has reported. "Even their former union leaders turned their hand at organizing the coca growers to obtain fairer prices from the drug barons." Coca-leaf production increased in Bolivia from 50,000 metric tons before the Sachs plan to 80,000 afterward—an increase of 60 per cent. Bolivia now produces considerably more coca leaf than Colombia.

Thus Bolivia under the Sachs plan did beat inflation, but the price has been continuing high unemployment, economic stagnation, labor revolt, a state of siege and a deepening involvement in the international drug market. Poor Poland: coca leaves won't grow there. Where will unemployed Polish miners turn? Some Solidarity members are thinking about Bolivia, Jeffrey Sachs's success story: "I would love to see Bolivia," Karol Modzelewski told the *New Yorker*'s Lawrence Weschler in Warsaw. "I just don't want to see Bolivia here."

The sad case of Bolivia demonstrates that stopping inflation is very different from sparking economic growth. The Sachs plan has a basic flaw: it seeks to achieve rapid economic growth by opening Poland to the "free market." But developing capitalist countries that have grown since World War Two have generally rejected the free market. West Germany kept its trade subsidies until the early 1960s, economist Doug Henwood has pointed out, and all of Western Europe maintained foreign exchange controls until the 1970s. Alice Amsden, an economics professor at the New School for Social Research and author of *Asia's Next Giant*, a study of Korean economic development, has observed that South Korea and Taiwan, those paragons of capitalist growth, have shunned the free market. Both have relied on strong government economic intervention that provides businesses with export subsidies, low-cost credit and protection from foreign competition. Thus the Sachs plan is not a growth plan, it's an anti-inflation plan that assumes capitalists will rush to invest in Poland once inflation is under control. The problem is that capitalists look for what economists call "comparative advantage," and Western capitalists have not been finding advantages in investing in Poland, despite headlines like this recent one from the *Wall Street Journal*: "Gold Rush: Capitalists Jam Poland: ... Money Is Pouring In." The text of that article told a different story: "With other Klondikes beckoning from Bucharest to Berlin, chances are Western business won't drop much cash in Poland very soon."

Solidarity hoped Polish-Americans would provide both investment capital and expertise for Poland, but the fiasco of Barbara Piasecka Johnson's Gdansk shipyard "rescue" suggests this route leads to a dead end. Johnson is the Polish immigrant maid who married the heir to the Johnson & Johnson pharmaceutical fortune and then inherited $350 million after his death. In 1989 she promised to rescue the Gdansk shipyard, birthplace of Solidarity, after the pre-Solidarity communist government announced plans to close it. Johnson declared she was ready to invest $100 million for a 55 per cent stake in the shipyard, keeping it open and saving workers' jobs. Lech Walesa himself proclaimed her offer "a model for other industries." If that's the model, Poland's marketeers are in deep trouble. In December 1989 Johnson submitted the details of her plan. It called for slashing the work force by more than half, freezing wages (the workers had expected an increase) and requiring a no-strike guarantee for five years. The workers, according to the *New York Times*, were "stunned and infuriated." The chief manager of Johnson's business affairs explained to them how the free market works: "She feels that her investments have to make a profit or else you should be investing in something else." Meanwhile, Solidarity had replaced the Communist government and agreed to run the shipyard as a state-owned company rather than liquidate it.

Poles had hoped that German capitalists would lead the pack of investors heading east of the Elbe, but rapid German reunification represents disaster for Poland's privatizers. The cost of reunification may be something like $600 billion, according to Gerhard Fels, who is director of the Institute for the German Economy in Cologne.

That means Germany, now one of the world's largest exporters of capital, may itself become a capital importer. The opportunities for profit in fusing the world's fourth and thirteenth largest economies are immense, and the project is likely to provide the biggest magnet for international capital investment over the next decade. Why invest in Poland, with its rebellious workers, obsolete factories and inexperienced government, when a reunifying Germany is beckoning?

Poland is not only having trouble finding investors; its economy is also crippled by foreign debt. Poland owes a monstrous $40 billion to the West as a result of the loans made to its Communist government during the 1970s in a previous effort to marketize the Polish economy. "This debt is totally unpayable," Sachs has said; any attempt to collect it would subject Poland to "economic serfdom for the next generation." Poland's creditors have established a debt relief schedule as a reward for the government's imposing one of the harshest austerity programs in history. But the Paris Club, made up of the seventeen Western creditor governments, did not cancel the debt, as Sachs insisted it must; instead the club rolled it over. That means the debt will remain an issue; Poland is still paying interest to Western lenders—at a nominal rate in 1990—but if the Poles change their mind about the Sachs plan, those same lenders will certainly retaliate and demand payment. Thus Poland learns the rules of the democratic community of Western nations. No doubt Sachs is right that Poland is incapable of paying its debts. But why does he think the same Western lenders, after being told they aren't going to get their money back, will now line up to offer new loans? They lost a fortune on bad loans to Mexico, Brazil and Argentina; the West's loans to Poland in the 1970s were made at a time when banks were floating in a sea of petrodollars. The situation now is entirely different because of the Federal Reserve System's new capital requirements for banks, which increase every year for the next three years. These requirements are difficult for many banks to meet, and force them to avoid "nonperforming loans" like the plague.

What about American government aid? The Bush Administration treats visiting Poles warmly but has coolly rejected Polish requests for money. When Bush visited the Gdansk shipyard in July 1989 Lech Walesa asked him for $10 billion in US aid. Bush offered only a minuscule $119 million, 1 per cent of what the Poles—and Jeffrey

Sachs—think they need. In the end Congress came up with $200 million. When Senator Bob Dole floated a trial balloon that involved increasing aid to Eastern Europe by cutting aid to Israel and other client states by a pitiful 5 per cent, the proposal sank like a stone. What about the Japanese? Will they invest in Poland? Not likely. They have always been averse to investing in high-risk situations; their favorite foreign investment is US Treasury bonds. The Japanese automaker Daihatsu pulled out of talks with a Polish car manufacturer in May 1990 because of what the Japanese company called "economic chaos" in Poland.

Eighty per cent of production in Poland is now in the state sector; under Sachs's shock therapy, those enterprises will be sold off to private investors as quickly as possible. How successful can such a passive privatization be? Margaret Thatcher holds the world record for privatization, but it took her a decade to sell off only a handful of state enterprises. Moreover, Thatcher's privatization scheme took place in the oldest capitalist country in the world. Poland seeks to sell off 100 state enterprises in 1990, most of them in bad shape. It isn't going to happen.

Strangely enough, the professor who convinced the Poles to follow Herbert Hoover rather than John Maynard Keynes doesn't consider himself a man of the right. "I see myself a liberal Democrat," he told me in an interview. Just back from a trip to Poland, in May 1990, Sachs remained relentlessly optimistic: exports were up 20 per cent compared with 1989 (Poland's worst year in recent history); unemployment had been exaggerated; the recent decline in Solidarity membership "is not indicative of its popular support"; the people "remain optimistic." (That same week the *Financial Times* reported "a growing sense of dread.") Asked whether Poland faces any significant problems, Sachs named only two: a possible slowing down of the privatization process, and Western creditors' reluctance to cancel debts. Despite Sachs's enthusiasm, Poland faces a grim future. No doubt some Poles will thrive in their new world of private greed. The majority, however, are more likely to suffer—especially the industrial workers, the backbone of the old Solidarity, with its egalitarian ethos. The big factories where they work will be the first to close under the Sachs plan. But by the time Poles realize their future looks more like Bolivia than Beverly Hills, it will be difficult to change course. The left-wing Soviet writer

Boris Kagarlitsky, who was recently elected to the Moscow City Council, argues that unemployment and economic decline will make the Polish working class, until recently so politically vibrant, more atomized and marginalized. Working-class resistance to the Sachs plan, he believes, is likely to appear too late to be effective. Unemployed workers without unions to protect them may then turn xenophobic, anti-Semitic and dangerous. Jewish candidates in the May 1990 local elections were greeted with "bursts of anti-Semitism," according to the *Financial Times*. If the fragile Polish democracy collapses into a right-wing authoritarian state in the next couple of years, Jeffrey Sachs and his capitalist shock treatment will share in the responsibility.

Since the shock treatment was first administered, Solidarity's approval rating in opinion polls has fallen—from 78 per cent in November 1989 to 47 per cent in March 1990. Austerity may be a necessity for Poland today, but a socialist government would give working people democratic powers in the factories and cities and let them decide how to spread the burden so that the poor don't suffer more than the rich. Polish workers remain fiercely anti-Communist, but Jeffrey Sachs needs to remember that Poland today, more than any other country in Eastern Europe, is a workers' state. Polish workers were the first in Eastern Europe to bring down a Communist government; they could easily be the first to bring down a post-Communist government.

The Nation, June 25, 1990

Postscript: The results of Poland's first year of free market reforms: industrial production declined 28 per cent in 1990 (compared to a decline of 3 per cent in 1989); inflation was 800 per cent in 1990 (it had been 250 per cent in 1989). By summer 1991 a deep recession was provoking mounting political unrest.

8

The Odyssey of Daniel Boorstin

When Daniel Boorstin retired in September 1987 as Librarian of
Congress, he ended a sojourn in the public eye that began in 1953 with
his testimony before the House Un-American Activities Committee as
a friendly witness. Although he avoided writing about this HUAC
experience in subsequent years, it subtly shaped his scholarship and
returned to haunt him at the two critical turning points in his career:
his decision to leave academia in 1969 and the 1975 Congressional
hearings on his confirmation as Librarian of Congress. Boorstin's
career demonstrates the political possibilities created by conservative
commitments, and also the intellectual cost of going to Washington—a
marked deterioration of his intellectual work.

It all began in 1953, when HUAC turned its attention to the universities; Harvard was at the top of its list, and Boorstin had been a
Communist for a year as a Harvard student. When the subpoena
arrived, Boorstin was a 39-year-old historian at the University of
Chicago. Although he was by then a conservative, there's no question
that Boorstin disliked McCarthyism. Unlike a few former Communists
who did not wait to be called, Boorstin did not volunteer information
and gave his testimony only after being subpoenaed and under threat
of a contempt citation. But he did give HUAC everything it wanted.
He named names of Communist Party members he had known—his
two college roommates and his adviser in history at Harvard, Granville
Hicks. (Only half of HUAC's other Harvard witnesses named names,
and only a quarter of all academics subpoenaed by HUAC did so,
according to Ellen Schrecker's authoritative study *No Ivory Tower*.)
Boorstin agreed with the committee that Communists should not be

allowed to teach, and he assured committee members that their inquiry did not threaten academic freedom. His collaboration reinforced the committee's assumptions and helped justify its persecutions.

The committee asked Boorstin how he expressed his opposition to Communism. "My opposition has taken two forms," he replied. "First, the form of an affirmative participation in religious activities, because I think religion is a bulwark against Communism. This has been expressed in my activities in the Hillel Foundation at the University of Chicago," he said. "The second form of my opposition has been an attempt to discover and explain to students, in my teaching and in my writing, the unique virtues of American democracy. I have done this partly in my Jefferson book, which, by the way, was bitterly attacked in the *Daily Worker* as something defending the ruling class in America, and in a forthcoming book called *The Genius of American Politics*. I have written articles and book reviews for *Commentary* magazine, which is a strongly anti-Communist journal."

The Genius of American Politics dealt with the broad sweep of political ideas across the three centuries of American history. The "genius" of American politics consisted of the absence of all ideology and doctrine. Boorstin made it clear in the book that anti-Communism was one of the ideologies that was alien to American political culture. He criticized cold war foreign policy, writing that the concept of "saving" nations and peoples by gaining their adherence to ideas was fundamentally totalitarian. And Boorstin strongly objected to McCarthyism.

Genius contains one striking anticipation of Boorstin's HUAC experience. In the "Suggestions for Further Reading" at the end of the book, Boorstin recommends Whittaker Chambers's memoir of his own HUAC experience, *Witness*. Chambers's picture of the man who names names is devastating:

> The ex-Communist informer ... sits in security and uses his special knowledge to destroy others. He has that special information to give because he knows those others' faces, voices, and lives, because he once lived within their confidence, in a shared faith, trusted by them as one of themselves, accepting their friendship, feeling their pleasures and griefs, sitting in their houses, eating at their tables, accepting their kindness, knowing their wives and children.... By the logic of his position in the struggles of his age,

every ex-Communist is an informer from the moment he breaks with Communism, regardless of how long it takes him to reach the police station.

When Boorstin recommended that Chambers be read, he had not yet been subpoenaed by HUAC, but he must have had some idea that sooner or later he would be on his way to the "police station"—in his case, the caucus room of the old House office building on Capitol Hill, where HUAC held the hearing in which Boorstin turned informer. None of the reviewers of *Genius*—including those in liberal journals— mentioned that Boorstin had testified before HUAC as a friendly witness. Subsequent writers about *Genius* have maintained that silence.

Boorstin's 1961 book, *The Image, or What Happened to the American Dream*, his best, gained deserved fame for introducing the concept of the "psuedo-event": "It is not spontaneous, but comes about because someone has planned, planted or incited it.... It is planted primarily ... for the immediate purpose of being reported or reproduced.... Its relation to the underlying reality of the situation is ambiguous.... Usually it is intended to be a self-fulfilling prophecy." The concept, as Victor Navasky pointed out in *Naming Names*, applies perfectly to the HUAC hearings. Although neither Boorstin nor his colleagues were writing about his HUAC appearance, it seems to have influenced his best work.

The rise of the New Left was the next crisis in Daniel Boorstin's life as a political thinker. At the University of Chicago, Boorstin's support for the war in Vietnam brought him into conflict with campus radicals. Boorstin's junior colleague in the history department, Assistant Professor Jesse Lemisch, used Boorstin's HUAC testimony in classes to illustrate the relationship between historical scholarship and political commitment. In 1966, Lemisch was fired; department chair William H. McNeill told him, "Your convictions interfered with your scholarship." Lemisch responded in public forums by pointing out that Boorstin had told HUAC that his scholarship served HUAC's political ends; why was it illegitimate for Lemisch's scholarship to serve different ones? Students for a Democratic Society members at the university distributed a leaflet in Boorstin's class quoting from his HUAC testimony and making Lemisch's point. That leaflet was then published in the journal *Radical America*.

Boorstin lashed back at the New Left, accusing its adherents of vandalism, violence and mindless activism—although in this case the connections they were making were hardly mindless. Boorstin's response to his student critics appeared in an article in *Esquire* in 1968, "The New Barbarians," where he wrote for the first and only time in his career about his experience in the Communist Party. The article contrasted the old left, which he praised for being truly radical, with the new. The Communists of the 1930s and 1940s, he wrote, "favored a reconstruction of American life.... They had a great deal to do with promoting a new and wider American labor movement, with helping FDR popularize the need for a welfare state, and with persuading Americans to join the war to stop Hitler"; they "did awaken and sensitize the American conscience.... That was radicalism." He wrote as one of "those of us who were part of it." One issue, as always, was avoided: in view of his comrades' achievements, why did Boorstin inform on them?

Boorstin was asking the New Left to do what his generation had done: engage in a "search for meaning," develop an ideology with "specific content," pose fundamental questions regarding community and society. But, as historian John Patrick Diggins later pointed out, in all of Boorstin's previous work he had argued that the development of explicit political ideas and values was fundamentally alien to the American character. His rage at the New Left blinded Boorstin to the central theme in his own work. "The New Barbarians" was Boorstin's swan song to academia. He resigned his chair at the University of Chicago in 1969, explaining later that it had become "less of a pleasure to go to the faculty-club luncheons and the afternoon teas when you had to sit through heated arguments over Vietnam." It's notable that this was a complaint not about being harassed by radical students but by colleagues. He got a position as director of the National Museum of History and Technology at the Smithsonian Institution in Washington.

Boorstin emerged from the 1960s with his world view unchanged. He was able to complete the intellectual project he had begun twenty years earlier: a three-volume comprehensive history of American culture and civilization grandly titled *The Americans*. In 1973 he published Volume Two, *The Democratic Experience*, a 600-page history of American culture during the century following the Civil War. When the narrative reached the 1950s it discussed foreign aid, atomic power and Sputnik but failed to mention McCarthyism, anti-Communism or HUAC.

President Gerald Ford nominated Boorstin in 1975 to be Librarian of Congress. Previously, the post had been an administrative one held by a prominent librarian; Ford's nomination of an active Republican and outspoken foe of the antiwar and civil rights movements set off a storm of controversy. The Congressional Black Caucus called Boorstin's nomination "disastrous," arguing that his remarks in the past showed "misunderstanding and misrepresentation of the goals of black and other activists" and that, "given Mr Boorstin's attitude on affirmative action," minority hiring at the library was likely to suffer. Black library employees, 2,500 strong, unanimously declared their opposition to Boorstin's confirmation on the same ground. The 35,000-member American Library Association also opposed Boorstin's nomination on the ground that the Librarian of Congress should be a professional library administrator.

So, Boorstin returned to Capitol Hill for a second Congressional hearing on his political and intellectual past, twenty-two years after the first one. In preparation for a confrontation with his critics, Boorstin had filled out a "clearance questionnaire" prepared by the White House counsel. Among other things it asked, "Have you ever had any association with any person or group ... which could be used, even unfairly, to impune [sic] or attack your character?" Boorstin answered, "Hearings before the Committee on Un-American Activities." It's notable that he listed as the black mark on his record his "association" not with the Communist Party but rather with HUAC. The Washington *Star* made the same judgment, reporting that "his listing of the names of fellow Harvard Party members is bitterly remembered by many."

At the hearings a spokesman for the Black Employees of the Library of Congress, Howard Cook, discussed Boorstin's political past. He quoted from "The New Barbarians" and commented, "Dr Boorstin seems to be suggesting that radicalism which had its roots in the Communist Party was all right.... Dr Boorstin has belonged to the CPUSA.... Dr Boorstin uses the fact that the Communists have a theory [to argue that] that makes them somehow better than the other radicals. I would like to remind you that the Communists have a theory and that theory is to destroy the United States." Here was an unexpected turn: one of Boorstin's black critics resorting to opportunistic Red-baiting. Oregon Senator Mark Hatfield asked: "I have heard from some of my more conservative constituents as to your membership in the Communist Party during 1938–39. I believe, while as a student instructor at Harvard, you were also studying Marxism." Boorstin in response launched into the only explicit statement he has made about his HUAC appearance since he testified in 1953. Joining the CP at the age of twenty-three was, he said, "part of the process of growing up. It was a very unimportant episode in my life." When he had been called before HUAC, he recalled, "it never occurred to me to take the Fifth Amendment. . . . It was my duty to respond. . . . I felt that in our country neither professors nor students are above the law." But in fact the law did not require naming names. Boorstin's defense of his actions in 1975 was, if anything, further to the right than his 1953 testimony had been. In any event, the Senate confirmed him, and in November 1975 he was sworn in.

Boorstin's move into the higher circles of Washington Republican politics coincided with a sharp deterioration in the intellectual quality of his work, as evidenced by his 1983 book, *The Discoverers*. An unexpected best seller, its first sentence read, "My hero is Man the Discoverer." The book told the story of "countless Columbuses," men who had "the courage, the rashness, the heroic and imaginative thrusts" to penetrate the unknown. Section titles in *The Discoverers* sounded as if they had come out of children's books: "Sea Paths to Everywhere" and "Inside Ourselves." Among Boorstin's countless thrusting Columbuses, in the chapter on "History as Therapy," was Karl Marx. Boorstin treated Marx with unexpected enthusiasm, but then everything in this uplifting book was upbeat. "Marx's Dutch mother . . . spoke German with an accent all her life," Boorstin told his readers, while Marx as a student in Bonn "spent 24 hours in the university jail . . . for drunken rowdiness." Those facts contribute nothing to explaining Marx's significance; apparently Boorstin felt that without colorful details readers might find his presentation of Marx's ideas boring. Because Boorstin presented ideas as "episodes of biography," he barely mentioned the historical context in which Marx worked. Marx was significant because of his internal "need to *know*," as one of the "men with an insatiable hunger for knowledge." His intellectual work, in Boorstin's view, had little to do with the revolutionary and working-class movements of his time; it was simply the expression of an innate drive. This approach creates nothing but obstacles to a historical understanding of Marx and his project.

Holding on to his place in Reagan's Washington became a full-time job for the Librarian of Congress. Reports surfaced of resentment at the library over "the high-style lunches and black-tie dinners he throws for congressmen and other dignitaries and over what is regarded as a thirst for publicity." The *Washington Post* quoted Ruth Boorstin as saying that her husband received a Christmas gift from President Reagan (a jar of jellybeans) and that Rupert Murdoch was interested in turning *The Discoverers* into a movie. The *Washingtonian* reported, "Recently he endeared himself to the White House by sending a clever, jesting note to Nancy Reagan praising her self-parody at the Gridiron Club dinner as a political event comparable to William Jennings Bryan's 'cross of gold' speech." There's nothing new about ambitious intellectuals flattering the powerful.

Boorstin's most controversial act as Librarian of Congress occurred in 1986, when, in response to Reagan budget cuts, he cut library hours by 30 per cent and eliminated most evening and weekend hours. "Dr Boorstin sought to make the library an elitist institution by closing it off to people who couldn't use it 9 to 5 weekdays,' said Russell Mokhiber, who chaired the Books Not Bombs Campaign to Save the Library of Congress, a group of library users. The library had been open evenings, Mokhiber pointed out, since 1897. The first day the library was scheduled to close early, more than a hundred demonstrators refused to leave and gathered in the ornate reading room "to express their love for the Library of Congress and their outrage at the early closing," Mokhiber said. William Hirzy, one of the protesters, summed it up in a speech: "Free access to information is a foundation of democracy."

Boorstin had left the University of Chicago in 1969 to escape precisely that kind of protest. He had criticized cuts in the library's 1986 budget, but instead of supporting the protests he reverted to the tactics of university administrators in 1968 and ordered the demonstrators arrested. Police charged eighteen of them with unlawful entry, but Boorstin wasn't satisfied; he also banned seven of the leaders from using the library. The seven challenged the ban in Federal court, and in July 1986, US District Court Judge Harold Greene issued a stinging rebuke to Boorstin, calling his action "utterly unconstitutional." "Perhaps in the Soviet Union or South Africa people are banned," Greene wrote in his decision, "but they are not being banned in the United States." He ordered the library not only to readmit the banned protesters but to pay their legal expenses. The protests proved to be effective; Congress appropriated almost $1 million to restore some of the library hours that Boorstin had cut.

Boorstin's Harvard class held its fiftieth reunion in 1984. In the "class report," each member presented his reflections; one quoted from Boorstin's HUAC testimony naming his Harvard college roommates. That entry was the talk of the gathering; some called it "inappropriate" but others said the essay was "great." The program listed a symposium with "Dan Boorstin, Librarian of Congress, who has been and done many other exalted things." After the class report referring to his HUAC testimony was published, Boorstin's symposium was canceled, and he did not attend the reunion.

His critics can find some satisfaction in the fact that Boorstin has never been able to escape fully the legacy of his HUAC testimony. To understand his career and scholarship, then, one must see Boorstin not just as the quintessential conservative historian of the 1960s, not just as the intellectual in power in Reagan's Washington, but as the friendly witness.

The Nation, September 26, 1987

9

Footnotes to History:

the David Abraham Case

Two senior historians, one at Yale University and one at the University of California, Berkeley, have devoted their time and professional reputations to destroying the career of a young Marxist historian, David Abraham, whose book, *The Collapse of the Weimar Republic*, published by Princeton University Press, has been found to contain numerous errors. In the past, debates among scholars have occasionally been vicious, but the Abraham controversy is more than a debate: it's a vendetta, and it's unprecedented. Abraham's critics, led by Professor Henry A. Turner Jr of Yale and Gerald A. Feldman of Berkeley, seek not just to expose Abraham's errors but also to make sure that he will never get another academic job and to persuade his publisher to withdraw his book; they have also argued that the University of Chicago should rescind his Ph.D. Lawrence Stone, Dodge Professor of History at Princeton, commented, "I've never seen a witch hunt like this in forty years in two countries." Natalie Zemon Davis, Henry Charles Lea Professor of History at Princeton, has seen something like it before: "In some ways it's reminiscent of McCarthyite hysteria."

These events reveal much about the position of Marxism in the history profession today, about the debate between old-fashioned positivists and interpretive historians on where historical truth lies, and about the current state of ethics in academia. In the course of researching and writing his book, Abraham misdated and misattributed one document, mistranslated another document in a way that distorted its meaning and treated a paraphrase of a third document as a quotation. He has also been accused of making dozens of lesser mistakes. Abraham has acknowledged his errors in print and has apologized for them. His critics, however, have not been satisfied. As historian Carl Schorske remarked, "They're not saying, 'Here's a serious error'; they're saying, 'Here's a lie, and I'll tell you why this guy lies.'" In accusing Abraham of fraud, his critics imply that he had to fabricate documents because his Marxist interpretation could not be sustained by the truth.

Stone, whose major work is in the hotly contested field of seventeenth-century English social history, has disputed Feldman's claim that good historians do not make mistakes, especially in their archival research. "When you work in the archives," he said, "you're far from home, you're bored, you're in a hurry, you're scribbling like crazy. You're bound to make mistakes. I don't believe any scholar in the Western world has impeccable footnotes. Archival research is a special case of the general messiness of life." Indeed, there is ample evidence that David Abraham is not the single bad apple in a barrel of virtuous footnoters. The publishers of the great British historian Sir Lewis Namier planned a second edition of his masterly *Structure of Politics at the Accession of George 3rd*. When editors checked the footnotes, Stone said, "I was told they found endless, constant, minor errors." Recently Emmanuel Le Roy Ladurie, France's most celebrated historian, has been criticized by the Vatican librarian for mistranslations and other errors in *Montaillou*. Perhaps Abraham's mistakes are more serious than those made by other archival researchers? "I can't think of another case in which an author's footnotes have been systematically checked in the archives," Stone said. "David's errors seem at the moment to be worse than others', but we can't be sure because nobody else's have been subjected to this kind of systematic scrutiny." Feldman and Turner disagree; each reports that his own work has been checked and upheld.

The campaign against Abraham was begun by Turner, a bitter opponent of Marxist history who had been working for years on a defense of German businessmen in the period immediately preceding the rise of Hitler. Turner became furious after hearing Abraham's work praised at a March 1983 colloquium on Weimar history at Harvard University. He wrote a letter attacking the book and sent it, along with photocopies of original documents that he said Abraham had misquoted, to colleagues in the United States and West Germany. One of the recipients, Arno Mayer, Dayton-Stockton Professor of

History at Princeton University, wrote Turner protesting his private campaign against Abraham. "You vent your anger at David Abraham for daring to publish a book on a topic on which you yourself have been working for years," Mayer wrote. "Have you no shame? Have you no sense of decency?" Feldman, the author of *Iron and Steel in the German Inflation, 1916–1923*, who had read Abraham's manuscript and recommended it for publication, sided with Turner.

Turner went public with his campaign against Abraham in the October 1983 issue of the *American Historical Review.* In a letter alleging that Abraham had forged a document showing business support for Hitler in the last days of Weimar, Turner reminded his colleagues that forgery was "among the gravest of scholarly offenses." It's hard to remember such a serious charge being made against another historian. Abraham then traveled to West Germany and found the document from which he had quoted. It had no signature and an imprecise date; he conceded in his *American Historical Review* response that his dating and attribution had been erroneous. Even those who agreed with Abraham's interpretation of Weimar felt that some of his research was sloppy and that his mistakes were not trivial. But there was a consensus that Abraham had successfully defended himself against the charge of forgery. Turner never apologized or offered a retraction for his allegations, and to many in the profession, he now looked like a man with an ax to grind: his own book had been pre-empted by a younger scholar whose Marxism he despised. At that point Turner ceded the front lines of the battle against Abraham to Feldman.

In 1982 Abraham had been recommended for tenure by the Princeton history department, but the dean's committee turned down the recommendation. Thus at the end of 1983, Abraham was on the job market, with a highly praised book, a dossier of references from prestigious historians and the dispute over his scholarly integrity resolved in his favor. It was then that Feldman began his campaign of letters and telephone calls to make sure that no university hired Abraham. His "Dear Colleague" letters were sent to dozens, perhaps hundreds, of historians in the United States and Europe. In its scope, methods and animus, the campaign is unprecedented in the history profession.

The University of Texas at Austin was the first of Feldman's targets. It invited Abraham for an interview but offered the job to someone else after hearing from Feldman. Then, after Catholic University's history department voted to recommend hiring Abraham, the department chair began receiving calls from Feldman—four or five in a two-week period, according to Prof. Timothy Tackett, a member of the search committee. "We were shocked," Tackett has said. "All his calls were unsolicited. He threatened to go over our heads to the administration." Among the unsolicited materials Feldman sent was a thirty-page attack on Abraham's scholarship, written by Feldman's former student Prof. Ulrich Nocken of the University of Düsseldorf. Back in 1976 Nocken had applied for the Princeton job that had been given to Abraham. The Nocken essay was "a diatribe," Tackett said. "Feldman told us it was forthcoming in the *Vieterljahrschrift für Sozial- und Wirtschafts-geschichte*, a reputable journal. It was impossible to ignore, but hard to verify in the short time we had. We were fuming, miserable and outraged." Thirteen of the department's fifteen members signed a document urging the administration to go ahead and appoint Abraham, but the dean decided against their recommendation.

A year later, Tackett and many of his colleagues at Catholic University were still bitter. "Later we learned that the Nocken piece was rejected by the journal that Feldman said had accepted it," he said. "It never has come out; maybe it never will. We were the victims of a vendetta." The University of California, Santa Cruz was next. Abraham was a leading candidate for a position there when Feldman intervened. The pattern was the same—four or five telephone calls to the department over the course of a month, the typescript of Nocken's attack, the unsolicited letters and the threats from Feldman that if the department didn't follow his advice, he would oppose Abraham's appointment at higher levels, including the system's Board of Regents. "I made it clear," Feldman said, "that I was not going to have Abraham appointed in this university system." Santa Cruz hired someone else. But thirteen members of the department signed a letter addressed to the American Historical Association, protesting Feldman's interference. Feldman also wrote Princeton University Press, Abraham's publisher, declaring that Abraham's book was "fraudulent and should be withdrawn from sale," and insisting that it not be adver-tised "on dust jackets, in journals, and in catalogues." If the press did not comply, Feldman wrote, "you should know that the request will be repeated by me in very choice company and ... a further decision to continue marketing the book will be made a matter of public record in what I write."

Perhaps the most extreme development in the case concerns Abraham's Ph.D. Feldman thinks the University of Chicago should rescind the degree, although he adds, "I have not made any such formal proposal up to the present time." Nevertheless, both the history department and the president's office at the university received at least some informal suggestions to that effect. Some time later the president of the university, Hanna H. Gray, filed a protest with the American Historical Association, describing Feldman's actions as a violation of professional norms. Even if he has not yet made a formal proposal that Chicago strip Abraham of his Ph.D., Feldman has told me that he would be happy to join in such an action—especially if he continues to be "harassed" by Abraham's supporters charging him with unethical conduct.

Feldman's duty, as he sees it, has been to alert the profession to what he views as Abraham's misconduct. Stanley Katz, Princeton Class of 1921 Bicentennial Professor of the History of American Law and Liberty, who joined in signing Gray's letter of protest to the AHA, disagrees. "Turner's letter to the *American Historical Review* gave the profession sufficient notice of the charges against Abraham," he has said. "It appeared well before any departments were considering hiring David. The burden is on those departments. If they consider it a problem, they may consult Turner or Feldman or others. Indeed they all were aware of the controversy and worried about it. It has yet to be shown that there's a single example of fabrication in Abraham's work. But if there had been a genuine hurry to bring a real offense to the attention of the profession, those concerned could have contacted the appropriate AHA division; they could have put something in the AHA newsletter, which has a shorter lead time than the *Review*. The obligation in a case like this is to use the formal communication mechanisms of the profession. There's no evidence that Feldman even considered these possibilities. His method was calculated not to inform but to intimidate."

In response to those charges, Feldman published an eighteen-page attack in the journal *Central European History*. He wrote that Abraham's "egregious errors, tendentious misconstruals and outright inventions" make the book a "menace to other scholars." He refused to "dignify"

Abraham's book with a discussion of its thesis. However, of the errors he attributed to Abraham, none are as serious as the misdated and misattributed document already discussed in the *American Historical Review*. In a 66-page reply in the same issue, Abraham apologizes for his errors, which he terms "inexcusable"; he distinguishes the minor from the major ones; he argues convincingly that he neither fabricated documents nor systematically misconstrued them; and he points out a couple of errors in Feldman's critique. Feldman follows with a 34-page rejoinder, terming Abraham's reply "an outrage" and "an insult to our profession." As for his own errors: "I have decided to forgive myself," he writes. Beneath the rhetorical smoke, Feldman quietly abandons several of his most serious charges, including fraud and forgery, without admitting he had been wrong.

Abraham's critics have also said that his "misinformation" begins with the dedication to his book: "For my parents, who at Auschwitz and elsewhere suffered the worst consequences of what I can only write about." His detractors point out that his mother, although imprisoned at Auschwitz, survived, and thus did not experience "the worst consequences." Arno Mayer's question "Have you no shame?" seems a particularly appropriate response to this criticism.

Many younger scholars see the vendetta against Abraham as a consequence of his Marxism, but it's more complicated than that. If Abraham had written a Marxist study of Weimar that didn't discuss the role of businessmen, Henry Turner wouldn't have bothered to check his footnotes. If he had written a Marxist theoretical essay on the Weimar state that didn't present archival evidence, Turner wouldn't have been interested. What aroused Abraham's critics was his having placed his empirical research on the politics of big business within a framework of Marxist theory.

Marxism is indeed an issue. The Nocken typescript distributed by Feldman alleges that Abraham follows the "official East German theory" of the rise of the Nazis by portraying industrialists as "mighty wirepullers" behind Hitler. (In fact, East German reviewers have attacked Abraham for "whitewashing the big bourgeoisie and its responsibility for barbarism and war.") Turner's book, *German Big Business and the Rise of Hitler*, finally published in 1985 by Oxford University Press, concludes with a diatribe against Marxist historians. He doesn't distinguish between the neo-Marxists who may be found in

American universities and Soviet or East German historians. All seek "to discredit and undermine societies with capitalist economies and to legitimize repressive anti-capitalist regimes." Feldman, on the other hand, denies that he opposes Abraham because he is a Marxist. He did recommend Abraham's book for publication, and in the past, he has directed dissertations by radical students.

Abraham's critics have focused their outrage almost exclusively on his research concerning the relationship between big businessmen and Hitler. In doing so, they've missed the point of his book. It is not an analysis of the growth of Nazism but a structuralist study of the success and failure of capitalist democracy: of how German elites won popular support from socialist and Catholic organized labor, and how this accord failed in the face of the Depression. "The collapse of the Republic and the Nazi assumption of power were by no means the same," Abraham writes in his conclusion. "That no stable ruling bloc could be organized under a democratic form of state did not, of itself, indicate that a fascist solution, whatever its nature, would follow." The fact that he focuses his research on structures rather than individuals has been widely praised in reviews and was the basis for the Princeton history department's decision to hire and then promote him.

The vituperative and wide-ranging attack on Abraham's book is, in fact, part of a larger debate between two kinds of historians—those who seek to identify broad levels of causation and those who confine themselves to a chronicle of events. The former group includes Marxists as well as structuralists, members of the Annales school and practitioners of cliometrics, all of whom seek to identify general causes beyond the acts and motives of individuals. As for the latter group: "Their attitude," according to Schorske, "is that because their footnotes don't contain errors, their understanding of history is correct."

The rise of different schools of historical interpretation signals the decline of a monolithic profession presided over by an establishment of "old boys." In the mid sixties, if the senior men at Yale and Berkeley said an assistant professor was no good, that would have been the end of the matter. The fact that three departments were interested in hiring Abraham in 1984, despite the opinion of two senior men, and that one actually voted to hire him, helps a little to explain Feldman's frenzy.

Abraham wanted Princeton University Press to publish a revised edition of his book in which he would correct the errors. Feldman has argued there would be nothing left of the book; Schorske disagrees: "The defects in David's book are glaring and inexcusable, but they are remediable and without any substantial impact on the unfolding economic and political analysis. When all the errors are corrected, the argument will stand exactly; the historical configuration will not change; the interpretive logic of the book will be upheld."

The Abraham controversy was widely reported in the *New York Times* and in *Time*. Feldman has said that people "admire my courage in pursuing this matter," and he is emboldened by this to call for a broadened effort to "clean up shop" in the history profession. Robert Tignor, chair of the Princeton history department, takes a different view of the consequences of the case's notoriety. He worries about its effect on young scholars: "The message is: Don't tread on the toes of established historians. Stay away from controversy. Don't take chances. The history profession is a sea full of sharks." It's also full of decent people who have come to Abraham's defense. Carl Schorske explains, "David Abraham is a guy who understands historical processes and has a subtle and refined interpretation. That's the reason why one wants to save him for the profession."

Postscript: In May 1991 David Abraham was appointed Associate Professor of Law at the University of Miami.

The Nation, February 16, 1985

Postscript: In 1986 Holmes & Meier published a second edition of *The Collapse of the Weimar Republic*. Unable to get a history job, Abraham enrolled in law school. In May 1991 David Abraham was appointed Associate Professor of Law at the University of Miami.

10

Bringing Nazi Sympathizers to the US:

Talcott Parsons's Role

Talcott Parsons, perhaps the most influential American sociologist of the twentieth century, worked with Army Intelligence officers and State Department officials after World War Two in an operation to smuggle Nazi collaborators into the country as Soviet studies experts. According to documents discovered by Charles O'Connell, a graduate student at the University of California, Los Angeles, Parsons went to Germany during the summer of 1948 and interviewed Russian exiles who had worked for the Nazis; along with Army Intelligence officers, he proposed ways to circumvent government policies that barred Nazi collaborators from obtaining US visas.

Parsons was teaching at Harvard University in 1948, but when he traveled to the American zone of occupied Germany that summer he entered the world of Nazis and collaborationist expatriates who desperately wanted to avoid prosecution for their crimes. They hoped to use their knowledge of the Soviet Union to obtain the protection of the US government, now committed to a cold war with the Russians. Klaus Barbie, the "Butcher of Lyons," traveled in this crowd, as is documented in the Marcel Ophuls film *Hotel Terminus*. Many of these Nazis and their abettors had already succeeded in convincing Army Intelligence officers and the newly established Central Intelligence Agency that the United States needed them; Talcott Parsons believed Harvard University needed some of them too, for its Russian Research Center.

Parsons, a sociologist whose structural–functional theory dominated the profession during the 1940s and 1950s, taught at Harvard from 1927 until his retirement in 1973. He died in 1979. He was president of the American Sociological Association in 1949 and served as chair of

Harvard's department of social relations from 1946 to 1956. He was the mentor of the next generation's leading sociologists, including Robert Merton, Kingsley Davis, Robert Bellah and Neil Smelser. The discovery of Parsons's efforts on behalf of Nazi collaborators is likely to inflame the debate over the political significance of his sociological theory. Parsons advocated a value-free sociology, arguing that social science had to purge itself of political values to achieve scientific status. His theory was ahistorical and highly abstract. During the 1960s, his work came under attack by a new generation of sociologists, who argued that his claims to "value-neutrality" masked a commitment to the status quo and to cold war ideology. The discovery of Parsons's recruitment of Nazi collaborators will strengthen that critique of his work.

The evidence of Parsons's postwar activities was discovered in the Harvard archives by O'Connell, whose dissertation is a study of the origins of the Harvard Russian Research Center. There he found ten letters Parsons wrote to a colleague, Professor Clyde Kluckhohn, head of the center. The letters report on Parsons's recruiting efforts in Germany and indicate that the most important of his Russian contacts was Nicholas Poppe, an expert on the languages of Soviet Asia who had been a professor at the University of Leningrad from 1925 to 1941. Parsons dedicated himself to obtaining a US entry visa and a Harvard appointment for Poppe—a difficult task, since Poppe was not only a Nazi collaborator but had been banned from entering the United States and had recently been the object of a US manhunt in Germany for extradition to the Soviet Union.

Poppe is a central figure in Christopher Simpson's recent book *Blowback: America's Recruitment of Nazis and Its Effects on the Cold War.* Poppe defected to the Nazis in 1942, the day they arrived in the Caucasus town where he was teaching. Simpson reported that Poppe "actively collaborated in the creation of the quisling government" in one of the ethnic minority areas, an administration that promptly expropriated Jewish property and murdered the region's Jews. In 1943 the SS brought Poppe to Berlin to work at the Wannsee Institute—the SS think tank where, in January 1942, the plans for "the final solution to the Jewish question" had been announced. The reports produced by Wannsee researchers were distributed to about fifteen top Nazi officials, including the military intelligence head on the eastern front, propaganda chief Joseph Goebbels and Hitler. Those reports, Simpson found, pinpointed the location and size of Jewish communities in the Soviet Union, thus assisting the SS in carrying out its campaign of extermination. Poppe's knowledge of the languages and ethnic groups in Soviet Asia would have made him useful for that project.

Poppe subsequently denied that his work at Wannsee aided the SS extermination program. In his memoirs he wrote that the Wannsee Institute's task "was to study various aspects of the Soviet economy, politics and science," and he claimed his work there dealt mainly with the "history, ethnography, culture and natural resources" of Siberia. That claim is "difficult to take at face value," Simpson writes, "in light of his strong expertise on the Caucasus region of the USSR, one of the most important focal points of the war at the time he was employed by the SS." In responding to charges that he had assisted the SS project of annihilation, Poppe reported an incident that inadvertently strengthens the case of his accusers. The Germans, he wrote in his memoirs, asked him whether a mountain tribe in the Caucasus, the Tats, were Jewish. Poppe reports that he informed the Germans that although the Tats practiced the Jewish religion, in fact they were ethnic Iranians; as a result of his report, Poppe says, the Tats were not exterminated. But if this was the kind of question the Germans were asking him, then it is clear that he was assisting the Nazi campaign to destroy the Jews.

The Poppe story is also told in a historic 1985 US General Accounting Office report, which confirmed that "Nazis and Axis collaborators were used to further US anti-Communist objectives in Europe—some immigrated to the United States." That report is best known for its account of the US protection of Klaus Barbie, but it also describes Poppe—although not by name—as one of "five Nazis or Axis collaborators with undesirable or questionable backgrounds who received some individual assistance in their US immigrations." After World War Two, Poppe took refuge in the British occupation zone. According to declassified Army Counter Intelligence Corps records obtained by Simpson, a top-secret memorandum dating from May 1947 reported that Poppe's presence in the British zone "is a source of embarrassment to British Military government, as the Soviet authorities are continually asking for his return as a war criminal. The British feel that Mr Poppe is valuable as an intelligence source and have asked ... if it is possible for US intelligence authorities to take him off their hands and see that he is sent to the US where he can be 'lost.'" Parsons made contact with Poppe a year later, and reported back to Clyde Kluckhohn the facts about "our friend Poppe."

A secret State Department letter regarding Poppe, dating from April 1948, instructed the Office of the US Political Adviser on German Affairs, in Frankfurt, to "arrange to have protection given to him and have him fattened up.... We shall be ready to lift him in about a month or two." A month later a telegram from the State Department's policy planning staff declared they knew Harvard was "anxious to get him." This initial effort to get Poppe into the United States did not succeed, as Parsons noted in a letter dated June 30, in which he reported that the State Department had refused Poppe entry even after a request from General Robert Walsh, director of intelligence in the European Command. Parsons then proposed another avenue to get Poppe into the United States. Edward Mason was a Harvard professor who served on the Russian Research Center's executive committee and also worked as a consultant to the State Department's policy planning staff. Parsons suggested that Mason be sent to enlist the help of George F. Kennan in gaining admission for Poppe. Kennan, a senior executive in the political warfare unit at the State Department, had just enunciated the containment doctrine that committed the United States to a cold war with the Soviet Union. Parsons's strategy worked: Kennan directly intervened to get Poppe into the country, a fact concealed for four decades until Simpson's book appeared last year. Poppe reported in his memoirs that he was flown out of Germany aboard a US military air transport plane; when he landed in Washington, DC, "a man sent by the State Department was standing on the airfield to meet me," he wrote.

Kluckhohn, acting on Parsons's advice, put Poppe up for a Harvard appointment, which the university's officials rejected. (Poppe later recalled that he had been turned down by Harvard "for political and some other reasons.") But in the fall of 1949, Poppe got a job as a professor of Far Eastern languages at the University of Washington, where he spent the rest of his career and where, according to Simpson, he taught many US intelligence agents.

But Poppe's activities were not limited to academia. He testified at the 1952 Congressional investigation of Owen Lattimore, who was probably the country's leading scholar on Mongolian society. Lattimore, director of the Walter Hines Page School of International Relations at Johns Hopkins University, was also a longtime State Department adviser with leftist sympathies. Joseph McCarthy had pledged that his whole anticommunist crusade would "stand or fall" on his charge that one man, Lattimore, had run a "Communist cell" in the Institute for Pacific Relations. Poppe was called by the Senate committee investigating Lattimore. He testified that many of Lattimore's studies of Mongolia were "very superficial," gave "a distorted picture of the realities" and were "not scholarly work." In fact Poppe had a private motive for joining McCarthy's attack on Lattimore, according to Simpson: he believed Lattimore had played a part in the State Department's initial denial of a US entry visa in 1948. Lattimore was eventually cleared of all McCarthy's charges against him, but Poppe's testimony helped provide academic respectability for McCarthyism.

Poppe was ninety-one years old in 1989, when thirty-two of his colleagues protested a *Seattle Times* article on Simpson's account of his collaboration with the Nazis. The colleagues described the Poppe they knew as "a gentleman, a compassionate human being, and one of the truly great scholars of this century."

Talcott Parsons knew that the man he called "our friend Poppe" had collaborated with the Nazis. He may not have known the details of Poppe's contribution—in particular his work for the Wannsee Institute. But he did know the British were embarrassed to have Poppe in their protection because of the charges against him, and he knew that the State Department had refused Poppe permission to enter the United States. The work Parsons did on Poppe's behalf indicates his willingness to overcome moral objections to collaboration, as well as his self-proclaimed "value-neutrality" in scientific norms, in the name of cold war activism.

Parsons developed relationships with other former Nazi collaborators on his German trip in 1948. Before he left Cambridge, an Army Intelligence officer had set up a meeting for him with Leo Dudin, a former professor of languages at the University of Kiev. In 1943, Parsons explained after the meeting, Dudin had gone to Berlin "and worked for the Propaganda Ministry writing scripts for broadcast to Russia. He got out just in time before the Russians came and has been in semi-hiding in Bavaria since." Dudin had served in the Vlasov Army, Parsons also reported, joining the Russians who fought for the

Nazis. The Vlasov Army was drawn mostly from prisoner of war camps; the Germans gave Soviet POWs a choice, according to war correspondent Alexander Werth: "[E]ither go into the Vlasov Army or starve." Though several thousand joined up, the overwhelming majority refused to go, and 2 million died in the camps. By 1945 about half of Vlasov's troops had come from the SS Kommando Kaminsky, a Byelorussian militia that had spearheaded the Nazis' annihilation of the 1943 Warsaw ghetto rebellion; their bestial conduct there offended even the German general Hans Guderian, who called for their removal from the field. If Parsons did not know the history of the Vlasov Army, whose veterans he was recruiting, he could have found out.

Another of Parsons's Vlasov Army contacts was Vladimir Pozdniakov, a former Red Army lieutenant colonel. Parsons explained that Pozdniakov was captured by the Nazis and "joined the Vlasov movement, where he became a full Colonel." Pozdniakov, according to a recent scholarly study, became chief of security for the pro-Nazi Committee for the Liberation of the Peoples of Russia, the political wing of the Vlasov movement. The Soviet Union listed Pozdniakov as one of seventy-three "war criminals and [persons] who collaborated with the enemy" whose extradition they sought from the American zone. Parsons reported back to Kluckhohn at Harvard that he had met not only with Poppe, Dudin and Pozdniakov but also with two US Army Intelligence officers who employed them; the intelligence officers, he reported, urged that the émigrés be brought to the United States, and Parsons suggested they be given jobs at Harvard. He called the notion "damned important." America's leading exponent of "value-free" sociology was here joining in a recommendation made by Army Intelligence officers that Nazi collaborators wanted as war criminals be given jobs at Harvard as Soviet studies experts.

Dudin and Pozdniakov did not get stateside jobs at Harvard in the end, nor did they get into the United States. But both were hired by Harvard's Russian Research Center to collect information about the Soviet Union from their displaced countrymen in Germany. Their reports, however, were of low quality, and their contract was not renewed in 1950. Dudin was reported in 1987 to have died. Pozdniakov published two volumes of Vlasov Army documents and memoirs in the early 1970s; his current status is unknown.

In the midst of his recruiting efforts, Parsons had a moment of doubt. In a June 1948 letter he wrote, "Perhaps I was a little hasty in my recommendations on the Dudin group.... Their political inclinations may be extreme—and yet—I want to go back to them with the wider perspective." This reconsideration concerned only the "political inclinations," not the past activities, of the people Parsons had put forward. He seems to have assumed that the cold war justified ignoring criticial questions about enlisting former Nazi collaborators as Harvard Soviet scholars. Was it right to help these people avoid prosecution for war crimes? Were they the kind of people who belonged on university faculties? Does a university have the same goals as the State Department and Army Intelligence in gathering information about the Soviet Union? Are former Nazi collaborators wanted by the Russians for war crimes likely to provide reliable information about the Soviet Union? Parsons's letters articulate none of these moral issues.

Parsons undertook his recruiting mission shortly after two key events that deepened the cold war, events that must have made his task seem especially urgent. In February 1948, Czechoslovakia's Communist Party, with the backing of the Red Army, took power, reinforcing fears about a Soviet military attack on Western Europe. "Russia, at this stage, is the world's No. 1 military power," *US News & World Report* proclaimed that April. "Russia's armies and air forces are in a position to pour across Europe and into Asia almost at will." In June the Soviet Union closed Western access to Berlin; the airlift of supplies was under way while Parsons visited American intelligence officers in Germany

Presumably, the justification for Parsons's recruiting efforts was the shortage of reliable information about conditions in the Soviet Union, information necessary to assess the threat it posed to US national security. At a time when anti-Soviet hysteria of the *US News & World Report* variety was spreading, accurate information about Soviet intentions and capabilities was especially important. But the people Parsons was enlisting were not good sources of information, because each had a nearly desperate personal interest in exaggerating the menace of the Soviet Union—since the Russians were pressuring the British and Americans to extradite them to face charges as war criminals. Of course, we don't know what the Parsons recruits told the State Department, the Army Counter Intelligence Corps and the CIA about the Soviet threat. We do know that the government greatly exaggerated the danger in 1948 and thereafter, relying in part on reports from such people. By materially assisting in this intelligence process, Talcott Parsons contributed to some of the most antidemocratic and anti-intellectual trends in postwar American political life.

Parsons's 1948 German trip raises some larger questions about the relationship between academic sociology and political life. Is there something about ahistorical social theory that leads its practitioners to "forget" the history of the Nazis' crimes? Is there something about "value-free" social science that leads its practitioners to ignore the value of bringing collaborators to justice? In the end, Parsons proves to be another case in a depressingly familiar story: that of leading liberal scholars in the United States making political commitments in the name of the cold war, blinding themselves to moral issues and making a mockery of their claims to objective scholarship.

The Nation, March 6, 1989

11

Poles, Jews, and Historians:

the Case of Norman Davies

In fall, 1987, a British historian of Poland filed a lawsuit against Stanford University, charging that its decision not to appoint him to a tenured professorship was an act of political discrimination. Norman Davies, a historian at the University of London, had accepted a visiting professorship at Stanford for 1986 after being assured that the department would vote him a $70,000-a-year chair in Eastern European history after his arrival. But according to Davies's attorney, former Representative Pete McCloskey, at the department meeting where his reappointment was discussed, "six Jewish professors ... stood up and castigated a single chapter" of Davies's book *God's Playground: A History of Poland*—the chapter on Poland's Jews. The historians' religion is relevant, according to Davies, because they claimed he distorted the history of Poland, was insensitive to the Jews and was an apologist for the Poles' conduct during the Holocaust. These criticisms, the suit argues, were false and derogatory and implied that Davies was anti-Semitic—and thus unqualified for work as a historian because he was unprofessional and biased. The suit also argues that Davies was the victim of discrimination, as his employer intended to control expression of his political views (a violation of the state labor code).

Davies's original suit, filed in May 1986, named not only Stanford University as a defendant but also individual historians who, he argued, had defamed him (Harold Kahn, a specialist in Chinese history; Paul Robinson, department chair at the time Davies was turned down; Alexander Dallin, a historian of Russia); Jon Adelstein, a graduate student who wrote a letter to the *Stanford Daily* criticizing Davies's work; several administrators; and twenty-nine additional

"John Does"—Stanford historians and others who, in Davies's view, had defamed him at the confidential department meeting but whose identity has been concealed. The original suit sought to collect damages from Professors Kahn, Robinson and Dallin and graduate student Adelstein as individuals, "based upon their respective net worths." His original suit was dismissed; his amended complaint drops the defamation charge against individuals but reasserts the discrimination charges against Stanford.

Davies's suits also charges Stanford with "negligent infliction of emotional distress," for which Davies seeks $3 million in damages. He cites specific acts—for example, Stanford vice president John Schwartz said there was "no merit to . . . the pernicious notion that if one's work is not deemed sufficient to merit appointment, one is defamed"—that inflicted $3 million worth of emotional distress on him. Moreover, Davies's suit charges that the defendants "met secretly and conspired among themselves" to "cause plaintiff severe emotional distress." Finally, Davies's suit claims that, when Stanford turned him down for a job, he incurred "damage to his reputation in the sum of $3 million." He also seeks triple punitive damages—$9 million—plus attorneys' fees for what he claims to have suffered.

Davies's claim that Stanford discriminated against him with the intent of controlling expression of his political views is more interesting. "The issue is very simple," McCloskey said. "Was he turned down because of his scholarship or because of his political views?" That indeed is the question. It would be wrong for Stanford to refuse to hire Davies on the ground that he advocated a political position, because advocacy is protected absolutely by the First Amendment. Stanford must evaluate his scholarly work, not his politics. Stanford has insisted its objection was not to Davies's advocacy of any political position. Provost James Rosse gave Stanford's official reasons for not hiring Davies in a seven-page, single-spaced letter: *God's Playground* crossed the line between scholarship and advocacy; as a result Davies's scholarly work had a "lack of objectivity," was "insufficiently analytical and tends to substitute rhetoric and irony for clear historical analysis and explanation," "lacked analytical rigor" and was "insufficiently critical." Stanford's historians have been instructed by their attorneys not to comment on the case, and none would.

But Davies has claimed that the official reasons only conceal the true motives of his critics, which were to deny him employment because of his political beliefs and creed. "I've been called anti-Polish by extreme Polish fanatics and anti-Semitic by extreme Zionist fanatics," Davies told me. "I don't take either of those charges seriously." In his original suit he sought to depose history department members to learn what they had said about him at the meeting. A California Superior Court ruled in favor of Davies; the university appealed, contending that the comments Davies alleged had been made about him were matters of opinion and therefore could not be subject to a defamation suit under the First Amendment. The California Court of Appeals agreed in January, ruling that you can't ask professors in court what they've said about one another's academic qualifications when they have been promised confidentiality. Attorney Steve Mayer of the firm Howard, Rice, Nemerovsky, Canady, Robertson and Falk, representing Stanford, called that "a resounding victory for academic freedom."

The American Federation of Teachers and the National Education Association both have taken a somewhat different position, calling for "open files"—complete disclosure of written materials used in the hiring and promoting of faculty. In a lawsuit unrelated to the one Davies filed, the University of California AFT sued the university to open its hiring and promotions files. The American Association of University Professors has taken an alternative stance, holding that written files should be open to candidates only where there is a *prima facie* case of discrimination—and the burden is on the candidate to demonstrate that case. But the AFT, the NEA and the AAUP have never argued, as Davies plans to, that candidates should have a right to question department members under oath regarding their "real" reasons for opposing an appointment. That was an untenable position, and the California court wisely rejected it.

Davies filed suit under California's Unruh Civil Rights Act, which prohibits discrimination by an employer based on creed or political orientation. The statute refers to religion and party affiliation; for example, a Republican boss can't fire workers for being Democrats. But Stanford's attorney Mayer has argued that all Stanford did was evaluate Davies's scholarship. The question that must be decided is whether the historical scholarship in *God's Playground* is good enough that discrimination becomes a plausible explanation for Stanford's rejection of him.

Davies is widely recognized as being among the world's leading historians of Poland—although there aren't many others. Almost half the voting members of the Stanford history department (the vote was 12 to 11) concluded that he was qualified for the chair. *God's Playground*, a two-volume work, covers a thousand years of Polish history; it displays impressive breadth and erudition. But his chapters on Jews in Poland during World War Two mix a dubious defense of Polish conduct during the Nazi occupation with an intensely anti-Soviet bias and some blame-the-victim arguments about the Holocaust. Polish anti-Semitism, Davies argues, was not responsible for Auschwitz; the Germans, not the Poles, destroyed Eastern European Jewry. Here Davies is absolutely correct. He has challenged Holocaust historians like Lucy Dawidowicz who see the "final solution" as the culmination of traditional European anti-Semitism. His criticism is also aimed at Claude Lanzmann, whose film *Shoah* seems to suggest that anti-Semitic Polish peasants had some responsibility for the death camps.

Although Davies is right in portraying the Poles as victims of the Nazis, his presentation of the Polish response to the presence of the death camps in their midst is deeply misleading. "To ask why the Poles did little to help the Jews," he writes, "is rather like asking why the Jews did nothing to assist the Poles." Well, let's ask what the Poles could have done to help the Jews. They could have saved Jews from the death camps by hiding them or providing them with forged documents. During the liquidation of the Warsaw ghetto, the forty-six days in the summer of 1942 during which 75 per cent of the 350,000 ghetto residents were put on trains to Treblinka, Poles could have cut the rail line. They could have supported the resistance movement in the ghettos by providing arms. They could have welcomed Jews into partisan units. They did none of these things.

Were the Poles capable of taking any of these actions? Davies argues that Nazi oppression made Poles helpless, as helpless as the Jews. He's right that Poles who helped Jews faced more risks than did non-Jews in the other Nazi-occupied countries. The only people deported from Nazi-occupied Poland to concentration camps in Germany between 1939 and 1941 were Poles, not Jews. And the Poles were subject to conscription by the Nazis for forced labor. Poles could be deported to concentration camps for concealing Jews and, beginning in late 1942, could be executed for it. But of course the Poles were not as helpless as the Jews. The Germans were tougher on Poland than on other occupied countries in part because the Poles had more ability to fight back. The Polish underground, the largest in Europe, was a well-organized force of 400,000 armed men who operated throughout the country. Poland's extensive forests provided excellent cover for guerrilla warfare. And the Poles had one additional reason to help the Jews—they were the first to learn the true purpose of the Nazi deportation of Jews.

Of course, some Poles did help Jews. As many as 20,000 Jews were in hiding in Warsaw outside the ghetto in 1942, according to Yisrael Gutman, a historian of Warsaw's Jews, and that was 5 per cent of Warsaw's Jewish population. They could not have avoided the Polish bounty hunters and extortionists without help from Poles, who were risking their lives. These Poles included intellectuals, devout Catholics and ordinary townspeople. Polish Communists, during the liquidation of the Warsaw ghetto, called on Poles to aid and conceal Jews who escaped. But these were exceptions to the general pattern. The Polish underground did not appeal to the Polish people to help Jews escape. It never adequately supported the resistance movement in the Warsaw ghetto. But the Warsaw ghetto uprising was the first armed, organized resistance to the Nazi occupiers; up to that point the Polish underground had done nothing. The revolt demonstrated that resistance was possible; it undermined the prestige and confidence of the Germans and impressed the Poles. It was in the interest of the Polish underground that the ghetto revolt survive as long as possible and take as great a toll of Nazi soldiers as possible.

Davies denies that the failure of the Polish underground to support the uprising was an expression of Polish anti-Semitisim. Writing in the *New York Review of Books*, he quoted a prominent Jewish survivor of the uprising, Marek Edelman, as describing the Poles as "a tolerant people." At the time Davies's article was published, Edelman's interview was available only in Polish, but it has since been translated. After the uprising, Edelman said, he escaped to the forests, where he was imprisoned by the Polish Underground Home Army, the AK. "The AK tried to have me executed, because being a Jew was a mistake." He went on to tell his interviewers, "Don't listen to me telling you such disgusting stories. They're not fit to print. Because, as you well know, the Polish people are very tolerant. Nothing bad ever happened here to national minorities." Thus Davies's evidence that the Polish people are very "tolerant" in fact supports what one might call a different interpretation.

Polish anti-Semitism was a Zionist myth, Davies argues, "a necessary instrument in the hands of the Zionist movement for persuading the Jewish masses to leave Poland for Palestine." But the evidence of anti-Semitism in Nazi-occupied Poland is overwhelming. On the streets of Warsaw, Gutman reports, "the attacks by individuals and gangs of Poles on Jewish passersby and apartment houses ... took on the proportions of a wave of pogroms." For example, an eyewitness reported that a thousand Polish hoodlums engaged in a weeklong attack on the Jews of Warsaw during Passover in 1940. Davies concedes that some Poles were anti-Semitic after 1939 but explains that they had been aroused by the Jews' welcoming of the Soviet occupation that year. In response to Jews who accuse the Poles of complicity with the Nazis, Davies refers to "the complicity of many Jews with the Soviet invaders." Thus Jewish conduct was responsible for "the marked increase in anti-Semitism in occupied Poland," and it is the Jews' own fault that the Poles didn't help them when the Nazis came. This argument appeared in, of all places, the *New York Review of Books*.

But when Polish Jews welcomed the Soviet occupation, it was not out of a desire to see Poland destroyed; it was out of the knowledge that the Red Army alone had the power to stop the Nazis and thus protect them. The Jews who welcomed the Russians were left-wing but not anti-Polish—they were anti-German and anti-Fascist. In part, the validity of Davies's argument about Jewish complicity with the Russians depends on one's assessment of Soviet policy in occupied Poland between 1939 and 1941. Davies warns readers not to "isolate the crimes of the Nazis from the parallel crimes of the Soviets, which were committed on an even grander scale and often on the self-same territories." Stalin's crimes against the Poles, Davies argues, consist of the deportation of 1.5 million Polish citizens to Russia between 1939 and 1941, half of whom, he estimates, died. Davies concludes that "Stalin was outpacing Hitler in his desire to reduce the Poles to the condition of a slave-nation." And, Davies argues, Poland's Jews helped Stalin enslave the Poles.

Davies's numbers seem to be exaggerated; a recent scholarly study reports the number of Polish deportees to be not 1.5 million but 880,000, half of whom were released in a 1941 Soviet amnesty. But the numbers game avoids the real question: was Soviet policy in Poland "parallel" to the Nazis' crime? The Nazis' crime was genocide; Stalin was seeking not to kill all the Poles but rather to prepare for the antici-pated Nazi invasion of Russia. The Russians did deport hundreds of thousands of Poles to atrocious camps, having identified them as potentially pro-Nazi and on a strategic frontier. This Soviet policy was terrible for the Poles who were deported, but it was not a policy of extermination of the Polish people. The Russians deported nearly a million Poles, but they left 19 million behind. Half a million Poles died in Soviet camps, but six million Poles died in Nazi camps. The Russians did not commit crimes against the Poles "on an even grander scale" than the Nazis.

In Nazi-occupied Eastern Europe, there was one ghetto resistance movement that achieved significantly more than the others: Minsk's. The key to its successes, as Reuben Ainszstein has shown in his monu-mental book *Jewish Resistance in Nazi-Occupied Eastern Europe*, was that the non-Jews provided more support for the ghetto fighters of Minsk than did their counterparts elsewhere. What made Minsk different? It was in Byelorussia, not Poland.

Davies's attorney, McCloskey, has argued that Davies is not anti-Semitic. "I submitted the key chapter of his book to a noted Jewish psychologist and his wife," he told me. "They tested it according to a technique of determining prejudice by evaluating adjectives. They found Davies applied equal numbers of laudatory and unfavorable adjectives to both Jews and Poles. I'm hoping to use them as expert witnesses." The idea that anti-Semitism exists in adjectives but not in historical arguments is, one might say, unconvincing.

Davies's claim that he is the victim of political discrimination echoes arguments made by radical scholars denied jobs or tenure. Since all scholarship has a political dimension, does that mean defenders of radicals like David Abraham ought to defend Norman Davies? Political issues certainly play a part in the Davies case; if no one cared about what happened to Jews in occupied Poland, no one would read Davies's chapter on the subject and find its faults. The left argues that academic hiring and firing should be based not on a candidate's politics but rather on the intellectual quality of his or her work; good historians who are radicals should not be denied jobs. But who decides what constitutes good history? Other historians and intellectuals. Judging the intellectual quality of scholarship, particularly in matters of interpretation, is highly subjective and open to prejudice, error and injustice. People disagree and argue. But there's no other way to decide; evaluating the quality of scholarship is what intellectuals do.

The objections to Davies concern the quality of his work as a historian. He distorts evidence to fit his conclusions (for example, the Edelman quote), he ignores evidence that disproves his arguments, and his thesis that Poles were as helpless as Jews under the Nazi occupation is simply untenable. There comes a point when a faulty interpretation is the equivalent of bad scholarship, and I believe that Davies's work passes that point. Thus, Stanford is not engaging in political discrimination by not hiring Davies. The historians who voted against him were fulfilling their responsibilities as intellectuals.

The Nation, November 21, 1987

12

Campus Capitalism:

Harvard Chases Biotech Bucks

Derek Bok, president of Harvard University, could hardly have put it better: educational institutions that promote business schemes "confuse the university's central commitment to the pursuit of knowledge and learning by introducing into the very heart of the academic enterprise a new and powerful motive—the search for commercial utility and financial gain."

That was in 1980, but the Reagan years appear to have changed the heart of the academic enterprise at Harvard. In September 1988 the university wrote a new chapter in the history of corporate–academic ties when it announced it would raise $30 million in venture capital to form a company to market the biotechnology research of the Harvard Medical School faculty. Other universities have been inviting biotech firms on campus, offering the profits from faculty research in exchange for funds and facilities. But Harvard has gone the next step by forming its own company—Medical Science Partners (MSP)—and reserving part of the profits for itself.

Harvard's unprecedented pursuit of profit reflects not only the *Zeitgeist* of the Age of Reagan but the new realities of biotechnology. Corporations and investors are desperate to gain access to university labs, because basic biotech research today is conducted almost exclusively in universities. It also reflects the past decade's privatization of discoveries deriving from government-sponsored research. Until 1980, the fruits of such research were public property. Patents on products developed under grants from the National Science Foundation or National Institutes of Health were for the most part held by the government. When Jonas Salk was asked who held the patent to his polio vaccine, he replied, "The people, I would say.... Could you patent the sun?" But the law was changed in 1980 to give universities exclusive rights to the products of government-sponsored research, including the rights to hold patents, issue licenses and collect royalties. Universities are thus doubly valuable to corporations interested in biotechnology profits. Not only are their labs the principal sites for biotech research but universities also have a right denied to corporations—the right to patent and license discoveries financed by the public. James Rule, a sociologist at the State University of New York at Stony Brook and an authority on the politics of biotechnology, pointed out in the fall 1989 issue of *Dissent* that "ideas developed at public expense and on behalf of public goals are being converted as rapidly as possible to private profit-making."

This search for profits can lead to violations of scientific procedures and scholarly ethics. For example, Washington University in St Louis made a deal with the Monsanto Company in 1982: the corporation invested $23.5 million in medical school research it hoped would produce marketable results; faculty members who received research grants gave Monsanto the rights to the product of their work, including the right not to market it and to conceal scientific discoveries that the corporation determined were threatening to its interests. Thus Monsanto held the right to delay disclosure of faculty research results for up to four years when executives felt the company might lose more than it would gain by marketing a new product, or when the company's competitors might benefit more from a particular discovery than Monsanto would. And faculty members had to promise Monsanto that they would not disclose the results of their research to the scientific community if that research was commercially relevant to Monsanto. Of course, this agreement violated scientific requirements for prompt dissemination of research results, necessary to permit repli-cation and to encourage prompt public benefit.

The most striking recent example of the fruits of university–corporate biotech research was Harvard's patent on a special mouse: half of all the females of this genetically altered rodent develop cancer. In April 1988, the Federal government granted Harvard the first patent on an animal for its mouse, which provides researchers with a more efficient way of testing cancer therapies. Because the mouse was developed by two Harvard Medical School researchers, the university holds the patent; but the Du Pont Company financed the research, and Harvard agreed to give the company the exclusive right to license and thus profit from the mouse. (The Harvard mouse patent triggered considerable controversy. Several members of Congress, along with farm groups, religious leaders and animal rights activists, argued that the Reagan Administration should not have established the policy of granting patents on animal species without public debate and in defiance of a request from Congress to delay such action.)

Until recently, faculty members who made discoveries with profit potential held the relevant patents jointly with their universities, and the discoveries were developed and marketed by corporations that put their own in-house researchers to work. Corporations paid royalties on the patents, which the professors shared with the universities that sponsored their research. Some universities take in substantial sums in royalties and licenses, among them Stanford, which earns more than $9 million annually. What's new in the Harvard plan is the way it puts the university in the role played, until now, by the corporation. Harvard's Medical Science Partners is a limited partnership that will support the research of its medical school faculty seeking to convert laboratory discoveries into marketable products. Harvard will hold the patents, and MSP will be granted exclusive licenses to market the discoveries it funds. Although the university will raise the capital, it won't invest any of its own money, but it will receive 10 per cent of the profits. The decisions about which faculty projects to fund will be made not by Harvard officials but rather by a former drug industry executive, Andre Lamotte, who will manage MSP and also receive 10 per cent of the profits.

But that's only the beginning. Lamotte's decisions will be subject to review by a mysterious entity called Ion Inc., a new, wholly owned nonprofit Harvard subsidiary, which will have the power to fire Lamotte. The officers of Ion Inc. will be university administrators; members of the Harvard Corporation (the university's secretive governing body); and members of the Harvard Management Corporation, the university's investment company (known recently for its reluctance to part with South African stocks). Ion Inc. in turn will receive recommendations from a special medical school academic review committee charged with evaluating the academic integrity and potential conflicts of interest in projects seeking support from Medical

Science Partners. This tangled web, Harvard officials insist, will somehow separate Harvard from the management of the fund while assuring that MSP does not violate university rules. But separating the profit-making enterprise from the university itself also creates an element of deniability for Harvard when conflicts of interest and ethical violations arise.

And they will arise—because even Harvard doctors can be greedy and corrupt. While Harvard spokesmen were defending the MSP plan, a conflict-of-interest scandal erupted involving a researcher at a Harvard-affiliated hospital. He had violated regulations of the university and the Food and Drug Administration by testing a drug that had not been approved for experimental use and in which he had a financial stake. Dr Scheffer C.G. Tseng had developed a vitamin treatment for a condition called dry eye, which he tested without FDA authorization on more than two hundred patients at Massachusetts Eye and Ear Hospital. The *Boston Globe* revealed in October 1988 that Tseng and his family held a substantial block of stock in Spectra Pharmaceutical Services, the company that manufactured the drug, and that they had made at least $1 million after Tseng announced his results were "promising." The drug has since proved to be ineffective. Two Congressional subcommittees have announced preliminary investigations, with Ted Weiss, chair of the House Human Resources and Intergovernmental Subcommittee, saying he is concerned about whether "Harvard adequately protected the patients" in the study.

Why didn't Tseng's Harvard overseers spot the problem? His supervisor, Harvard Medical School Associate Professor Kenneth Kenyon, also owned stock (at one time worth $340,000) in the company. Kenyon also touted the new drug as "promising," though Tseng's research was clearly faulty and may have been fraudulent. After the conflict of interest was discovered, Harvard Medical School Dean Daniel Tosteson ordered Kenyon to give up all benefit from his Spectra stock, but took no other disciplinary action. When Harvard itself stands to profit from the work of its researchers, the pressures to violate scientific and ethical rules will be more intense and cases of what Harvard casually calls "faulty oversight" will be more common.

In 1980 the Harvard faculty objected loudly when a plan similar to MSP was proposed—leading president Bok to proclaim that the pursuit of profit is incompatible with the purposes of the university. This time the best-informed and fullest critique of the new plan came not from the faculty but from Harvard Watch, a Ralph Nader-sponsored project headed by Robert Weissman, an undergraduate. In October 1988, the organization released a nineteen-page dissection of the Medical Science Partners proposal, arguing that Bok's objections to the 1980 plan remain altogether relevant in the present case. Harvard officials responded with assurances that no ethical problems will arise—after all, university guidelines state that "faculty members have a responsibility to maintain the scholarly character of their research." Harvard Medical School Dean Tosteson, in a letter to the *New York Times*, described the new profit-making firm as simply a "fund" that will "combat disease" and "improve human health." Who could object to that? The guidelines also state that faculty members must not make agreements with MSP to "restrain publication" or "provide for the holding of any information in confidence." But what if, instead of making an agreement to keep their research secret, they just happen to keep their research secret? The pressures toward secrecy will quickly grow as Harvard's investors commit vast resources toward developing patents or products worth millions of dollars.

The university also defended the new firm by arguing that it will serve the public interest—primarily by filling something Harvard calls the "development gap," a gap between basic research funded by the NIH and the NSF and corporate research to develop commercial applications. Stephen Atkinson is one of the Harvard officials whose job includes defending the MSP plan. He has a title that didn't exist before the biotechnology revolution hit the campus: Director of the Office of Technology Licensing and Industry-sponsored Research at Harvard Medical School. He told Harvard Watch that capitalism doesn't work when it comes to linking basic medical research findings to commercial potential, and thus the public needs Harvard's Medical Science Partners. But does the "development gap" really exist? Biotechnology is a field where venture capital firms constantly seek high-risk, high-return investments of precisely the type that would fall under this rubric. Even if the gap is real, Harvard Watch argues, projects that risk-oriented private capital refuses to fund will not be promising sources of profit for the university. MSP is supposed to make a profit, and thus will have an incentive to avoid products that fall into the gap. The firm's commercial orientation clearly undermines its claim to serve the public interest.

University officials have worked hard to dispel the notion that Harvard is "going into business." "There will be no control [by the university] over the investment decisions of that company," explained John Shattuck, Harvard vice president for government and community affairs. Harvard Watch's Weissman replied that the real problem is not that Harvard will control the company but that Harvard will tailor its own activities to benefit the company—by keeping profitable discoveries secret, by hiring and promoting faculty with profit-making potential, by devoting lab space and other resources to profit-oriented rather than basic research. Harvard Watch also maintains that the university should make public all documents of Ion Inc. and the medical school academic review committee that is charged with oversight, including reports submitted by professors participating in MSP. "If the documents can't be made public," Weissman argued, "then the proposal does not satisfy academic requirements for preserving the free flow of information and MSP is not a project Harvard should be involved in." Thus far the university has refused to agree to make the documents public.

Even the *New York Times* attacked Harvard—a rare event—for the MSP plan. The paper argued in an editorial that the university's pursuit of profit threatened to undermine its pursuit of "pure knowledge." Harvard Watch made a similar case: by joining the biotech industry, the university is abandoning its self-proclaimed role as an independent critic of society. This "ivory tower" conception of the university was discredited long ago, of course, partly by Clark Kerr's description of the "multiversity" that serves diverse social ends, and partly by 1960s radicals who showed the varied ways that universities serve the needs of corporations. (One current example: when farm workers organized a union in California, the University of California, Davis, stepped up its research on "labor saving" devices that would help agribusiness eliminate workers' jobs.) Of course, the university also provides a home for social critics and planners of alternative policies, including a few who publish in *The Nation*. But although the university has never existed in isolation from social and political forces, the present aggressive trend toward profit-making is genuinely a new step.

And it is a step that could well threaten hallowed scholarly criteria for hiring and tenure. Bok has declared that there is "no possibility that the appointment process would be affected in any way by the fund." But suppose a young scientist does work lacking in real intellectual or scientific significance; suppose, moreover, that he doesn't show up for class, and harasses women who work in his lab. But the corporate managers say he's developing marketable discoveries that will make big profits; if he's denied tenure, he'll take his ideas to another university, which will get rich instead of Harvard. The medical school may not be able to resist pressures to grant tenure to such a person.

The opportunities for marketing faculty research, of course, need not be limited to biotechnology. Why not go all the way and make the university itself a corporation—sell stock in Harvard? If the Nabisco name is worth $25 billion, imagine what investment bankers would pay to own part of the Ivy League. Other prestigious universities would follow suit. Those with weak profits would become takeover targets; to restore investor confidence, they would sell off divisions with lackluster earnings, putting the philosophy, classics and German literature departments on the auction block. Scholarship would be channeled into fields where there's a strong merchandising potential, like literary theory. Other universities would market humbler intellectual products—happy histories by Daniel Boorstin—with an "everyday low price" strategy. Never again would political scientists with Third World pacification programs simply give their work to the government for free. Now, universities could form limited joint partnerships with other corporations to market such plans, and then use the profits to invent ever newer forms of social control.

The Nation, January 2, 1989

13

The CIA Goes Back to College

Is the teaching of college courses by officers of the Central Intelligence Agency a threat to academic freedom? That's only one of the questions raised by a new CIA program that places agents on university faculties as visiting scholars, which has become the target of protests at the University of California, Santa Barbara. The agency's Officer-in-Residence Program was described by a CIA official in a letter to UCSB's political science department as an effort to "enhance CIA's recruiting efforts by providing an opportunity for experienced officers to serve as role models, [and] to counsel interested students on career opportunities with CIA." Under the program, the CIA selects and pays the salary of the agent and the university provides an academic appointment—an unusual arrangement for universities that generally insist on autonomy in making appointments and on the intellectual independence of faculty members.

The program came to light at UCSB when faculty in the political science department protested the appointment of CIA officer George Chritton Jr, a thirty-year agency veteran, to a two-year term as a lecturer, teaching departmental courses on intelligence gathering. Some 800 students attended a rally and 150 students joined a sit-in at the chancellor's office in November 1987, calling on the university to sever its ties with the CIA program; 38 students were arrested.

CIA spokesman Bill Devine said in an interview that the program is not secret, but he refused to identify the six universities that currently have CIA officers in faculty positions or reveal the spooks' names. Two other institutions, however, have acknowledged their participation in the program; the Georgetown University School of Foreign Service and the Lyndon B. Johnson School for Public Affairs, at the University of Texas, Austin. Devine said that one other university is already participating in the program; UCSB political science chair Cedric Robinson says he was told by the CIA that it is the John F. Kennedy School of Government, at Harvard. Devine also said two more universities have appointments "in the pipeline" for the spring or fall 1988 semesters; one of them is George Washington University, according to Robinson. The identity of the sixth university is unknown.

At the University of Texas's LBJ school, a spokesman identified the CIA officer in residence as James McInnis. Max Sherman, dean of the school, said "There's been no problem" with protests against the CIA's presence there. "The Central Intelligence Agency is a major agency of the Federal government," he said, "and we don't want to be prejudiced for or against them." At Georgetown, officials identified Noel Firth as the CIA officer on the faculty, a "research associate," and Harold Bean as his predecessor in the program. UCSB president David Gardner told *The Nation* that critics of the CIA appointment were making "arguments for 'guilt by association' ... parallel to those used in 1949 when the Regents of the university barred members of the Communist Party from teaching by imposing a loyalty oath. It should not be one's personal affiliations or political views that determine such appointments but rather the canons of the academic profession, which are concerned with the individual scholar's freedom to seek the truth and impart it."

UCSB Chancellor Barbara Uehling rejected a unanimous recommendation from an academic senate committee that the university terminate its participation in the CIA program. "I firmly believe that a university must guarantee that differing points of view, especially those that are unpopular, can be heard and debated," she said. "To subject prospective appointees to political or ideological tests is antithetical to this essential purpose." She accepted a recommendation from the political science faculty downgrading Chritton's appointment from "visiting lecturer" to "visiting fellow." He will not be allowed to teach his own courses but will serve as a resource person available to deliver lectures in courses taught by others, although she held out the possibility that he may teach courses during a second year. According to Uehling, Chritton "is prohibited from recruiting for the agency." But CIA spokesman Devine said that although Chritton "won't be interviewing—we have other people who do that," he "is there if somebody reaches out to him" about a career with the agency.

Chritton's defenders, including Dean Mann, the former political science chair who hired him, have said critics of the CIA Officer-in-Residence Program are threatening academic freedom. That argument has become the center of campus debate. "People are confusing academic freedom with freedom of speech," said Todd Gooch of the Student Legislative Council, who was arrested in the sit-in. "No one is denying Mr Chritton his right to speak. But academic freedom is different; it's reserved for those who have demonstrated the capacity to act according to the standards of the academic community. The official university regulations on academic freedom state that 'the university is founded on faith in intelligence and knowledge and it must defend their free operation.' But CIA agents are prohibited from participating in the free operation of knowledge. Mr Chritton is obliged by law not to provide certain information; he may be obliged by the agency to provide disinformation. The people who are using 'academic freedom' against us don't understand what academic freedom is."

"Freedom of speech is not the issue," added Jaime Acton, director of the campus student lobby and the first student to be arrested. "People can speak on the campus without having an official affiliation. We've invited him to speak, to debate; he hasn't accepted. He said, 'I'm here to teach, not to debate.' The issue is his affiliation with the faculty. It legitimizes the CIA and discredits the university to provide a formal academic position for a CIA representative." Active CIA officers in academic positions might report to the agency about campus activists or foreign students or faculty, argued anthropologist Tom Harding. "His [Chritton's] presence creates a chilling effect on campus." Executive Order 12333, signed by President Reagan in December 1981, effectively authorizes CIA domestic activities for the first time in its history. At the time, the agency claimed it was not going to spy on American citizens at home, but the order does allow the CIA to engage in "undisclosed participation" in domestic groups, activities and organizations. The college classroom could be the site of such undisclosed activity.

Critics reject the parallel between the current controversy and the McCarthyite purges of the campuses in the 1950s. Communists were fired from university positions on the ground that they were members of a disciplined organization with secrets to keep and thus could not be trusted to teach freely. No one established the validity of these charges in the cases of Communists who were dismissed. But, in the CIA Officer-in-Residence Program, historian Leonard Marsak argued, "we have an individual who is a member of an organization that has in fact committed illegal acts, who is under discipline with secrets to keep, and so is in no position to teach freely, as the university rightly requires."

Chritton lacks the usual qualifications for a teaching position in the political science department. He earned a BA in 1955 from Occidental College in Los Angeles, according to CIA spokesman Devine, and was a graduate student at Princeton University. He served in the Air Force and has thirty years' experience in what Devine called "a variety of CIA management jobs." According to the book *Dirty Work: The CIA in Western Europe*, edited by Philip Agee and Louis Wolf, Chritton joined the agency in 1960. His subsequent posts included Ankara, Turkey, from 1963 to 1965, under State Department cover as an embassy attaché and political officer—just before the massive government repression of the late 1960s. He served in Katmandu from 1967 to 1969, and Malta from 1972 to 1974. He has told students his area of speciality is Africa. (When students tried to consult their library's copy of *Dirty Work*, they found it had been checked out by Chritton for the entire year.) Chritton has appeared in an international relations class, where he took questions from students. "People asked about links between the CIA and Iran/*contra* affair," said Dan Zumwinkle, a member of the Associated Students Legislative Council and a student in the class. "Chritton is a congenial older man; he chuckled and said, 'I'm not very familiar with that area.' He's pretty good at evasion."

"It's not hard to see what they are doing," said Jan Sallinger-McBride, a Ph.D. student in political science who is active in the student movement. "They sent us a man who is pleasant to talk to, a deacon in his church. He doesn't look anything like a killer. People think, 'That jolly little fat guy couldn't have done anything much.' His normality is one of the best weapons they have.

"Santa Barbara is part of a CIA pilot program," Sallinger-McBride argued. "The reaction on the first four campuses to the Officer-in-Residence Program will determine its future at other universities. We want to prevent decisions like this from being made in secret at other schools, without the knowledge or consent of their university communities."

Meanwhile, student opposition to UCSB's ties to the CIA continues to grow. Two weeks after the sit-in and arrests, CIA critic John Stockwell spoke in the largest hall on campus to an overflow crowd of 1,000 people. The next day 300 attended a rally and mock funeral for academic freedom. The day after that a debate between supporters and detractors of the CIA was scheduled. Santa Barbara in the 1980s has been known more for its surfers than its student activists; that image, along with the image of today's students as Reaganites, apparently needs to be revised.

The Nation, December 12, 1987

14

Dollars for Neocon Scholars:

the Olin Money Tree

The John M. Olin Foundation is pouring millions of dollars into universities in an effort to reshape the curriculums, take the intellectual initiative away from the academic left and give scholarly legitimacy to Reaganite social and economic policies. The 1988 report of the foundation lists grants of $55 million, most of which help underwrite university programs "intended to strengthen the economic, political, and cultural institutions upon which ... private enterprise is based."

The list of Olin beneficiaries reads like a who's who of the academic right: Alan Bloom, the 1960s-hating author of the 1987 best seller *The Closing of the American Mind*, is getting $3.6 million to run the University of Chicago's John M. Olin Center for Inquiry into the Theory and Practice of Democracy. Harvard University professor of government Samuel Huntington, best known as a Vietnam War strategist, is getting $1.4 million to establish the Olin Institute for Strategic Studies on campus, along with $618,000 to support the Olin Program in National Security Affairs and $100,000 for his own Olin Research fellowship—a total of $2.1 million. Neoconservative ideologue Irving Kristol received $376,000 all for himself; this cash supported him first as the John M. Olin Distinguished Professor at the New York University Graduate School of Business Adminstration, and then as the holder of a John M. Olin Fellowship at the American Enterprise Institute in Washington. Among the fellows there is Robert Bork, Ronald Reagan's failed Supreme Court nominee, who collected $163,000 in 1988 as occupant of the John M. Olin Chair in Legal Studies.

Olin and several smaller conservative foundations provide a vital link between universities and the political world of Republicans in government, right-wing think tanks and conservative publications. They provide fellowships that give academic respectability to ideologues like Robert Leiken, a leading defender of the Nicaraguan *contras*. They buy time off from teaching for conservative scholars to develop arguments justifying right-wing policies, and then help push those ideas into the public discourse, where they can do conservatives some political good. Allan Bloom, for example, brought Francis Fukuyama, deputy director of the State Department's policy planning staff, to his Olin Center at Chicago in 1988 to give a paper, "The End of History?" In it, Fukuyama proclaimed the total victory of the West in the cold war. This paper was then published in the *National Interest* (Summer 1989), a quarterly that has received $1 million from Olin and is edited by Olin donee Irving Kristol. The journal published responses to Fukuyama by Olin grant recipients Bloom, Kristol and Huntington; the "debate" got picked up and featured on the *New York Times* Op-Ed page, in *Time* and in the *Washington Post*.

The end of history, however, is not the Olin foundation's principal preoccupation. The foundation has committed $5.8 million in current grants toward establishing and supporting a program innocuously called "Law and Economics." This field, founded at the University of Chicago in the late 1960s, applies the principles of "free market economics" to the law. Yale Law School is the biggest recipient of Olin grants supporting this movement: law professor George Priest is getting a total of $1.5 million for fellowships, lectures, journals and programs under his direction, including $464,000 for himself. The law schools at the University of Chicago, Stanford University and Harvard University are getting close to $1 million each for their Olin programs. The University of Virginia, Duke University, the University of Pennsylvannia and the Massachusetts Institute of Technology are getting roughly half a million dollars each for theirs. The Olin foundation considers these programs worthwhile because they provide a rationale for right-wing economic policies designed to "get government off our backs."

The goal of the law and economics field is a society in which conflicts are resolved not by government rules or communitarian values but by unregulated markets that set prices on different activities. The field is based on the assumption that human beings are inherently selfish; altruistic behavior, such as giving to "undeserving" welfare mothers, is explained away or dismissed as merely another form of selfishness. The preoccupation is with the cost of desirable ends: hardly anyone wants accidents, but we must be careful not to overspend on preventing them. Critics on the left, such as Mark Kelman of Stanford Law School, have said the "ideological task" of the new field is to prove that the "egoistic cacophony" of the marketplace eventually produces "social harmony."

It might seem hard for any law school to resist Olin's big bucks, but the University of California at Los Angeles did reject an Olin program in law and economics in 1985 after trying it out for a year. The Olin program at UCLA, like the foundation's programs elsewhere, provided John M. Olin Fellowships to students; these students were required to take special new courses where they would learn the law and economics gospel. The courses were directed by John M. Olin Scholars—faculty members receiving Olin money. Olin fellowship students were also required to attend the John M. Olin Symposium in Law and Economics, which brought prominent right-wing advocates to the campus, among them Bork and Supreme Court Associate Justice Antonin Scalia. The principal objection to the program at UCLA, in the words of the law school's curriculum committee, was that Olin was "taking advantage of students' financial need to indoctrinate them with a particular ideology." Professor Christine Littleton, a committee member, told her colleagues that if law and economics is worth studying the school should develop its own program and then seek support for it, instead of accepting the Olin foundation's program and hoping it would not "seriously offend notions of academic value." (Olin did find others at UCLA willing to accept its money and the strings that come with it: economist J. Clayburn LaForce and management professor James Wilson are getting $1 million to establish the Olin Center for Policy at UCLA's Graduate School of Management.)

Walter Williams, a black neoconservative, received $200,000 from the Olin foundation. Williams, an economist at George Mason University in Fairfax, Virginia, has lamented the fact that South Africa's government "owns coal-to-oil conversion plants, railroads, the telephone company, and other major industries." He maintains that Bishop Desmond Tutu, who says he wants socialism for South Africa's future, is already living under a socialist government, which, Williams argues, is the source of many of the problems Tutu has been struggling against. Williams writes a syndicated newspaper column that spreads the free-market gospel, explaining in one of them that the market "reduces human conflict far better than government does." *Human Events*, the extreme right-wing weekly, praised Williams's columns for arguing that "success in the market is color-, sex-, and race-blind and it virtually always comes from pleasing one's fellow man."

Historian François Furet received an Olin grant of $470,000 as director of the John M. Olin Program in the History of Political Culture at the University of Chicago. Furet is the pre-eminent historian in France working to discredit the Marxist interpretation of the French Revolution, which has dominated French scholarship on the revolution for most of this century. During the 1989 bicentennial celebration of the revolution, the French media promoted Furet as the celebration's quasi-official historian. Furet's main thesis is that revolution is obsolete in today's world. In Daniel Singer's words, "For Furet's version to stand, democracy as a concept must be stripped of any economic and social context." Furet was a Communist in his youth; as an old political infighter, he now brings his zeal and strategic sense as a former party member to fight the academic left.

And of course there is Allan Bloom. Bloom's frankly elitist book, supported by Olin grants, described the 1960s as a decade of nihilism and despair. The Bloom operation at the University of Chicago explains in a brochure that its purpose is to provide "a forum for the reconsideration and analysis of the fundamental principles and current practices of American politics ... in an atmosphere of dispassionate and impartial reflection." Two dispassionate and impartial thinkers who have participated in the reconsidering and analyzing are Scalia, eager to reconsider *Roe v. Wade* (presumably his Olin honorariums didn't compromise the independence of the judiciary), and Wilson, co-director of UCLA's Olin Center for Policy.

Olin has funded Peter Collier and David Horowitz, authors of *Destructive Generation: Second Thoughts About the Sixties*, who got $200,000 for the 1987 "Second Thoughts" conference of 1960s apostates. And the foundation gave $163,000 to Michael Novak, a conservative Catholic writer whose 1987 book, *Will It Liberate?*, attacks liberation theology and argues that socialism is "a form of self-immolation ... like rushing willingly into death." Novak's 1984 book, *Freedom with Justice*, was

102

praised by *National Review* for arguing that "the sin of the Left is that it refuses to appreciate ... the world as it is." *Contra* promoter Robert Leiken got a $75,000 John M. Olin Research Fellowship at Harvard's Center for International Affairs, where he is engaged in "work on media treatment of the conflict in Central America."

Academics on the left, struggling with student papers, staying up late to finish tomorrow's lecture and working weekends on that big article, look enviously at their ideological antagonists, who are freed from time-consuming tasks by generous grants from Olin and other dispensers of neocon largesse. And why shouldn't leftist scholars be envious? Who wouldn't want Allan Bloom's $3.6 million to support his or her intellectual work? The issue, however, is larger than mere envy. Competition between right and left in the marketplace of ideas has been distorted by right-wing money. The Olin foundation is testing the hypotheses that money talks, and that the sound of money talking will drown out critical voices on the left. No doubt somewhere a Distinguished Olin Professor is trying to explain why that's a good thing for the body politic.

The Nation, January 1, 1990

15

Accuracy in Academia:

Reed Irvine Rides the Paper Tiger

After seven months of existence Accuracy in Academia, the organization seeking to root out the dissemination of "disinformation or misinformation" by radical professors, looks like a paper tiger. News stories in 1985 reported that the organization had an annual budget of $160,000, plans for a staff of twenty-five and a network of freelance informers at 160 colleges and universities. Matthew Scully, associate editor of AIA's bimonthly newsletter, recently said, "Lots of things that were announced have never come to pass. The organization has switched gears. We're now a journalistic venture.... If someone told me today they were setting up a nationwide network of classroom monitors, I'd say it was a ridiculous idea." Recent AIA newsletters bear out Scully's account. Virtually none of the stories come from student monitors' reports about professors' classroom statements; for the most part they are accounts that have appeared in print elsewhere. When you call AIA's number in Washington, the person who answers says you've reached the group's parent organization, Accuracy in Media. If AIA has an annual budget of $160,000, why can't it afford its own telephone?

So far AIA's attacks on radical professors have, if anything, backfired. The organization's first newsletter reported on "an unidentified midwestern professor" whose lecturers on Latin American history criticized US policy in the region. "We didn't print her name," executive director Les Csorba explained, "because when we interviewed her she was cooperative; she agreed to distribute some material we offered documenting Sandinista atrocities." That sounds like a case of successful intimidation. The professor in question, Mary Karasch of Oakland University in Rochester, Michigan, tells the story differently:

When Reed Irvine [the head of Accuracy in Academia as well as Accuracy in Media] called me, I said I would distribute their material in the classroom. I do explore controversies, and I hadn't thought through AIA's offer. But they never sent their material. Then, last month, Les Csorba came to the campus to debate our dean and brought me a copy of the material they wanted me to hand out, along with a phone number in Washington to call to get copies for the one hundred students in my class. After reading the material, I concluded it was inappropriate for my students. My union, the American Association of University Professors, advised me that I should not change my syllabus on the basis of pressure from outside political groups.

The case received extensive coverage in the local media, most of it strongly supportive of professors' rights, Karasch told me. A few pro-AIA letters to the editor were also printed. She said that the entire academic community at Oakland—the student council, the faculty and the administration—all opposed AIA. When a television station prepared a fifteen-minute special on the group, its reporters had trouble finding a student to defend the organization, although they eventually succeeded. "My colleagues who go back to the fifties say it's nothing like the McCarthy days," said Karasch. "In this area at least, the people have grown and changed."

The target of AIA's March 1986 newsletter, its third, was Linda Arnold, a historian at Virginia Polytechnic Institute and State University in Blacksburg, Virginia. Although AIA focused on Arnold as a result of a student complaint, the newsletter did not attack anything she said in class. Instead it objected to what she told Irvine when he called to confront her about the text she was using in her introductory course, Howard Zinn's *The Twentieth Century*. The newsletter criticized the book for portraying "American heroes" such as Henry Ford and Douglas MacArthur as "villains."

Arnold recalls receiving a phone call from someone who said, "My name is Reed Irvine; I work with AIA. Do you have a few minutes to chat?" She wasn't sure who he was, and agreed to talk.

We ended up arguing for an hour, mostly about Zinn's book. Three times he asked, "Don't you think the book should be burned?" I said I'm against book burning. He told me he would like to send somebody down to lecture, with a critique of Zinn; I said no. I told him if he was so interested in the subject he should teach his own course. He said I should be teaching about the entrepreneurial spirit, for instance the people who created McDonald's. I told him I'm more interested in the people who eat at McDonald's. He never asked permission to quote what I regarded as private comments.

AIA urged its followers to complain to the school's president, William Lavery, that by assigning Zinn, Arnold was not presenting "the fundamental facts and interpretations of American history." Lavery told me his policy in such cases is "to let the faculty member know, ask for their response, then support their views and protect to the hilt their academic freedom." He also said he would let the faculty know they do not have to respond to inquiries like Irvine's. In any case, although associate editor Scully says the organization printed 10,000 copies of the newsletter, Lavery has received "only four or five letters complaining about Arnold." The small number of letters reveals a lot about AIA's weakness. From the beginning, AIA said that Howard Zinn, who teaches at Boston University, was one of the professors whose classroom it was interested in monitoring. But the AIA report on Zinn is limited to a critique of his book; it contains nothing about his teaching or political activities.

The target of the second newsletter, published in January 1986, was David Abraham, the Marxist historian who has been attacked by several members of the profession allegedly for the errors in his book *The Collapse of the Weimar Republic*. Most of the article about him consists of previously published quotations, some of them going back as far as 1983. It does not report any complaints by student informers, but it does include an interview with a professor—Yale University historian Henry Turner, who worked with AIA in order to breathe new life into his three-year-old vendetta against Abraham.[1] In the interview Turner attacked those who criticized his conduct in the Abraham case; he also provided AIA with material from his files. Turner thus became the first, and apparently the only, historian to go against the American Historical Association's resolution condemning AIA's activities as a "threat to academic freedom." (I attempted to reach Turner for a comment, but he did not return my calls.) Richard

---

1. See chapter 9.

Kirkendall, head of the AHA professional division, which is monitoring AIA's attacks on historians, commented, "I'm surprised that Turner would cooperate with a group like AIA. It contradicts his stated position on the careful use of sources. These people are careless in their handling of documents."

The report on Abraham contains a number of inaccuracies. The lead sentence states that Abraham is "a Princeton University professor"; in July 1985 he became a visiting associate professor at the New School for Social Research. The report implies that Hanna Gray, president of the University of Chicago, is a "radical historian," although she's in the mainstream. Turner's ally, historian Gerald Feldman, of the University of California, Berkeley, is quoted as referring to German President Paul von Hindenberg as "Hinderberg." It seems Abraham is not the only one who makes mistakes.

Another AIA target, historian Terry Anderson of Texas A & M University, sued the organization. Anderson, who won the college's teaching award in 1984, was quoted in an AIA story in November 1985: "I do not believe in the institution of marriage.... I'm an atheist.... I am not patriotic toward Texas A & M, the flag or America." Csorba and Scully wrote: "Lucifer himself could not have framed his credo any better. But such erudite comments make us wonder just what a man does revere who has no wife or party or country or God." The story is "totally inaccurate," according to Anderson. "They never checked any of those quotes with me. They say I'm an athiest; in fact I'm a humanist. They say I'm not patriotic; in fact I'm a Vietnam vet." AIA took the quotations from Texas A & M's *Battalion* and sent the story to "a couple of hundred campus newspapers across the country," Csorba said. "Ten or twelve reprinted it," he added, including the University of Maryland's *Diamondback*, the *Arizona Daily Wildcat* and Hofstra University's *Chronicle*.

Anderson's suit for defamation and libel was filed in Minnesota, since the University of Minnesota's *Daily* was one of the newspapers to publish AIA's story. Anderson's attorney, William Harper, explained, "Although Terry has tenure at Texas A & M, AIA's untrue depiction of him might affect his employability if he sought another job." Anderson was seeking exemplary and punitive damages. Csorba said, "Our story is accurate. The papers that published it are the ones to be sued, if anyone is."

Only one AIA victim, its first, made the national news: political scientist Mark Reader, a 52-year-old tenured associate professor who had taught at Arizona State University since 1968. Reader was singled out not because of a report from a student but because Scully wrote attacks on Reader for a local newspaper in Arizona before Irvine hired him. Thus from the beginning, AIA's newsletters have been recycling old stories. Reader is no Marxist; he describes himself as "a whole-earth person who believes that we are at the end of the old ideologies of capitalism and Communism." In his view, "the need is now for a gentler, a more tolerant people than those who won for us against the ice, the tiger and the bear." It's hard to call that statement "inaccurate." Irvine charged him with teaching "fears of nuclear war, power and weapons." The president of Arizona State, J. Russell Nelson, said he "was not going to pay any attention" to AIA, and that was that.

The prototype for AIA seems to have been Students for a Better America, a right-wing group at the University of California, Davis, headed by Les Csorba, which began a campaign against visiting history professor Saul Landau in January 1985. Asked whether he achieved his goals, Csorba commented: "I wanted to get the university to bring Jeane Kirkpatrick to speak; her anticommunist views would balance Landau's. I failed at that. But I did contribute to an awareness at Davis of what Landau had done." The most ominous aspect of Csorba's campaign was his distribution of information on Landau's political activities going back twenty years. Landau suspected the material had come from his Federal Bureau of Investigation file, but Csorba insisted that it all came from published sources, including James Tyson's *Target America*, a column by Rowland Evans and Robert Novak and the *Congressional Record*. Much of this concerned Landau's alleged role in the Venceremos Brigade, an organization of Americans helping with Cuba's sugar harvests since 1970, which Congressional investigators subsequently sought to link to "domestic terrorism." It's likely that the FBI supplied material on Landau to Evans and Novak and to the House Un-American Activities Committee, but Csorba seems to have had no direct access to the FBI files.

It is noteworthy that none of the three AIA newsletters published

thus far have reported on their targets' past political activities or statements. When Csorba was asked to explain this difference between his
campaign against Landau and AIA's tactics, he said, "At Davis I was
on my own. My role here is to publicize what's going on right now.
We're not concerned about these people's histories; we want to
promote balance in the classroom today."

Those who fear AIA believe it may be following in the footsteps of
Red Channels, the private anticommunist publication which printed
information about left-wing memberships and activities of writers,
actors and others during the 1950s and became a quasi-official enforcer
of the Hollywood blacklist. AIA initially had similar ambitions. Not
long ago Csorba, sounding like a junior Joe McCarthy, boasted, "I
have a list of over a thousand radical, commie professors I've compiled
over the last three years." And Accuracy in Media, which started out as
the letterhead and post office box of a right-wing crank, recently
commanded an hour on PBS and space on the Op-Ed page of the *New
York Times*.

Irvine sees the media and the universities as the two major bastions
of liberal thought in America; he hoped the same strategy and tactics
that had proved effective against one would also work against the other.
But although professors are more likely to say outrageous things than
newscasters, the networks are more vulnerable to pressure. No TV show
has tenure, and more are sensitive to audience response in the form of
declining ratings or cards and letters. Universities offer an amorphous
target. Unlike TV shows, they are widely dispersed and do not enter
people's living rooms. It is easier for Reed Irvine constituents to get
mad as hell at Dan Rather than at Howard Zinn. Finally, the pace of
change and response at universities, unlike television stations, is very
slow. For all these reasons, the tactics that won Irvine a respectful
hearing from broadcasters have been firmly rejected by academics.

AIA is hard-pressed to find any prominent academic supporters. Its
literature gives the impression that Boston University president John
Silber, notorious among university administrators for his dictatorial
style and Reaganite political ambitions, has endorsed the organization.
Silber has denied it. Teachers should not expect to be immune from
criticism, he said. "No professor, it seems to me, should be intimidated
by Accuracy in Academia. If the presence of AIA on campus restrains a
professor from distorting the truth, then it will provide a benefit to

those who care about the true purpose of a university. If, on the other hand, AIA goes off on witch hunts against professors merely because they hold left-wing positions, it will quickly discredit itself." Some of the strongest criticism of AIA have come from neoconservatives. Midge Decter, a member of the National Advisory Board of Accuracy in Media, called AIA "wrong-headed and harmful" in a *New York Times* Op-Ed piece; Harvard historian Richard Pipes, a Polish émigré and former National Security Council Soviet affairs expert, condemned the group on the ground that "what goes on in the classroom is sacrosanct"; and Reagan's Secretary of Education, William Bennett, said AIA was a bad idea that could only make martyrs of those it attacked.

It's not that the neocons disagree with AIA's diagnosis of academic life. Indeed, many of the people who denounced the New Left as anti-intellectual now argue that unrepentant New Leftists are taking over the intellectual life of the universities. They are concerned because the organization's main achievement to date consists of mobilizing the political center to defend the academic freedom of leftist professors from attacks by right-wing kooks. The American Association of University Professors and at least ten other official higher-education groups, including the American Historical Association, the Organization of American Historians and the American Council on Education, have said AIA is "clearly inimical to the principle of free expression of views by all members of the academic community." Nothing could be more damaging to the neocons, who've spent years trying to persuade the center that it's the left rather than the right that threatens the integrity of the university by injecting external political issues into academia.

AIA has apparently intimidated a few academics, as have right-wing students acting on their own, ostentatiously monitoring classes and threatening to turn in their professors. But Reed Irvine in effect admitted that the quality of student reports has been low when he told a television interviewer that "students say a lot of things" and that their claims require verification. It may be that many self-selected informers are retaliating for bad grades rather than exposing "inaccuacy." Some targets of these threats have been shaken; others now begin their courses denying bias and affirming their patriotism. But the record of the past six months should reassure them. Midge Decter put it pretty well: "Bias is something that anyone with opinions can be accused of. How can a person without opinions be qualified to teach?"

The Nation, April 5, 1986

16

History Wars:

Why the Right is Losing in Academe

The attention focused on Accuracy in Academia has obscured a more significant siege on radical scholarship mounted recently by neoconservatives who believe they can do a better job fighting the academic left. The problem with AIA, Midge Decter wrote in a *New York Times* Op-Ed article, is that its attack comes from "outside the university"; AIA head Reed Irvine should leave the fighting to the insiders, to conservative professors who can criticize radical scholarship in the name of upholding standards and defending the university from the intrusion of politics. The field of history has become a great battleground. Part of the intellectual legacy of the 1960s was the rise of social history, examining the experience of workers, blacks and women, their struggles for equality and the obstacles they encountered, and the decline of traditional political and diplomatic history, which focus on leaders and their policies.

Neocons favor the latter approach, but they have criticized the new social history on political as well as scholarly grounds. One of the most prominent early proponents of social history, Princeton University historian Lawrence Stone, came under fire in June 1985, in a lengthy article in the *New Criterion* by Norman Cantor, a newcomer among the neocons. A medievalist at New York University, Cantor purported to prove that Stone "is an English Marxist." He declared that because of Stone's "peddling" the "pure Marxist line in historiography," Princeton has become "a central school for indoctrination of the young in Marxist ideology." The evidence includes Stone's defense in *The Nation* of David Abraham, the Marxist historian who has been assailed,

112

allegedly for the errors in his book on Weimar Germany.[1]

Cantor's blast drew chuckles from historians across the political spectrum because Stone is widely known as a liberal. He has been willing to work with Marxist students, but he's best known for a 1979 essay in which he expressed his antagonism to Marxist history, calling for a "return to narrative." Eric Hobsbawm, a real English Marxist, rejected that idea at a symposium last fall at the New School for Social Research: "The first item on the agenda of radical history is to resist this return to the historical *stone* age."

As a political historian, Cantor might well oppose the social history Stone has written and encouraged, but that doesn't explain his Red-baiting. That probably had something to do with a 1968 *New York Review of Books* article in which Stone criticized Cantor's book *The English: a History of Politics and Society to 1760*, an old-fashioned constitutional history. "The book is clearly not about the English, not about how they lived and died, ... not about their thoughts, beliefs, and superstitions, not about their social structure or social mobility," Stone declared. "It is scarcely credible that a historian would even attempt such a thing in the mid-twentieth century." Moreover, Stone pointed out, the book's preface suggested that a graduate student of Cantor's had assembled the text from Cantor's lecture notes. Cantor waited eighteen years before striking back. By doing so, he was able to make use of a forum—the neocon journal of combat—that barely existed in 1968, or indeed in 1978, and that enabled him to give his personal pique a political veneer.

Princeton historian Robert Darnton has objected to Cantor's use of "Marxist historian" as an epithet. In a letter to the editor that the *New Criterion*'s Hilton Kramer published, he correctly termed Cantor's charge "a revival of McCarthyism." He added in an interview: "Marxists as well as non-Marxists have a place within academic communities. Liberalism includes the right to hear the other side. In claiming to defend liberalism, Cantor is in fact betraying it." Several leading conservative scholars have denounced Kramer for publishing Cantor's absurd attack on Stone. Gertrude Himmelfarb, professor of history at the City University of New York, wrote that the Cantor piece

---

1. See chapter 9.

"unwittingly distracts attention" from the real Marxists. J.H. Hexter, head of the Center for the History of Freedom at Washington University in St Louis and a vigorous polemicist against the academic left, declared that in reaction to the political radicalism of the 1960s, "I began a slow quiet crawl to the right—and there I find Norman Cantor. Guess I'll start crawling back."

Despite this criticism, Kramer is unrepentant. Asked whether Cantor made a mistake in calling Stone a Marxist, Kramer replied, "Absolutely not." In the magazine's March 1986 issue the editors explained that Cantor "did not accuse Stone of being a traitor either to his native country or to his adopted one" (Stone was relieved to learn that). They criticized Himmelfarb's letter for failing to trace the connection between Marxism and social history, and instructed her to "find an opportunity to explore this important subject on some future occasion."

If Kramer read magazines besides his own, he would know that Himmelfarb has already done that. In the February 10, 1986, issue of the *New Republic* she wrote a lengthy attack on British Marxist historians. In a 1984 article for *Harper's* on the relationship between Marxism and social history, she lamented that the Marxist view that political conflicts express social and economic differences "has so penetrated the culture that it might well be said, 'We are all Marxists now.'" Not quite all: Himmelfarb has argued that history should be understood as the "considered reflection and judgment" of "statesmen" about "the national interest and the public welfare." That's the way all the Nixons and Kissingers hope to be treated by historians.

The worst example of the new history Himmelfarb could find was a question on the College Board Advanced Placement examination in American history: "How and why did the lives and status of Northern middle-class women change between 1776 and 1876?" In that type of question, Himmelfarb wrote, women are "demeaned" because attention is directed to the "ordinary" aspects of their lives—work, family, social relations. There's a term for her attitude: ̄elitism.

Himmelfarb's *New Republic* article, narrower in scope than the one in *Harper's*, focuses on the links between British Marxist historians and the Communist Party. She reports that the distinguished journal *Past and Present* was founded by members of the Communist Party Historians' Group in 1952 and that Eric Hobsbawm remains a party member. Those facts, she says, are "little known." Actually, Hobsbawm discussed both topics in an essay six years ago, as has *Radical History Review*, in interviews going back to 1976 and in the edited collection *Visions of History*, published in 1984.

Himmelfarb is less interested in Marxist historians' scholarship than in their politics. She repeats the cliché that they are "bound by a pre-determined schema that applies to all periods and events." Yet she praises E.P. Thompson for his "eloquent, richly textured" account of working-class development; she credits Hobsbawm for an "impressive personal accomplishment and formidable contribution"; and she compliments Rodney Hilton for revising Marx's interpretation of the feudal peasantry to "make them worthy of sympathy and respect." All these writers, she observes, have abandoned a simple economic determinist version of Marxist theory; all are more interested in culture and politics than in the mode of production. So what happened to the "pre-determined schema"?

All the historians in question except Hobsbawm left the Communist Party thirty years ago. They should have left earlier, Himmelfarb says, during "the highly publicized purges and trials of the 1930s." That criticism is especially unfair to Thompson, who was ten when the purges began, in 1934. Although all of them—Thompson in particular—have rejected what they define as Stalinist history, that's not enough for Himmelfarb, because they remain men of the left. Himmelfarb objects strongly to Thompson's refusal to follow what he calls the "well-worn paths of apostasy," or become a "Public Confessor and Renegade." For Himmelfarb, if you're not her kind of anti-Communist, you're a Stalinist dupe. The greatest failing of the British Marxist historians as historians, she writes, is that they have not undertaken an analysis of Stalinism. Thompson, she suggests, should set aside his biography of William Blake to write about the Soviet "Doctor Plot" of 1952–53, and Christopher Hill should stop thinking about Milton and get to work on Lysenko. In the end, Himmelfarb is guilty of the crime she charges the radicals with committing: bringing a political agenda into historical scholarship.

The group of conservative historians who publish the journal *Continuity* see their audience as being composed of what editor Paul Gottfried described in 1983 as "non-Establishment i.e. non-leftist historians." The targets of their wrath, however, are not just radicals and

Marxists. One article criticized Winston Churchill for arguing in *The Gathering Storm* that Stalin was forced into the Nazi–Soviet pact by the West's actions at Munich; another chastised Arthur Schlesinger Jr for defending President Truman's "limited responses to Soviet advances in the Balkans and Iran." The magazine devotes considerable space to defending the Confederacy and lambasting "Northerners, and Southerners who thought like Northerners," who have "invaded the field of southern history." Even the journal's founding editor, Aileen Kraditor, was faulted for writing in her recent book *The Radical Persuasion*—an assault of leftist historians—that working conditions in factories in the early twentieth century were "brutal" and "dangerous" and that factory owners had "arbitary power."

Who reads *Continuity*? Virtually no one. *Ulrich's Guide to Periodicals* reports that the journal has a circulation of 300; *Radical History Review* ten times that. If there is an audience for *Continuity*'s brand of right-wing history, it does not seem to be among academics who read scholarly journals.

The Reagan Administration has its own agenda for the humanities, laid out by Secretary of Education William Bennett. At a neoconservative gathering in 1985 he said that the nation's schools have left students "intellectually defenseless" against radical critics. And he called for an "intellectual initiative" that would transmit his kind of American values through an emphasis on the teaching of American history.

That initiative was spelled out in a 42-page report issued by the National Endowment for the Humanities in November 1984. The nation's colleges and universities, according to the report, should convey "the accumulated wisdom of our civilization." The core readings in American history should be the Declaration of Independence, *The Federalist Papers*, the Constitution, the Lincoln–Douglas debates, the Gettysburg Address—plus, Bennett added, the Bible. As the bicentennial of the Constitution approaches, this political debate is likely to heat up, the left teaching about the Bill of Rights, the right arguing that the Founding Fathers opposed gun control and favored school prayer. The Reagan agenda is objectionable because it would have students study the Declaration instead of the experiences of working people, blacks and women.

116

The neocons are right about one thing: there's a tremendous gap between the political currents of the Age of Reagan and the intellectual life of the universities. The field of history provides the most contested terrain, and the clearest evidence of the intellectual strength of the left. In the past several years an impressive number of prizes have gone to radical and feminist historians. Leon Litwack won the 1980 Pulitzer Prize for *Been in the Storm So Long*, a study of blacks' experiences of emancipation following the Civil War. Columbia University's Bancroft Prize has been awarded to Mary Ryan for *Cradle of the Middle Class*, a study of how family patterns shaped nineteenth-century American social structure; Suzanne Lebsock for *The Free Women of Petersburg*, a study of status and culture in the antebellum South; and Jacqueline Jones for *Labor of Love, Labor of Sorrow*, a history of black women from slavery to the present. Recent prizes of the American Historical Association and the Organization of American Historians have gone to Nick Salvatore for his biography of Eugene V. Debs; Ira Berlin and associates for *Freedom: A Documentary History of Emancipation 1861–1867*; and Sean Wilentz for *Chants Democratic*, a study of working-class culture and politics in New York City before 1850.

The appeal of left-wing scholarship was evident at a New School symposium titled "Agenda for Radical History" and sponsored by the school's Eugene Lang College. Eric Hobsbawm said radical history's "most widely recognized achievement has been to win a place for the history of ordinary people, common men and women." Christopher Hill spoke of the "importance for radical historians of seeing history as a whole" and of creating "a sense of retrospective solidarity with all that's gone before us." Perry Anderson of *New Left Review* argued that the strength of Marxist history lay in its adherence to a theory that addresses the issue of causation; E.P. Thompson declared the radical project was "finding the 'reasons' of social unreason." Joan Wallach Scott of the Princeton Institute for Advanced Study criticized all of them for paying lip service to the history of women. One thousand people attended; it's inconceivable that any panel of conservative historians could attract an audience of even half that size.

The Organization of American Historians has elected several leftists to its presidency in recent years: Eugene D. Genovese in 1978, William Appleman Williams in 1980, Gerda Lerner in 1981 and Leon Litwack in 1986. The same year the American Historical Association elected its first woman president, Natalie Zemon Davis of Princeton, who is also an editorial associate of the *Radical History Review*. At the Organization of American Historians' annual meeting in New York City in April 1986, fourteen past and present officers drew up a petition opposing aid to the *contras*. The signers included the current president and two past presidents, Anne Firor Scott and Arthur S. Link. "We deplore President Reagan's distortion of history for political purposes in describing the Nicaraguan contras, whose systematic abuse of human rights has been documented by independent observers, as the 'moral equivalent of the founding fathers,'" they declared, condemning aid to the *contras* as "a continuation of a long history of US intervention in the internal affairs of Central American and Caribbean nations."

Cast against this background, neoconservatives in academia are not only on the defensive; they are steadily losing ground. That helps explain the growing nastiness that marks their writing: Norman Cantor's lame joke that Lawrence Stone and other Princeton historians "want to drive to the barricades in their Ferraris," and the recent remark in the *American Scholar* by British constitutional historian Geoffrey Elton—Himmelfarb's exemplary historian—that the history of women is "written by fanatics" and that the late Joan Kelly, author of the posthumously published *Women, History and Theory*, was "beatified" by women's historians after she died of cancer, "a charismatic disease in such circles." Especially in the crucial field of American history, radical and feminist historians have made their work the center of discussion and debate; their ideas and their agenda for the field can no longer be dismissed or ignored. The recent neoconservative attacks on radical scholarship are evidence not of the weakness of the academic left but of its strength.

The Nation, May 24, 1986

17

School for Spooks: Yale and the CIA

Robin Winks, a Yale historian of the British empire and an authority on spy fiction, knows that some people think intelligence services do more harm than good, and that anti-Soviet spy stories somehow tend to increase when US–Soviet relations are improving, but those are not issues in his book *Cloak and Gown*.[1] Instead, it documents the link between Yale and the CIA with a series of meticulously researched portraits.

Winks reports that more graduates of Yale than of any other university have gone into the Office of Strategic Services and the CIA, including at least forty-two members of the class of '43. Why? The OSS and CIA, Winks says, wanted "young men with high grades, a sense of grace, with previous knowledge of Europe ... an ease with themselves," "a certain healthy self-respect" and "independent means." Yale is a good place to look for such characters—which is also why people said that "OSS" stood for "Oh So Social." The OSS and CIA relied for recruiting on what they called "the P source": professors. The principal recruiters of Yale undergraduates into the CIA were masters of residential colleges (Winks himself is master of Berkeley College). The masters' job, Winks writes, was to teach young men "what it meant to 'play the game.'" During the 1940s and early 1950s the most important CIA recruiter on the Yale faculty was Arnold Wolfers, professor of international relations and master of Pierson College, an aristocractic

---

1. Robin Winks, *Cloak and Gown: Scholars in the Secret War, 1939–1961* (New York: William Morrow, 1987).

Swiss exile who entertained visiting dignitaries like Dan Acheson by playing Dixieland jazz with his wife.

Wallace Notestein, the leading American historian of Britain during the 1930s and 1940s, was equally important as a CIA recruiter, Winks reports; he taught young men to think about the relationship of history to the "real world." Four of his students went on to become Yale history professors, college masters and CIA recruiters in the 1950s. Other professors became intelligence operatives themselves. Harvard diplomatic historian William (Bull) Langer joined the service after suffering an anxiety attack during a 1938 lecture on the Italian peasantry. "A break from Cambridge and from teaching was precisely what he needed," writes Winks, so Langer went—where else?—to the OSS research and analysis division, and later served as assistant director of what was by then the CIA. Under Langer the CIA contracted out research projects to institutes at Stanford, Berkeley, Columbia, Princeton, the University of Denver and Yale, and enlisted anthropologists, archaeologists, art historians and other academics to use their fieldwork for CIA intelligence-gathering purposes.

Yale's playing fields also served as recruiting grounds: "Coaches were at least the equal of masters in being the leaders of men." Crew coach Allen (Skip) Walz was a major CIA recruiter; he also brought in National Football League players who had been cut from teams and needed jobs. He eventually left the CIA to become an executive at Canada Dry.

What is intelligence? Yale historian and CIA veteran Sherman Kent believed that 95 per cent of "the things our state must know" could be found in the library—the Yale library—without covert means. In 1951, as head of the CIA's Office of National Estimates, he set out to prove this thesis, putting five members of the Yale history department to work for twelve weeks to see how much they could glean about US military capabilities from public sources. (One of them was David M. Potter, who later became an eminent historian on the faculty of Stanford University.) The resulting "Yale Report" turned out to be 90 per cent correct in its inventory of the gross order of battle. President Harry Truman was on a secrecy kick at the time, accused by Republicans of trying to muzzle the press. He seized on the Yale Report as evidence of the need for press restrictions, claiming it proved that 95 per cent of the government's classified information was already in print. A CIA official arrived at Yale posthaste and told the five scholars to turn over to him every bit of paper they had used. Right-wing leaders charged that Yale historians were "subversively" showing how to steal the nation's secrets.

A quarter of Winks's book is devoted to James Angleton, Yale '41, head of CIA counterintelligence during the 1950s and 1960s. Angleton left the agency after the 1975–76 Church committee hearings revealed that he had headed CIA operation HT/LINGUAL, under which the agency had opened American mail since 1955 had kept a watch list of two million citizens, in violation of its charter. Defending himself before the committee, Angleton said, "It is inconceivable that a secret intelligence arm of the government has to comply with all the overt orders of the government." In spite of that, Winks can hardly restrain his admiration for Angleton, describing him as "incredibly attractive," the greatest mind in the history of counterintelligence and a "theoretician of human nature." Yet Angleton worked for years with Kim Philby, had lunch with him weekly and never suspected him of being a Soviet spy. Indeed, the failure of the head of US counterintelligence to suspect Philby led some to conclude that Angleton himself was a KGB mole; the CIA investigated him for two years before deciding that he wasn't.

Angleton began his career with the OSS during Word War Two in Italy, where his father had been a prominent American businessman; his jobs included keeping an eye on OSS agents who seemed sympathetic to the Communist partisans. He stayed on after the war, using CIA money to keep the Italian Communist Party from winning elections in the late 1940s and 1950s. Every year, $10 million to $30 million was paid not only to the Christian Democrats but to "splinter groups that might divide the Communists," and for "straightforward bribes." Claire Sterling, *New York Times* correspondent and self-appointed expert on Soviet disinformation, was a reporter for the Rome *Daily American* at the time; Winks writes that she was rumored to be working for Angleton. But that, too, is OK with Winks; he calls her "a courageous and enterprising investigative journalist."

Angleton went on to run a pathetic covert action which sought to overthrow Albania's Enver Hoxha and restore King Zog. Sixty agents were parachuted into Albania in 1950 and 1951; Angleton and his superiors dreamed they would start an Albanian national uprising that would "strike a spark in other eastern European countries." Virtually all the agents were caught. Angleton's other work as a "theoretician of human nature" involved 1962 Soviet defector Anatoly Golitsin, who claimed to be a powerful KGB official and who reported that the KGB had a mole high up in the CIA. He also claimed the Sino-Soviet split was a ruse, the Prague Spring a sham and Averell Harriman a Soviet agent. This led many in the CIA to question his reliability, including agency director William Colby. But not Angleton. He went to his death believing Golitsin was right, not only about the Sino-Soviet split but about Soviet penetration of the agency. Winks, trying to show that Angleton was "in some measure nonetheless correct," considers the possibility that Colby was the mole. Evidence: Colby fired Angleton, who wanted to find the mole. And Colby "surrendered the CIA's family jewels" to the Church committee in 1975, admitting CIA activities in violation of its charter and promising to end them.

If Angleton was a paranoid anticommunist, Donald Downes, Yale '26, was a socialist when he went into the OSS; he ended up embittered by what he learned about American compromises with Fascism in north Africa, Spain and Italy. He had plenty to be bitter about: J. Edgar Hoover started a Federal Bureau of Investigation file on him which is said to have grown to more than 2,000 pages, and the FBI hounded him until the end of his life, spreading rumors that he was a Communist and a drug dealer.

In 1943, Eisenhower was worried that Allied forces in north Africa were vulnerable to an Axis attack launched from Spain. The Spanish Foreign Minister was pressing Franco to enter the war on the Axis side, and Franco was friendlier than ever with Hitler and Mussolini. Downes built a network to prepare for sabotage inside Spain if the Germans sent an army through. "Downes's Ducks" (about fifty men and a dozen instructors) were mostly anti-Franco Spanish exiles recruited in Mexico and American veterans of the Abraham Lincoln Brigade. He looked for more recruits in Vichy concentration camps in the Sahara, where large numbers of Spanish Republicans were being held in "torture holes" and where the life expectancy was twenty months. The camps were unknown to the public; Downes and some of his Ducks interviewed 2,000 prisoners and tried to persuade the American authorities to close the camps, with no success. When he tried to get some inmates released to work in his sabotage network,

Allied headquarters refused. Finally, he helped those he wanted most to escape.

Downes's Ducks were infiltrated into Spain in OSS Operation Banana in July and August 1943. They provided a "long list of priceless information," including the Spanish order of battle, the movement of Spanish artillery by sea and data on German activity at Spanish airports. But the operation violated British and American pledges not to conduct espionage against neutral Spain, and when the British Foreign Office found out about it, they ordered that all Allied support be withdrawn. One group of "Banana boys" waiting to be picked up from a Spanish beach by a British ship was left stranded, and shortly thereafter Franco's forces raided the Banana safehouse in Málaga. A siege followed in which twelve policemen and eight Banana boys were killed.

Ten surviving Banana boys were tortured, and named Downes and Arthur Goldberg as the men who had recruited them. Before dying at the hands of Franco's police, they revealed their local Republican network; the Falangist government arrested 261 anti-Franco activists and executed 22. The American Ambassador to Madrid, Carlton J.H. Hayes, formerly a historian at Columbia, objected strongly to Operation Banana, and Franco was given an official US apology. A British officer Winks interviewed dismissed Downes's Ducks as "Communist desperadoes bent on settling old scores with Franco." The operation brought the largest single loss of OSS operatives in all of World War Two.

Why did so many historians have ties to the CIA? Winks refers to the "hard gemlike flame with which historians were meant to burn." I must confess I've never seen historians burning that way, but maybe things are different at Yale. Winks also argues that historians confront the same kinds of problems as the CIA, searching for appropriate evidence to answer questions about government. The problem is that Winks is looking for the answer in the methodology of history, instead of in its social and political dimensions. Ivy League historians became CIA agents in the 1950s not because their methodology was appropriate but because they had already gone through a selection process for a profession that was Waspy and elitist and shared the assumptions of diplomats and officials. Once history graduate departments opened up in the 1960s to people from outside the elite, the profession's links with the CIA came under sharp attack, from which the agency has never recovered.

Although the subtitle indicates that *Cloak and Gown* covers the period up to 1961, it's mostly about the OSS in World War Two, with a few brief sections on the CIA. The book doesn't cover Asia, so there's nothing on the role of Yale men in Indochina in the 1950s; it doesn't deal with the CIA's overthrow of Mohammed Mossadegh in Iran in 1953 and the installation of the Shah, or with the successful CIA coup against Guatemala's government the next year, or with the Bay of Pigs fiasco. Winks does report that the Yale CIA men he interviewed condemned agency mail-operating, inteligence-gathering on American citizens and attempts to assassinate Castro—not because they were wrong, but because they failed and thus brought the agency into disrepute. That says something about the morality and ethics Yale taught its undergraduates.

Winks ends by declaring that he sought to answer two questions in the book: whether there is an American imperialism, and whether the CIA's effort to give historical scholarship a "social utility" compromised the discipline. Unfortunately, the book hardly touches on either of those questions. It does provide irrefutable evidence that Yale has been entwined with the CIA for decades. Historians of Harvard and Princeton now have an obligation to those institutions to show that Yale did not stand alone when the CIA called.

The Nation, September 5, 1987

PART III

The Campus Left

18

Law Profs Fight the Power

Minority legal scholars have become the target of an attack in the *Harvard Law Review* that has aroused anger among law professors who study civil rights.[1] Its author, Randall Kennedy of Harvard Law School, is himself black. Kennedy criticizes those who argue that "intellectual contributions of scholars of color are wrongfully ignored."

Kennedy's attack reflects that fact that something genuinely new is happening in the world of minority legal scholarship: a body of work is appearing that is radically different from the typical law-review fare, not only in content but also in form. "The traditional way of doing legal scholarship doesn't do justice to our experience," said Harvard Law School professor Derrick Bell. "We need new ways of addressing a situation many of us feel is abominable. But minorities who are trying to blaze new trails in legal academia are meeting opposition and silencing."

The work challenges the way knowledge is constructed by the legal profession and addresses the relationship between knowledge and power. Articles by the new legal scholars of color draw explicitly on personal experience, include storytelling and family history, and mix dreams and fantasies with the more familiar apparatus of scholarly citations and analysis of cases and court decisions. In the process, the authors—like many feminist scholars—reveal much more about their own lives than one finds in conventional legal writing. "Mainstream

---

1. Randall Kennedy, "Racial Critiques of Legal Academia," *Harvard Law Review*, vol. 102, June 1989.

legal scholars write as if there's only one way of knowing the world," according to Mari Matsuda of the UCLA Law School. "They all write with the same universal authoritative voice. But when you read Chuck Lawrence and Pat Williams, you feel you have a personal relationship with them and with their families; you get an idea of what it was like for them growing up. Scholarship for them is not an abstract intellectual process divorced from experience." The profession's response to the emerging minority legal scholarship, she argued, "is like the first responses to the work of Jackson Pollock or Charlie Parker: Some people say, 'It's self-indulgent, I don't know what it means, I don't like it, it's no good'; others say, 'This is brilliant.'"

Bell is the best known and most prolific of this group. In 1985 the *Harvard Law Review* published his "Civil Rights Chronicles" (included in his book *And We Are Not Saved*[2]), which provided the first and in many ways still the most important example of the new voice and form of minority legal scholarship, posing a radical alternative to the standard article.[3] Bell describes the pieces as a "fantasy" in which he has created a second voice in addition to the author's, to pose radical criticism of civil rights law, including his own work and commitments as a legal scholar. At the same time, the dialogue between his voice and the second in the "Chronicles" bristles with 214 footnotes, which demonstrate the massive legal scholarship Bell commands.

The "Chronicles," Bell wrote, were told to him by "Geneva Crenshaw," a civil rights lawyer and activist from the 1960s who has "strange and allegorical visions." In "The Chronicle of the Celestial Curia," Geneva criticizes reliance on the courts for social justice. "Doesn't your lingering attachment to civil rights litigation stem from the exciting and rewarding career it has offered you?" Geneva asks Bell. He replies, "I must confess ... that few of those we represented have been able to achieve the status we have gained as a direct result of our efforts on their behalf. For many of us, that realization tinges even

---

2. Published by Basic Books, 1987.
3. In addition to the individual articles cited here, see also *Minority Critique*, issue of *Harvard Civil Rights Civil Liberties Law Review*, vol. 22, spring 1987, with articles by Richard Delgado, Maria Matsuda and Patricia Williams.

the greatest personal success with a bitterness that outsiders may have difficulty understanding." To find such a statement in the *Harvard Law Review* is astonishing.

In "The Chronicle of the DeVine Gift," Geneva argues that even if qualified black candidates were available for jobs at an elite, pre-dominantly white law school, the white faculty would limit the minority presence to 25 per cent of its numbers. Bell then asks whether the courts would accept such a limit under the doctrine of the "tipping point," according to which the New York City Housing Authority was for several years allowed by the Federal courts to limit the number of apartments it made available to minorities on the ground that without such limits the number of minority residents would reach the "tipping point," and whites would move out—thereby creating a newly segregated community. Bell asks, if the tipping point applies to housing, why wouldn't it apply to law school faculties?

Kennedy has criticized Bell, arguing that his "Chronicle" substitutes "mere assertion" for "a careful, detailed exposition," and that Bell "avoids a central issue," the "pool problem"—the small pool of qualified minority applicants—which Kennedy defines as the "apparent inability" of minority scholars, for a variety of reasons, to meet law school employment criteria "that seem innocuous and relevant" but have "disastrous consequences for minority candidates." Unless Bell can show that enough qualified minority candidates exist to fill 25 per cent of Harvard's law faculty positions, Kennedy argued, the "Chronicle" is "absolutely self-defeating." In an interview Bell replied, "I'm not forgetting the pool problem. Hell, everybody knows about the pool problem. In the article I go beyond that. I talk about the resistances hiding behind the pool problem. I explained this to Kennedy, but he continues to say I've avoided the pool problem."

Richard Delgado, of the University of Wisconsin Law School, set off the current controversy with a March 1984 article in the *University of Pennsylvania Law Review*, "The Imperial Scholar." Bell called it "an intellectual hand grenade, tossed over the wall of the establishment as a form of academic protest." Delgado analyzed the work of the most-cited scholars in civil rights law—all white males—and found that their citations were primarily of one another, with very few citations of minority scholars. "Paul Brest cites Laurence Tribe. Laurence Tribe cites Paul Brest and Owen Fiss. Owen Fiss cites Bruce Ackerman, who cites Paul Brest and Frank Michelman, who cites Owen Fiss and Laurence Tribe and Kenneth Karst ... an inner circle of about a dozen white, male writers comment on, take polite issue with, extol, criticize, and expand on each other's ideas," Delgado writes. By failing to cite the work of scholars of color, he argues, those voices have monopolized the field and made it difficult if not impossible for minorities to break into their elite ranks.

Mari Matsuda makes a somewhat different case in her spring 1988 article in the *Harvard Women's Law Journal*, "Affirmative Action and Legal Knowledge," in which she calls for "specific action to end the apartheid in legal knowledge.... Human beings learn and grow through interaction with difference, not by reproducing what they already know," she writes. "A system of legal education that ignores outsiders' perspectives artificially restricts and stultifies the scholarly imagination." Where Delgado emphasized that the white elites ignored minority legal scholarship, Matsuda emphasizes that some of the most relevant writing by people of color and women is found not in law-review articles but in "position papers, briefs, speeches, op-ed pieces and other non-academic publications," including fiction, history, biography and autobiography written by people of color. Most important for Matsuda, "The new voices will emphasize difference."

Kennedy, a contributor to *The Nation*, was recently voted tenure at Harvard. Among the scholarly works he submitted for his evaluation was a draft version of his *Harvard Law Review* article. There he criticizes the new minority scholars because they have "this eager yearning to perceive and celebrate ... differences between racial groups"; because their celebration of difference has had the "negative consequence" of "segregat[ing]" people of color "from the main currents of American culture." They are making "racial generations" that "derogate from the individuality of persons insofar as their unique characteristics are submerged in the image of the group to which they are deemed to belong." He singles out Matsuda, arguing that she "simply *presumes* that any scholar of color will have undergone the experience ... [of] racial victimhood."

Patricia Williams, one of the new black legal scholars, responds, "Randy's article is a representative response from the academy to new black voices. He is saying, 'Prove that racism exists.' I'm not going to do that. I take American history as given, and work with the results. In the ideology of legal style this is called 'unscholarly'—especially if it's done in the first person." Delgado says, "I disagree strongly with the view that minorities do not have a distinctive experience. They can place themselves outside it, they can disregard their experience. That's what he has done." Nell Painter, a black historian at Princeton University, points out that Kennedy's article arguing that blacks do not share a distinctive experience begins with a quotation from Ralph Ellison. "That's characteristic of the way black scholars write about race—they endow other black voices with authority," Painter says. "I'd be very surprised to see a white scholar start a law review article, or any scholarly article, by quoting Ralph Ellison."

Bell points out that "Randy's own work has been influenced by the fact that he is black. He went after an article of Benno Schmidt's, showing that Benno had glossed over some egregious things Supreme Court Justices of the teens and twenties had done on race. He showed they were some of the worst racists around. He did the same thing in his article on the death penalty. Not only did he criticize the majority of the Court for refusing to give weight to statistical evidence that was overwhelming in its proof that blacks who kill whites are more likely to get the death penalty than any other group, but he also criticized the dissenters who beat their breasts about the decision but did not acknowledge that the Court has never reversed a criminal decision on the basis of racial discrimination in the harshness of the penalty. That's the kind of contribution a scholar of color should be making, and that's the kind Randy has been making, and it's the kind I hope he will go back to."

Kennedy's most powerful argument is that Delgado fails to identify specific works by scholars of color that "deserve more recognition." The article Kennedy criticizes was published five years ago; in the past two years significant new work by minority scholars has appeared. Clearly Bell, Delgado and Matsuda are producing important work, and they are hardly the only ones. When other legal scholars are asked about people of color who are doing outstanding work, they suggest many additional names. Three that are on virtually everyone's list are Patricia Williams, Charles Lawrence and Kimberlé Crenshaw.

Williams, who has joined the University of Wisconsin law faculty, writes in an intensely personal voice that is unlike anything that's ever appeared in law journals; she has attracted the attention not only of legal scholars but of literary critics like Harvard's Barbara Johnson, who says Williams "writes with a short story writer's sense of pace and vividness, with a literary theorist's sophistication and with a lawyer's attention to detail and passion for justice." The best example of Williams's work is the essay "On Being the Object of Property," which appears in her book *The Alchemy of Race and Rights*. It is impossible to paraphrase, partly because she draws on different styles of persuasion and makes connections on more than one level.

The essay begins with William's great-great-grandmother, a slave in Tennessee impregnated by her master when she was eleven years old. Williams connects that experience with the Baby M case, in which a surrogate mother was denied custody of the baby she bore under contract to a middle-class couple: "My great-great-grandmother's powerlessness came about as the result of a contract to which she was not a party; Mary Beth Whitehead's powerlessness came about as a result of a contract ... that she signed ... yet which, over time, enslaved her," and "made her and her child helpless in relation to the father." Under slavery, black people were bought and sold; now "it is white children who are bought and sold, [and] black babies have become 'worthless' currency to adoption agents—'surplus' in the salvage heaps of Harlem hospitals." Unlike Bell's "Chronicles," Williams does not illustrate arguments through storytelling. "I borrow devices from fiction," Williams explains, "but I don't fictionalize. I use my own dreams, hallucinations and fantasies, as a way of empowering less authoritative ways of speaking."

Lawrence, also a black civil rights scholar, teaches at Stanford University and is best known for "The Id, the Ego, and Equal Protection: Reckoning With Unconscious Racism," published in the *Stanford Law Review* (vol. 39) in January 1987. His article begins with the kind of personal narrative that has become a hallmark of the new minority scholarship: "It is 1948. I am sitting in a kindergarten classroom at the Dalton School." The teacher is reading *Little Black Sambo* to the five-year-olds:

> I remember only one part of the story, one illustration: Little Black Sambo is running around a stack of pancakes with a tiger chasing him.... I ... have heard the laughter of my classmates. There is a knot in the pit of my stomach. I feel panic and shame.... I am slowly realizing that, as the only black child in the circle, I have some kinship with the tragic and ugly hero of the story—that my classmates are laughing at me as well as at him.

I am thirty-three. My daughter, Maia, is three. I greet a pink-faced, four-year old boy on the steps of her nursery school. He proudly presents me with a book he has brought for his teacher to read to the class. "It's my favorite," he says. The book is a new edition of *Little Black Sambo.*

Lawrence goes on to challenge current doctrine that requires plaintiffs in discrimination cases to prove that the laws they are challenging were passed with an explicit "discriminatory purpose." With this requirement, Lawrence writes, "The Court creates an imaginary world where discrimination does not exist unless it was consciously intended." But a great deal of racism in our society is unconscious. Lawrence draws on Freudian theory and cognitive psychology, which suggest that some beliefs are "so much a part of the culture, they are not experienced as explicit lessons." Thus, "requiring proof of conscious or intentional motivation ... ignores much of what we understand about how the human mind works," Lawrence writes. "It also disregards both the irrationality of racism and the profound effect that the history of American race relations has had on the individual and collective unconscious." His conclusion is that the requirement of proving conscious intent should be abandoned; "equal protection doctrine must find a way to come to grips with unconscious racism."

Crenshaw, who teaches at the UCLA Law School, is best known for "Race, Reform, and Retrenchment," an article in the May 1988 *Harvard Law Review* that is less personal and more directly political than the work discussed above. In it she criticizes both neoconservatism and the leftist Critical Legal Studies school; both, she argues, fail to appreciate the force of racism in American society. The "Crits" maintain that the pursuit of equal rights has crippled black struggle: blacks ought to fight for concrete goals like jobs and good schools and housing, the Crits argue, not for abstract legal principles like equal rights. In making this their goal, the Crits say, blacks participate in the legitimation of liberal ideology that functions to justify existing structural inequalities.

Crenshaw's response to the Crit's bashing of rights discourse is devastating: The problem for blacks is not the legitimation of liberal ideology but rather that they are "coerced into living in worlds created and maintained by others. ... The ideological source of this coercion is not liberal legal consciousness, but racism." Although liberal legal ideology may serve as an obstacle to some goals, the fight for black rights—however abstract an end—plays a vital role in "combating the experience of being excluded and oppressed." Rights that other Americans took for granted were denied to blacks; as a result, Crenshaw writes, "Blacks' assertion of their 'rights' constituted a serious ideological challenge to white supremacy."

Kennedy, in an interview, said that minority legal scholars like Bell and Delgado "are engaged in interest-group ethnic politics—the familiar move of playing the race card," and that he is "impatient with it, tired of it." Several of the leading white civil rights scholars, however, have a different view. Frank Michelman at Harvard is one of those Delgado had singled out in 1984 for not citing minority scholars. Asked to comment on the controversy, he replied, "Delgado and Matsuda have written forceful pieces; they raised important issues and caused me to think hard about those issues." Paul Brest, Dean of Law at Stanford, another of those Delgado identified in his article as not citing minority scholars, said, "Derrick Bell and Chuck Lawrence have influenced in a significant way the way I think about race discrimination. I think getting away from the traditional law review mode is almost always a good thing; to the extent that it illuminates ideas that simply wouldn't come forward, it has to be good. *And We Are Not Saved* has power because it is not an analytic article with lots of footnotes."

Kenneth Karst of UCLA Law School, author of a new book, *Belonging to America: Equal Citizenship and the Constitution,* added: "What I find so compelling about the work of these minority scholars is the way they put the reader in touch with the feelings of real people— particularly in Derrick Bell's 'Chronicles.' These writers are providing a kind of moral translation of their experience into terms that legal doctrine can deal with in addressing the harms of exclusion."

"The debate is about voice," Delgado concludes, "about making everybody speak one language. Certain cries of pain lose of lot in the translation. The whole idea of the dominant legal discourse is to limit the range of what you can express, the range of argument you can make. It requires that everything be buttressed by authority, by looking to the past. What happens in the law reviews is important because they are the perfect place to explore a broadening of the dominant discourse. For Kennedy to take us to task for urging experimentation with and broadening of that discourse is singularly unfair."

Legal scholars, Matsuda writes, need to develop "new skills of listening" to learn about minorities' experiences: "The voices bringing new knowledge are sometimes faint and self-effacing, other times brash and discordant.... We should strive to understand their origin and listen carefully for the truth they may hide." The outsider's voice, she concludes, "is likely to change the way we understand the world."

The Nation, September 4–11, 1989

19

Free Speech for Campus Bigots?

In a classroom discussion at the University of Michigan in 1989, a student said he considered homosexuality a disease treatable with therapy. The university summoned him to a disciplinary hearing and charged him with violating the school's new regulations prohibiting speech that "victimizes" an individual on the basis of "sexual orientation." The American Civil Liberties Union took the university to court, and District Court Judge Avern Cohn ruled in September 1989 that the new rules violate the First Amendment's free speech guarantee.

The Michigan case typifies the debate now raging among liberals and others on the left as US campuses grapple with a marked rise in slurs and actions that are antigay, antiwoman and racist. The question at the center of the debate is, how do colleges and universities protect free speech and at the same time combat the increase in abusive language by the dominant white male group? Understandably, the victims of such harassment are demanding that their institutions do much more to make campuses what they ought to be: places that are free of discrimination, that foster and celebrate diversity. The new regulations at the University of Michigan were promulgated in response to such demands after a series of incidents on that campus— including the broadcast of racist jokes on the school radio station—that are just a part of the increase in offensive speech on campuses in the 1980s. The evidence continues to accumulate.

At the University of Connecticut in December 1987 eight Asian-American students on the way to an off-campus, semiformal dance were harassed for forty-five minutes by a group of "very large football players who were just dying to get us to fight them," one of the victims related. "They spit on us ... called us 'Oriental faggots' and sang 'we all live in a yellow submarine.'"

At Arizona State University in Tempe, in April 1989, a black student, Toby Wright, got into a fight with a white member of the Sigma Alpha Epsilon fraternity, Sean Hedgecock, outside the SAE house. Wright maintained he heard Hedgecock say, "Fuck you, nigger." More than two dozen SAE members came out of their house and surrounded Wright and two other blacks, chanting, "Coon. Nigger. Porchmonkey." The police arrived, broke up the confrontation and later reported that Hedgecock "kept making racial slurs and threats," including a threat to "get those niggers" and "kill them." Hedgecock denied the charge. Later the same night, around 1 a.m., two other black students on fraternity row were confronted by Hedgecock, who shouted, "Those are the niggers! They're back!" A mob of 2,000 poured out of fraternity-house parties and surrounded the two blacks as ten to fifteen fraternity men beat them. Within four minutes the police arrived again, sprayed Mace to clear the street and took the two blacks into custody in handcuffs, later releasing them.

Putting up with offensive speech is a price its targets must accept for the privilege of living in a free society. Many white males try to dismiss these kinds of abusive behavior as harmless frivolity. White students at the University of Connecticut told their Asian-American classmates that their harassers were "just drunk, trying to have some fun." The police chief at Arizona State denied the mob attack on blacks was racially motivated; he called it a "fight" caused by "hot weather."

These latter views suggest that white people don't understand that racist speech hurts. "We have not listened to the real victims," Stanford Law School professor Charles Lawrence told a recent ACLU conference. Richard Delgado of the University of Wisconsin Law School refers to "words that wound"—speech that interferes with the abused students' ability to study and learn, undermines their self-respect and leads to feelings of defensiveness, anger, shame, helplessness, and to a withdrawal from campus activities. The United States is virtually alone in the world in providing governmental protection for racist hate speech, wrote Mari Matsuda, a professor at the UCLA Law School, in the August 1989 issue of *Michigan Law Review*. Britain's Race Relations Act of 1976 criminalized incitement to discrimination and incitement to racial hatred, including "threatening, abusive, or insulting" written matter or public speech. Canada has outlawed inciting hatred against a group when a breach of peace is likely to follow. Australia and New Zealand also have legal restrictions on racist speech. Countries outside the common-law tradition have similar laws: in Sweden "agitation against ethnic groups" is a crime defined as "contempt ... with allusion to race, skin color, national or ethnic origin or religious creed." If all these countries are trying to protect minorities from offensive speech, why can't the United States?

Even First Amendment absolutists recognize some limits on freedom of speech. The law protects people against defamation and libel, Matsuda wrote, because lawyers and lawmakers "understand the way false speech damages their standing in the community and limits their opportunities, their self-worth, their free enjoyment of life.... To see this and yet fail to see that the very same things happen to the victims of racist speech is selective vision." It won't be easy to design protections against offensive speech on campus, but Matsuda makes a strong case that we must try, because such speech does "real harm to real people" who deserve protection and redress.

Two different approaches to prohibiting offensive speech and harassment, one broad and one narrow, are currently being debated at colleges and universities. The first prohibits students from engaging in a wide variety of abusive behavior. At the University of Connecticut, for instance, students may now be punished for the use of "derogatory names, inappropriately directed laughter, inconsiderate jokes, and conspicuous exclusion [of another student] from conversation." At the University of Pennsylvania students may be punished for using any language that "stigmatizes or victimizes individuals" and "creates an intimidating or offensive environment."

The University of Michigan policy that was struck down by Judge Cohn was one of the broadest. Established in 1988, it prohibited "any behavior, verbal or physical, that stigmatizes or victimizes an individual on the basis of race, ethnicity, religion, sex, sexual orientation, creed, national orientation, ancestry, age, marital status, handicap or Vietnam-era veteran status." Prohibited speech included that which "has the purpose or ... effect of interfering with an individual's academic efforts." A handbook titled "What Students Should Know about Discrimination and Discriminatory Harassment" included examples of conduct that would be punished. One of them read, "A male student makes remarks in class like 'Women just aren't as good in this field as men,' thus creating a hostile learning atmosphere for female classmates." The judge examined university records of enforcement of the policy and found three cases in which "students were disciplined or threatened with discipline for comments made in the classroom setting." Judge Cohn did not declare that all offensive speech is protected by the First Amendment. "What the University could not do," he ruled, was "establish an anti-discrimination policy that had the effect of prohibiting certain speech because it disagreed with ideas or messages.... Nor could the University proscribe speech simply because it was found to be offensive, even gravely so, by large numbers of people."

The broad policies have been the target of fierce criticism by civil libertarians. Although the regulations limiting racist speech on campus are designed primarily to protect blacks, the victims of these ordinances probably will *be* blacks, argues Ira Glasser, national executive director of the ACLU. "Louis Farrakhan is likely to be the first," Glasser says, because the leader of the Nation of Islam calls Judaism a "gutter religion." That means his speech could be banned under the broad rules because it is abusive and stigmatizes people because of their religion in a way associated with past discrimination—the kind that led to the Holocaust.

The narrow approach seeks to deal with the concerns of the civil libertarians by permitting all public speech and prohibiting only the most threatening and inflammatory cases of face-to-face abusive speech: direct, intentional verbal assaults, personal confrontations where angry or hateful epithets are hurled at particular students. Some legal scholars argue that prohibiting this kind of speech is allowable under the "fighting words" doctrine, created by the Supreme Court in the case of *Chaplinsky v. New Hampshire.* In that 1921 ruling, the Court declared that it is permissible to ban words that "by their utterance inflict injury or tend to incite an immediate breach of the peace." The University of Wisconsin, Pennsylvania State University and the nine-campus University of California system have adopted the narrow policy, prohibiting only fighting words and allowing all other expressions of offensive speech.

The narrow regulations are frustrating to student targets of abusive attacks, who turn to their school administrators for help in coping with racial harassment. Under the narrow rules, Wisconsin cannot punish a fraternity that held a mock "slave auction," with pledges in blackface, because the fraternity members did not directly confront blacks. Nor could Michigan punish the campus disc jockey who broadcast racist jokes.

The "fighting words" standard adopted by the Supreme Court may provide a legal basis for criminalizing abusive speech, but civil libertarians do not accept the doctrine. In *Chaplinsky* a Jehovah's Witness had been distributing religious literature on a street corner in Rochester, New Hampshire; he told a police officer, "You are a God damned racketeer" and "a damned Fascist and the whole government of Rochester are Fascists or agents of Fascists." He was arrested and convicted for making these statements, and the Supreme Court upheld his conviction, declaring that he had uttered "fighting words." Civil libertarians feel that *Chaplinsky* was wrongly decided, arguing that it should not be a crime to call a cop a fascist. They also point out that the courts seem to be employing the "fighting words" test quite selectively. For example, a notorious invocation occurred in fall 1989, when Chief Justice William Rehnquist cited the doctrine as a justification for banning flag burning. Thus the doctrine has been invoked by the Court to protect cops and to prosecute flag burners, but not to protect gays, women and minorities from cruel speech and harassment.

Some critics, including Matsuda, have also objected to the "fighting words" doctrine because it provides a male-centered standard: insults can be prohibited when they provoke violence by men. Such a doctrine could define some racist, sexist or homophobic insults as non-actionable, Matsuda argued, because the victims did not respond with violence. Women especially do not respond to verbal abuse with physical counterattacks; instead, she said, they try to avoid situations where they are abused and internalize the damage.

The ACLU is opposed to both the broad and narrow rules. "We're against every version of campus restrictions on racist speech we've seen," said Glasser. "We think they are all unconstitutional.... Freedom of speech is being made the scapegoat for problems the people in power don't know how to solve." Glasser objected especially to the way the University of California's "fighting words" regulation distinguishes between words that express an idea, which are protected, and words that "simply injure and intimidate," which are prohibited.

Who, Glasser asked, is going to decide which words don't express an idea and thus can be banned? "We live in a racist society," Glasser insisted, "which is why you can't trust the people in power to make distinctions about which speech should be permitted. We just got through eight years of a national government that believed affirmative action was reverse discrimination against whites. We have a Supreme Court that basically endorsed that view. Ours is still a white society defending its historical racism. We can't control how they will interpret these rules. No one should have any confidence in our law-enforcement apparatus. To rely on the Supreme Court and the dominant political majority to make good decisions about restricting speech is to live in a dream world."

More ACLU litigation is planned. The University of California "fighting words" policy is "probably a violation of the First Amendment," said Ramona Ripston, executive director of the ACLU of Southern California. "I would like to see the ACLU come up with a policy that protects students from some kinds of harassing speech. After all, we believe the workplace should be free of sexual harassment. We don't see banning explicitly sexual posters in the workplace as a violation of the First Amendment. But unless the University of California can answer the questions we've raised, we will go to court to challenge the constitutionality of the present regulations. Still, I would like to find a way of crafting a policy that would get at some racist speech without impinging on the First Amendment."

Thomas Grey, a constitutional law expert at the Stanford Law School and a civil libertarian, has written a set of narrow guidelines that are regarded by minority advocates as the most thoughtful in meeting the ACLU's objections and in identifying "the point at which protected free expression ends and prohibited discriminatory harassment begins." Under his proposed regulations, a university's commitment to free expression requires that "students tolerate even expression of opinions which they find abhorrent." But Grey acknowledges that such a commitment collides with another equally important principle, the university's efforts to achieve equal opportunity, which also has a constitutional basis: the Fourteenth Amendment's guarantee of equal protection under the law. Under Grey's proposed regulations, drafted in October 1989, speech constitutes harassment when it satisfies three criteria: (1) It must be "intended to insult or stigmatize an individual

... on the basis of their sex, race, color, handicap, religion, sexual orientation, or national and ethnic origin." Political fighting words— calling a cop a fascist—are not actionable; this rule thus represents a narrowing of the Supreme Court's "fighting words" standard. (2) The insult must be "addressed directly to the individual"; there are no penalties for racist statements made to public audiences in lectures, in the student newspaper or on the radio station, or for abusive remarks made, for example, among an all-white fraternity group when the targets of the slurs are not present. (3) The insult must "make use of 'fighting' words or non-verbal symbols," those "commonly understood to convey direct and visceral hatred or contempt." Thus speech can be prohibited when it is "about individuals, directed to those individuals, and expressed in viscerally offensive form."

Inevitably, each criterion raises questions. The requirement of intentionality, for example, would allow the white fraternity boys at Arizona State who used the epithet "nigger" to defend themselves by arguing, "We were just kidding. Can't you take a joke?" The requirement that fighting words must be used in order for the offense to be punishable leaves unpunished extreme expressions of racial hatred that, in the judgment of disciplinary officials, do not meet the criterion because expressions of opinion are and ought to be protected by the First Amendment. Moreover, the fighting words are not identified in Grey's proposed regulations. He is confident, however, that everyone knows what they are: " 'Black son of a bitch' won't do it," Grey said in an interview; " 'Nigger' will." Legal thinkers pride themselves on the law's ability to make distinctions, but a black undergraduate is unlikely to see much difference in this one. Therefore, any set of regulations must be specific about the prohibited speech.

Grey staunchly defends his proposed regulations against the First Amendment absolutist position. "Do you really think someone ought to be able to go to a black person, call him a nigger to his face and not have that be a breach of the peace? Do you want our universities to tell black students that kind of behavior should be protected? That's not sensible." Racist public speech may well be even more damaging to minority students than private insults. But, said Grey, the "other side of the balance cuts in at this point. Speech directed at the public should be protected."

Although the ACLU plans to continue to fight restrictions on abusive speech, that doesn't mean the organization thinks the phenomenon should be ignored. "We are very unhappy at the way all concern for the problem of race relations on campus has been channeled into this debate about curbing speech," Glasser said. "[White] kids on campus today grew up at the time when our leadership made it fashionable to be racist. Suddenly they are eighteen years old, living in dorms with blacks, and we expect them to speak to their black classmates across a cultural chasm not of their making. It's appalling that universities, of all places, are restricting speech when they should be teaching kids of different races how to talk to each other." On this point, most people on the left agree. Prohibiting fighting words, Stanford's Grey conceded, "absolutely does not deal with campus racism in a significant way. You're never going to be able to do that with discipline. These rules are like bias-crime statutes, which treat racially motivated crimes as separate, more serious offenses. These rules provide an effective way of saying we take this seriously. They are symbolic, and that's important." How to provide that protection without setting dangerous precedents is a subject that has only begun to be explored. Meanwhile, offensive speech continues to isolate and wound its victims. Minority students deserve protection from such attacks.

But whatever the short-term solution to the problem of words that wound—and let's hope that a creative solution will yield a sanctuary for both free speech and human dignity—the critical need is for a long-term commitment by the universities to extirpating students' racist behavior. The rise of campus racism and other abusive behavior in the Reagan years indicates that white students need to be educated. This ought to be possible at institutions dedicated to education. Courses on the history of race relations in America should be added to the requirements for graduation (they already have been at some universities); orientation programs for incoming students must address the issue of cultural diversity on campus explicitly and frankly; more minority faculty must be hired, which means more minority students must be attracted to Ph.D. programs. Minority advocates and civil libertarians agree that these are the real weapons for fighting racist speech on campus.

The Nation, February 26, 1990

20

Racial Hatred on Campus

The Boston Red Sox had just lost the 1986 World Series to the New York Mets. At the University of Massachusetts, Amherst, hundreds of students, many of them drunk, poured out of the dorms. White Red Sox fans began shoving Mets fans who were black; soon a white mob of 3,000 was chasing and beating anyone who was black. Ten students were injured. Joseph Andrade recalls thinking, "My God, my life is being threatened here—and it's because I'm black."

The U-Mass explosion—on October 27, 1986—may be the most emblematic outbreak of student hatred of the 1980s. But it is by no means the only one. The upsurge in campus racism is the most disturbing development in university life across the nation during the past decade. More than anything, it reveals how white attitudes toward minorities have changed on campus during the Reagan years, even at institutions that historically have been bastions of liberalism.

At the University of Michigan, Ann Arbor, for example, the campus radio station broadcast a call from a student who "joked": "Why do blacks always have sex on their minds? Because all their pubic hair is on their head.... Who are the two most famous black women in history? Aunt Jemima and Mother Fucker." At Dartmouth College, the *Dartmouth Review* attacked a black music professor, William Cole, describing him as "a cross between a welfare queen and a bathroom attendant." Then four *Dartmouth Review* staff members confronted Cole after a class in February 1988 and, in front of his students, apparently attempted to provoke him into a fight. Esi Eggleston, a black student who witnessed the confrontation, told PBS's *Frontline*: "That moment let me know that there are people in this world who hate you just because of your color. Not dislike you, or choose not to be friends with you, but hate you." At the University of Wisconsin, Madison, a fraternity held a "slave auction" as part of a pledge party in October 1988. At UCLA white and Chicano students fought on campus in spring 1989, during a student election. At Purdue, a black academic counselor found "Death Nigger" scratched on her office door. A headline in a recent issue of the *Montclarion*, the student newspaper at Montclair State College in New Jersey, read, "Attention focused on racial tension at MSC."

Why is all this happening now? Shelby Steele, a black associate professor of English at San Jose State University, tends to blame the victim. He has argued that the problem on campus is not white racism but rather black "feelings of inferiority," which give rise to "an unconscious need to exaggerate the level of racism on campus—to make it a matter of the system, not just a handful of students." Instead of "demonstrating for a black 'theme house,'" Steele wrote, black students "might be better off spending their time reading and studying."

Duchesne Paul Drew, a Columbia University junior who is black, offers a different explanation: "Reagan was President during the formative years of today's students." When Reagan was elected in 1980, this year's freshman class was ten years old. Their political consciousness was formed while the White House used potent code words and attacked social programs to legitimize a subtle racism. Columbia students report that racist remarks are seldom made to blacks but frequently are heard in conversations among whites. The litany is that black people tend to be criminals, drug addicts and welfare cheats; that they don't work; and that black students aren't as smart as whites. This, of course, is the image of blacks George Bush sought to project in his campaign to succeed Reagan. The Republicans' Willie Horton television ads featured a photo of the convicted black rapist released from prison in Massachusetts while Democratic candidate Michael Dukakis was governor; Horton went on to commit another rape. The ad suggesting that blacks are rapists and murderers played not just in living rooms but in dormitories and student centers for most of the fall semester. Undergraduate viewers may have been even more vulnerable to the Horton propaganda than was the rest of the TV audience, because most of them lacked the experience and knowledge required to challenge racist imagery—especially after eight years of Ronald Reagan.

The Reagan Administration gave its blessing to the *Dartmouth Review*, the best-known purveyor of campus racism and intolerance. The *Review* (which is not an official Dartmouth publication) boasts that several of its former staff members have gone on to prestigious jobs in Reagan's Washington: one became a speechwriter for President Reagan, another for Vice President Bush. *Dartmouth Review* columnist and president Keeney Jones penned a notorious racist parody, "Dis Sho Ain't No Jive Bro," that purported to quote a black student at Dartmouth: "Dese boys be sayin' that we be comin' here to Dartmut an' not takin' the classics. You know, Homa....' Jones was subsequently hired as a speechwriter for Secretary of Education William Bennett. The editor who published that column, Dinesh D'Souza, went on to a career as a policy analyst in the Reagan White House.

This legitimization of racism has been accompanied by other developments. Admission to top colleges, including some public universities like the University of California, Berkeley, and UCLA, has become fiercely competitive: Berkeley had 21,200 applications to its 1987 freshman class, and enrolled 3,700—14 per cent. Many students with straight A averages in high school were denied admission. At the same time, some college campuses are beginning to reflect the diversity of the American population: Berkeley's incoming class in 1987 was 12 per cent black, 17 per cent Latino, 26 per cent Asian and only 40 per cent white. This new alignment comes as a shock to many white students, especially those who grew up in all-white, middle-class suburbs. Some of them respond to campus racial diversity by proclaiming that all blacks and Latinos have been admitted under affirmative action programs and thus are taking places away from "more qualified" whites. That argument is often turned around, however, as a justification for hostility toward Asians, who are criticized for being supercompetitive.

University administrators at many campuses prefer to ignore racial incidents or keep them out of the news, but antiracist student organizations have successfully focused attention on the problem. After the U-Mass incident following the World Series, campus officials at first denied that race had played any part in what the campus police termed a brawl among sports fans. That made it hard for black students to follow Shelby Steele's advice and spend their time "reading and studying." Not until students demonstrated did U-Mass chancellor Joseph Duffey admit that his campus had a racial problem. At Penn State, 89 students were arrested at a campus sit-in in April 1988. At U-Mass in February 1988, two hundred students held a five-day sit-in; at Wisconsin in November 1987, 100 protesters marched outside the Phi Gamma Delta ("Fiji") fraternity house, where a racist incident had occurred, chanting, "Hey, Fijis, you can't hide, drop the sheets and come outside!" As a result of dozens of scenes like these, the student campaign against racism has provided the focus for campus politics at many colleges and universities.

Campus antiracist activists have put forward a variety of strategies. One of these identifies the problem as ignorance among white kids, many of whom grew up in isolated lilywhite suburbs and need to learn about the diversity of American culture. Advocates of this approach insist that all students should take a course in ethnic studies or cultural diversity, often taught by newly hired minority faculty members. The Universities of Indiana and Minnesota each require two courses in US cultural pluralism; the University of Wisconsin, Madison, has established a one-course ethnic studies requirement and the University of California, Berkeley, has established a similar measure. Minority student organizations across the country enthusiastically support an ethnic studies requirement for graduation. Charles Holley, co-president of the Black Student Union of the Madison campus, has argued that the courses teach "what minorities are all about, where we came from, what we feel." The student government officers at Berkeley, in a joint statement, declared that "students commonly graduate without reading the work of a minority author, studying under a minority professor, or having learned the vital histories of people of color. In a state that will soon have a non-white majority, such an undergraduate experience dangerously perpetuates false stereotypes."

Another strategy focuses on the empowerment of targets of violence. Much racial harassment typically goes unreported, even though it makes life miserable for minority students. When these students have their own campus centers and organizations, they don't have to suffer in isolation; they can—and increasingly do—rally their forces against their antagonists. In the aftermath of racial flare-ups minority students have frequently demanded university support for such centers. At

U-Mass, participants in winter 1988's sit-in called on school administrators to renovate New Africa House as a cultural center for minority students.

A third strategy strives to reduce campus violence in general as a way of thwarting racial violence. Jan Sherrill, director of the Center for Study and Prevention of Campus Violence at Towson State University, in Maryland, argues that American culture condones violent means of resolving disputes as a legitimate form of male self-expression. Reagan's oft-proclaimed "values" glorified the macho response to international problems. Terrorism at a disco in Berlin? Send the Air Force to Tripoli to bomb Qaddafi. Men longed to join the President in saying, "Go ahead, make my day." A media culture of exploding cars, free-swinging cops and bone-crunching sports is re-inforced by campus norms that say it's OK for young men to get drunk, wreck their dorm rooms and slug it out with one another. A program at Towson State's Richmond Hall has focused on reducing property damage in the dorm and violence of all kinds between students by setting strict rules and giving residents responsibility for enforcing them. As a result, there have been no racist incidents or attacks on gays or women this academic year in the dorm, which has become "a violence-free zone," according to Sherrill. It's not yet clear whether incidents elsewhere on campus will decline.

On many campuses, racism is endemic to the fraternity subculture. The house that held the slave auction at Madison, Zeta Beta Tau (ZBT), is predominantly Jewish and had itself been a target of an attack: members of Fiji crashed a ZBT party, beat three persons and taunted them with anti-Semitic slurs. In another racist incident involving fraternities on that campus, a Kappa Sigma party in 1986 had a "Harlem Room," with white students in blackface, watermelon punch, graffiti on the walls and garbage on the floor. Racism among fraternities is fostered by the fact that most are completely segregated, and it is exacerbated by rituals of heavy drinking on party weekends. In November 1988, the Chancellor at Madison, Donna Shalala, established a Commission on the Future of Fraternities and Sororites, which is to recommend ways to reduce their racist and sexist behavior. The possibilities, Shalala said, range from attacking "substance abuse" as a cause of "misconduct" to elimination of the Greek system altogether.

A more problematic strategy for reducing campus racism focuses on criminalizing racist speech, which constitutes the most prevalent form of harassment. At the University of Michigan, Ann Arbor, interim president Robben Fleming implemented a new code in 1988 that allows university administrators to place on probation, suspend or expel students engaged in "discriminatory" behavior, including racist speech. Under the code, the student who told the racist "jokes" over the radio would be put on probation; if he made "other blatantly racist remarks" while on probation he could be suspended or expelled. Most of the university Regents support the code, the *Michigan Daily* reported, as do several deans and professors. But the student representatives of the University Council have denounced the proposal as a "terrible misuse of power," and the United Coalition Against Racism, a student group that has demanded university action against racial abuse, has voiced a similar sentiment.

At Madison ZBT was cleared by the student government disciplinary committee of all charges of violating university rules against racial discrimination. Committee chair Rana Mookherjee said of the fraternity's slave auction, "There is no rule you can write to eradicate bad taste and insensitivity." Many minority students expressed outrage at the decision; one was in tears. A spokesman for the Madison campus's Minority Coalition, Peter Chen, said, "By hiding behind the issue of free speech, the administration is making this campus safe for racism."

The protection of offensive speech will always cause frustration, but it nonetheless provides an important lesson in the meaning of the First Amendment. Campus leaders need not limit themselves to defending the First Amendment just because of constitutional barriers to criminalizing offensive speech, however. On the contrary, they have an obligation to speak out, forcefully and frequently, explaining why racist speech is objectionable. At Madison, Chancellor Shalala did that: although fraternity members have a First Amendment right to objectionable speech, she said, "using slavery as a basis for humor should be offensive to every American."

Donna Shalala began her term as chancellor in February 1988 by announcing the "Madison plan." It calls for the University of Wisconsin to double the number of minority undergraduates over the next five years; create 150 financial aid packages for low-income students; raise $4 million in private money to increase the scholarship endowment and another $4 million to endow 25 new minority graduate and professional fellowships; hire 70 new minority faculty members over the next three years, more than doubling the current number; and require ethnic studies courses in each college. In addition, the university pledged to hire or promote 125 minority academic staff members over the next three years. Shalala budgeted $4.7 million to implement this program over the next three years, part of which must come from new appropriations, which the Wisconsin Legislature is currently considering.

The Minority Coalition at Madison criticized the plan for failing to establish a strong racial harassment policy, an adequate multicultural center or antiracism workshops during student orientation. But the goals, the budget and the timetable make the Madison plan one of the most far-reaching attempts to overcome institutional racism undertaken by any major university. The University of Wisconsin's effort is important, among other reasons, because of the school's size: it has the fourth largest student body in the nation, numbering about 44,000. It's especially heartening that Wisconsin is making such an extensive commitment at a time when people feel beaten down and defeated by eight years of losing battles against the Reagan White House.

Unfortunately, the promises made at Madison and at other progressive institutions to hire more black faculty run up against a major obstacle: the small pool of available black college teachers. These men and women are being intensely wooed, and Madison's recruitment successes will inevitably hurt the campaigns on other campuses. The shortage of black faculty is part of a larger problem—the declining number of blacks in higher education, from the undergraduate through the professorial ranks. Most talented black undergraduates opt for law or medicine or business over academia—and why not? The prospect of spending years as an isolated, underpaid, overworked assistant professor is not an inviting one. The Madison plan addresses this problem in several ways: by pledging that the university will work with local high schools to improve their graduation rates; will in the future recruit twice as many minority students to its freshman class and provide them with financial support to help them stay through graduation; and will double the number of fellowships for graduate and professional schools, to encourage minority students to finish dissertations.

Defensive administrators at colleges and universities across the country argue that the recent spread of racism on campus shows only that the university is a part of American society, which itself seems to be increasingly racist and violent. That's true, but it shouldn't provide an excuse for educators who prefer to wait for the larger society to change. More universities need to make the kind of commitment demonstrated by Chancellor Shalala at the University of Wisconsin if they are going to overcome the racism that has stained the campus during the Age of Reagan.

The Nation, February 27, 1989

21

Looking Back, Moving Ahead:

Students Today and the Sixties

A debate over the meaning of the 1960s rages in the new student movement. For Amy Eppler, a 1986 Yale Law School graduate, the 1960s provide an alternative point of reference for activists in a yuppie world. "It's important for us to see ourselves not as part of the 'me generation' but as connected to the past. I'm proud to be part of a continuum with earlier activists," she said. "And we've learned from the past. The Yale divestment movement today is not just made up of students: unionized employees and community members are working with students to fight the university's South Africa policy. What we are doing at Yale today is better than what happened here in the sixties."

This desire for continuity—expressed graphically in 1985 by 400 pro-divestment students at UCLA who arranged a special screening of *The War at Home*, the 1979 antiwar documentary, while occupying the administration building one night—is a mark of how the current student movement diverges from its precursor. "The film made us feel that we're part of the same struggle," said Carla Zeitlin, a participant. But what made the New Left new, largely, was its break with the elders. In 1962 Students for a Democratic Society was officially the youth organization of the League for Industrial Democracy. After the Port Huron convention, the board of the LID attacked the kids, fired SDS president Tom Hayden and decided to censor all SDS materials.[1] Shortly before, Irving Howe and Lewis Coser had condemned the nascent New Left in the pages of *Dissent*. When Richard Flacks

---

1. See chapter 28 below.

brought the news of Port Huron to Leo Huberman of *Monthly Review*, Huberman told him, "It's much more important whether Fidel Castro can defend his revolution than whether American youth think anything." SDS founders reacted by sharpening their sense of themselves as a "new" left.

Today's student activists do not face that kind of opposition from their New Left elders. On the contrary, they see themselves and are seen as a part of the same tradition. In particular, the students at Rutgers University who helped plan the national student convention in February 1988 sought the advice of veterans. John Grele said, "Our ties to sixties activists are an important resource for us. They have helped us greatly. Personally, I've gotten the most out of talking with Mark Rudd, Al and Barbara Haber and Abbie Hoffman." Christine Kelly added, "The sixties people who have been most helpful to us have offered advice, but they respect our autonomy. They are there when we need them, but they aren't interfering if they aren't asked. We've been impressed with their support. Abbie has been good. Barbara Ehrenreich has been really enthusiastic from the beginning."

The Rutgers students have done some serious thinking about what they can learn from the 1960s, mainly from the collapse of SDS. "The New Left's candor and openness set a model for us," said Jonathan Stein, another student who worked on the convention. "We hope to avoid the pitfalls that befell them, especially sectarianism." Kelly agreed. "The sectarians won out in SDS in the late sixties because they were the hardest workers. We have to develop our theoretical and historical understanding, but we have to focus on the hard work of building a movement, of developing a generation of activists. Abbie Hoffman has prodded us in this direction. The way to defeat the sectarians is to work harder than they do." She pointed to another lesson current activists have learned: "The women are not going to be making the coffee this time around.... The biggest difference has been the women's movement. We have women in leadership positions."

But the legacy of the past—and the eager help of aging SDSers—can be a burden as well as a benefit to young activists. "For us, the sixties are an overwhelming presence that can't be escaped," said L.A. Kauffman, a Princeton student who worked on divestment and on the campus *Progressive Review*. "The prevailing conception of the sixties constrains our ability to do politics now. We're told we're a remnant of something that was once great. We're told we are trying to re-create the past, which is impossible. We are asking ourselves, How is it possible for us to develop our own definitions, instead of being absorbed within this older conception?" Other activists I interviewed felt the same way. "We have a media-created burden of comparing ourselves to the sixties," said a leader of the antiapartheid movement at Yale, "Our actions are constantly measured against them. Before the arrests here over divestment, I thought my generation could never match the sixties. In the sixties, students led the progressive movement. That's no longer true in the peace movement or in the movement concerned with Central America. But Cornell had 1,100 arrests in 1985. Nothing like that happened there in the sixties. For the first time it made me think that maybe we could do it; maybe students could lead the country away from supporting the South African government."

Still others resented being asked to compare the two eras. Another Yale activist, Nathan Light, said, "The administration here is thinking about the sixties. We aren't." His classmate Jennifer Yardley said, "How do we really compare with sixties campus movements? We're totally non-violent; that's different. We use the tactics of civil disobedience and confrontation; that's similar. But what's the point of comparing the two?" Beyond the weight of left tradition, today's activists confront media images of that earlier radicalism as something essentially useless and self-indulgent. "I hear people saying very little was accomplished," observed Julian Fischer, a student at the Oakwood School, in North Hollywood, California. "John Cougar Mellencamp said on an MTV interview that the sixties was a dishonest time. He said, 'We screamed a lot, but really all we did was get stoned.'"

Another difference between the generation is that in many respects the culture that emerged two decades ago is still alive. New Leftists rejected more than the politics of their elders; they also rejected the life style—in favor of sex, drugs and rock and roll. In American culture, and even in middle age, New Leftists remain on the same side as today's students. It's more than a matter of the revival of miniskirts and the color chartreuse. The music is still popular. The Beatles' version of "Twist and Shout" was on the charts recently—as heard in the film *Ferris Bueller's Day Off*. A student at John Jay College in New York told historian Mike Wallace he wished he had been older in the 1960s, "so I could have heard the Grateful Dead in three decades, not just two."

Paul Simon and Stevie Wonder sell records to a new generation. Rock is no longer the palace of the young; its fans range in age from fifteen to fifty-five. Some left-wing students explicitly identify with the 1960s counterculture. At Purdue University in West Lafayette, Indiana, guys with shoulder-length hair wearing tie-dyed T-shirts are militantly anti-Reagan. They won't listen to Prince or Bruce Springsteen; for them no one has ever surpassed Jimi Hendrix. For other self-styled hippies, the embrace of an earlier era extends to its drugs of choice. At Princeton and elsewhere they reject cocaine as a "yuppie performance drug" in favor of marijuana and LSD.

Thus, today's student activists must grapple with their relationship to the culture of the 1960s as well as its politics. In both spheres, the challenge is to learn from and be inspired by the previous generation while finding their own identity and direction.

The Nation, March 26, 1988

22

Freshman Activists

The Age of Reagan seems to be coming to an end on the nation's campuses: 37 per cent of the 1990 freshman class reported that they "participated in organized demonstrations" last year, according to an authoritative poll—more than double the percentage of the late 1960s. "Influencing social values" was "a very important goal" to 41 per cent—an all-time high (the 1960s peak was 34 per cent, in 1969 and 1970). Eighty-six per cent of all college freshmen thought the government wasn't doing enough to control pollution, 68 per cent said the government wasn't doing enough to promote disarmament and 65 per cent supported abortion rights—the highest ever, up from 53 per cent in 1979.

What gave 1989's high school seniors the idea that they ought to fight the power and exercise their First Amendment rights? School issues provoked many demonstrations in 1988–89, as students marched against dress codes and in support of popular minority teachers and officials threatened with firing. The dismissal of a black superintendent was the focus of the recent Selma, Alabama, sit-in by black high school students. In Los Angeles, 10,000 high school students took part in sit-ins and protest marches during a two-week teachers' strike in 1989, with many of the students actively supporting the teachers' demands—the largest wave of student-led protests in the LA schools in twenty years.

Fewer of the 1990 freshmen told the poll they were interested in majoring in business than any entering class during the previous five years, and the number who said it was "very important" or "essential" to "be successful in my own business" declined to 45 per cent, its lowest point in more than a decade. "The great surge of popularity of business majors and careers that we witnessed during the 1970s and 1980s has ended," the pollsters concluded. Crime and drugs were the only areas in which a majority of first-year students held Reaganite views: only 21 per cent opposed the death penalty, compared with 58 per cent in 1971; 17 per cent favored legalized marijuana, an all-time low, down from a peak of 53 per cent in 1977.

The study, conducted annually since 1966 by UCLA's Higher Education Research Institute and the American Council on Education, involved 296,000 freshmen at almost 600 two- and four-year colleges and universities; it was statistically adjusted to represent all 1.6 million first-time, full-time students entering college in fall 1989. Students filled out a four-page mutiple-choice "Student Information Form" on which the political questions were camouflaged. The form included a list of twenty-five "activities"; students were asked to check those they had engaged in. "Participated in organized demonstration" came between "won a varsity letter for sports" and "was bored in class."

So the *Zeitgeist* has shifted. But it's not shifting back to the sixties: there's no Vietnam War to provide a unifying focus for protest today, and no leaders of student protest have captured national media attention. Today's freshman activists find themselves in a more intellectually nurturing campus environment than did their predecessors of twenty-five years ago. More faculty members are teaching about power and inequality than ever before, and the campus left of the eighties leaves a respectable legacy of fighting for divestment and against campus racism. The eighties were a hard decade—but the times they are a-changin'.

The Nation, April 16, 1990

23

Divestment Report Card:

Students, Stocks and Shanties

The 1985–86 academic year was a good one for the campus divestment movement. The biggest victory came in July 1986, when the University of California Board of Regents voted to sell all $3.1 billion of its stock in companies that do business in South Africa. That's by far the largest divestiture by any university in the country, more than the combined total from the 120 private and public colleges and universities that have decided to divest either partially or totally. The California action, said Peter Duignan of Stanford University's Hoover Institution, "is going to make it difficult for any other university president to hold out."

The California Regents made their move at the urging of Republican Governor George Deukmejian. His chief of staff explained that divestment was a "moral imperative" for the Governor. "You don't grow up listening to the story of the Armenian genocide without having deep empathy for oppressed people wherever they may be," he said. But Deukmejian was Armenian last year, when he vetoed a divestment bill passed by the State Assembly. Los Angeles Mayor Tom Bradley, Deukmejian's challenger in the November 1985 elections, called the Governor's change of heart an election-year flip-flop designed to deprive Bradley of a potent issue. Republicans hope Deukmejian's move will keep him from losing support among college-age voters.

University of California students put divestment on the Regents' agenda and kept it there. At Berkeley in April 1986, when police attacked two dozen shanties at 2.30 in the morning, some students linked arms and resisted arrest, while others erected barricades to stop police buses. The next day students rebuilt the shanties, and the university drew on fourteen different police forces to mount a 3 a.m. attack. Students fought for hours; by 7.30 one hundred of them had been arrested and many injured. The Berkeley City Council then voted unanimously to stop sending its police to suppress antiapartheid demonstrations on campus. Deukmejian, in switching positions on divestment, apparently sought to avoid militant demonstrations on campus during the campaign season.

For the campus divestment movement, 1985–86 was the year of the shanties, makeshift structures disrupting the campus landscape of tidy quadrangles and plazas, symbolizing the viciousness of apartheid and the oppression of South Africa's blacks. The shanties have also come to symbolize the campus activism of the 1980s. They have appeared not only at schools with long radical traditions, like the University of Wisconsin, Reed College and Columbia University, but also in unexpected places, like the University of Utah, the University of Florida at Gainesville and Purdue University.

The power of the shanties was evident in the opposition they provoked. At Utah and Johns Hopkins University shanties were set on fire; at Dartmouth College they were attacked by right-wing students wielding sledgehammers. At Yale University departing president A. Bartlett Giamatti emerged from a birthday luncheon in April to see students setting up shanties. Enraged, he yelled that he'd have the structures torn down. When the police came, at 5.30 in the morning, they arrest 78 people blocking their path; at noon that day 1,500 people joined in a protest rally, and two days later more than 150 anti-apartheid demonstrators had been arrested. The events followed the 1960s paradigm: radicals confront administration; administration calls police on campus; formerly apathetic students are radicalized en masse. Yale learned that lesson in the 1960s and did not arrest students during those years, when Kingman Brewster made the school a model of liberal political engagement. Recalling the Brewster era, 150 faculty members protested the arrest of students and a faculty committee recommended that the shanties be rebuilt. A municipal court judge later dismissed all charges against the students. Freshman activist Jennifer Yardley told me, "The administration used bully tactics in the middle of the night to destroy something important. That's what outraged students." Eric Arnesen, another undergraduate, summed it up: "The shanties worked."

Yale's divestment movement has one significant accomplishment beyond mobilizing students: it has forged a link between students, campus workers and New Haven's black community. The employees' union, strengthened by a militant strike in 1984, has been active in the divestment campaign, and more than one hundred local people were arrested in the antiapartheid protests. Benno Schmidt, who took office as Yale's president on July 1, 1986, came from the faculty of Columbia University, which in 1985 promised to divest completely by 1987. He ought to know that divestment works. Nevertheless, he declared his opposition to divestment and a new season's cycle of student protests and arrests began. At Harvard University not only did students build shanties in the hallowed yard; alumni also challenged the administration's South Africa policy—and won the first round. Harvard Alumni Apartheid (AAA) elected a pro-divestment candidate, Gay Seidman, to the board of overseers, one of two bodies that officially govern the university. Seidman was the first woman president of the *Crimson*, graduated summa cum laude in 1978, spent five years in southern Africa writing and teaching, and is now in a Ph.D. program in sociology at Berkeley.

AAA leaders had placed three pro-divestment candidates on the ballot by petition, challenging the official slate, and they wondered why Seidman was the only one to be elected. Because the election was in effect a referendum on divestment, they had assumed that the three would either all win or all lose. Before the vote the AAA had asked that the ballots be counted by a neutral party, such as the League of Women Voters or the American Arbitration Association. Instead, the Harvard administration appointed its own accounting firm, Coopers and Lybrand, and opened some of the ballots before giving them over to be counted. "Harvard clearly had the motivation to cheat," said AAA coordinator Chester Hartman. "They also had the opportunity to cheat."

When Harvard announced the results, it reported a turnout of only 27 per cent, up from 21 per cent the previous year. (The record, 33 per cent, was set in 1969, when Norman Mailer and Henry Norr, a leader of Students for a Democratic Society, ran as insurgent candidates with no get-out-the-vote effort.) The state attorney general was asked in June 1986 to investigate possible vote fraud.

Divestment was also debated during 1985–86 at Randolph-Macon

Woman's College in Lynchburg, Virginia; St Mary's College in Notre Dame, Indiana; and Alabama A & M University. At the University of Utah, Connie Spencer, a senior majoring in political science, told me that in February 1986 she had been complaining to her friends about how hard it was to get their small divestment group going. "Then three of us read about Dartmouth and how the shanties galvanized things there. We said, 'We'll do the same thing.' So we put up two shanties over the weekend." Within weeks their group had grown to thirty. "Then some white South African students tried to tear the shanties down. Then a Molotov cocktail was thrown at one shanty while people were in it. Then murals painted on the shanties by art students were sledgehammered. Then gasoline was poured on a shanty and set on fire." Each time the shanties were repaired or rebuilt.

Chase Peterson, the university's president, called in Spencer and other divestment leaders and told them that as a result of the attacks on the shanties the university was about to lose its liability insurance; therefore, the shanties had to come down. The students refused to remove them and they sued the university. "This will shock your socks off," Spencer told me. "We won." US District Court Judge Aldon Anderson ruled in August 1986 that the shanties are protected by the First Amendment. The university may establish "reasonable restrictions" on the time, place and manner in which shanties are used, but it may not order them dismantled. That precedent could protect shanties on other campuses. "A lot of students don't agree with us but feel we have the right to do it," Spencer said. "Our biggest critics are Mormon Church missionaries who've been to South Africa and tell us it's not so bad there. Of course, the Mormon Church is up to its eyeballs in South African investments and has a horribly racist background, so we have to fight that."

At Duke University, in Durham, North Carolina, the trustees voted in May 1986 for total divestment if apartheid was not abolished by the following January. They rejected a process of evaluating individual companies' policies toward South Africa. Peter Wood, a history professor who helped draft the proposal the trustees passed, argued that "university actions should be based on the conduct of the South African government and not the behavior of the corporations themselves." Trustee David Maisel agreed: "Divestiture, unlike selective divestment, makes clear what we actually desire—a real change in the government system in South Africa." Students had been pressing the divestment issue at Duke since 1978 but never mobilized large numbers of supporters. When they built shanties in spring 1986, the administration ordered the arrest of six students who had defied a ban on staying overnight in the shanties. The university argued that staying overnight was "hazardous." But a local judge threw the university's case out of court, and the student activists gained respect and sympathy.

The Southern civil rights movement, past and present, figured significantly in Duke's decision to divest. While the student protests were under way, the immense Duke chapel was used for the induction of Rev. Benjamin F. Chavis Jr as executive director of the United Church of Christ's Commission for Racial Justice. Chavis, a prominent black activist minister, praised the courage and commitment of the students who had been arrested. As he called those students to the pulpit, the audience, mostly from neighboring black communities, gave them a standing ovation. The significance of the event was not lost on Duke's trustees, many of whom are Southerners who want to avoid rekindling the racial struggles of the 1960s.

At the University of Texas, Austin, hundreds of students (182 in one day alone) were arrested in antiapartheid protests in April 1986. At the University of Illinois's Urbana-Champaign campus 60 people were arrested outside a trustees' meeting at which divestment was rejected and students were ordered to dismantle a shantytown. At the University of Wyoming in Laramie students persuaded the trustees to divest totally. At Utah State University students voted 1,000 to 800 in favor of total divestment. At Bryn Mawr College, 200 students occupied the administration building, and 50 stayed overnight; the next day the trustees voted for partial divestment.

At Brown University four students fasted in the choir loft of Manning Chapel, calling for total divestment; the university "dis-enrolled" them after nine days. An official explained that the administration was concerned about its liability for the students' health. Paul Zimmerman, a sophomore member of the group, said, "It is no longer useful to appeal to the conscience of our university." In April 1986, Bucknell University's trustees offered antiapartheid students travel expenses so that they could visit the headquarters of companies that do business in South Africa and talk to executives—thus advising the students, Don't tell us, tell them. The students kept up the pressure, and six weeks later the trustees declared they would divest totally the next year. At Swarthmore college trustees voted for conditional divestment but cut faculty salaries 1 per cent in case the post-divestment rate of return on investment fell—thus advising the faculty, You'll pay for this.

In these debates South Africa raises the same kind of issue that Mississippi did during the early 1960s: students' disappointment with university policy in both cases was brought to a flash point by what Todd Gitlin, a member of the executive committee of Harvard's AAA, called "a volatile mixture of racism and hypocrisy." Like the segregated South in 1962, South Africa has a power structure that is unjust, and it is also distant from the daily lives of most college students. Still, those who think the student divestment movement should come up with a strategy to link its actions to domestic racial issues are asking too much, especially when civil rights leaders and organizations themselves have found it easier to unite on divestment demands than on domestic policy proposals.

If the campus divestment movement addresses an issue that is distant, it nevertheless poses radical questions for America about economic democracy. How should socially generated wealth be invested? Who should have the power to decide? Matthew Countryman, a Yale senior and divestment leader, told me: "Students here are learning about the nature of this institution. Yale University doesn't practice the social and moral ideals we are taught in the classroom. It's run undemocratically. It supports existing power and privilege in the world." Most campus divestment activity, however, is centered not on radical questions but on a liberal definition of apartheid as a purely moral issue. The pre-eminent question is, how can you organize a portfolio to provide the highest rate of return without investing in certain immoral stocks? The significance of even that question should not be underestimated, however; recognizing that there are moral limits on making money is a considerable achievement in the age of Reagan. If it's immoral to profit from exploiting blacks in South Africa, maybe other kinds of exploitation are immoral too.

At a Columbia divestment teach-in in 1985, a liberal investment banker who explained strategies for managing a portfolio without stock investment in South Africa was one of the most popular speakers, prompting dozens of questions. The school administration was partly responsible for the students' interest, since it had defined the issue as "fiduciary responsibility," arguing that students were too ignorant to understand the necessity of investing in South Africa. Students felt they needed to learn investment strategies to defend their position. In fact, the Boston Company's South Africa Free Equity Index, which compares the companies in the Standard and Poor 500 that have employees in South Africa against those that do not, shows no difference in the total return on investment of each over a period of two and a half years beginning in 1984. But what if investments in South Africa did make more money? You might also increase your rate of return by investing in child labor or slavery.

The divestment movement is going to win. The day will come when US corporations pull out of South Africa, either because the costs of staying become greater than the costs of leaving, or because Congress forces them to withdraw. What will the divestment movement do with such a success? Can it spark a broader, more sustained and more radical movement, the way civil rights did in the 1960s? So far the experience with success has not been encouraging. At Columbia the movement has recapitulated part of the history of the 1960s, as black and white activists bicker over leadership and the less political students fade away. The students who were radicalized prior to the divestment campaign remain active; the rest do not.

Divestment leaders know what's needed. Joshua Nessen, student coordinator of the American Committee on Africa, said, "The focus of the divestment movement has to be broader. We need to find ways of building political and material support for liberation movements. We need to focus more activity on stopping US funding for Unita; we need to link Reagan's support for Unita with his support for the *contras*." Moving in that direction, the Berkeley Faculty for Divestment recently changed its name to Faculty Against Apartheid and is emphasizing support for the African National Congress and other liberation movements.

South Africa could also provide the starting point for a wider campaign for democratic control of social wealth. Harvard's Alumni Against Apartheid may argue for a systematic affirmative investment program, according to Todd Gitlin, in which part of Harvard's endowment would be invested in socially valuable activities and projects.

DIVESTMENT REPORT CARD

Matthew Countryman concludes: "Before last spring I thought you couldn't compare my generation with that of the sixties. The vast majority of students today weren't prepared to take risks. In the sixties students led the nation in challenging an unjust government policy. That hasn't been true for the nuclear freeze movement or the opposition to *contra* aid. But it has become true for divestment. Today's students have come out of the woodwork."

The Nation, October 11, 1986

24

Campus Voices, Right and Left

Political conferences can be disorienting. At a meeting of an organization called the National Association of Scholars, for example, one does not expect to find advertisements for the Dix Gun Works catalogue, chocolate-chip cookies in a "spectacular" Statue of Liberty tin ("the perfect gift") and a videocassette entitled "How to Raise Your Self-esteem." Nor at a left-wing gathering on anticommunism, does one anticipate hearing praise for the American press from a Communist journalist. But for all the surprises, these two recent conclaves went a long way toward illuminating the preoccupations and obsessions of the right and the left as they steeled themselves for combat in the Age of Bush.

"Reclaiming the Academy: Responses to the Radicalization of the University" was the title of the conference held by the National Association of Scholars, which is not really a large national association but a small group of conservative professors funded by the right-wing Olin and Scaife foundations. They espouse what their statement of purpose calls a "renewed assertiveness" against feminism, ethnic studies and literary theory. The meeting, held over the weekend of November 12–13, 1988, in the fading splendor of the Roosevelt Hotel in midtown Manhattan, was attended by nearly three hundred people and looked like an ordinary faculty gathering: older men in tweed jackets, a few women, a single black. Besides the "Liberty Tree Catalogue" with its gun and cookie ads, the book exhibits displayed literature about the English Language Amendment to the Constitution ("ELA" to its proponents, a little-known anti-immigrant proposal that would make English the official language of the US) and the scholars' new journal,

Academic Questions, the first number of which features Barnard College historian Rosalind Rosenberg, who seems to be a hero in these circles for standing up for Sears Roebuck when the company was charged by the Equal Employment Opportunity Commission with sex discrimination (see chapter 4 above).

In a large room with green walls, dusty chandeliers and torn carpets, the scholars' president, Stephen Balch, opened the conference by announcing that it was "the beginning of a movement ... to end the servitude of the university to forces with contempt for intellectual values." Balch, a fast-talking man, looks a little like Woody Allen and told a few jokes: the goal of the left faculty, he said, is to turn the whole curriculum into "oppression studies." The audience guffawed appreciatively. Balch said the organization's aims included "informing communities about the quality of higher education in their areas," which seems to mean trying to get local right-wing groups to attack ethnic studies programs and campus women's centers. He concluded his call to arms by lamenting that "unlike the ideologues of the left, we did not see campus political struggle as part of our vocation." Another speaker hit the same dour note, reporting plaintively that right-wing students today "envy student radicals for their sense of commitment."

Next came Herbert London, a New York University dean and columnist for the *New York City Tribune,* sister paper of the Rev. Sun Myung Moon's *Washington Times,* and newly announced Republican candidate for mayor of New York City. He denounced the "Derridaization of the curriculum," including "Marxism and minimalism." Minimalism? The trouble with including literature by women and non-whites in the core curriculum, he argued, is that "it does not lead us toward our true humanity." London posed the big questions: "What must we do to give our lives value [and] certify that we are not headed for a meaningless death?" The answer, implicit in the rest of his talk: fight feminism. Keynote speaker Jeane Kirkpatrick branded the scholars' academic enemies "the fascist left." But the scholars' real hero was Alan Kors, a rumpled, bearded intellectual historian at the University of Pennsylvania who was a Princeton University student during the 1960s. "The immediate threat to academic freedom," he proclaimed, "comes from antiharassment policies, racial awareness programs and the enshrinement of 'diversity' as a value for the university." The antiharassment policies in question prohibit unwanted sexual remarks or actions in the classroom, among other places. Kors sees these policies as threatening professors' academic freedom, since a student could complain that a lecture contained "unwanted sexual remarks." The new "academic totalitarians" behind these policies, Kors said, are "the women's centers, the lesbians and gays."

The racial awareness programs Kors attacked have been a typical university response to outbreaks of racial tension or violence on campus; Kors denounced such programs as efforts at "thought control." Waving his arms and yelling about the dangers of "tolerance and diversity," Kors urged his fellow association members to "use ridicule" against blacks, gays and feminists. The audience cheered. "Our opponents are filled with resentments born of marginality," he concluded. In fact, the conference demonstrated that it is the right-wing faculty who are filled with resentment, because they know it is they who have been marginalized—by the intellectual energy and commitment of the academic left.

While the National Association of Scholars snarled in New York City, more than 1,300 people gathered in Cambridge, Massachusetts, to discuss "Anticommunism and the US: History and Consequences" at a conference sponsored by the Institute for Media Analysis held at Harvard University. Many thought anticommunism was losing its rationale, since Reagan himself had given up his "evil empire" talk to praise Mikhail Gorbachev. The *Boston Herald* provided a stiff antidote to this view; columnist Dan Feder suggested that "a group of roaches [had] scheduled a meeting to protest the effects of DDT."

Three generations of roaches milled around Harvard's glass and concrete Science Center: old leftists, 1960s movement people and today's student activists. The different generations had different agendas: the old Communist Party members talked about the costs of anticommunism over the past forty years; one silver-haired man argued, "We gave something to America nobody else did," and another said poignantly, "Anticommunism ruined my life." The younger people focused more on the way anticommunism today impoverishes American political culture. Arlene Goldbard, founder of the Institute for Cultural Democracy, maintained that "anticommunism has shrunk our ability to imagine and discuss alternative futures."

David Montgomery, a labor historian at Yale University who had been a CP union organizer in the 1950s, recalled for the audience the progressive agenda of 1945: full employment based on government planning and investment; increased union organizing; a fair employment law to protect black workers; national health insurance; public housing; world peace based on cooperation with the Soviet Union through the United Nations. What happened to that agenda? In 1946 the Republicans won control of Congress for the first time since the Depression by launching a campaign against "Communism, corruption and chaos." And in 1948 Truman followed suit. The "missing agenda" of 1946, Montgomery argued, provides the clearest measure of the costs of anticommunism.

The conference was a celebration of old left heroes and victims: Cheddi Jagan, former Prime Minister of British Guyana, twice overthrown by Central Intelligence Agency-backed coups; 85-year-old Virginia Durr, one of the few white people in Alabama to support the Montgomery bus boycott in 1954 (called before the Senate Internal Security Subcommittee, she told its chair, Senator John Stennis of Mississippi, "You're common as pig tracks"); Jack O'Dell, Martin Luther King Jr's direct mail fund-raiser. President Kennedy personally told King to fire O'Dell, whispering, "He's a Communist," and King reluctantly did. Today O'Dell is director of international affairs for the National Rainbow Coalition.

At the Friday evening symposium, seven panelists grappled chaotically with the topic of who sets the news agenda. An unlikely lovefest developed between Karl E. Meyer, an editorial writer at the *New York Times*, and fellow panelist Gianfranco Corsini of Italy's Communist daily, *L'Unita*. Meyer boasted of his longtime friendship with Corsini, and the Italian, in turn, praised both Meyer and the mainstream press Meyer works for, lauding it for the vast amount of information it offers each day. He then rambled on for so long that panelists William Styron and Alexander Cockburn nodded off.

The conference featured a Cockburn family panel. "Which Cockburn is that—the good one or the bad one?" a liberal journalist asked. The "good" one is Patrick, former Moscow correspondent for the London *Financial Times*, now at the Carnegie Endowment for International Peace; wearing a dark blue suit, he bore a striking resemblance to the middle-aged T.S. Eliot. The "bad" Cockburn is, of course, *The Nation*'s Alexander; he wore a florid Hawaiian shirt to avoid, he explained, "the KGB look." One Cockburn argued that "the eternal verities of 'the Soviet threat' will not be undermined by the realities of *glasnost*. The American military budget is based not on Soviet actions but on America's economic needs." The only way to cut military spending, he concluded, is to challenge corporate power directly. Another Cockburn criticized Soviet secrecy, exemplified by Russia's attempt to conceal the Chernobyl disaster. The failure of that cover-up, he argued, was a turning point toward a greater openness in reporting events. (When this analysis was denounced as "anti-Sovietism" by one member of the audience, one of the brothers said, "Patrick, say something nice about the Soviet Union.")

One of the sharpest debates took place at the culture panel. Meredith Tax, a feminist and author of the novels *Rivington Street* and the recently published *Union Square*, asked why the personal experience of Communist Party life had not been explored in American novels with the kind of insight European writers like Doris Lessing have shown. "I don't think it's the ghost of Joe McCarthy," she said. "I think it's the ghost of Joe Stalin, a Stalinist way of thinking about the US and about literature that still has a hold on many minds. Censorship is bad, but self-censorship is worse. The truth will not hurt anything that deserves to be cherished." Howard Fast, a former Communist and blacklist victim and a bestselling author, disagreed strenuously with Tax, whom he accused of "slanders against the party." Fast concluded, "Communism should not be written about by examining its sores.... We were a handful of people who moved this country. We must put *this* into books."

The panel "Radicals and Anticommunism" examined the question, how can the left make critical judgments about the Soviet Union and the CP without echoing or adding to official anticommunism? Anne Braden, for forty years an activist in the Southern civil rights movement, posed the question well but had no answer. Richard Healey, executive director of *Nuclear Times*, said the peace movement ought to criticize Soviet missiles in Eastern Europe and that such criticism should not be attacked as "Red-baiting," which he called "a term that avoids thought." The next speaker was Judith Leblanc, national organization secretary of the CP, USA. She said "anticommunism is a weapon to undermine the struggle of the working class against capitalism." People believe the country has become more conservative under Reagan, but "the Communist Party has a more accurate feel for where the people are.... Mass thinking is shifting to the left.... We have confidence in the forward motion of the working class." So much for the issue of left-wing criticism of the party.

Old leftists dominated many of the question periods, and various people argued that "anti-Sovietism is the most virulent form of anti-communism," or that "you have to look at the source of anti-communism: capitalism," or that "the Frankfurt School were international pimps for the bourgeoisie." This rhetoric annoyed many younger radicals, reminding them of why they had broken away from the old left in the 1960s. Carl Bernstein (of Woodward, Bernstein and Watergate) came out as a Red Diaper baby. "I am a child of the old left," he announced. "The FBI came to my bar mitzvah." His father, he said, was director of organization for the United Public Workers, a union of federal employees expelled from the AFL–CIO for being "Communist dominated." The elder Bernstein served as counsel to 700 Federal employees called before Security Loyalty boards seeking to purge reds from government beginning in the Truman years. "The laundry business took a turn to the left in the 1950s—because people like my father went into it after losing their jobs." Bernstein has written a book, *Loyalties*, telling the story of his family's life under the blacklist.

The conference ran with surprisingly few glitches, unusual for the left. The inevitable problems were met with good humor. The second day a thousand people sat down for lunch, or tried to, in Harvard's cavernous old Memorial Hall, where the speakers were John Henry Faulk and Jessica Mitford. The food ran out before everyone was seated, and late arrivals wandered hungrily among the tables. Those who managed to get lunch shared it with the less fortunate. Princeton English Professor Andrew Ross called this "an experience of primitive communism."

The conference was financed by grants from eight foundations and twenty-six individuals, including ecologist Abby Rockefeller. The ice cream was donated by Ben & Jerry's.

The Nation, December 12, 1988

PART IV

Radical History

25

Radical Historians and the Crisis in American History, 1959–1980

Most historians profess to believe in the pursuit of truth, but as members of a profession they are also engaged in the legitimation of knowledge, in the definition of who is a historian and who is not, what history is and what it is not. The definitions themselves are products of historical forces. Over time they change. The purpose of this article is to examine that process by focusing on the profession's initial rejection of the school that called itself "radical history" in the 1960s, and the subsequent limited acceptance of that school in the 1970s and 1980s.

During the 1960s, a new generation of scholars, a new intellectual community, formed itself out of its own experiences and concerns— notably the civil rights and antiwar movements. Among the prominent members of that community were historians who developed a critique of, and an alternative to, the ways American history had been constructed. Some intellectual leaders of the group made self-conscious use of Marxist theory, organizing their work around issues of class relations and ideology. The majority did not, but all took those issues seriously. In general, radical historians have focused on issues of exploitation, domination and oppression; they have argued that existing patterns of domination are not natural or immutable, but rather have historical origins; thus they can be abolished. In seeking

Research support for this article was provided by the American Council of Learned Societies. The author wishes to thank Eric Foner, Sean Wilentz, Jesse Lemisch, Christine Stansell, Perry Anderson, Michael P. Johnson, Daniel J. Walkowitz and Peter Novick for their comments, Susan Armeny of the *Journal of American History* for her editing, and Bill Billingsley for his research assistance.

those historical origins, they have focused on ordinary people rather than political elites, on groups rather than individuals, and on human agency rather than on abstract or general processes of change. Fierce debates have sometimes broken out among radical historians. New subjects and methods developed in response to intellectual and political changes during the 1960s and 1970s, and one task of this chapter is to trace the way radical historians' definitions of their work have changed.

Marxist historians, it has been written, are "obsessed by an ... exclusively economic interpretation" of history. They "force evidence to fit their pre-conceived opinions" and "ignore such materials as do not support [their] point of view." They believe in "the simple single factor explanation" of history as "the function of economic motives." Therefore, it was argued, Marxist history is *not* history.[1]

The dominant voices in the history profession described radical work in this way until the mid 1960s. Sometimes the profession specifically stigmatized Marxist history writing; just as often, mainstream critics projected Marxism's supposed sins onto all sorts of radical scholarship. Indeed, most of the statements quoted above appeared between 1959 and 1961 in scholarly reviews of two books by William Appleman Williams, *The Tragedy of American Diplomacy* and *The Contours of American History*—books that presented radical, but not really Marxist, interpretations. Harvard University professor Frank Friedel, reviewing the book, called Marxism "an outmoded over-simplification." Oscar Handlin reviewed *Contours* in the official journal of the predecessor to the Organization of American Historians (OAH) and informed the profession that "large sections" of the book were "farcical" or "altogether incoherent," and that Williams may have "intended [*Contours*] as an elaborate hoax." The *American Historical Review (AHR)* reviewer, Foster Rhea Dulles, called Williams's *Tragedy* "argument rather than history," and the reviewer in the *American*

---

1. Foster Rhea Dulles, review of *The Tragedy of American Diplomacy* by William Appleman Williams, *American Historical Review*, 64 (July 1959), pp. 1022–3; C.A. McClelland, review of *The Tragedy of American Diplomacy*, *American Political Science Review*, 53 (December 1959), p. 1195.

Political Science Review declared "this book cannot be taken seriously as history." Less than twenty years later, the Organization of American Historians elected Williams its president.[2]

The profession's initial dismissal of Williams and his subsequent election to the OAH presidency provided an exemplary case showing how historians define significant problems and appropriate methods for solving them, and how they change those definitions. The history profession as a community of scholars draws the line separating history from non-history and exercises sanctions over those who do not conform to its definition. Williams had masterfully reinterpreted the main lines of American history, but the profession regarded his work as non-history because he did not use the concepts and methods that defined acceptable discourse. The rejection and eventual acceptance of Afro-American and women's history revealed the same phenomenon.[3]

In 1985 some of those most visible a decade later as radical historians were unknown, scattered at schools that lacked graduate programs: Eugene D. Genovese was teaching at Brooklyn Polytechnic Institute, Herbert G. Gutman at Fairleigh Dickinson University, Christopher Lasch at Williams College, Warren I. Susman at Reed College. A decade later, all had been hired at major universities, and two decades later radical articles were appearing in scholarly journals, and some younger radicals were being hired by history departments and given tenure. Radical history continued to be challenged and criticized, often

---

2. Eugene D. Genovese characterized William Appleman Williams as a non-Marxist radical because he posed a conflict between "the individual" and "the community" rather than between classes and because he neglected Marx's concept of exploitation. See Eugene D. Genovese, "William Appleman Williams on Marx and America," *Studies on the Left*, 6 (January–February 1966, pp. 70–86). Frank Freidel, review of *The Contours of American History, Christian Science Monitor*, August 17, 1961, p. 7; Oscar Handlin, review of *The Contours of American History, Mississippi Valley Historical Review*, 48 (March 1962), pp. 743–5. John Higham protested that Handlin's review was "tasteless and irresponsible ... a scandalously intemperate polemic." See John Higham, "Communication," *Mississippi Valley Historical Review* 49 (September 1962), pp. 407–8; Handlin rejected the criticism, ibid., p. 408.

3. See August Meier and Elliot Rudwick, *Black History and the Historical Profession, 1915–1980* (Urbana, 1986). No comparable study yet exists for women's history, although the need is obvious. The new political history and quantitative history offer examples of other new schools that met initial resistance and then acceptance.

vehemently, but it had become part of the history profession, no longer excluded.[4]

How did radical historians establish their place in the profession? How did radical history enter the dialogue among American historians? It would be comforting to the profession to argue that the history profession excluded radical history before 1965 simply because it was bad history, and that when radicals began doing good history, the profession accepted and indeed honored them and their work. Thus the profession excluded Herbert Aptheker but admitted Genovese; it excluded Philip Foner but admitted his nephew Eric. The relevant comparison, however, is not between Aptheker's *American Negro Slave Revolts*, published in 1943, and Genovese's *The Political Economy of Slavery*, published in 1965; it is between *American Negro Slave Revolts* and the work of Ulrich B. Phillips, the dominant work of the time, which looked at slaves through the eyes of "the dominant class of the South," to whom Phillips dedicated one of his books. One might also contrast W.E.B. Du Bois's Marxist-influenced *Black Reconstruction*, published in 1935 and ignored for decades by the history profession, with the openly racist work of the Dunning school, part of the regular curriculum for decades.[5]

Good work does not insure acceptance for a new viewpoint. Scholars' definitions of "good work" embody assumptions about method, focus, purpose and agenda—assumptions that are not often made explicit or systematically articulated. Indeed, one characteristic of a successful school is that members do not need to defend their

4. For example, see Jonathan M. Wiener, "Class Structure and Economic Development in the American South, 1865–1965," *American Historical Review*, 84 (October 1979), pp. 970–92, and the ensuing exchange: Robert Higgs "Comments," ibid., pp. 993–7; Harold D. Woodman, "Comments," ibid., pp. 997–1001; and Jonathan Wiener, "Reply," ibid., pp. 1002–6. See also Michael Merrill and Michael Wallace, "Marxism and History," in *The Left Academy: Marxist Scholarship on American Campuses*, edited by Bertell Ollman and Edward Wernoff (New York, 1982), vol. 2, pp. 202–41.

5. Ulrich B. Phillips, *A History of Transportation in the Eastern Cotton Belt to 1860* (New York, 1908); Herbert Aptheker, *American Negro Slave Revolts* (New York, 1943); Eugene D. Genovese, *The Political Economy of Slavery: Studies in the Economy and Society of the Slave South* (New York, 1965); W.E. Burghardt Du Bois, *Black Reconstruction: an Essay toward a History of the Part Which Black Folk Played in the Attempt to Reconstruct Democracy in America, 1860–1880* (New York, 1935).

assumptions about significant problems and appropriate methods; their work consists of solving problems whose significance is widely accepted. The conventional explanation overlooks the crucial problem: how were a new generation of historians able to do radical work within a profession that rejected it as not history? How did the history produced by radicals in the sixties and later accepted by mainstream historians get written in the first place? The problem has two sides: the formation of a new generation of history students, mobilized by the civil rights and antiwar movements to challenge prevailing conceptions of the American past, and a transformation in the history profession, which changed its definition of history to include issues and problems that had previously been defined as non-history.

Before the sixties, the history profession, unlike some fields in social science, had never had a substantial group of radical scholars; some leftist scholars of the thirties and forties abandoned a Marxist orientation, including Merle Curti, Louis Hartz and Richard Hofstadter.[6] A few historians lost their jobs during the fifties, as McCarthyism swept the country; most of the rest of the profession proved to be easily intimidated. The Progressive school, with its sympathies for radicals and democratic movements and its attention to economic causes, had remained open to radical work. But the consensus history influential in the fifties with a few notable exceptions celebrated the absence of radical challenges to the status quo, portraying America as "a relatively homogeneous society with a relatively conservative history," in John Higham's words. Instead of seeing the United States as divided between privileged and excluded groups, Richard Hofstadter, David Potter, Louis Hartz, Daniel Boorstin and others emphasized continuity and stability.[7]

The picture of American universities as powerful sources of oppo-

---

6. On Hofstadter's Communist Party experience, see Susan Stout Baker, *Radical Beginnings: Richard Hofstadter and the 1930s* (Westport, 1985).

7. John Higham, *History: Professional Scholarship in America* (Baltimore, 1965), p. 221. Louis Hartz lamented America's uniformity; Daniel Boorstin celebrated it. The profession included critics of consensus scholarship: John Higham, "The Cult of the 'American Consensus,'" *Commentary*, 27 (February 1959), pp. 93–100. C. Vann Woodward, "The Populist Heritage and the Intellectual," *American Scholar*, 29 (Winter 1959–60), pp. 55–72.

sition to McCarthyism has been shattered by recent scholarship. When American universities resisted investigation by anticommunist congressional committees, their officials generally defended themselves by claiming that the university was capable of excluding Communists and unrepentant ex-Communists on its own. And that public claim seems to have masked a secret relationship between each of the major universities and the Federal Bureau of Investigation (FBI), in which they traded information about faculty members' political activities and ideas.[8] In California, for example, periodic harassment of leftists and former leftists was transformed into a permanent, quasi-legal "purge machine." In 1952, twenty-eight private and public colleges and universities, including the University of California and Stanford University, agreed to collaborate with the state legislature's Committee on Un-American Activities and install on each campus an official responsible to the committee. In the first year of operation, this system resulted in more than one hundred dismissals or resignations and the prevention of about two hundred new appointments. Private organizations also dedicated themselves to monitoring the political activities and opinions of university professors, reporting to the House Committee on Un-American Activities (HUAC) or to the FBI professors whose lectures criticized HUAC or failed to criticize the Soviet Union strongly enough.[9]

M.I. Finley, a historian of ancient Greece, was teaching at the Newark campus of Rutgers University in 1951 when he was identified as a Communist by Karl Wittfogel, a historian of China, testifying before the Senate Internal Security Subcommittee. Wittfogel said that Finley, while a graduate student at Columbia University during the thirties, had run a Communist study group. Finley, called before the same committee, testified that he was not a member of the Communist Party but invoked the Fifth Amendment when asked if he had ever been one. The Rutgers Board of Trustees declared that pleading the

---

8. Sigmund Diamond, "The Arrangement: the FBI and Harvard University in the McCarthy Period," in *Beyond the Hiss Case: the FBI, Congress and the Cold War*, edited by Athan G. Theoharis (Philadelphia, 1982), pp. 341–71; Sigmund Diamond, "Heeling for Hoover: God and the FBI at Yale," *The Nation*, April 12, 1980, pp. 423–8; Ellen Schrecker, *No Ivory Tower: McCarthyism and the Universities* (New York, 1986).

9. David Caute, *The Great Fear: the Anti-Communist Purge under Truman and Eisenhower* (New York, 1978).

Fifth as Finley had done was "cause for immediate dismissal" and fired him—the first time an American university fired a faculty member for relying on the constitutional privilege against self-incrimination. Finley was then blacklisted; no American university or college would hire him. In 1958 the history department of Cornell University nominated Finley for a position, but President Deane W. Malott rejected the nomination. Finley found a job at Cambridge University in England, where he was eventually knighted for his distinguished scholarship.[10]

Daniel Boorstin, an American intellectual historian at the University of Chicago, took a different course when subpoenaed by HUAC in 1953. He gave HUAC everything it wanted: he named names of Communist Party members he had known—his two college roommates and his adviser in history at Harvard, Granville Hicks; he declared that he agreed with the committee that Communists should not be allowed to teach; and he assured committee members they were not threatening academic freedom.[11] Boorstin went on to write some of the fundamental works of consensus history and then to serve as Librarian of Congress. Among these Boorstin named was his college roommate, Richard Schlatter, who at the time of the hearings was teaching American history at Rutgers, which had fired Finley for taking the Fifth. When Schlatter was subpoenaed, he told the committee in a private executive session that he had contacted everybody he was planning to name and had gotten permission to name them. The committee did not ask him to appear at a public session, apparently wanting to avoid publicizing his strategy for answering their questions.[12]

W.A. Williams was not subpoenaed by any congressional committee, but he was a target for McCarthyites at the University of Oregon, where he taught from 1952 to 1957. "Various people there tried to make life miserable for me and some other people on the campus," he explained. "They got rid of at least three of us." He accepted an offer from the University of Wisconsin, one of the few major universities that did not fire faculty members for their political

---

10. Schrecker, pp. 171–2, 179, 273, 293.

11. See chapter 8. For Boorstin's testimony, see Eric Bentley, ed., *Thirty Years of Treason* (New York, 1971), pp. 604–5.

12. Schrecker, p. 196; Richard Schlatter, "On Being a Communist at Harvard," *Partisan Review*, 44 (December 1977), p. 612.

views during the McCarthy years. Then William's publisher, George Braziller, refused to publish his new book, *The Tragedy of American Diplomacy*. In 1960 HUAC subpoenaed the manuscript of *The Contours of American History* as the book was about to go into galleys. HUAC sent Williams's name to the Internal Revenue Service; "the IRS worked me over for the better part of twenty years," William reports, starting with an effort to tax a grant he received from the left-wing Rabinowitz foundation.[13]

Few targets of McCarthyism were attacked because their scholarship was radical. Virtually all were charged with association with the Communist Party; most such associations had taken place in the past, often in student days a decade or two previously, and many of those attacked had long ceased their connection with the organized left. But the attack on radicals and radical ideas proved to be effective in intimidating academics, and the consequences for the profession were profound. A chill spread across the intellectual landscape: avoiding controversy became prudent; criticism of American institutions or practices could endanger one's job. Faculty members played it safe, avoiding topics in their teaching and research that might arouse the Red hunters.[14]

The institutions of the history profession took part in the anti-communist hysteria. In the early fifties, for instance, the Bancroft Prize was awarded to a poorly written, minor book on the grounds that it showed "the inapplicability of the Marxist theory of the class struggle."[15] During the fifties the official history journals—those published by the American Historical Association (AHA) and the

---

13. "Interview with William Appleman Williams," in Henry Abelove et al., eds., *Visions of History* (New York, 1984), pp. 132, 134–5. The interview was originally published in *Radical History Review* no. 22 (1979–80), pp. 65–92.

14. For a survey of "apprehension" and "patterns of caution" among academics, including 681 historians, see Paul Lazarsfeld and Wagner Thielens Jr, *The Academic Mind* (Glencoe, 1958), pp. 192–265.

15. The book was Arthur Holcombe, *Our More Perfect Union: From Eighteenth-Century Principles to Twentieth-Century Practice* (Cambridge, Mass., 1950). The committee that year awarded the prize to two books, the other being Henry Nash Smith, *Virgin Land: the American West as Symbol and Myth* (Cambridge, Mass., 1950). For an account citing the correspondence of the prize jury, see Peter Novick, "American Leftist Historians," paper delivered at the annual meeting of the American Historical Association, December 1978, p. 30 n29 (in Jon Wiener's possession).

OAH—placed the work of the small number of radical and Marxist historians outside the bounds of historical scholarship. Williams was not a Communist; he was an independent radical. But the *AHR* did not consider his book *The Tragedy of American Diplomacy* in its "Reviews of Books" section. Instead, a one-paragraph critique appeared in the section titled "Other Recent Publications." Williams's work received the same treatment for several years. When *The Great Evasion* appeared in 1964, arguing that the history profession had evaded Marxism, the *AHR* did not review the book at all. The *Journal of American History* (*JAH*) gave it a one-paragraph summary in the "Book Notes" section, where it appeared along with *Humor of the Old Southwest, Secret Loves of the Founding Fathers* and *Bark Canoes and Skin Boats of North America*.[16]

During the sixties, in response to the social and political upheavals that swept American society and politics, new groups of historians formed; the work they did presented not so much new facts as a different set of significant problems requiring study, and different notions of what constituted a solution. They proposed a new radical history. They callenged not only the mainstream of the profession but also the scholarship produced by historians with ties to the Communist Party. The received orthodoxy of historical materialism, and the interpretation of history that went with it, had been unquestioned in the party. The model of the disciplined Bolshevik called for a stern and wooden style. The party had no firm line on American history, but its political shifts required shifting interpretations of the history of popular struggle, class alliances and ruling-class intentions and capabilities. The subjects of Soviet history, Communist Party history, twentieth-century labor history and the work of Marxist historians unconnected with the party received the most dogmatic treatment.[17] The New Left history that would challenge the profession during the sixties began with the shattering of the Communist Party. And the most powerful blows to Communist orthodoxy in the United States were struck, not

---

16. Foster Rhea Dulles, note on *The Tragedy of American Diplomacy* by William Appleman Williams, *American Historical Review*, 64 (July 1959), pp. 1022–23; "Book Notes," *Journal of American History*, 51 (March 1965), pp. 763–77.

17. Eric Hobsbawm, "The Historians' Group of the Communist Party," in *Rebels and Their Causes: Essays in Honour of A.L. Morton*, edited by Maurice Cornforth (London, 1978), pp. 21–47.

by HUAC or Joe McCarthy, but by Nikita Khrushchev. His 1956 acknowledgment of the crimes of Stalin, together with the Soviet army's invasion of Hungary, destroyed American Communists' intellectual world.[18]

The English Marxist historian E.P. Thompson, whose book *The Making of the English Working Class* has been the most important exemplar of radical history since its publication in 1964, has described the conditions under which an alternative community of radical scholars could flourish: "some territory which is, without qualification, their own; their own journals, their own ... centers: places where no one works for grades or for tenure but for the transformation of society: places where criticisms and self-criticism are fierce, but also mutual help and the exchange of theoretical and practical knowledge; places which pre-figure in some ways the society of the future."[19] An alternative community of radical historians began to take shape after 1956, when intellectuals leaving the Communist Party joined with leading independent radical scholars. For American historians we can locate its origins precisely. In 1957 William Appleman Williams came to the University of Wisconsin in Madison; his graduate seminar provided the intellectual arena in which New Left history in the United States first developed. If radical students at Wisconsin worked for grades, they also engaged in the mutual help, community building and political thinking Thompson described as essential to the development of radical scholarship.

Madison had a strong Progressive, isolationist tradition that combined intellectual work with political commitment. By the early 1950s, Madison was already a center of intellectual resistance to cold war politics and scholarship, resistance that stood outside both the Marxist and the liberal traditions. Merle Curti wrote the history of American peace movements; Merrill Jensen defended the Confederation democracy; William Hesseltine studied politics and became a contributing editor of *Liberation* magazine, a radical pacifist monthly.

---

18. Joseph R. Starobin, *American Communism in Crisis, 1943–1957* (Cambridge, Mass., 1972); Jon Wiener, "The Communist Party Today and Yesterday: an Interview with Dorothy Healey," *Radical America*, 11 (May–June 1977), pp. 25–45.

19. "An Interview with E.P. Thompson," *Radical History Review*, 3 (fall 1976), p. 25.

20. Paul Buhle, "Memories of Madison in the Fifties," *Radical History Review*, 36 (1986), pp. 101–3.

None had been silenced by McCarthyism.[20]

Herbert Gutman went to Madison in 1950 after what he later called "a brief, intense if uneventful involvement with the orthodox Communist movement" and the completion of an MA at Columbia with Hofstadter. At Wisconsin he studied with Jensen, Curti, and Howard Beale ("my Madison guides," he later called them) and worked as Curti's research assistant, helping prepare an essay on Charles Beard as a historical critic. "The Madison years made me understand that all my left politics had not prepared me to understand America west (and even east) of the Hudson River," Gutman recalled in 1982. "The progressive historians ... helped me unload my dogmatic blinders." Warren Susman, a Wisconsin graduate student at the same time as Gutman, recalled that Hesseltine always asked students to write on their prelims about the use of the army to deal with American internal political questions. "The fear of totalitarianism came together with a fear of excessive government power of any kind," he recalled.[21]

Williams had been a political activist before he became a historian. A naval officer during World War Two, he had worked with the civil rights movement around the naval air training base in Corpus Christi, Texas. As the cold war began, he decided to go on to graduate school in history "to try and make some sense out of what the hell was going on." His 1950 dissertation at Wisconsin examined American–Russian relations. He published a key article, "The Legend of Isolationism in the 1920s," in 1954 in *Science and Society* and expanded its central thesis into *The Tragedy of American Diplomacy*. Published in 1959, the book argued that the roots of American foreign policy lay in the imperial expansion of corporate capitalism, which consistently opposed revolutionary movements in other parts of the world.[22] But Williams had little involvement with Marxist theory or Communist politics.

---

21. Herbert G. Gutman, "Learning about America,' ibid., p. 104; Warren Susman, "The Smoking Room School of American History," ibid., p. 107.

22. William Appleman Williams, "The Legend of Isolationism in the 1920s," *Science and Society*, 18 (winter 1954), pp. 11–20. "Interview with William Appleman Williams," p. 129. At the same time Williams criticized those who "make the fundamental error of equating economic determinism with Marxism." See William Appleman Williams, "A Note on Charles Austin Beard's Search for a General Theory of Causation," *American Historical Review*, 62 (January 1956), p. 63.

The students at Williams's seminar who set out most self-consciously to challenge consensus history sought to address problems of economic, social and political development that were specifically American. In 1959 Williams's students started their own journal, *Studies on the Left.* Over the next eight years, its editors included Martin Sklar, Lloyd Gardner, James Weinstein, James O'Connor, Stanley Aronowitz, Staughton Lynd and Eugene D. Genovese; its associates included Joan Wallach (later Scott) and Susman. In the editors' first statement they described themselves as "radicals"; although they did not refer to themselves as Marxists, they objected to scholars who "shroud in secrecy the now radical fact that the US economy is capitalistic." The prevailing conception of "objectivity," they wrote, expressed the world view of "the scholar satisfied with—or browbeaten by—things as they are." Those who "stand opposed to established institutions and conventional conceptions" and who therefore "possess an unconcern for their safety or preservation" could achieve a more genuine objectivity. "The radicalism of our time ... 'does not consist in the things that are proposed, but in the things that are disclosed,'" they wrote, quoting a stunningly appropriate line from—of all people—Woodrow Wilson.[23]

Studies on the Left published articles by Gabriel Kolko, Aileen Kraditor, Conor Cruise O'Brien, and a host of graduate students who criticized the beats, praised Fidel Castro's revolution, and debated American communism. The journal's most important contribution was a theoretically self-conscious reinterpretation of American history, supported by an impressive series of research monographs. The editors first presented this "corporate liberalism" thesis in 1962. They argued that the central theme of American history was the global expansion of United States capitalism. The entire legacy of popular movements had to be understood within this context. Their most important political conclusion was that virtually all popular and protest movements had been incorporated within the expanding capitalist system, instead of undermining it.

Studies on the Left wanted to make history illuminate the present. Its editors argued that liberalism, the ideology by which the corporate elite had established its hegemony, was becoming increasingly authori-

---

23. "The Radicalism of Disclosure," *Studies on the Left*, 1 (fall 1969), pp. 2–4.

tarian. The corporate liberalism thesis suggested that the principal obstacle to the further democratization of American society was not the far right (represented at that point by the John Birch Society), but corporate capitalism. The decisive element in American politics, the *Studies on the Left* editors argued, was the political sophistication of American corporate leadership, acting in its own long-range class interest by developing a liberal ideology. The New Deal provided an exemplary case of the conservative achievements of liberal reform and had included the leadership of the labor movement, which won real concessions. Capitalists achieved their domination over the working class above all by means of ideology. By seizing the initiative in calling for reforms, corporate capitalism turned popular protest movements toward strengthening liberalism; as a result popular movements seldom challenged capitalism on socialist grounds.[24]

Gabriel Kolko published the first and in many ways the strongest of the monographs based on the corporate liberalism thesis. In *The Triumph of Conservatism*, he examined Progressivism, which previous historians, Progressive and consensus alike, had described as a democratic movement for popular control of giant new corporations. Kolko showed that many Progressive "reforms" had been initiated by corporate capitalists who enlisted state power to rationalize an economy where uncontrolled competition created unstable and unpredictable conditions. Kolko's work combined exhaustive archival research with an intellectual ruthlessness in seizing on crucial questions and demolishing the consensus historians' interpretation of Progressivism.[25]

The corporate liberalism thesis addressed a central Marxist concern—the links between economic and political power in a capitalist democracy—and argued that orthodox Marxism failed to grasp the new forms of capitalist domination. The capitalist class in the contemporary United States, it asserted, ruled not just by force but also by providing a rational organization of the economy to limit structural

---

24. "Editorial Statement," *Studies on the Left*, 7 (January–February 1967), pp. 10–12.

25. Gabriel Kolko, *The Triumph of Conservatism: a Reinterpretation of American History, 1900–1916* (Glencoe, 1963). On more recent work developing the corporate liberalism interpretation, see Frank Brodhead, "Social Control," *Radical America*, 15 (November–December 1981), pp. 69–77.

crises and to meet some social needs that would be neglected under laissez-faire capitalism. The corporate liberalism thesis made fifties American politics intelligible: the incorporation of working-class challenge and the easy destruction of radical movements by McCarthyism. It took seriously the problematic of consensus history, while attacking its pious nationalism and whig optimism. And when the liberal Kennedy and Johnson administrations committed the country to an imperialist war in Vietnam, advocates of the corporate liberalism thesis could claim decisive empirical confirmation.

Genovese's *The Political Economy of Slavery* revealed his intellectual ties to the corporate liberalism interpretation advanced in *Studies on the Left*. His analysis of the antebellum South emphasized ruling-class hegemony and working-class integration, elements at the center of the corporate liberalism thesis regarding the industrial North. Like Kolko, he rejected the conclusions of Marxist historians who had written in the 1930s and 1940s. Kolko argued that Philip Foner's portrayal of working-class resistance to capitalism was mistaken; Genovese showed that Herbert Aptheker's picture of black resistance to slavery was similarly erroneous. Genovese drew on the theory of the mode of production to focus on the class relation between master and slave, and to portray slave society as fundamentally different from northern capitalism. He showed the pressures and limits arising out of the slave mode of production, which pushed the South's ruling class toward crisis and war.

The reviews of Genovese's book in the scholarly journals were mostly negative. Some suggested that Genovese was a bad historian because he was a Marxist; the rest argued that Genovese had some worthwhile things to say despite his Marxism. The reviewer for the *JAH*, Joe G. Taylor, wrote that *The Political Economy of Slavery* contained a "good essay" on livestock; as for the rest of the book, "its few virtues are far outweighed by its many faults." The *Journal of Southern History* reviewer, Thomas P. Govan, a member of the editorial board, wrote that Genovese "is either unaware of the facts, misunderstands what they mean, or is simply unwilling to permit them to alter his preconceived opinions." The *William and Mary Quarterly*'s reviewer, Melvin Drimmer, declared that Genovese's "over-all thesis is overstated and simplified, tied to a rigid philosophy of social change, based on questionable and hypothetical reasoning, widely at variance with historical fact, and presented with an arrogance which blinds him to even his own evidence." *History and Theory*'s reviewer, Theodore R. Marmor, declared that Genovese's work was characterized by "a combination of empirical acuteness and theoretical confusion." Genovese's argument for Southern distinctiveness would have been more effective, the reviewer declared, if he had relied, not on Karl Marx, but on the essay on "National Character" in the 1954 *Handbook of Social Psychology*. In the *AHR* Carl Degler praised the book for "exposing the hidden assumptions and the flaws in the logic or evidence" of earlier studies. The "weakest element [is] the assumption ... that the planters as a group were conscious of their class interests," Degler wrote. That of course was the heart of Genovese's Marxist analysis. [26]

Only two reviewers understood the significance Genovese's work would have in breaking down the consensus that Marxist theory had no place in historical scholarship. Neither review appeared in a professional journal. David Potter in the *Saturday Review* called Genovese's book "one of the landmarks of Southern historiography ... one of those books that rearrange basic concepts." He praised Genovese's exploration of the master–slave relationship and accepted the argument that the relationship distinguished the South from the capitalist North. Genovese later commented that the Potter review "probably had more to do with establishing my *bona fides* than anything else."[27] Only one favorable review explicitly referred to Genovese's Marxism: Stanley Elkin's lengthy essay in *Commentary*. Elkins's treatment of Genovese's Marxism was remarkable. Beard was not a Marxist, he began: "he could never grasp the subtle relationship between class interest, ideological conviction, and political action which Marx and Engels insisted upon." Genovese was a genuine Marxist. Elkins declared that he was "thoroughly persuaded" by Genovese's argument on the

---

26. Reviews of Eugene D. Genovese, *The Political Economy of Slavery*, by: Joe G. Taylor, *Journal of American History*, 53 (June 1966), p. 36; Thomas P. Govan, *Journal of Southern History*, 32 (May 1966), pp. 231–4; Melvin Drimmer, *William and Mary Quarterly*, 24 (January 1967), pp. 160–63; Theodore R. Marmor, *History and Theory*, 6 (no. 2, 1967), pp. 253–60; Carl Degler, *American Historical Review*, 71 (July 1966), pp. 1422–3.

27. David Potter, "Right to Defend the Wrong Reasons," *Saturday Review*, January 1, 1966, pp. 33–4; Ronald Radosh, "An Interview with Eugene Genovese: the Rise of a Marxist Historian," *Change*, 10 (November 1978), pp. 31–5.

distinctiveness of slave society, the obstacles to capitalist development posed by slavery, and the South's internal crisis as the root of secession. Elkins described Genovese's writing as "open-minded and flexible." He stated his own position: "the South reflected a flawed form of capitalism, and the flaw was race."[28]

While the *Studies on the Left* group was arguing for the key role of corporate liberalism in American history, other radical historians were developing other interpretations. Herbert Gutman and David Montgomery belonged to the same generation as the *Studies on the Left* group, and, like several of its editors, had had ties to the Communist Party. Neither Gutman nor Montgomery, however, was associated with *Studies on the Left*; both worked in relative obscurity during the period—Gutman at Fairleigh Dickinson, Montgomery at the University of Pittsburgh. Both had been victims of McCarthyism. Gutman, as a graduate student at Wisconsin in the early fifties, had independently developed a position similar to E.P. Thompson's. Gutman's first essay, "The Workers' Search for Power in the Gilded Age" appeared the same year as *The Making of the English Working Class*, but he did not become a leader of radical historians until later in the sixties. Gutman focused on the way the American working class was "made and re-made" by successive waves of immigration and on the defensive roots of class consciousness and resistance to capitalism among workers. He inspired a generation of younger scholars to seek out in new ways the roots of American working-class life.[29]

---

28. Stanley Elkins, "The Fatal Flaw," *Commentary*, 34 (July 1966), pp. 73–5. The state of the profession in 1966 is also revealed in the critical response to the chapter on the American Civil War in Barrington Moore Jr, *Social Origins of Dictatorship and Democracy: Lord and Peasant in the Making of the Modern World* (Boston, 1966). See Jonathan M. Wiener, "Review of Reviews: *Social Origins of Dictatorship and Democracy*," *History and Theory*, 15 (May 1976), pp. 146–75.

29. Herbert Gutman, "The Workers' Search for Power in the Gilded Age," in *The Gilded Age: a Reappraisal*, edited by H. Wayne Morgan (Syracuse, 1963), pp. 31–53. Gutman called himself a socialist, but not a Marxist, in "An Interview with Herbert Gutman," *Radical History Review*, 27 (May 1983), pp. 205–6, 214–15. Gutman was subpoenaed by HUAC in 1953 and quizzed about his membership in the Communist Party, his participation in the 1948 presidential campaign of Henry Wallace, and his work as a counselor at Camp Kinderland. He denounced the committee and refused to answer its questions. See US Congress, House, Committee on Un-American Activities, *Investigation of Communist Activities: New York Area—Part 5 (Summer Camps)*, 84 Cong., 1 sess., August 1, 1955, pp. 1394–400.

Gutman later distinguished himself even among his radical and Marxist peers by the strength of his commitment to genuinely democratic education, to bringing the new labor history he had pioneered to trade unionists, labor educators and community college teachers. This work culminated in the American Working Class History Project, a multimedia curriculum on American social history designed for workers and working-class students. Gutman also served as an exemplary figure for radical graduate students. "He showed us," Sean Wilentz wrote, "that you didn't have to obey *their* rules to partake of the life of the mind."[30]

Montgomery provides another link between the Old Left and the New. He had been a Communist trade-union organizer during the fifties. Blacklisted by employers for his union activity, in 1960 he decided to become a historian. *Beyond Equality* uncovered the working-class movement for social changes beyond those acceptable to the Radical Republicans. Closer to the spirit and scholarship of Marx than anything the New Left produced, *Beyond Equality* demonstrated that one of the most critical periods of American history could not be understood without taking into account the political demands of workers.[31]

Within a few years of the founding of *Studies on the Left*, the political reality it sought to comprehend had undergone a dramatic transformation. In 1960–61 black students in fifty-four cities across the South joined the sit-in movement, stirring student political consciousness across the country. In 1965 twenty-five thousand people turned out for the first antiwar march on Washington, called by Students for a Democratic Society (SDS); henceforth the war in Vietnam dominated university political life. The Student Nonviolent Coordinating

---

30. Sean Wilentz, "Herbert Gutman, 1928–1985," *Village Voice*, August 6, 1985, p. 42. See also Joan Wallach Scott, "Remembering Herbert Gutman," *Radical History Review*, 34 (January 1986), pp. 108–12.

31. David Montgomery, *Beyond Equality: Labor and the Radical Republicans, 1862–1872* (New York, 1967); "An Interview with David Montgomery," in Abelove et al., pp. 167–83. David Montgomery, "The Working Classes of the Pre-Industrial American City, 1780–1830," *Labor History*, 9 (Winter 1968), pp. 3–22, was widely reprinted in anthologies in the early 1970s.

Committee's (SNCC) grass-roots organizing in the heartland of segregation inspired SDS to start organizing poor people in northern cities. The rise of the antiwar movement, the civil rights movement in the South, and the wave of ghetto rebellions in Los Angeles, Newark, Detroit and elsewhere shattered the consensus school's assumption that in the United States the fundamental problems had been solved; they forced the issue of race, ignored by the dominant historians of the 1950s, into the forefront of American life.

The civil rights and antiwar movements gave participants an experience of making history from below. It gave them an appreciation of the popular capability to challenge elite domination—an appreciation lacking in the earlier, more pessimistic studies adopting the corporate liberalism thesis. The revival of political opposition among the most oppressed (blacks) and the most incorporated (students) required analysis; it suggested a different sense of how history was made: not simply by elites, from the top down, but in the interaction of social groups holding power in different forms. A second wave of New Left history now appeared, dubbed by one of its leading voices, Jesse Lemisch, as "history from the bottom up."[32]

The civil rights and antiwar movements rapidly became a source of intellectual energy for those developing critical perspectives on consensus history. In the early stages much of that critical work did not come from Marxists. One crucial early challenge addressed the prevailing picture of abolitionists as psychologically disturbed fanatics. Martin Duberman made clear the connections between activism and the new scholarship in the opening sentence of his 1962 essay "The Abolitionists and Psychology." Historians with a "heightened concern with the pressing question of Negro rights," he wrote, had undertaken a reevaluation of the abolitionists "who in their own day were involved in a similar movement of social change." He emphasized that this scholarship was relevant to the movement: "About both them and ourselves we are asking anew such questions as the proper role of agitation, the underlying motives of both reformers and resistants, and

---

32. Jesse Lemisch, "The American Revolution Seen from the Bottom Up," in Barton J. Bernstein, ed., *Towards a New Past: Dissenting Essays in American History* (New York, 1967), p. 3.

the useful limits of outside interference." In the same period Leon Litwack published *North of Slavery*, which challenged the assumption that the North treated blacks with "benevolence and liberality."[33]

In one of the great coincidences of history writing with history making, Thompson's *The Making of the English Working Class* was published in 1963, to be read by students inspired by the example of SNCC and ready to begin their own movement to challenge corporate liberalism. Thompson had left the British Communist Party after 1956 and helped found *New Left Review* in 1959, the same year *Studies on the Left* was organized. The *New Left Review*'s commitment to constructing an independent and critical Marxist theory and history, politically engaged with concrete political issues, was strikingly similar to that of the *Studies on the Left* board.[34] Thompson's book, meanwhile, showed how people whom historians had described as mobs, deviants, and eccentrics had been intelligible and intelligent agents of history. He showed that ordinary working people had developed an articulate culture of resistance to capitalist exploitation and that they had created it out of their own cultural and ideological traditions; it was not the creation of a "vanguard" political party.

Through the Vietnam teach-in movement of 1965, practitioners of the new historical scholarship forged a link to political activism. Williams helped organize the University of Wisconsin teach-in and spoke to two thousand students there; at the Berkeley teach-in, Staughton Lynd spoke to twelve thousand. At the Washington National Teach-In on May 15, 1965, one hundred campuses connected by a radio hookup held simultaneous teach-ins. Christopher Lasch, then teaching at the University of Iowa, questioned the teach-ins' political effectiveness but nevertheless saw them as potential sources of a new left, cutting across generational divisions. Teach-ins, he wrote in *The Nation*, "represent precisely the mingling of age groups

---

33. Martin Duberman, "The Abolitionists and Psychology," *Journal of Negro History*, 47 (July 1962), pp. 183–91; Leon F. Litwack, *North of Slavery: the Negro in the Free States, 1790–1860* (Chicago, 1961), p. vii.

34. E.P. Thompson, *The Poverty of Theory* (London, 1978), pp. i–v; John Saville, "The XXth Congress and the British Communist Party," in *The Socialist Register, 1976* (London, 1976), pp. 1–23; David R. Holden, "The First New Left in Britain" (Ph.D. thesis, University of Wisconsin, Madison, 1976).

which has to occur before an effective Left can take shape."[35]

The Rutgers teach-in helped earn Genovese the full attention of the profession. Genovese was among the most politically outspoken of the *Studies on the Left* editors. In 1965 Richard M. Nixon attacked him for his opposition to the war in Vietnam. In a speech at the Rutgers teach-in, Genovese said, "I do not fear or regret the impending Vietcong victory in Vietnam: I welcome it." The Republican gubernatorial candidate demanded that the Democratic governor fire Genovese from his tenured job. Nixon came to the state to campaign for the Republicans and asked a cheering American Legion audience, "Does an individual employed by the state have a right to use his position to give aid and comfort to the enemies of the US in wartime?" The legionnaires roared back, "No!" Nixon beamed. Nixon sent a copy of his speech calling for Genovese's firing to his supporters around the country. Later he told White House speechwriter William Safire, "I know you and the rest of the intellectuals won't like it ... but somebody had to take 'em on."[36]

The incumbent governor and the Rutgers administration publicly defended Genovese's right to teach. The Democrats won in a landslide, and the American Association of University Professors gave Rutgers its Alexander Meikeljohn Award for not firing Genovese. He, however, describes the aftermath differently: after the Nixon attack, the Rutgers administration "made clear to me that I was going to be a second class citizen in salary and in promotion possibilities." He resigned and went to Sir George Williams University in Canada. Genovese's *The Political Economy of Slavery* appeared the day after the New Jersey gubernatorial election. The *New York Times*, the *Washington Post*, the *New York Herald*

---

35. For the text of the talks by William Appleman Williams and Staughton Lynd, see Louis Menashe and Ronald Radosh, eds., *Teach-Ins: USA Reports, Opinions, Documents* (New York, 1967), pp. 45–49; Christopher Lasch, "New Curriculum for the Teach-Ins," *The Nation*, October 18, 1965, pp. 239–41.

36. "Rutgers Dispute Looms as Central Issue in Jersey," *New York Times*, October 17, 1965, p. 84; New Jersey Legislature, General Assembly, "Report to the General Assembly of the State of New Jersey re Professor Eugene D. Genovese and the 'Vietnam Teach-In' at Rutgers University on April 23, 1965," p. 1 (Documents Division, Princeton University Library, Princeton, NJ). See also Arnold Beichman, "Study in Academic Freedom," *New York Times Magazine*, December 19, 1965. William Safire, *Before the Fall: an Inside View of the Pre-Watergate White House* (Garden City, 1975), p. 22. See also "Mr Nixon in New Jersey," editorial, *New York Times*, October 27, 1965, p. 42; and Richard M. Nixon to editor, ibid., October 29, 1965, p. 42.

Tribune, the *Saturday Review* and *Commentary* all ran reviews of the controversial historian's scholarship. "In all probability," Genovese said, they "wouldn't have reviewed the book at all if it hadn't been for the political notoriety."[37]

If the Genovese case at Rutgers showed that universities would sometimes protect radical scholars facing outside political pressure, the experience of Lynd at Yale demonstrated that universities could end the careers of radical historians who were also activists. Lynd, the most important radical organizer among the New Left historians, was fired by Yale in 1968; despite his important work on the history of American radicalism, no university would hire him. The firing and blacklisting of Staughton Lynd marked a key moment in the formation of radical history and contributed to the adversary relationship between radicals and the mainstream of the profession.

During the Mississippi Freedom Summer project in 1964, Lynd had served as director of the Freedom Schools, a project that enrolled two thousand black children in thirty-one summer schools. In April 1965 he chaired the committee that organized the first antiwar mass march on Washington. While he was an assistant professor at Yale, Lynd travelled to North Vietnam in 1965 with Tom Hayden and Herbert Aptheker in defiance of a State Department ban. At the same time he helped shape the new radical scholarship as an editor of *Studies on the Left* and author of *Class Conflict, Slavery and the United States Constitution*, a collection of essays written from a neo-Beardian perspective, and *Intellectual Origins of American Radicalism*, which began with prerevolutionary Nonconformist thought and concluded with the abolitionists, uncovering early examples of civil disobedience and articulate critiques of private property and the state.[38]

When *Intellectual Origins of American Radicalism* was published in May 1968, editors quickly assigned reviewers to explain what the New Left's most politically active historian had to say about the past. *Time* gave the book a full-page review, complete with pictures of Tom Paine and the author; predictably, the magazine ridiculed Lynd's commitments along with his scholarship, calling him "the Brooks Brothers

---

37. Radosh, "Interview with Eugene Genovese," pp. 31–35, 32.

38. On Lynd and the Freedom Schools, see Clayborne Carson, *In Struggle: SNCC and the Black Awakening of the 1960s* (Cambridge, Mass., 1981), pp. 109–10, 119–21; and Howard Zinn, *SNCC: the New Abolitionists* (Boston, 1965), pp. 247–50.

man as revolutionary." J.H. Plumb, writing in the *Saturday Review*, described Lynd's book as a "valuable" part of the "revolution in American historical studies" that had begun. "Lynd provides a useful corrective to [Bernard] Bailyn," he declared. Robert Middlekauff reviewed Lynd's book in the *New Republic*, respectfully summarizing its thesis and rejecting Irwin Unger's criticism that Lynd's work had an "exaggerated present-mindedness." Richard B. Morris, reviewing *Class Conflict, Slavery, and the United States Constitution* in the *New York Times Book Review* that same month—May 1968—declared that the book's "carefully researched conclusions" were "sound and sensible." David Donald wrote the strongest review of the book: "Of all the New Left historians," he wrote, "only Staughton Lynd appears able to combine the techniques of historical scholarship with the commitment to social reform."[39]

Reviewers in the scholarly journals treated Lynd's *Intellectual Origins* with surprising respect. The *JAH* reviewer, Charles A. Barker, called it "strong," writing that "the author's belief in conscience and freedom enlarges his own awareness of processes which scholars are slow to discuss." Henry F. May, reviewing the book in the *AHR*, wrote that Lynd's book "gains from his passionate involvement"; he found Lynd "convincing" in arguing his central thesis, "that the libertarian and

---

39. Staughton Lynd, *Intellectual Origins of American Radicalism* (New York, 1968); Staughton Lynd, *Class Conflict, Slavery, and the United States Constitution* (Indianapolis, 1967); "For the Gentleman Rebel," *Time*, July 5, 1968, p. 67; J.H. Plumb, "Perspective," *Saturday Review*, June 29, 1968, pp. 23–4; Robert Middlekauff, "Reconstructing Society from Below," *New Republic*, July 20, 1968, pp. 39–40; Richard B. Morris, review of *Class Conflict*, in *New York Times Book Review*, May 26, 1968, pp. 10–11; David Donald, review of *Intellectual Origins* in *Commentary*, 46 (August 1968), p. 79. In a review, Genovese attacked *Intellectual Origins* as "a travesty of history." Lynd "presents himself as a spokesman for the New Left," he wrote, "but he has only the right to present himself as a spokesman for a particular tendency of it"—non-Marxist radicals whose position Genovese described as "moral absolutism" (Eugene D. Genovese, in *New York Review of Books*, September 26, 1968, p. 79).

40. Reviews of *Intellectual Origins* by Charles A. Barker, *Journal of American History*, 55 (December 1968), pp. 633–4; Henry F. May, *American Historical Review*, 74 (February 1969), pp. 1077–8. Even Irwin Unger treated Lynd respectfully, writing of the "imagination of flexibility" in his work which could "tell us important things about complex historical events" like the Confederation. Irwin Unger, "The 'New Left' and American History: Some Recent Trends in United States Historiography," *American Historical Review*, 72 (July 1967), p. 1259.

essentially religious strain in American radicalism has indeed been the most powerful and consistent."[40]

When Yale denied Lynd tenure in 1968, its decision made the national news; the *New York Times* quoted him as saying, "I think their reasons were at least in part based on my outside activities." Edmund S. Morgan and C. Vann Woodward replied to his charges in print, defending the Yale history department's action. Lynd spent 1967 and 1968 searching for a teaching post in the Chicago area. He was recommended for appointment by the history departments at Northern Illinois University, the University of Illinois-Chicago Circle, Chicago State, Roosevelt University, and Loyola University; at each institution, the administration rejected him. The Chicago State Board of Governors stated that his trip to Hanoi was the reason for their action; the rest gave no reason. Lynd concluded that he was being blacklisted because of his antiwar activism. He became a community organizer in Chicago and enrolled in law school. Lynd's struggle to stay in the profession, his firing by Yale, and subsequent blacklisting exposed the costs of activist commitment, strengthening radicals' conviction that the university was part of the status quo and thus "a social institution to be confronted," in the words of the *Radical America* editors, rather than "a place where critical scholarship may be carried on."[41]

Radical history reached a watershed with the Socialist Scholars Conferences, the first of which was held at Columbia University in 1965. The conference organizing committee, chaired by Helmut Gruber of Brooklyn Polytechnic, included Louis Menashe and Marvin Gettleman from Brooklyn Polytechnic, Ann Lane from Sarah Lawrence College, and Genovese and Susman from Rutgers. The first conference statement of purpose declared: "We wish to show our students, our colleagues, and our fellow Americans in non-academic areas that alternative socialist interpretations have a validity, a vitality, and an integrity which have unfortunately been underestimated too

41. *New York Times*, June 7, 1968, p. 42; Edmund S. Morgan and C. Vann Woodward, "Academic Freedom: Whose Story?" *Columbia University Forum* (Spring 1968), p. 42. In 1976 Lynd began to practice labor law in Youngstown, Ohio, to fight the closing of Youngstown's steel mills, and to write about working-class history. On his experiences after Yale, see: "Staughton Lynd," in Abelove et al., pp. 147–65; "'New Left Historians' of the 1960s," *Radical America*, 4 (November 1970), p. 84.

long." The organizers had hoped to attract an audience of 150 or 200; almost 1,000 faculty and students attended. The intellectual high point of the conference, according to *Studies on the Left*, was Susman's paper, "Conservatism in American Life," which argued that radicals could learn more from conservatives than from liberals. Liberals had "retreated to gross empiricism"; conservatives understood "the value of ideology," the value of an "analysis of the nature of the total reality of our world." Susman recalled in 1985 that the absence of programmatic proposals in his paper outraged some in the audience. One angry person "grabbed the audience microphone at the end of the session. 'If this is the way socialist scholars behave,' she shouted, 'long live the peasants and workers!' "[42]

A confrontation between Lynd and Genovese suggested the extent to which radical historians were divided. Lynd, speaking on "The Future of Socialism," argued the possibility for the "maturation of a revolutionary crisis in the US as an increasingly predatory foreign policy generated resistance at home." Genovese challenged Lynd sharply, arguing that "socialist scholars ought to concentrate on intellectual work as part of a struggle that might take a century to mature."[43]

The 1966 Socialist Scholars Conference organizing committee was chaired by Menashe and included Paul Sweezy, editor of the independent Marxist *Monthly Review*, Philip Foner, and James Weinstein of *Studies on the Left*. It attracted 2,000 participants, who saw a deepening conflict between the organizing committee and younger radicals seeking a politically engaged scholarship. Genovese gave a paper on slavery that opened, "American radicals have long been imprisoned by the pernicious notion that the masses are necessarily both good and revolutionary, and by the even more pernicious notion that if they are not, they should be."[44] He was criticizing Aptheker's *American Negro*

---

42. Helmut Gruber, "Marxism in the American University, 1945–82: a Deceptive Triumph," in International Conference of Labour Historians, *Tagungsbericht XIX* (Vienna, 1984), p. 4. The Susman incident is recalled, and the paper reprinted, in Warren I. Susman, *Culture as History: the Transformation of American Society in the Twentieth Century* (New York, 1984), pp. 55, 63, 73.

43. "From the Editors: Socialist Scholars Conference," *Studies on the Left*, 5 (fall 1965), pp. 3–7.

44. Eugene D. Genovese, "The Legacy of Slavery and the Roots of Black Nationalism," *Studies on the Left*, 6 (November–December 1966), p. 3.

Slave Revolts, but soon he and others would direct the same criticism at the works of radicals studying history from the bottom up.

For the 1967 Socialist Scholars Conference, the organizers issued a new statement of purpose, expressing concern about the massive turnout of activist students: "The SSC is not a political organization. Meetings are designed for maximum expression of scholarly ideas unencumbered by partisan purposes, political rhetoric or polemic. Members are agreed that, however great the need for political commitment and action on the part of all Americans, not least among scholars, the Socialist Scholars Conference is not the proper vehicle for such an effort." Nevertheless 3,000 people showed up for the 1967 conference, held at the Hilton Hotel in New York City. The unprecedented numbers attending the Socialist Scholars Conferences and the intellectual seriousness of the programs demonstrated that radicals in the university had reached the point of critical mass by 1965–66.[45]

SDS actively promoted radical history during those years, bringing the energy and commitment of the civil rights and antiwar movements to historical issues. The history produced under its auspices had a more activist and more optimistic perspective than the work of the *Studies on the Left* group. In December 1965 SDS had authorized the creation of the Radical Education Project (REP) to educate the thousands of people joining the organization. SDS leaders were already lamenting the "astonishing lack of political sophistication and knowledge among younger and newer recruits," who were more interested in action than in ideas. SDS leaders hoped the REP would redress that balance. The project described itself as "an independent education, research and publication program, initiated by Students for a Democratic Society, devoted to the cause of democratic radicalism and aspiring to the creation of a new left in America." In the late sixties, the

---

45. Gruber, "Marxism in the American University", p. 16. In an effort to restore the conference to its original scholarly purpose, the 1968 meeting was moved from New York City to Rutgers, and attendance fell to six hundred people, mostly academics. But the strain between scholarly and activist commitments deepened. The steering committee was expanded to include New Left and movement people; it committed the 1969 conference to an activist orientation, declaring that the events were part of "the struggle for a socialist America", ibid., p. 50. The 1970 organizers issued no statement of purpose, and that year's conference was the last. See also George Fischer et al., *The Revival of American Socialism: Selected Papers of the Socialist Scholars Conference* (New York, 1971).

project published close to a hundred pamphlets, selling at between ten and twenty-five cents, many of which dealt with historical subjects.[46]

Among the SDS–REP pamphlets was Jesse Lemisch's *Towards a Democratic History*, published in 1966. Lemisch discussed historians who disliked "history written with a bias favorable to an elite" and who studied "the common man"; he included Thompson; Kolko; Lynd; Alfred F. Young, who studied workers in eighteenth-century New York City; Norman Pollack, who criticized Hofstadter's negative portrayal of populism; and Stephan Thernstrom, who studied social mobility among nineteenth-century Massachusetts workers. As a group they demonstrated the possibility of a different kind of history, based on non-elite sources. He called their approach to research "democratic," because it was based on "respect and sympathy for the majority." This new history demonstrated that "the common man has in fact had an ideology, that that ideology has been radical, and that conditions have been objectively bad enough so that a radical critique has been a sound one." The protest movements of the sixties had shown that history "can happen from the bottom up"; the time had come to apply that lesson to historical scholarship, to write what he called "history from the bottom up."[47]

The journal *Radical America*, founded in 1967 by the SDS Radical Education Project as "An SDS Journal of the History of American Radicalism," provided a key link between the second generation of New Left historians and activists. Like *Studies on the Left*, it was edited and published by University of Wisconsin students, but by a cohort that had grown up in the sixties rather than the fifties. From the beginning *Radical America* debated American history. In its second issue, Joan and Donald Scott launched an attack on Lemisch's call for "a democratic history." The Scotts, writing from the perspective of the older *Studies on the Left* group, of which Joan was a member, expanded Genoveve's critique of leftist histories of slavery, arguing that it applied also to "history from the bottom up." Lemisch, they argued, was propounding a "myth of the people as glorious revolutionaries."

46. Wini Breines, *Community and Organization in the New Left, 1962–1968* (New York, 1982), p. 91. The description appears on the cover of Jesse Lemisch, *Towards a Democratic History*: a Radical Education Project *Occasional Paper* (n.p., [1966]).

47. Lemisch, *Towards a Democratic History*, pp. 4, 5.

Thompson and Thernstrom were exemplary radical historians, the Scotts argued, "not because their substance is the 'common man,' but because their questions provide us with a new way of looking at history. Their radical sympathies raise radical questions about all kinds of people."[48]

Lemisch responded that he did not advocate viewing the people as glorious revolutionaries, and that the key problem facing radical historians was to find a method "to explore the all-important connections between the ideology of the inarticulate and their activity." "History from the bottom up" was such a method, he argued. It assumed that "the ideology of the inarticulate" was rational and might "offer a sounder critique of the society in question than [that of] the articulate."[49] The exchange between Lemisch and the Scotts was an early expression of a debate that would engage radical and Marxist historians for the next decade and beyond.

The relationship between scholarship and activism, which Lynd and Genovese had debated at the first Socialst Scholars Conference, was raised in the AHA in 1969 when the radical caucus proposed that the historical associations take a stand against the war in Vietnam. The radical caucus thereby posed a frontal challenge to the assumptions governing the history profession. It mobilized historians on the left to an unprecedented degree and provoked bitter dissension not only between radicals and the mainstream but among radicals as well. In 1969, 2,000 people attended the AHA business meeting; the previous year 116 had appeared. The vote on condemning the war was "evenly divided." The radical caucus ran the first opposition candidate for AHA president in the 85-year history of the organization; Staughton Lynd got 30 per cent of the vote.[50] Opponents of the antiwar resolution, including Genovese, argued that as a matter of principle it was improper for professional associations to take an official stand on a political issue. Both the AHA and the OAH subsequently declared

---

48. Paul Buhle, "American Radical History: a Progress Report," *New Left Notes*, January 13, 1967, p. 2; Joan W. Scott and Donald M. Scott, "Toward History: a Reply to Jesse Lemisch," *Radical America*, 1 (September–October 1967), pp. 38, 42.

49. Jesse Lemisch, "New Left Elitism: a Rejoinder," *Radical America*, 1 (September–October 1967), pp. 44, 46, 47.

50. R.R. Palmer, "The AHA in 1970," *American Historical Review*, 76 (February 1971), p. 2.

they would not meet in states that had not ratified the Equal Rights Amendment, and both have recently divested their portfolios of stock of companies doing business in South Africa. Those political stands were taken without opposition from those who had criticized the radical caucus for its antiwar proposal.

The radical caucus's critique of the profession was expressed most fully in Lemisch's essay "Present-Mindedness Revisited: Anti-radicalism as a Goal of American Historical Writing since World War II," presented at the 1969 AHA meeting. The piece was a passionate response, documented with 305 notes, to the argument that radical historians' political commitments undermined their work as scholars. Lemisch demolished the claim that the left was injecting politics into a profession otherwise characterized by objectivity and political neutrality. Leading historians had often taken political positions in their work, Lemisch showed; they tended to be cold warriors who enlisted history in the fight against communism. He drew parallels between the scholarship of Allan Nevins, Samuel Eliot Morison, Daniel Boorstin, Arthur Schlesinger Jr and Oscar Handlin, and their involvement with political causes: Boorstin, for example, had coop-erated with HUAC, Schlesinger's 1949 book *The Vital Center* had helped shape cold war ideology, and Handlin was an outspoken supporter of the war in Vietnam.[51]

Lemisch submitted his essay to the *AHR*; obviously the *AHR* was not going to publish it, but the response of editor R.K. Webb could hardly have done more to confirm Lemisch's thesis. The essay, Webb wrote, "unjustly" convicted "a good many of my close friends" of "historical derelictions." Lemisch's evidence, Webb argued, should be interpreted as revealing, not a pattern of political commitments among leading historians, but rather "indiscretions or lapses or outrageous gaffes by some." Lemisch then submitted his piece to the *JAH*; the response if anything exceeded that of the *AHR*. An anonymous reader for the journal wrote, "I don't know how you can tell him that he simply cannot do this, and that he certainly cannot do it in the pages of

---

51. The essay was eventually published in Jesse Lemisch, *On Active Service in War and Peace: Politics and Ideology in the American History Profession* (Toronto, 1975), pp. 73–4. On its presentation, see Ronald Radosh, "Annual Set-to: the Bare-Knuckled Histor-ians," *The Nation*, February 2, 1970, pp. 108–9.

the *Journal.* He probably believes that he can, which says something about how far he and his ilk are estranged from civilization." Editor Martin Ridge advised Lemisch to read the story of Diego Rivera's painting a portrait of Lenin into a mural at Rockefeller Center in 1933; Nelson Rockefeller had the mural destroyed. Ridge was suggesting that expecting the *Journal of American History* to publish Lemisch's piece was like expecting the Rockefellers to include Lenin in the Rockefeller Center mural. Lemisch concluded that his point had been proven: the official journals consciously played the part of the Rockefellers when confronting an intellectual challenge from below.[52]

The year 1969 marks a great divide in the history of the New Left and in New Left history. Nineteen sixty-eight had been a year first of tremendous hope and then of defeats and disasters for the left: the Tet Offensive, the student revolts in Paris and at Columbia University, and the Eugene McCarthy campaign; but then the assassinations of Martin Luther King Jr and Robert Kennedy, the nomination of Hubert Humphrey against the background of a police riot in the streets of Chicago, and the election of Richard Nixon. The disintegration of SDS in 1969 was especially significant for radical historians; SDS had been the national organization of campus radicals, developing a critique of American society (in terms of participatory democracy) and debating strategies for protest and resistance.

Together these events brought a renewed sense of the tenacity of structures of oppression, past and present, a renewed sense of the power of the status quo to perpetuate itself. The New Left's interest in Marxism grew in response. *Radical America,* which had appreciated history from the bottom up, now declared, "we find Marxism the most useful starting point." History from the bottom up "has distinct limitations if it is not linked with an overview of the way the lower classes

---

52. For Martin Ridge's letter and anonymous referee's report, see Lemisch, *On Active Service,* pp. 3–5. *JAH* editorial correspondence and referees' evaluations written before 1979 are closed "for the lifetime of the author unless the reviewer explicitly sanctions opening," by vote of the OAH executive board. The referee in question has refused to give permission to open the Lemisch file and make known his identity (Joan Hoff-Wilson to Jonathan M. Wiener, February 20, 1987 (in Wiener's possession); David Thelen to Wiener, June 3, 1987).

have related to the rest of society." The Marxism *Radical America* adopted was the unorthodox variant developed by E.P. Thompson—a Marxism that valued working-class culture and consciousness and strove to integrate class analysis with the cultural concerns growing out of black nationalism, feminism, and youth culture.[53]

A second conclusion the *Radical America* editors drew from the disasters and defeats of 1968–69 was that the student movement had collapsed because it was too far removed from ordinary working men and women. "In one way or another, blue-collar America had to be an essential part of our future constituency," the editors concluded, and the journal began publishing a series of articles on working-class history that continues today.[54]

The *Radical America* editors also presented a critique of the history profession. It seemed to them "a bad combination of a gentleman's clubhouse and a bureacracy"—a gentleman's club "not simply because there are scarcely any women ... but also because of its upper-class tone that is carried over from the days when history was written principally by wealthy men of leisure." For younger men struggling to advance their careers, the history profession became "the source of all values." The editors also charged the profession with "social irresponsibility" in its scholarly work. "It operates for the most part on two levels: dry monographs, usually accessible only to other historians ... and patriotic textbooks, written in a manner that is very careful not to disturb anyone's comfortable notions about the status quo."[55]

In the next several years *Radical America* published historical studies of labor radicalism among steelworkers, saleswomen, pullman porters

53. "Introduction: Special Issue on Radical Historiography," *Radical America*, 4 (November 1970), pp. 2, 3; James Green, ed., *Workers' Struggles, Past and Present: a 'Radical America' Reader* (Philadelphia, 1983), pp. 3–23, quoting "Special Issue on Radical Historiography," *Radical America*, November 1970. That issue indicated the editors' turn toward Marxism. It included Paul Buhle, "American Marxist Historiography, 1900–1940," ibid., pp. 5–36; Paul Richards, "W.E.B. DuBois: Evolution of a Marxist," ibid., pp. 37–66; James O'Brien, "The Legacy of Beardian History," ibid., pp. 67–80; and "New Radical Historians in the Sixties: a Survey" ibid., pp. 81–106. Other essays published that year included Michael Meerpol, "William Appleman Williams' Historiography," *Radical America* (August 1970), pp. 29–49.
54. Paul Buhle, "Introduction to '15 years of *Radical America*,'" *Radical America*, 16 (May–June 1982), p. 4.
55. "Introduction," *Radical America*, 4 (November 1970), pp. 2, 4.

and the unemployed; studies of conflicts within American labor along gender, race and class lines; studies of the constant tensions between trade-union organizations and self-directed labor militancy. *Radical America* helped show that American working-class history was, in the words of Casey Blake, "far richer, far more turbulent, and far more complex than anyone would have imagined from its treatment at the hands of earlier historians, including those on the left."[56]

Women's history developed alongside the radical history of the sixties. The tie was first expressed at *Radical America*, which published a "Women's Liberation" issue in 1970 and a pioneering monograph, "Women in American Society: an Historical Contribution," the next year. The authors, Mari Jo Buhle, Ann G. Gordon and Nancy Schrom, introduced their sixty-page essay by linking women's history to feminist activism: women, they said, were "returning to historical questions in a search for their collective identity and for an analysis of their condition." The civil rights movement provided a model: "blacks have shown the role history plays in defining a social movement." The goal of women's history was to "define the '*specificity*' of their oppression." The article "gained immediate currency as the most important single article we had published," editor Paul Buhle later wrote, and it was reprinted steadily for the next five or six years. "A feminism informed by history" became *Radical America*'s "principal orientation for the 1970s," and the journal published work by Mari Jo Buhle, Sara Evans, Linda Gordon, and Sheila Rowbotham.[57]

The professional journals treated some of the first monographs in women's history with the same hostility and disdain than they had bestowed on early works of radical history. The treatment of Linda Gordon's *Woman's Body, Woman's Right*, published in 1976, was especially brutal. The book argued that reproductive freedom for women was not a problem of science overcoming nature, but a problem of power, a political and social problem; it argued against orthodox Marxism for the irreducibility of gender as an analytic cate-

---

56. Casey Blake, "Where are the Young Left Historians?" *Radical History Review* (no. 28–30, 1984), p. 117.

57. Mari Jo Buhle, Ann G. Gordon and Nancy Schrom, "Women in American Society: an Historical Contribution," *Radical America*, 5 (July–August 1971), p. 3; Buhle, "Introduction to '15 Years of *Radical America*,'" pp. 3–5.

gory; it argued with Marxism for class analysis, showing how the experiences and needs of women differed according to class; and it concluded with a call for political organization and activity to achieve reproductive freedom and sexual equality.[58]

Gordon had made her commitments clear in her acknowledgments. Edward Shorter, reviewing the book for the *Journal of Social History*, ridiculed them: "The members of the Bread and Roses Women's Collective, the Marxist-Feminist Conference Group, and the *Radical America* editorial board, whom Gordon acknowledges fulsomely in the preface, will doubtless beam approvingly" at her work, Shorter wrote; "other readers may have trouble suspending disbelief." For Gordon, Shorter declared, as for Ann Douglas and Carroll Smith-Rosenberg, "The name of the game becomes getting the goods on the chauvinists." "Gordon slams into the 'professionalization' of birth control, ... flails away at the punching bag of 19th century 'male' medicine," and "sneers at any kind of libertine behavior that may have happened before the 1970s." But it was Shorter who slammed and sneered—in a journal that claimed to represent the new histories.[59]

The official journals treated *Woman's Body, Woman's Right* in a similar fashion. The *AHR* reviewer, J. Stanley Lemons, declared, "history was enslaved to politics for this book." Gordon's argument was "thrust upon the reader," he complained, implying that women are not supposed to do the thrusting in the history profession. He objected not only to her feminism, but also to her Marxist framework—her "use of Marxist jargon," as he put it. "Like baseball and cricket," the review concluded, "history and political polemics have different rules." Lemons thus declared in the official journal that writing history out of feminist and radical commitments was against the rules of the profession. David M. Kennedy made the same argument in the *JAH*. His review called *Woman's Body, Woman's Right* "breathtakingly obtuse," a book that "degenerates into simple cant... [and] sneering canards." His conclusion about Gordon's work adopted precisely the formulation used to bar radical history from

---

58. Linda Gordon, *Woman's Body, Woman's Right: a Social History of Birth Control in America* (New York, 1976).

59. Edward Shorter, review of Gordon in *Journal of Social History*, 11 (winter 1977), pp. 270–72.

the profession a decade earlier: "This is not history."[60]

Radical America was a political magazine that included historical articles; the first journal devoted exclusively to radical history appeared in 1974: the *Radical History Review* published by MARHO, the Middle Atlantic Radical Historians' Organization. In an early statement, the editors explained, "The growth of the *Review* reflects the emergence of a new generation of Marxist historians in the United States.... The collapse of the student-based movement of the sixties, and the failure of its strategic vision, left many people on the Left in despair, but inspired in others a mood of introspection, a hunger to analyze the development of a society which seemed so unjust yet so resistant to basic change." In this context, "many people made their first serious study of Marxism, not in the quest for a new orthodoxy, but in an effort to understand the complex interrelationships between institutional and cultural change which dominant liberal *and radical* paradigms could not explain."[61]

The journal has recently distinguished itself by publishing a series of interviews with Thompson, Williams, Gutman, Montgomery, Natalie Davis and others, exploring the relationship in their work between historical scholarship and political commitment. The *Radical History Review* has also distinguished itself by an attention to public history that has set the journal against the increasing specialization that separates the profession from a public interested in its past. The editors' discussions of the theory and practice of public history also challenge the packaging of the past for public consumption by governments and corporations. The MARHO Forum in New York City has over the last ten years presented almost 150 talks, open to the general public, on radical history.[62]

---

60. J. Stanley Lemons, review of Gordon in *AHR*, 82 (October 1977), p. 1095; David M. Kennedy, review of Gordon in *JAH*, 64 (December 1977), pp. 823–4. Today Gordon is a professor at the University of Wisconsin and in 1987 she was elected to the Nominating Board of the Organization of American Historians. She remains an editor of *Radical America*. An adequate discussion of the process by which women's history won acceptance by the profession requires a separate paper.

61. "Introductory Statement," *Radical History Review*, 3 (fall 1976), p. 2, emphasis added.

62. The author is a member of the *Radical History Review* editorial collective. For the MARHO position, see "Editors' Introduction," *Radical History Review*, 28–30 (1984), pp. 5–12. For the interviews, see Abelove et al. For MARHO essays on public history, see Susan Porter Benson, Stephen Brier and Roy Rosenzweig, eds., *Presenting the Past: Essays on History and the Public* (Philadelphia, 1986).

A turning point in the profession's recognition of radical history came in 1967, when the *AHR* published an entire article attacking radical history: Irwin Unger's "The 'New Left' and American History." The editors had solicited the advice of David Donald, who argued that it should not be published because "the historians whose work [Unger] discussed were not of sufficient consequence to merit extended consideration in the pages of our major professional journal."[63] The historians included Williams, Genovese, Lasch, Kolko, Litwack, and Thernstrom. The editors did not accept Donald's advice.

Unger's article warned of the danger the new historians posed for the profession. "We see at present only the tip of the iceberg," he wrote. "Beneath the surface still lies the main mass of young radical scholars," those "just now completing their training at the major cosmopolitan graduate schools." Soon they would "have to be reckoned with by their professional elders." Unger's purpose was to help prepare the professional elders for this reckoning. He urged "the senior men" to extend to the New Left historians the "courtesy of judging them." And he outlined how to do it: The New Left historians raised "useful" questions about the "agonies" and "ills" of the United States. But they were "bad tempered"; "most disturbing of all," they had "a contempt for pure history." They needed to learn that history must be "allowed to speak for itself." Their questions came, not from "the *natural* dialogue of the discipline," but rather from "the outside cultural and political world."[64]

The ambivalence of the journal became clear the next year, when the editors decided to publish two reviews of *Towards a New Past*, an anthology that declared itself an "anti-text." The book brought together the varieties of radical scholarship developed during the preceding decade. Aileen Kraditor wrote that Lasch and Genovese were the best and Lemisch the worst of the contributors, and that the

---

63. David Donald, review of Barton J. Bernstein, ed., *Towards a New Past, AHR*, 74 (December 1968), p. 531. Unger's paper had originally been presented at the 1967 meeting of the Organization of American Historians.

64. Unger, "The 'New Left' and American History,", pp. 1260, 1261, 1262–3, emphasis added. After excoriating New Left historians, Unger tried to make money off them, publishing his own anthology of their work: Irwin Unger, ed., *Beyond Liberalism: New Left Views of American History* (Waltham, 1971).

volume was "provocative" and "refreshing." That was the favourable review.[65]

Donald wrote the unfavorable review. "The historical profession has already paid these writers more attention than they deserve," he wrote. "Hereafter their effusions might better be publicized in the obscure partisan periodicals to which they frequently contribute." He was writing about James McPherson and Thernstrom as well as Genovese and Lasch and Barton Bernstein. The "New Leftists ... need to re-evaluate their attitudes," Donald declared. They should "cease to claim that they are the voice of outraged youth" and "end their plaintive laments that the 'power structure' of the historical profession ignores them" (although ignoring them was exactly what Donald proposed). If Genovese, Lasch, et al. changed their attitudes, then the profession should allow them "a significant share in the writing of American history." These remarks were published in the profession's official journal.[66]

Nevertheless, during the early seventies many radical historians got jobs and eventually tenure. Doors were also opened to other new histories: Afro-American, women's, quantitative, interdisciplinary; but of all the changes in the profession, the institutionalization of radical history was the most remarkable. As political crisis undermined the profession's commitment to the prevailing conception of history, leading historians began redefining the field in a way that opened the door to radical history. This process began when important figures expressed a loss of confidence that consensus history asked the important questions and provided adequate answers. Hofstadter, the most eminent of the founders of consensus history, was the most important to articulate that doubt. While Donald and Handlin were denouncing New Left history, Hofstadter was writing *The Progressive Historians*. That project might seem an escape from the turmoil of the

---

65. Aileen Kraditor, review of Berstein in *AHR*, 74 (December 1968), pp. 529–31. For Lemisch's response and Kraditor's rejoinder, see "Communications," *AHR*, 74 (June 1969), pp. 1766–9.

66. Donald, pp. 531–3. He added a ritual disclaimer: "the profession, dull and complacent, needs the concern for ideas, the social involvement, and the passion these dissenters exhibit." *Towards a New Past* received other hostile reviews: see Charles Mullett in *Journal of Southern History*, 35 (February 1969), pp. 77–80.

day into the ivory tower. But it was also a response to the crisis of consensus history, to the challenge from radical historians. Frederick Jackson Turner, Charles Beard and Vernon L. Parrington had taken "their cues from the intellectual ferment of the period from 1890 to 1915, from the demands for reform raised by the Populists and Progressives, from the new burst of political and intellectual activity that came with these demands." Hofstadter and his generation, responding to a different historical situation, found Progressive history irrelevant and created a new history. Now, new political debates and demands for reform were making another new history relevant; the established forms of history no longer "inspired one young man after another to take up history as a profession."[67] The phrases describe the rise of the Progressive historians but implicitly refer to the new crisis in the profession.

In March 1968 Hofstadter read the last chapter of his book manuscript at Harvard's Charles Warren Center for Studies in American History. The consensus school, he declared, did not provide "a satisfactory general theory." Consensus historians had been motivated by "the search for a usable past ... responsive to the problems of foreign policy in the early phases of the cold war." That was a telling response to critics like Unger who denounced the New Left for seeking a usable past, instead of practicing "pure history." Historians, Hofstadter wrote, needed to ask "a set of new questions" about "the complex texture of apathy and irrationality that holds a political society together": "Whose participation in a consensus really counts? Who is excluded from the consensus? Who refuses to enter it? To what extent are the alleged consensual ideas of the American system ... actually shared by the mass public?" Such an account would be very much like the work radical historians were doing; it would restore to the center of the historical stage "our slave insurrections, our mobbed abolitionists and lynched Wobblies, our sporadic, furiously militant Homesteads, Pullmans, and Patersons; our race lynchings and ghetto riots."[68]

---

67. Richard Hofstadter, *The Progressive Historians: Turner, Beard, Parrington* (New York, 1968), p. xii.

68. Ibid., p. 453. Hofstadter and a Columbia graduate student published a documentary history of American violence. The student is now an editor of *Radical History Review.* See Richard Hofstadter and Michael Wallace, eds., *American Violence: a Documentary History* (New York, 1970).

Hofstadter brought a historical perspective to the profession's immediate crisis. "Once in each generation," he observed, "the American people endured a crisis of real and tumbling severity"—the Civil War, the 1890s, the 1930s. "Now, in the 1960s, it is in the midst of a dangerous major crisis the outcome of which I hesitate to predict." "The urgency of our national problems seems to demand, more than ever, that the historian have something to say that will help us," he wrote. Presentmindedness had "often brought with it a major access of new insight.... At their best, the interpretive historians have gone to the past with some passionate concern for the future." Winston Churchill and Leon Trotsky, for example, wrote "great histories." French historiography has a "marvelous vitality derived from the controversial heritage of the French revolution." No other argument for including radicals within the historical profession could have been more powerful.[69]

Potter, a consensus historian of Hofstadter's stature and a political conservative, reviewed Hofstadter's book in the *New York Review of Books* in 1968. He recognized a kinship between it and New Left works. The work of historians became irrelevant, Potter argued, not because of its "specific defects," but rather from "their being caught in the intellectual riptide which occurs when society is replacing one image of itself with another."[70] The sentence referred to Turner, Beard, and Parrington, but Potter was also referring to himself and Hofstadter. It expressed a loss of confidence in the historical scholarship of the fifties, the scholarship exemplified in his own book, *People of Plenty*. That loss, characteristic of a vital segment of the profession, undermined the commitment to consensus history among other historians, and led to a breakdown in prevailing definitions of what was—and was not— history. It gave radical historians a chance.

While some prominent historians questioned whether consensus history asked the important questions and provided adequate answers, others explicitly advocated including radicals within the history profession. C. Vann Woodward was among the most important. His work, going back at least to *Origins of the New South*, published in 1951, had

---

69. Hofstadter, *Progressive Historians*, pp. 459, 465.
70. David Potter, "The Art of Comity," *New York Review of Books*, December 5, 1968, pp. 46–8.

always posed a critique of and an alternative to the consensus school. In 1960 he wrote a blurb for *Studies on the Left*. In the same issue in which Jean-Paul Sartre and Che Guevara appeared, Woodward was quoted: "It is a welcome sign that graduate students are still alive and kicking in spite of all the professors can do to anesthetize them."[71] His willingness to open the doors to debate with radical historians had been evident in 1966, when he participated in the second Socialist Scholars Conference. There he joined Aptheker in commenting on Genovese's paper "The Legacy of Slavery and the Roots of Black Nationalism" and began by noting that a lack of respect for age and authority characterized left-wing politics as well as the Ivy League. "In this conflict, I naturally identify with Mr Aptheker, since we are of the same generation," he said. He praised Genovese for "the blow that he has struck for scholarly candor, skepticism, irreverence and independence."[72]

Woodward wrote a long, serious evaluation of Bernstein's *Towards a New Past* in the *New York Review of Books* in 1968. Acknowledging that "many older historians would bridle at being branded 'establishment' or 'consensus,'" he declared that it would be a "mistake" for the profession to ignore or dismiss the radical historians. "They deserve a full hearing and a close reading," he wrote. "They have much to say that is relevant to the correction of a complacent and nationalist reading of our past." In one of his most memorable statements, Woodward concluded that, if the radical historians sometimes "opposed the inevitable" in American society, "the inevitable needs all the opposition it can get."[73]

---

71. *Studies on the Left*, 1 (spring 1960), p. 5.
72. C. Vann Woodward, "Comment on Genovese," *Studies on the Left*, 6 (November–December 1966), pp. 36, 38, 40. Woodward subsequently led a fight to prevent Herbert Aptheker from teaching a student-initiated one-term seminar on W.E.B. Du Bois. See Jesse Lemisch, "If Howard Cosell Can Teach at Yale, Why Can't Herbert Aptheker?" *Radical History Review*, 3 (spring 1976), pp. 46–8. A resolution calling on the OAH to investigate the Yale history department's rejection of Aptheker passed in a mail ballot, but the Yale department indicated that "Yale University policy forbids disclosure of the discussions and reasons for decisions about appointments." See "The Yale–Aptheker Resolution," *OAH Newsletter*, 4 (July 1976), p. 5. On the controversy, see "Southern History and the Politics of Recent Memory," *Radical History Review*, 38 (April 1987), pp. 143–51.
73. C. Vann Woodward, "Wild in the Stacks," *New York Review of Books*, August 1, 1968, pp. 8–12. For another positive review of Bernstein, see John A. Garray, in *New York Times Book Review*, May 12, 1968, p. 1. Woodward subsequently changed his

Other established historians joined in redefining the field to include radical history. The editors of new journals launched to overcome the limitations of existing scholarship adopted editorial policies different from those of the official journals. Most important was the *Journal of Social History*, which began publishing in 1967 under the editorship of Peter Stearns. The founding editorial board included not only committed opponents of radical history, notably Oscar Handlin, Nathan Glazer, and Robert Nisbet, but also Genovese, George Rudé, and Reginald Zelnick. The board's composition and several essays in the first two volumes made it clear that radical history was part of social history.[74] *Labor History* and the *Journal of Interdisciplinary History* also published the best radical work as part of social history—and criticized it as such. Their editors—Milton Cantor in the former case, Robert Rotberg and Theodore Rabb in the latter—played a crucial role in redefining the field.

As the barriers began to fall, some historians who had insisted that radical history was not history abandoned that position. Donald was the most important. His own work underwent a striking transformation: the first volume of his Charles Sumner biography, published in 1960, portrayed Sumner as psychologically disturbed; it received a great deal of criticism from radical historians. The second volume, published in 1970, portrayed Sumner as a heroic fighter for black rights. Later he praised Litwack's *Been in the Storm So Long* and other radical histories of the post-Civil War South.[75]

Marxist Perspectives appeared in 1978; never before had a scholarly

position, writing that the sixties New Left and the redhunters who attacked the university in the fifties "had much in common." C. Vann Woodward, "The Siege," *New York Review of Books*, September 25, 1986, p. 10.

74. Eugene D. Genovese, "Materialism and Idealism in the History of Negro Slavery," *Journal of Social History*, 1 (summer 1968), pp. 371–94; Richard Tilly, review of *The Making of the English Working Class* by E.P. Thompson, *Journal of Social History*, (spring 1968), pp. 288–93; James McPherson, review of *The Political Economy of Slavery* by Eugene D. Genovese, ibid. (spring 1968), pp. 280–85; James T. Lemon and Gary B. Nash, "The Distribution of Wealth in Eighteenth-century America," *Journal of Social History*, 2 (fall 1968), pp. 1–24; Robert Wiebe, review of *The Corporate Ideal in the Liberal State* by James Weinstein, *Journal of Social History*, 2 (winter 1968), pp. 174–76.

75. David Donald, *Charles Sumner and the Coming of the Civil War* (New York, 1960); David Donald, *Charles Sumner and the Rights of Man* (New York, 1970); David Donald, review of *Been in the Storm So Long* by Leon F. Litwack, *New Republic*, June 9, 1979, pp. 32–3.

journal with so many distinguished editors made its adherence to Marxist theory so explicit. Although the editors included anthropologists and sociologists, the organizers were overwhelmingly historians, led by Genovese. An editorial statement signed by Genovese and Susman challenged the assumption that prevailing forms of historical scholarship posed the significant questions and provided adequate answers. Marxism, they argued, could "pose the questions which intellectuals must face if they are not to abdicate their responsibility to interpret the world and thereby to contribute toward changing it for the better." The journal published articles by Hobsbawm, Lasch and Montgomery; John W. Womack on "The Mexican Economy during the Revolution," Eric Foner on "Class, Ethnicity, and Radicalism in the Gilded Age" and Linda Gordon on "Politics, Social Theory, and Women's History." Among the regular departments was "From the Other Shore"—offering essays critical of Marxism by Schlesinger, Stanley Engerman, John P. Diggins, and others. Despite its intellectual vitality, and an offer by Cambridge University Press to become its publisher, Genovese decided that issue 10 would be the journal's last. Published in 1980, it listed 125 editors and organizational secretaries at colleges and universities in 30 states—the clearest measure that the boundary separating Marxism from the history profession had disappeared.[76]

During the mid seventies, as some doors opened to radical history, the job market for historians collapsed, leaving many radical historians unemployed or working in non-tenure track situations. Some talented radicals, from Staughton Lynd to David Abraham, have been denied tenure or turned down for jobs under murky circumstances. Radicals in the eighties face renewed opposition from a variety of sources, including right-wing politicians, freelance Red hunters, a few entrenched and fearful older colleagues, and neo-conservative intellectuals emboldened for a time by Ronald Reagan's 1984 landslide.[77]

---

76. Eugene D. Genovese and Warren Susman, "Editorial Statement: a Note to Our Readers," *Marxist Perspectives*, 1 (spring 1978), pp. 4–5. When the journal ceased publication, it had 3,500 subscribers and sold an additional 1,000 copies as single issues (*New York Times*, February 1, 1981, p. 16).

77. "The David Abraham Case: Ten Comments from Historians," *Radical History Review*, 32 (1985), pp. 75–96; see also chapter 9. On the opposition to radical history in the eighties see chapters 15 and 16.

And of course radical historians have hardly been a unified, harmonious group; they have been divided by a variety of issues—for example, the debate between Marxist structuralism and humanism. They have diverted their energies, as in the destructive feud between Genovese and Gutman in the early seventies, and they have abandoned their achievements, as in the closing down of *Marxist Perspectives*. And radical historians continue to face unavoidable conflicts between intellectual and activist commitments. The pressures to conform to institutional standards of scholarly productivity are immense and difficult to resist. Radical historians have responded to these pressures in different ways.

Some work at reaching wider audiences through films or museum exhibits, through their writings for *The Nation* and the *Village Voice*, and through the American Social History Project's curriculum for working-class students. Some engage in campus political battles around divestment or unionization. Some argue that their first commitment must be to developing the quality of radical scholarship. Most have a strong commitment to undergraduate teaching. Despite new attacks from without and intermittent conflicts within, radical history in the age of Reagan occupied the strongest position it has ever held in American universities.[78]

In the conventional view, this transformation is evidence that the profession is a meritocracy, the radicals should be congratulated for

---

78. On the debate between Marxist humanism and structuralism, see Jon Wiener, "Marxist Theory and History: Thompson and Althusser," *Socialist Review*, 10 (July–August 1980), pp. 136–44. On Gutman and Genovese, see Ira Berlin, Introduction to "Herbert G. Gutman and the American Working Class," in Herbert G. Gutman, *Power and Culture: Essays on the American Working Class* (New York, 1987), pp. 46–52, 55–9; Eugene D. Genovese, "Solidarity and Servitude," *Times Literary Supplement*, February 25, 1977, pp. 198–9; Eugene D. Genovese, "The Debate over *Time on the Cross*: a Critique of Bourgeois Criticism," in Elizabeth Fox-Genovese and Eugene D. Genovese, *Fruits of Merchant Capital* (New York, 1983), pp. 136–71. Around 13 per cent of historians described their political orientation as "left" in a 1984 survey. See Stephen H. Balch and Herbert I. London, "The Tenured Left," *Commentary*, 54 (October 1986) p. 43. Kent Blaser argues that radical historians have failed to form and transmit a new paradigm, but his criteria for success are so high that no school of history has attained it: "for the school to be successful or hegemonic ... it must be able to socialize followers over several generations." Kent Blaser, "What Happened to New Left History?: Part 1, An Institutional Approach," *South Atlantic Quarterly*, 85 (summer 1986), pp. 283–96, especially p. 289.

doing work so good that the profession had to accept them, and the profession should be congratulated for recognizing the good work even when it challenged the mainstream. But the foregoing suggests the inadequacy of the meritocratic thesis: the profession had to transform the prevailing definition of "good work" before radical historians could be judged on their merits. The profession's agenda was transformed when established historians observed—and experienced—the social and political upheavals that swept American society and politics. Partly in response to pressure from their students, partly in response to their own experiences and their own intellectual work, many of them abandoned the assumption that the prevailing historical scholarship posed the significant questions and provided adequate answers. The consensus about the boundaries of history that had consolidated historians' loyalties and commitments disintegrated. The profession's willingness to defend the boundary that had separated "history" from non-history was undermined. During this crisis the profession re-defined the field in a way that included radical historians' conceptions of the significant problems requiring study.

Today's radical history arose in a particular historical context, against the background of the civil rights and antiwar movements; it developed as a critique of a particular body of scholarship—consensus history. Radical history, that is to say, does not present "truth" in any transcendent sense; it is itself a historical product. As E.P. Thompson has written, today's radical historians "are as much subject to our own time's formation and determinations as any others. If our work is con-tinued by others, it will be continued differently."[79]

Journal of American History, Fall 1989

---

79. E.P. Thompson, "Agendas for Radical History," *Radical History Review*, 36 (1986), pp. 41–2.

26

Crossing the Lines: Taylor Branch

Gives the Movement Its Due

At the first observance of the new Martin Luther King federal holiday in 1986, a bust of King was installed in Statuary Hall in the US Capitol alongside forgotten senators and statesmen; "We Shall Overcome" was played by the Marine Band, fresh from the invasion of Grenada. Vice-president Bush spoke at Ebenezer Baptist Church in Atlanta, the King family's church, endorsing "King's dream of equality and non-violence." Taylor Branch's book provides the antidote to this hypocrisy.[1]

Do we really need another 1,000-page book about King to accomplish that, especially after David Garrow's 800-page Pulitzer Prize-winning biography, *Bearing the Cross?* Garrow is a phenomenally energetic researcher, but his approach to King's life was deeply flawed. His King is a Christ-like figure who, as his title suggests, bore the cross of racism, anticipated his own crucifixion, and apparently died for our sins. Branch gives us a completely different sense of King's political character, and so of the civil rights movement as a whole. Garrow neither placed King in the larger context of the movement nor assessed his role as organizer and political thinker. Branch sees King as the most prominent among many extraordinary movement strategists, tacticians, and political leaders. By refusing to treat him as a unique figure, by giving the movement its due, by recounting the actions of little-known local heroes and showing how King learned from the many protests that arose without his direct involvement, Branch is able

---

1. Taylor Branch, *Parting the Waters: America in the King Years, 1954–1963* (New York: Simon & Schuster, 1988).

to show his real contribution. The result is probably the best book ever written about the civil rights movement.

Branch begins by placing King in the context of the black church, with its long-standing tradition of activism. Among King's predecessors at the Dexter Avenue Baptist Church in Montgomery was the Rev. Vernon Johns, unknown to historians until Branch discovered him but famous among Montgomery blacks as the grandson of a slave who had killed his master. In 1949 Johns put up a notice outside his church advertising the following Sunday's sermon, which was to be on "Segregation After Death"; he was immediately summoned by the police chief to come down to headquarters and explain what he meant. Happy to oblige, Johns preached to the chief and officers present about Christ's parable of the beggar Lazarus and the rich man Dives. When he finished, he later reported, there was "not a dry eye in the station house." Johns personally challenged bus segregation in Montgomery years before King came to town, demanding his money back when told to give up his seat to a white; he also ordered food in a white restaurant, after which "a gang of customers ran to their cars for guns and chased him out." When King arrived in Montgomery, he took up the pulpit of a minister so brave that whites regarded him as crazy.

But the church also expressed contradictory elements in black life. The strongest black opposition to King came from the National Baptist Convention, and the story of that conflict is told for the first time in Branch's book. The six-million-member NBC had provided the arena where both King's father and grandfather gained national standing; its 1960 convention brought 35,000 blacks together under one roof. King hoped to mobilize the NBC's power against segregation, and because he was too young to challenge longtime president J.H. Jackson, he and other civil rights ministers supported another challenger for the post. A yearlong struggle over credentials and procedures came to a head at the NBC's 1961 gathering in Kansas City. Convinced that they were about to be robbed of the vote, the King forces entered the convention hall in a "flying wedge" of several hundred preachers, storming toward the podium in a "thundering mass" while King waited outside. Several hundred preachers on the opposing side rushed to protect their candidate, and a huge battle ensued, in which hundreds of ministers "shoved, wrestled and slugged each other" for almost an hour. The fighting ended only when eighty Kansas City riot police showed up, along with Kansas City's 300-pound mayor. One of the key lieutenants of the anti-King forces suffered a fractured skull in the battle and died two days later.

King's opponent won reelection, and King was promptly stripped of his office in the NBC—a punishment close to excommunication. The victorious Jackson told the press that the ministers who supported King were "hoodlums and crooks." King would not address the NBC again in his lifetime, and Jackson turned its power against most of King's subsequent civil rights campaigns. For the rest of King's life, Branch reports, he mourned his failure to win this crucial institutional base for the civil rights movement.

Branch also pays close attention to King's relationship with local civil rights struggles and their organizers, and his chapter on the Montgomery bus boycott is an example of the way his careful reporting refines the received view of events. American history students asked to explain the origins and significance of the boycott are expected to write that it was started by Rosa Parks, a black seamstress in Montgomery who, one day in 1955, refused to give up her seat on the bus to a white man, as the law required; she was arrested, and her arrest sparked a massive and eventually successful bus boycott that propelled Martin Luther King to leadership of the new civil rights movement and demonstrated the power of nonviolent direct action tactics. Recently, however, some historians have argued that Rosa Parks was not just a seamstress but a trained activist, the secretary of the Montgomery chapter of the National Association for the Advancement of Colored People who had spent a week at the Highlander Folk School studying interracial cooperation. These historians point out that two women before her had been arrested for refusing to give up their seats, and report that local NAACP president E.D. Nixon had decided not to use their cases to challenge the bus segregation law because they were not strong enough to be defendants. This revisionist case holds that the arrest of Rosa Parks was part of a much more deliberate and organized challenge to segregation than the world knew at the time. Branch resolves the controversy by showing that Rosa Parks's action was indeed spontaneous, and that the local NAACP head decided only later to make her arrest a test case.

Branch's discussion of the sit-ins also places King in the context of the movement as a whole, showing how he learned about strategy from student activists. When black students in Greensboro, North Carolina, lined up at all-white lunch counters and refused to leave until they were served, their protests were initially viewed as reckless and futile provocations even by the black press; the NAACP Legal Defense Fund refused to support those who were first arrested. Branch shows that King was almost alone among established civil rights leaders in praising the students for their political maturity: "What is fresh, what is new in your fight is the fact that it was initiated, led, and sustained by students," he said. "You now take your honored places in the world-wide struggle for freedom." The student sit-ins, Branch argues, represented a major strategic advance over King's campaigns—an advance whose significance he appreciated. The students had done something King had only thought about: they challenged the segregation laws by seeking out a confrontation. Not until six years after Montgomery would King adopt the strategy of selecting targets, deliberately creating issues and planning campaigns in advance. Branch emphasizes that during that period he did not initiate civil rights campaigns; he responded to urgent requests for support from campaigns already underway.

Parting the Waters also puts King in the context of national politics, exploring in detail his frustrations with white liberals who knew segregation was wrong but who criticized the civil rights movement for "moving too fast." The most important of these liberals were the Kennedys. Even Branch is not completely immune to the Kennedy myth: "King and Kennedy," he writes, "were like a pair of ill-fated lovers, with similar interests but mismatched passions." But Branch does know that Kennedy did not have a genuine interest in civil rights; he considered the demand for "freedom now" to be just as irresponsible as the calls for "segregation forever." Only in the battle against Communism did Kennedy think the US should "pay any price, bear any burden." In the struggle for black rights he never asked the American people to make any such commitment. Kennedy had no civil rights program; he refused to fulfill even the modest pledges of the 1960 Democratic platform, and appointed blatantly racist federal judges in the South, starting with Harold Cox, who called black people "baboons." During the Freedom Rides, the Birmingham church bombings, and the riots at Ole Miss, Branch portrays King and the Kennedys watching each other, dealing through go-betweens, mobilizing different kinds of resources to test each other's commitments and limits.

King's most insidious opponent in Washington was J. Edgar Hoover—a story first told in Garrow's earlier book, *The FBI and Martin Luther King*. Acting on information provided by Hoover, Kennedy himself demanded that King "get rid of" his friend and strategist Stanley Levison, along with Jack O'Dell, his top direct mail fundraiser. "They're communists," JFK whispered—although Hoover had no evidence to back up the charges. Branch appreciates the significance of this act, with which "the Administration laid claim to govern not only King's hiring practices but also his friendships, even the advice he could seek and the words he could hear."

In an effort to find some evidence that King was associating with Reds, Hoover proposed to Attorney General Robert Kennedy that King's home, office, and hotel rooms on the road be wiretapped. Kennedy approved Hoover's request, Branch argues, partly because it would provide him with advance information about King's political plans. Those wiretaps and bugs eventually turned up evidence of King's extramarital sex life—evidence that Hoover later tried to use to blackmail and destroy him and that provided the most sensational parts of David Garrow's book. Garrow presented the material the FBI gathered on King's sex life (Hoover called him a "tom cat") without interpretation or analysis; Branch, to his credit, examines the way King struggled to understand his conflicting impulses. The small circle of peers and advisers closest to King, Branch writes, saw his "sexual adventures as a natural condition of manhood, or of great preachers obsessed by love, or of success, or of Negroes otherwise constrained by the white world."

King came close to talking about his sexual affairs publicly, Branch shows, in sermons at Atlanta's Ebenezer Baptist Church. "Many of you here know something of what it is to struggle with sin," he said. "In this moment of despair you decided to take your problem to God.... You discovered that the evil was still with you. God would not cast it out." King went on to discuss legendary sinners who, in Branch's words, "redirected the torment of their inner confessions to produce historical miracles." King scholars have long puzzled over the sources of his unwavering commitment to nonviolence, his refusal to hate his opponents. Garrow attributed it to a religious conversion experience;

Branch's argument about the sources of King's moral strength is more complex and more persuasive. King's painful awareness of his own moral failings drove him to do public good and enabled him to see opponents not as the incarnation of evil but as people not unlike himself.

Branch weaves his analysis and interpretation into a powerful and moving narrative—the story of the Freedom Rides, the sit-ins, and the monumental Birmingham campaign, with its fire hoses and police dogs turned on black demonstrators and the arrest of thousands of black children. The book is full of telling details: in Albany, Georgia, one of the hundreds of places where civil rights marchers were jailed, a woman named Marion King—no relation to Martin—joined a group outside the Mitchell County jail, singing freedom songs and waiting to visit those who had been arrested. The sheriff ordered them to move, and Marion King, six months pregnant, in maternity clothes, her two children in her arms, didn't move fast enough. "The sheriff slapped her sharply across the face," Branch writes. "Three-year-old Abena went sprawling from her arms to the pavement. One-year-old DuBois shrieked. As the sheriff slapped her again, the deputy kicked her in the shins, knocking her feet from beneath her, and then kicked her several times more on the ground." The brazen public beating of the pregnant wife of one of the pillars of the Albany black community horrified even the most hardened veterans of police brutality; her husband and friends sobbed with rage over their inability to defend her. In his telling of this small incident, Branch manages to suggest the dimensions of what was at at stake in the black freedom movement.

Branch's book ends in 1963, with the march on Washington and the Kennedy assassination. Another volume is promised, which will deal with the period when King turned his efforts to northern cities and adopted a frankly socialist critique of American society. In 1967 he said, "the problem of racism, the problem of economic exploitation, and the problem of war are all tied together." He said that "something is wrong with capitalism as it now stands in the US," and that we needed "a radical redistribution of economic and political power." In the words of Vincent Gordon Harding, the first director of the Martin Luther King Jr Center in Atlanta, King sought "to help find the ways by which the full energies and angers of the poor could be challenged, organized, and engaged in a revolutionary process that would open

222

new creative possibilities for them and for the nation."

Jesse Jackson has been walking the line between the goals of empowerment and inclusion King set out in the mid sixties and the miserable realities of politics in the age of Reagan. Jackson today is far more prominent, and commands far broader support than King ever did in his lifetime. That's a result largely of King's achievements: by leading the fight to destroy segregation and win black voting rights, he made it possible for a black presidential candidate to win 6.6 million votes and the second-highest delegate total in 1988's Democratic primaries.

After eight years of Reagan, the King years look immensely bright. Branch's book is a reminder that although the black freedom struggle of the fifties and sixties moved mountains to abolish legal segregation in the South, King's actual victories in the nine years covered by this book were few—bus desegregation in Montgomery, desegregation of downtown Birmingham—and he suffered some major defeats. Branch shows not only what made for the historic victories, but how King kept on when things were bad. "No lie can live forever," King told Fisk University students in Nashville in 1961. "Let us not despair. Work together, children. Don't get weary."

Village Voice, December 27, 1988

27

The Liberal Imagination and

the Antiwar Movement

From its inception, the sixties antiwar movement was a battle between liberals and radicals, so it shouldn't come as a surprise that historians of the movement are refighting that battle. *Who Spoke Up?*,[1] the first full-length history of Vietnam protest, has been getting a lot of coverage from reviewers who agree with its thesis—that radicals undermined the movement's effectiveness.

The book is a chronological narrative of demonstrations that made page one of the *New York Times*, plus interviews with two dozen movement heavies ranging from Dr Spock to Cora Weiss to Rennie Davis. The title comes from I.F. Stone. Future generations, he wrote, will ask us the same question we ask about Nazi Germany: who spoke up? The implication is that everyone who spoke up was a hero. But for Nancy Zaroulis and Gerald Sullivan there were two categories of protestors— decent, ordinary, patriotic citizens who spoke up to "save the nation's honor," and radicals, who exploited the Vietnam issue to advance their own goals, ideological or personal. Those who hated America because of what we were doing to the Vietnamese "were no longer of the antiwar movement even as they were no longer of America," the authors declare. And "the antiwar movement was not a movement of licentious counter-culturals."

Zaroulis and Sullivan begin their history with the protest of Norman Morrison, the 32-year-old Quaker who set himself on fire outside the Pentagon in 1965. The implication is that the radical movement was

---

1. Nancy Zaroulis and Gerald Sullivan, *Who Spoke Up? American Protest Against the War in Vietnam, 1963–1975* (New York: Doubleday, 1985).

always self-destructive. Repeatedly, the authors write as if the movement's own failings and weaknesses were responsible for the war's continuing. They bring back to life the vicious liberal denunciations of campus radicals, for whom Vietnam was "a neglected or at best a peripheral issue, invoked usually as a standard of gruesome horror against which to measure and minimize the violence perpetrated by protesters." The authors see the 1969 Harvard strike (in which I participated) as a typical case. Here their narrow vision approaches blindness: they consider our central demand, the abolition of ROTC (Reserve Officers' Training Corps) a separate issue from the war. As for their conclusion that the strike "demoralized" the "Harvard community," Harvard as a single community had long since ceased to exist. The administration was demoralized, but everybody I knew was exhilarated. And the authors neglect to report that the strikers won: after forty years at Harvard, ROTC was abolished.

Ideological knife-sharpening also seems to have influenced the authors' choice of interviewees. The only person they quote on the last days of Students for a Democratic Society, and on the Harvard strike, is Jared Israel, then of the Progressive Labor Party. I knew this guy, a strident sectarian. You couldn't find a less sympathetic figure to represent student radicalism. (Even PL turned against him: the authors report that he was subjected to a PL star-chamber proceeding in 1973, charged with—who would have guessed?—"male chauvinism.")

Some balance is provided by interviews with lefties like Dave Dellinger, Sidney Peck, and Tom Hayden. But much of what they say (or at least are quoted as saying) rehashes the mind-numbing story of behind-the-scenes struggles over strategy and tactics (People's Coalition for Peace and Justice versus National Peace Action Coalition in 1971) and the even more frustrating negotiations with the government over turf (would the Washington demonstrators get the Ellipse or be confined to the Washington Monument grounds). Like mainstream history from above, this version misses the experience of participants. The march on the Pentagon, for example, is told from the vantage point of organizer Peck, angry that the day turned out to be so disorganized and spontaneous. But that spontaneity was precisely what made the event so thrilling.

While building their case, the authors do present some fascinating information. At the 1968 Democratic national convention, when

Senator Abraham Ribicoff denounced "Gestapo tactics on the streets of Chicago," the TV showed Mayor Daley shouting back, off-mike. The authors cite lip-readers who report Daley's response: "Fuck you you Jew son of a bitch you lousy motherfucker go home." And they include some great examples of liberal attempts to silence radical protest. My favorite is SANE(Committee for a Sane Nuclear Policy)'s refusal in 1965 to approve demonstration signs reading "Bring the GI's home now"; they insisted on "New action to speed negotiations."

Certainly the left suffered its share of self-inflicted disasters that need to be re-examined—the failure of the 1967 New Politics conference, the biggest gathering of antiwar and civil rights groups ever held; the preoccupation with Third World revolutions as models for America; the collapse of SDS. But to blame radicals for failing to stop the war is to forget who had the power. Indeed, some movement disasters were undoubtedly government-inspired. For example, the 1970 attack on Wall Street demonstrators by two hundred "construction workers" was universally seen as evidence of working-class support for the war— which is how Zaroulis and Sullivan tell it. But recently released Nixon White House tapes suggest that the event was organized at the president's instigation. Vietnam era opinion polls consistently showed that working-class people were more likely to favor an immediate end to the war than college-educated people, who had learned about the need for "experts" and the danger of "simple solutions."

What did the antiwar movement accomplish? Zaroulis and Sullivan don't try to answer the question; for them, it's enough that the movement existed. They do retell a revealing story: when the computer experts at the Pentagon recommended that Hanoi be bombed back to the Stone Age, Johnson replied, "I have one more problem for your computer—how long will it take five hundred thousand angry Americans to climb that White House wall out there and lynch their president if he does something like that?"

The legacy of the Vietnam protest is the movement to end US intervention in Central America, considerably more successful than its counterpart a decade ago. The Kennedy administration had 10,000 US troops in Vietnam, and 600 Americans dead in combat, before an opposition movement surfaced; until 1966, exactly two senators opposed the war. Today Congress has limited the Reagan administration to 68 advisers in El Salvador, and has been trying to cut off funds for the "Vietnamization" of Nicaragua.

Liberals concerned about intervention in Central America may look to this book for lessons. It tells them the Vietnam protest movement was weakened by cultural and political radicals. It's hard to imagine a more destructive message at a time when the peace movement needs all the radical intelligence it can get.

Village Voice, February 19, 1985

28

The New Left as History

Three new books on the sixties and their origins set a new standard for serious scholarly study of that era.[1] James Miller provides the best and intellectually most fruitful definition of the subject: the sixties constituted an explosion of democracy, a popular challenge to established authority in the state, the university, and the family, a renewal that, in its sweep and intensity, ranks beside the era of Andrew Jackson and the New Deal. Students for a Democratic Society occupies the center of this history because it articulated the crucial concept of the decade: "participatory democracy."

Each author seeks to explain what was new about the New Left— how the activists of the sixties distinguished themselves from the old left. Each discusses the New Left's rejection of anticommunism, including the anticommunism of veterans of the thirties left. Each addresses the argument that the New Left ended up repeating the mistakes of the old left. Each brings different strengths to this history.

Maurice Isserman is an historian and author of *Which Side Were You On?*, a study of American communism during World War Two. He answers a compelling question in his new book: why wasn't a New Left organized in 1956? The Port Huron statement, which effectively launched SDS, did not appear until 1962. In 1956, experienced

---

1. Maurice Isserman, *If I Had a Hammer . . . : the Death of the Old Left and the Birth of the New Left* (New York: Basic Books, 1987); James Miller, *"Democracy is in the Streets": From Port Huron to the Siege of Chicago* (New York: Simon & Schuster, 1987); Todd Gitlin, *The Sixties: Years of Hope, Days of Rage* (New York: Bantam Books, 1987).

Communist Party activists had just left the party after Khrushchev's acknowledgement of Stalin's crimes; the Montgomery bus boycott had recently showed the possibilities of popular non-violent action and established Martin Luther King as its spokesman and most skilled practitioner; McCarthyism had peaked and then receded without becoming fascism. The time for a non-Communist left seemed to have arrived. In England this was the moment of independent revolutionary Marxism, with the organization of the *New Reasoner* with Alasdair MacIntyre and E.P. Thompson, and then the *New Left Review*.

The possibility of an American New Left was raised by, among others, the *National Guardian*, which ran a headline in October 1956: "The New Left: What Should it Look Like?" and reported on a meeting between Earl Browder and Norman Thomas. In their conception, a New Left would not be a student movement, but rather a regrouping of adult radicals, experienced in the struggles of the thirties and forties; their ideas and strategies would be new. Even in 1959, when Michael Harrington reported to the Young People's Socialist League National Executive Committee on "the prospects for a New Left in the United States," students were not at the top of this list; he pointed to the battle of the trade union federation AFL–CIO against "right to work" laws, the success of SANE, and the growth of the civil rights movement, as well as to activist students.

Isserman's book is a fascinating history of the false starts and bungled opportunities that delayed the emergence of a New Left until the sixties: Max Shachtman's aborted effort to bring ex-CPers into a revived Socialist Party; radical pacifists' preference for moral gestures over political organizing; SANE's capitulation to McCarthyism. The book begins by recounting the familiar story of the CP in the fifties, and describes how the events of 1956 initially brought some leaders to attempt to transform the party from within, to make it a New Left. As those efforts were defeated, the party lost two-thirds of its membership, a far more devastating loss than anything McCarthyism had inflicted.

Here was the first real opportunity to create a New Left, as many people at the time observed. Herman Benson of the Independent Socialist League wrote in *New International* in 1956:

Thousands of Communists have devoted their full mature life to the fight for a world of socialism, as they saw it, risking personal well-being, gaining experience in the class struggle. Are they now to be scattered to the winds and squandered?

One of the most potentially significant New Left projects was Shachtman's proposal that his ISL and its youth group merge into the Socialist Party and recruit former Communists. The SP at that point had perhaps a thousand members, whom, it was thought, might be drawn into an "all-inclusive" socialist movement, "the Socialist Party of Eugene Debs," which would then become the organization for a New Left in America. But when the merger was finally consummated in 1958, Shachtman showed no interest in recruiting ex-Communists. Holding fast to his lifetime of sectarianism, he preferred to hold power over a tiny group than to risk losing control to a broader movement.

The place of *Dissent* in "the death of the old left and the birth of the New Left" occupies almost fifty pages of Isserman's book. Irving Howe and the other *Dissent* editors, Isserman argues, spent the fifties waiting for a New Left to appear, hoping they could contribute to its development and help it avoid the mistakes of the old left. They anticipated many early New Left themes. But their preoccupation with their own political past undermined their ability to engage with the New Left when it did take shape; as a result, during the sixties the *Dissent* editors "lost the political opportunity for which they had been waiting for a lifetime." This is a brutal statement, but it's true. Sixties veterans can learn from the case of *Dissent* and work to have a more fruitful engagement with the next generation of radicals.

Partly because the old left rejected the new, Isserman argues, radical pacifists ended up having much more influence on the spirit and tactics of the New Left. The New Left was never very socialist, but it did embrace the deeply moral stance of the pacifists, who had demonstrated their commitments to putting themselves on the line to challenge injustice. The spirit of the people who tried to disrupt nuclear submarine launchings, Isserman argues, was reborn a decade later in the Weathermen: for both, "effectiveness" and "organizing" didn't count; ordinary politics had failed, the hour was late, one had a moral obligation to confront evil. What Irving Howe and other critics of the New Left mistook for Stalinism, Isserman argues, was in fact the legacy of that ultimate American, Henry David Thoreau.

Compared to the old leftists, the pacifists had some crucial advantages in appealing to young people in search of radical politics. Pacifists did not have the left's legacy of internecine warfare, they did not specialize in the crushing rhetorical denunciations that Howe and others, schooled in New York's sectarian hothouse, directed at the nascent New Left. And the threat of nuclear annihilation gave the pacifist mission a new urgency in the decades after Hiroshima. The pacifists advocated a radicalism of means as well as ends. Moreover, their advocacy of nonviolent tactics gained the charisma of the civil rights movement, of Martin Luther King; pacifists organized the Congress on Racial Equality (CORE), which pioneered the use of civil disobedience to challenge segregation. Isserman's history of radical pacifism and its influence on the New Left is his most significant contribution.

SANE was organized in 1957 as a political education group, one which would not practice direct action tactics. Within a year SANE had 130 chapters and 25,000 members. In spring 1960, SANE held the biggest antiwar gathering since the 1930s at Madison Square Garden, attended by 17,000 people. Nathan Glazer wrote in *Commentary*, "SANE might grow into a really powerful force in American politics." Then the Red-baiters went to work. Senator Thomas Dodd, vice chair of the Senate Subcommittee on Internal Security and a leading opponent of a nuclear test ban, charged that the chief organizer of the Madison Square Garden rally was a Communist. Under the leadership of Norman Cousins, SANE pledged the next day to purge its ranks of Communists and require that all local chapters adopt new charters enforcing the purge. The membership objected strenuously; twenty-five out of fifty local chapters in New York refused to comply; many prominent radical pacifists resigned, including Muste, and younger activists turned against the organization. That, Isserman shows, ended the possibility that SANE could have become the vehicle of a New Left in the 1960s.

The sudden example of the sit-in movement in 1961 inspired young radicals to turn from the nuclear threat to address issues of racism, poverty and injustice in domestic society; no single-issue peace group could be the vehicle of their politics. Now SDS took center stage with its 1962 Port Huron statement. Isserman's achievement is to show that this New Left was genuinely new, largely because of the failure of older radicals to organize an adult New Left after 1956.

231

James Miller is a book and music critic for *Newsweek* and editor of the magnificent *Rolling Stone Illustrated History of Rock and Roll*; he is also a political theorist and intellectual historian, author of a book on Sartre and Merleau-Ponty and of *Rousseau: Dreamer of Democracy*. His focus on participatory democracy as the central political concept of the sixties makes for a brilliant study of the ideas and actions of New Left activists. The book is beautifully written; who would have thought that a study of the Port Huron Statement could be a page-turner?

"Democracy is in the Streets" addresses the argument that the New Left was anti-intellectual. The Port Huron Statement, Miller demonstrates, remains a document of intellectual substance twenty-five years after it was written. Much of Miller's book is an analysis of the adventures of the Port Huron Statement through years of social and cultural upheaval, as SDS turned from protest to resistance to revolutionary rhetoric. Young people in SDS and elsewhere, Miller argues, tested the limits of democracy during the sixties. Miller focuses first on the experience of the key people who drafted the Port Huron Statement; one of the strengths of the book is the way it recaptures their "excitement and sense of adventure." The central figure in the book is Tom Hayden—rightly, because he wrote the Port Huron Statement draft, and because he proved to be perhaps the most articulate leader of this movement without leaders. The concept of participatory democracy came from Arnold Kaufman, one of Hayden's teachers at Michigan—from Kaufman's 1960 essay "Participatory Democracy and Human Nature," published in *Nomos III: Responsibility*. This fact should give hope to every philosopher and theorist working away in obscurity, hoping that his or her ideas could become the rallying cry of a generation of young people.

Only fifty-nine people showed up at the 1962 Port Huron conference. Mostly they were midwestern college kids from Michigan, Oberlin and Swarthmore. The statement they drafted began, not with a Marxist discussion of the state of capitalism, but with an evocative description of young people's lives in middle-class America and their discovery of the hypocrisy of the powerful; that section was followed by a forthright affirmation of what they valued in relationships and societies. It was a great beginning.

232

Michael Harrington was at Port Huron as the 34-year-old "youth leader" of the League for Industrial Democracy—SDS at that point was officially their youth organization. Harrington returned to an LID board meeting, packed with ILGWU veterans, Social Party leaders and officials of the Jewish Labor Committee, and led an all-out attack on the Port Huron convention for being "outside the basic principles of the LID." The big issue: SDS had allowed a Communist to be "seated at the convention and given him speaking rights"; its statement had "placed the blame for the cold war largely on the US" and had "bitterly scored [American] foreign policy." The board decided to fire Hayden as SDS president, censor all SDS materials and appoint a new "student secretary" of SDS who would abide by LID politics.

Recently Paul Berman, reviewing Miller's book in *The New Republic*, argued that the LID leaders were right: SDS should have banned Communists from membership. That would have made it impossible for the Progressive Labor Party to take over SDS in 1969, Berman argues. The decision not to ban Communists "sold the New Left down the river."[2] That's a perversely ahistorical position, which fails to appreciate the significance of SDS's refusal to institutionalize internal McCarthyism. Gitlin explains it best: the rejection of anticommunism was "the crucible of a political identity" for the New Left; what haunted kids who grew up in the fifties was not Communism but McCarthyism. Harrington told Miller he soon came to regret treating the "kids" from Swarthmore and Oberlin and Michigan "as if they were old Trotskyist faction fighters following a line." In Harrington's recent memoir of Port Huron, published in the New Left *Socialist Review*, he writes of his own "stupidity" in criticizing the SDS draft for being soft on Communism; today, he writes, he finds himself completely in agreement with its remarks on that subject.[3]

The response of other institutions of the old left to the Port Huron Statement was not much better than that of the LID, Miller shows. The independent Marxist *National Guardian* refused to run an article on the conference by Richard Flacks, who today teaches sociology at the

2. Paul Berman, "Don't Follow Leaders," *New Republic*, August 10/17, 1987, pp. 28–35.

3. Michael Harrington, "Between Generations," *Socialist Review* 93/94 (May–August, 1987), pp. 152–8.

University of California, Santa Barbara, and who remains a political activist. "They perceived LID as a right-wing social-democratic organization," he recalled. "So how could their youth group amount to anything?" Leo Huberman of *Monthly Review* told Flacks, "It's much more important whether Fidel Castro can defend his revolution than whether American youth think anything." For SDS, the LID actions suggested that it was not the political right that was trying to silence them, but rather their old left sponsors; the effect on the Port Huron leaders was to sharpen their sense of themselves precisely as a "New" left.

What did participatory democracy mean? The Port Huron Statement called for a political system in which "the individual shares in those social decisions affecting the quality and direction of his life." For some the concept suggested democratic socialism; for others, a new form of political organization distinct from anything known to the old left. Miller shows that in the beginning the concept had two distinct elements: first the advocacy of a face-to-face community of trust, friendship and stability; while for other SDS founders, participatory democracy meant an experimental collective testing the limits of democracy, a project that necessarily involved tension and upheaval. Within SDS its meanings changed, Miller argues: by 1964 it meant rule by consensus; by 1965 it was offered as a radical alternative to representative institutions, a weapon in the struggle against hierarchy and authority.

In 1987, *Socialist Review* published a symposium on the Port Huron Statement on its twenty-fifth anniversary that is an essential supplement to Miller's book. In his contribution, Richard Flacks emphasizes the political strategy expressed in the statement: it did not argue that a mass student movement could transform America; in fact it called for a coalition, spearheaded by a revitalized labor movement, drawing on the moral force of the civil rights movement, for which students and intellectuals would provide skills.[4] The weaknesses of non-student parts of that proposed coalition explained a great deal about the trajectory SDS followed in the later sixties.

---

4. Richard Flacks, "Port Huron: Twenty-five Years After," *Socialist Review* 93/94 (May–August 1987), pp. 140–47.

Two-thirds of Miller's book deals with the period before the first SDS antiwar march on Washington, held in April 1965. The organizers expected a few thousand; between 15,000 and 25,000 turned up—the first sign that a mass student movement was about to appear. Paul Potter gave the key SDS speech: "What kind of system is it that justifies the US or any country seizing the destinies of the Vietnamese people and using them callously for its own purpose? ... We must name that system. We must name it, describe it, analyze it, understand it and change it." The speech, Miller writes, captured "the moral passion and restless question that constituted the heart and soul of the New Left." Potter himself later explained, "I refused to call it capitalism because capitalism was for me and my generation an inadequate description of the evils of America—a hollow, dead word tied to the thirties.... I sensed there was something new afoot in the world that we were part of that made the rejection of the old terminology part of the new hope for radical change in America."

Participatory democracy now became the banner of a new generation of members, who gave it a different meaning. Staking their own claim to power within SDS, they called for an end to all authority, hierarchy and bureaucracy, and argued that SDS should begin at home. Grassroots initiative should replace leaders; SDS should make sure it did not become a new political party of the left. Thus the next convention voted a referendum on whether to abolish the national office. One national officer of the older generation, Steve Max, warned against the trend: "To destroy formal structures in society is unfortunately no small task. But to do so in one's own organization is not only possible but easy."

Meanwhile, back at the national office, nobody was opening the mail or running the mimeo machine. The "democratization of office work" had been a disaster. New president Paul Booth wrote at the end of 1965, "what is amazing is that the organization refuses to admit the fact that it plays an important role in American politics, and as a consequence, refuses to create responsible mechanisms from week to week."

At the end of 1965 women first began challenging their treatment by the male leadership of SDS; the history of this development has been written by Sara Evans in her 1980 book, *Personal Politics*. SDS women drew on the ideas of participatory democracy to argue that SDS men had excluded women from full participation, even though the group's

235

community organizing projects in particular had depended on women as organizers of welfare mothers.

"The vision of political freedom that had once inspired [SDS members'] enthusiasm and moral confidence now was mired in paradox and contention," Miller writes. "The prevailing hostility to elites ... made the creation and preservation of institutional safeguards against the abuse of authority by elected officers perversely difficult; a growing mood of militance made sober discussion of such issues all but impossible."

Hayden went to North Vietnam with Staughton Lynd and Herbert Aptheker in 1965, and found the Vietnamese putting "participatory democracy" into practice. Miller is sympathetic to Hayden's account, arguing that at the time Hayden and Lynd visited Hanoi, the Communist Party there, in order to withstand the total war unleashed by the Americans, made popular political participation "a prized feature of revolutionary organization." Hayden today hasn't abandoned that position, despite his move to the right on other issues. "What I saw was true," he told Miller; "I wasn't fooled. I saw people in a state of epic transformation, making an ultimate sacrifice against apparently invincible odds."

Following the concept of participatory democracy into the late sixties does not provide an adequate basis for understanding the implosion of SDS. It wasn't the flaws in that concept that led to the movement's demise; here Miller's book becomes less of an explanation and more of a chronicle, especially of Hayden's actions. Miller took his title "Democracy is in the Streets" from the headline of one of Hayden's preconvention manifestos from Chicago in 1968. The goal of the demonstrators, according to the manifestos, was to "face the Democratic Party with its illegitimacy and criminality." "In 1968 the game is up," Hayden wrote. "Our victory lies in progressively demystifying a false democracy." Even in this crisis, Miller points out, "democracy" provided the ideological keystone to SDS leaders.

SDS's experiment in participatory democracy faced a powerful antagonist: J. Edgar Hoover's FBI. Hoover declared that the SDS activist was "a paradox because he is difficult to judge by the normal standards of civilized life.... His main reason for being is to destroy, blindly and indiscriminately, to tear down and provoke chaos." Thus the FBI launched its COINTELPRO program to disrupt the New

Left. COINTELPRO was discovered in 1971 when heroic anti-FBI activitists removed over a thousand documents from the Bureau's office in Media, Pennyslvania. The program included an effort to use false information to provoke internal dissension and factionalism among activists, including reports that Tom Hayden was a government agent; sending phony "concerned alumnus" letters to university trustees seeking to get faculty sympathetic to SDS fired; and working with cooperative reporters to publish stories about the "scurrilous and depraved nature" of New Left life. The FBI in 1970 ordered investigations of every member of SDS.[5] Participatory democracy did not prove to be an effective way to resist the FBI COINTELPRO campaign; in measuring SDS's achievements and disasters, COINTELPRO requires scrutiny, yet Miller devotes only a single sentence to it. (Gitlin has a better sense of the significance of FBI disruption.)

For Miller, "The death knell for the Movement sounded ... on May 4, 1970, [when] National Guardsmen opened fire on students demonstrating on the campus of Kent State University. The bullets were real. The days of revolutionary fantasy were over.... The New Left collapsed, plummeting into cultural oblivion as if it had been some kind of political Hula-Hoop." Here Miller is unconvincing. Those bullets did not silence the New Left; on the contrary, the protests that followed the Kent State killings were monumental. The largest student strike in American history erupted, mobilizing 500 campuses and four million students. They stopped the American invasion of Cambodia and prevented Nixon from attempting anything like it again.

Miller concludes his book by showing that the principal architects of the Port Huron Statement have remained political activists on the left, learning from their experiences and holding fast to their visions of a better society. That's a necessary corrective to the media's recent infatuation with Jerry Rubin's turn toward Wall Street. What explains

---

5. Richard Gid Powers, *Secrecy and Power: the Life of J. Edgar Hoover* (New York, 1987), p. 449; Geoffrey Rips, *The Campaign Against the Underground Press: PEN American Center Report* (San Francisco, 1981), pp. 61, 68; Frank Donner, *The Age of Surveillance* (New York, 1981), pp. 232–7; Charles Brennan, testimony before the Church Committee Hearings, September 25, 1975, quoted in Senate Select Committee to Study Government Operations with Respect to Intelligence Activities ("Church Report"), *Final Report*, Book 2 (94 Cong., 2 Sess., 1976), pp. 8–9.

the New Left's demise? Miller shows it was not the consequence of flaws in the concept of participatory democracy. The collapse of the New Left was caused not so much by its own weaknesses or errors, he argues, but rather by "the almost hopeless difficulties and immense strategic quandaries posed by the economic, social, and political forces it wished to counteract."

Todd Gitlin is a Berkeley socialist, author of *The Whole World is Watching*, an indispensable book on the media and the New Left; he also served as an early president of SDS and an organizer of the first antiwar march on Washington in 1965. *The Sixties* is the most am-bitious of the three books under consideration. Gitlin's greatest achievement is his ability to convey the feelings and passions of the era, the ecstatic high and the despair, better than any book I know. It's remarkable that at the same time he is able to analyze the strengths and weaknesses, achievements and limitations, of each key moment of the New Left.

Gitlin also describes his own personal experiences as a New Left leader, beginning with Harvard Tocsin at the time of the 1960 Washington Action to protest the Bay of Pigs invasion, through the early days of SDS, and then as one of the elders who watched the younger generation take the organization toward revolutionary politics and implosion. He draws not just on his memories, but on letters to and from friends, which make for some of the most powerful material in the book. But because Gitlin's book follows his own experiences, it slights the parts of sixties history that he didn't take part in: draft resist-ance, Vietnam Veterans Against the War, the 1967 Pentagon demon-stration, Berkeley before October 1967, the Vietnam Summer project, the 1967 National Committee for a New Politics convention, the Harvard strike, the Stonewall rebellion, as well as the entire liberal antiwar movement, from the 5th Avenue Peace Parades to the 1968 McCarthy campaign to the 1969 Mobilization in Washington. Each of these gets no more than a paragraph from Gitlin, while every phase of the internal turmoil of SDS gets a chapter. These omissions are signifi-cant in a book whose title lays claim to comprehensiveness.

Gitlin traces some of the characteristic problems and failings of the New Left to its very newness, to the defeat and collapse of the left in the fifties. The result of the absence of an adult left, he writes, was a movement led by 22-year-olds who alternated between a belief that students *were* the revolution, and a belief that students were incapable of achieving anything, that they needed to identify the revolutionary class and join with it. Critics could—and did—say "I told you so" when SDS in Gitlin's phrase "slid into romance with the other side." But Gitlin argues that this "tendency" was "not the only one, not final or unopposed even in SDS," and that its significance was exaggerated by supporters of the war and by the media. The movement's "Third World turn" "began in McComb, Mississippi, and led to the Mekong Delta," Gitlin writes in a penetrating discussion of the problem. Young activists admired seemingly powerless people who were struggling to free themselves from opponents of immense evil and power. SDS started out recognizing their suffering and defending their right to rebel. In South Vietnam the NLF was the most popular force, the Vietnamese had compelling reasons to support it, and it represented in Gitlin's words "the least bad practical alternative for Vietnam"—on these points the New Left had a firmer grasp of the reality of the war than its critics. The Vietnamese resistance to American imperialism *was* heroic—like the Russian resistance to Hitler's invasion or the Spanish Republic's fight against fascism. The mistake for the New Left was to defend the North Vietnamese leaders and government uncritically.

The Other Side, Tom Hayden and Staughton Lynd's book about their trip to North Vietnam, provides the best example of the New Left's thinking in this regard. Lynd told Gitlin that he now regards it as "a poor book"; two years after writing it he concluded the North Vietnamese had lied to him when they told him they had no troops fighting in the South. Nevertheless Gitlin finds the book's "refusal to honor the standard cold war demonology touching, naive, and saddening." The Hanoi government was not committed to freedom; but that was not a reason to support the repressive Saigon government. Gitlin ends up agreeing with the conclusion of Lynd and Hayden's book: "If the United States is genuinely concerned to promote freedom for the North Vietnamese, it should stop bombing them."

Liberals see the assassination of Robert F. Kennedy in 1968 as the end to the chances that the sixties might have led to a positive conclusion. Gitlin is skeptical of this interpretation, recalling the Kennedy–McCarthy debate a week before the 1968 California primary: Kennedy implied that antiwar Senator Eugene McCarthy wanted to impose "coalition with the Communists" on the Saigon government; when McCarthy said he wanted to build public housing in the suburbs, Kennedy replied, "You say you are going to take ten thousand black people and move them into Orange County." This did not sound like a man who was about to transform American politics.

One of Gitlin's most striking personal recollections concerns Chicago during the 1968 demonstrations: fleeing from cops and tear gas in Grant Park one night, Gitlin found himself running with Jules Feiffer, a McCarthy delegate from New York; "I introduced myself, and we decided to run together." They took shelter in the Hilton cocktail lounge, where Studs Terkel and William Styron invited Feiffer and his friend for a drink. Gitlin guzzled a Bloody Mary, then ran back onto Michigan Avenue to continue the battle. Commitment to the struggle took precedence over networking with the intellectual big shots.

Gitlin's heyday in SDS was 1960–65; by 1967 he was out of college, cut off from the new SDS leadership, and increasingly despairing over the state of the movement. His account of the late sixties expresses that despair. But for younger people the most thrilling days were yet to come: for them 1968 was the beginning, and the mass student strike that followed the Kent State killings the most moving event they had ever seen. In the spring of 1969 alone, 300 universities and colleges, with a third of all American students, saw significant demonstrations. Other radicals of Gitlin's generation didn't share his despair: Paul Buhle, for instance, speaks for many when he writes in his new book *Marxism in the USA* that these "would be the best years of our lives."[6] Still, Gitlin's account of the political despair and nihilism of the late sixties makes those feelings comprehensible. The failure of SDS's Economic Research and Action Project to organize an interracial coalition of the poor; the irrelevance of participatory democracy in an imperial nation at war; the urgency of the moral task facing the antiwar movement, and the monumental obstacles to our success; the apparent lack of results for the largest political mobilization in the nation's

---

6. Paul Buhle, *Marxism in the USA: From 1870 to the Present Day* (London, 1987), p. 239.

history—all this led to a conclusion Gitlin himself drew in 1968: "The politics that makes sense to me now aims to stop this country, not change it; to help revolutionaries, not pretend to be them."

When he examines the late sixties, Gitlin's sense of proportion becomes skewed: a book titled *The Sixties* devotes less than a page to the October 15, 1969 moratorium in Washington, attended by half a million people; less than two pages to Woodstock, attended by half a million people—but it spends virtually a whole chapter on the Weather Underground. Gitlin obsessively chronicles their every move, demonstrating over and over the ways they embodied the worst of the movement. Yet he acknowledges that they had about a hundred people when they went underground. One might conclude that the activists of the day demonstrated admirable political sense in this virtually unanimous refusal to join the Weather Underground.

One of the greatest strengths of Gitlin's book is his examination of the relationship between political radicals and the counterculture. While the movement confronted illegitimate authority, using discipline and organization to try to change the world, communes and collectives sought to transform people here and now by putting new values into practice, "exuberant, fitful, and flawed attempts to live a new way of life." To his credit, Gitlin does not portray the two positions as necessarily contradictory; he shows the intersections and mutual influences, the efforts by activists on both sides to bring the two together.

The two strands of sixties radicalism came together in 1969 in Berkeley People's Park. Gitlin skillfully analyzes the significance of this battle that has always seemed peculiarly Californian to outsiders. The construction of a park on unused University of California land, he explains, broke down the divide that had separated straight from hip, student from non-student: People's Park "touched some deep hunger for a common life." Work there was "a joy, not a job. . . . On weekends up to 3,000 people a day came to carry sod, to plant, to install swings, to cook and eat huge vats of stew and soup, to play." Gitlin recalls the park as a bit of "anarchist heaven on earth." Then the Alameda County Sheriff's deputies showed up and opened fire with shotguns, keeping up their fire for several hours; at least fifty demonstrators were shot, one of whom died and another of whom was permanently blinded. "It was one thing to theorize about the university's commitment to its property," Gitlin writes, "but no one had anticipated shot-guns." After a night of fury, Governor Ronald Reagan sent 3,000 rifle-bearing National Guardsmen into Berkeley, declared a curfew, and prohibited public gatherings of more than three people. The sixties' deepest dreams and darkest fantasies came true at People's Park.

Alan Brinkley, reviewing Isserman and Miller in the *New York Review*, argued that "the seductive appeal of the counterculture under-mined the New Left far more effectively than its own political blunders." The New Left failed, he writes, because its members had always been searching for self-fulfillment, and found more immediate gratification in the counterculture.[7] In fact, the counterculture put into practice many of the key political values of the New Left. Gitlin shows how they did it: in institutions like underground newspapers, free schools, food co-ops and women's health groups. He reports that by 1973, for instance, radicals had created 800 free schools—which did provide self-fulfillment, but also took genuine commitment and hard work. These counter-institutions provided what Gitlin calls "ways of settling down for a long haul." In many ways this settling down was as successful as anything the politicos undertook: counter-institutions kept participatory democracy alive as a standard against which to criti-cize the work place, the state and the family. Gitlin's brief argument about the legacy of the counterculture is one of his most important contributions, and shows some of the ways the sixties transformed American society. Through the counterculture, "a loose anti-authori-tarianism was normalized"; the lives of women, gays and children were transformed.

What remains to be written about the sixties? These three authors have covered the history of the origins of the New Left from the late fifties through the Port Huron generation. We need to know about the middle sixties, when the New Left was a mass movement: a book arguing that the *real* sixties came after the Port Huron generation. We need to examine again the political problems the New Left faced: how to maintain a position that is independent and critical of undemocratic

---

7. Alan Brinkley, "Dreams of the Sixties," *New York Review*, October 22, 1987, pp. 10–16. Quote from p. 16.

governments like Hanoi's, while fighting to end America's imperialist interventions; how to balance militant tactics with an appeal to the undecided, how to turn outrage into organizing; how to understand what student radicals can accomplish in the absence of an adult left.

We need a book on the spread of participatory democracy beyond SDS, through the rest of the New Left, into the counterculture, to draft resistance groups, health clinics, law communes, free schools, feminist groups, underground newspapers, drug crisis centers, food co-ops—all tried their hand at direct democracy and rule by consensus. As Gitlin writes, "anthropologists declared their independence of the CIA, city planners consulted for community organizations, priests and nuns married, soldiers confronted officers, reporters confronted editors, patients confronted doctors, wives confronted husbands, children confronted parents." In each case we need to assess the failures, defeats and disasters as well as the achievements. The history of this broader process of democratization and assertion of rights during and after the sixties, which often had little to do with the organized left, is the next task facing historians of the sixties.

Radical History Review, Fall 1988

29

Chicago '68 Revisited

The historic confrontation between police and antiwar youth outside the 1968 Democratic National Convention in Chicago provided the climax to a year of radical student mobilization so massive that it is still dizzying to contemplate it. Students demonstrated against the war at a record two hundred colleges and universities, including Columbia in New York City. In the months before the convention, grassroots antiwar sentiment forced Lyndon Johnson to withdraw from his own reelection campaign. Then Martin Luther King was assassinated in Memphis, ghetto riots broke out in a dozen cities, including Chicago, and Robert Kennedy was assassinated in Los Angeles, ending liberal hopes for a successful antiwar candidacy.

In the midst of that tumultuous time, a small group of long-haired dope smokers in New York's East Village were dreaming up some truly radical political ideas. Giving themselves the name "Yippies," they sent out a call to all young people opposed to the war to come to Chicago in August for a "festival of life" outside the Democratic National Convention. Most of the organized antiwar movement opposed the Yippie plan as irresponsible and provocative. In terms of numbers, the demonstration turned out to be a flop; the Yippies had hoped for half a million people, but only 10,000 showed up.

It was the police riot that made the demonstrations historic. Mayor Richard Daley, last of the great thick-necked political bosses in America, put 12,000 police on twelve-hour shifts, had 12,000 more National Guardsmen and army troops called up, armed them with rifles, bazookas and flame throwers, and ordered them to shoot to kill. The cops beat not only demonstrators, but also bystanders, convention delegates and newsmen. It was all live on TV; viewers saw Hubert Humphrey win the nomination in a sea of blood. And when Senator Abraham Ribicoff of Connecticut took the convention podium to denounce Mayor Daley's use of "Gestapo tactics in the streets of Chicago," the Mayor yelled back, "Fuck you you Jew son of a bitch you lousy motherfucker go home!"

Instead of telling "the" story of the demonstrations, David Farber's book *Chicago '68*[1] tells three separate tales. He gives us the events as seen first by the Yippies, led by Abbie Hoffman and Jerry Rubin; then by "the Mobe"—the National Mobilization To End the War in Vietnam, headed by Dave Dellinger and Tom Hayden, which sought a more organized confrontation; and finally by Mayor Daley and the police. Farber thus shows that, in the streets outside the convention, three sharply different views of reality met head-on. But the author has also gone a step further, presenting each narrative in the voice of its central figures. Thus the Yippies' segments feature words like "rapping" and "goofing," while in the Mayor Daley chapters Farber writes about the need to "respond to provocations" with "firmness."

Farber is at his best explaining the much-maligned Yippies. They wanted to create forms of political expression that would convey more life and feeling than protest marches and picket signs. They had an optimistic confidence that young people could overcome America's ugliness and brutality. They brought the spirit of play to the world of politics. Tactically, they staged outrageous media stunts to expose the pretensions and dullness of routine politics.

In contrast, the Mobe argued that you had to organize, to bring the power of the people into a dramatic confrontation with the power of an unjust and oppressive state. The police, for their part, Farber explains, believed that they, not poor people or blacks, were—in the words of LA's police chief at the time—"the most downtrodden, oppressed minority in America." The head of the American Federation of Police explained that cops facing civil rights and antiwar demonstrators saw themselves "at war with an enemy just as dangerous as the Viet Cong in Southeast Asia."

In three concluding chapters of analysis, Farber praises the antiwar

1. David Farber, *Chicago '68* (Chicago: University of Chicago Press, 1988).

forces for their "courage and heart" while criticizing their "unworkable politics." What the nation got instead was Richard Nixon, who won the election by mobilizing what he called the "silent majority" of white people against the poor, the young and the black. That politics was eminently "workable"—it's still working for George Bush today, twenty years after Chicago '68.

LA Weekly, November 18–24, 1988

30

Black Social Experience and

Radical Politics in Alabama

All God's Dangers: the Life of Nate Shaw is the autobiography of an illiterate black tenant farmer who was "much of a man."[1] Nate Shaw was eighty-four years old when he spent several months telling his life's story to Theodore Rosengarten, a young white radical from the North. The central event in Shaw's life was an act of political resistance during the Depression: he and several other members of the Alabama Share-croppers Union had a shootout with local sheriffs. While his family and community do not like him to talk about his political past, the shootout still dominates Shaw's conception of himself; with Rosengarten, he set himself the task of justifying and explaining how it came to be that "on a Monday evenin, in December of '32," his Smith and Wesson revolver "squalled like a wildcat," forcing the sheriffs' deputies to "outrun the devil away from there." The explanation becomes the story of Shaw's life: put to work in the fields when he was nine years old, becoming an independent small property-owner through his own determination and strength, suffering oppression and injustice, fighting back, serving twelve years in prison, and returning to a changed world. "I got so much to tell," he says, and this book is the result.

The critical praise for *All God's Dangers* has focused on Nate Shaw as a heroic black person. Few have examined the social basis of his deter-mination to resist, or the political ideas with which he explained and justified his action. The value of the book lies not only in the discovery

---

1. Theodore Rosengarten, *All God's Dangers: the Life of Nate Shaw* (New York: Knopf, 1974).

of an authentic black hero, but also in what it suggests about the ways in which a particular social experience shaped a political consciousness that was not unique to Shaw, but rather one which has been characteristic of people in Shaw's position in Europe as well as America—the non-Marxist radical populism of small property-holders.

Unlike the great majority of his black neighbors, Shaw accumulated a considerable amount of property, which gave him relatively more independence from the local white ruling class of planters and merchants. The first half of the book is the story of young Shaw's systematic triumphs over injustice and adversity; they turned him from a propertyless sharecropper into a prosperous farmer who had "got as high as four head of stock and a two-horse wagon and a rubber-tire buggy. I was prosperin," he tells us. His first year on his own he raised five bales of cotton; his second, six; and his third, "good God I made eight bales of cotton.... I was saving myself a little money at the end of each year, getting a footin to where I wouldn't have to ask nobody for nothin."

Economic independence was Shaw's goal—to be independent of white planters and merchants, to own his own means of production (although he did not express it in that phrase). The first moment of his rise he identifies as the purchase of his own mule: "I came up from the bottom then," he says. The ownership of a mule made it possible to stop sharecropping and start renting, which freed Shaw from the close supervision landlords gave to sharecroppers. As a sharecropper, he bitterly resented his landlord saying, "you ain't got sense enough to know this, you ain't got sense enough to know nothin.... I got my own way of doin, but he calls it ignorant and disobeyin his orders." As a renter, "I planted and worked what I wanted to," Shaw says.

He describes in great detail and with great pleasure his accumulation of farm equipment—replacing his Boy Dixie brand "old timey weak plow" with a new Oliver Goober iron-beam plow, which "stood up with big mules and cut deep." But it was not just ownership of draft animals and tools that was crucial to economic independence. Shaw says it simply: "You had to have land." Thus he struggled to acquire his own fertile farmland, to get off the "little old rocky-assed rough places" landlords assigned to blacks, and it was this struggle for land ownership that was to culminate in the shootout.

Shaw tells us not only about the purchase of farm equipment, but about the acquisition of household goods, of which he recalls both the price and the brand name: his Wetter's cooking stove, which cost $50 just after World War One; the sewing machine and record player he bought for his wife for $67; his "dinin safe" (which held dishes), which cost $13; and the object of great pride, his Dixie brand rubber-tire buggy, for which he recalls he paid $187.50.

But this buggy too was only a step: "I was climbin up in the world like a boy climbin a tree." He became one of the first blacks in his part of Alabama to buy an automobile—a new 1926 Ford—and was among the first to need a two-car garage when he bought a 1928 Chevrolet. Shaw is somewhat defensive about having been the only black in his community with a new car in 1926. "I didn't buy that car to try and get bigger than nobody else. I didn't buy it to show myself rich—I weren't rich. I bought it to serve my family and I knowed I was entitled to anything I wanted if I had the means to get it." Here Shaw is unconvincing. He chose to become the only black with a new car in 1926 not just to provide transportation for his family, but to indicate to his neighbors his status as a prosperous man. The importance Shaw assigns to all these goods was apparently perceived by his black neighbors, one of whom, we learn, accused Shaw of "worshipping" his own property. Shaw interprets this as an expression of resentment and jealousy by a less successful farmer, but the incident suggests that Shaw's status as a man of property, which has been emphasized here, was clearly evident to his community.

Shaw's relative economic independence was a consequence not so much of his success as a cotton farmer as of his prosperity in other activities. Like his father before him, he hauled logs for the lumber company, the income from which he invested in his farm. Lumber hauling itself offered a degree of freedom from the oppressiveness of landlord–tenant relations. As he explains, "If the sun got too hot I'd set down if I wanted to. Nobody to tell me not to." Indeed, planters objected to blacks' hauling lumber for this reason. The *Mobile Daily Register*, most authoritative voice of planter interests in the state, complained as early as 1883 that declining plantation profits were caused by blacks who "have abandoned working in the fields and haul wood for a living.... It is this thriftlessness, this want of energy that makes the problem of labor so difficult to solve in the South." This planter lament described Shaw's father better than Shaw himself, while

Shaw invested his income from timber hauling in his farm, his father combined work in the lumber industry with hunting and fishing in a way that made it possible for him to escape labor in the cotton fields (although he did insist that his wife and children work there).

Shaw found intrinsic pleasure in lumber hauling: "I loved that work.... If that lumber was good lumber, it was a pleasure to load—it'd load smooth and it had a nice scent. It waked you up to haul that lumber." But he insists that, however much he enjoyed the work and the relative freedom of lumber hauling, "I absolutely had my heart in farming." He hauled lumber only to make money to invest in his farm.

Shaw also made extra money as a peddler. For several years he drove his wagon into town once a week to sell "milk, nice homemade butter, sometimes syrup, eggs, vegetables too.... Winter, I'd load up stove wood, cut, cured, and dried, sell it in person." But he emphasizes again that this work was a supplement rather than an alternative to farming: "I never did love a sellin job but I could get somethin out of it ... so I done it. I was a cotton farmer." While he prefered farming to selling, he prefered not to grow cotton: "If I could have made a livin raisin vegetables and corn crops ... I'd a let the cotton alone. But I just couldn't realize it." Indeed, Shaw takes greatest pleasure not in recalling his cotton crops, but in his other agricultural pursuits: "I raised big crops of peas, old unknown peas, speckled peas, and a pea they call the iron pea, that was the heaviest weight pea I ever used ... them iron peas was the top peas of all. They was just a little old clay-colored pea. I raised my own honey.... Mostly these bees I had was this Italian bee, big yellow bee. I also had these little old black bees, call him the swamp bee.... Italian bee is a quieter bee than a black bee; swamp bee, that's a ill little devil." The obstacles to full-time vegetable farming, as he describes them, came from a racist marketing system which restricted blacks to growing cotton. "They had a little rule—the white people cut the colored people clean out of sellin fruits and vegetables."

In addition to hauling lumber and peddling, Shaw made money by making baskets, a craft he learned from his father. "Basketmakin is a special labor with me," he explains. "I can make any kind of basket, most you want to see—fish basket, feed basket, clothes basket, market basket, cotton basket, any sort of basket in reason." His profits from basketmaking paid for his first buggy in 1907, and he continued to make baskets while talking to Rosengarten in 1971.

In explaining his success at accumulating small property, Shaw emphasizes the importance of his using time efficiently. "You got to get out there and hustle and watch the time, be on time the first time.... Some folks don't use the time God gives em; that's why they're liable to come up defeated." This Franklinesque argument can only be considered an expression of a classically bourgeois sense of time.

Shaw describes with acute insight those blacks who did not gradually accumulate property as he did: he sees them as suffering from the legacy of slavery, which "taught the colored man to take what come and live for today." Such a man "didn't look ahead to profit himself in nothin he done. Is it or not a old slave act?" For Shaw, genuine emancipation means self-discipline, the denial of immediate gratification in favor of the accumulation of property—an orientation Max Weber described as the "Protestant ethic" and Freud approvingly called the "reality principle." But Shaw also found pleasure in the sensuous reality of an abundant land; he, like many entrepreneurs in other situations, does not fit the ascetic bourgeois Puritanism Weber and Freud identified:

My daddy would catch fish, great God almighty. Catch em in baskets, two or three baskets.... And he'd get some steel traps and go down to the creek—trap eels. Fish, eels, wild turkeys, wild ducks, possums, coons, beavers, squirrels.... But he wouldn't shoot a rabbit ... just didn't fancy rabbits out of all the beasts of the forests and fields....

I didn't never want for no vegetables, what I had I growed em. Okra, anything from okra up and down—collards, tomatoes, red cabbages, hard-headed cabbages, squash, beans, turnips, sweet potatoes, ice potatoes, onions, radishes, cucumbers—anythin for vegetables. And fruits, fruits for eatin purposes and cookin, pies, preserves—apples, peaches, plums, water-melons, cantaloupes, muskmelons ... cut em open and scrape the seed out of em, sprinkle if you like a little salt over em. Sometimes I've seen people sprinkle a little black pepper too....

Cheese would grease the paper wrapper through and through. Real cheese, crumbly cheese, cheese with a hole through the center, sharp cheese, mild cheese....

I went out and dug a well ... a good well of water, cold, clear, no wiggle-tails.

Similarly, he regarded his mules with an enthusiasm and affection that would have been inappropriate for a stereotypical Puritanical bourgeois: "The first we ever called our own," he recalls, was "that Lu mule." Silas was "fractious ... it didn't do to play with him, just treat him nice like you treat a person." Old Haggard was a "scoundrel", "my Mattie mule" was "just as pretty as a peeled onion," "that Mary mule ... was the devil on hinges ... but she was as good a workin mule as ever was hitched up.... O, she was a piss ripper"; Vernon's mule was "a stinkin good mule but she was one of those wild rattlers"; and his last one was "that Kizzie mule": "when I got to where I couldn't put in a day's plowing ... I'd sit down on my plow many a time, and she'd stand there. She understood." Shaw sums up: "O, my mules just granted me all the pleasure I needed, to see what I had and how they moved."

For Shaw, the pleasure he took in his property and his appreciation of the abundance of the land merged into an unselfconscious picture of the good life, expressed in a memorable image: "the limbs of that plum tree would just lean over with great big purple plums.... O, it was a beautiful tree, right to the northwest of my car-shed, two-car shed; had that '26 Ford and that '28 Chevrolet stationed close to that plum tree."

While Shaw is proud to describe himself as a relatively independent man of property, he makes two crucial distinctions. First, he sees himself as a man of small property, to be distinguished sharply from big property holders. "I wanted to boss my own affairs," he says, "but I never did let it hit me to want to be a big man, ownin this, that, and the other." Second, he sees himself as a worker, not a propertied man of leisure. "I was a workin man; whatever I had, it come to me through my labor", "this whole country knowed me for my work." When he was told he worked too hard, "that fretted me.... I said, 'I got to work. I'm born to work.'" At eighty-four years, too weak to plow, Shaw says, "I'm yet a laborin man; I makes baskets." These two social distinctions are the key to his political world view, which is radical and populist rather than class-oriented. As a small-propertied working man, Shaw favors an alliance of people like himself with propertyless workers against the rich and powerful, a position which must be distinguished from the Marxist strategy in which the propertyless are to unite against the propertied. Shaw sees the political world not as a class conflict, but rather as a struggle of "little people" of different classes against the "big man." "Who is the backbone of the world? It's the laborin man, it's the laborin man. My God, the big man been on him with both foots all these years and now don't want to get off him. I found out all of that because they tried to take I don't know what all away from me." The radical and populist politics that formed the basis for his political resistance identify him not as a unique or isolated hero, but as a characteristic independent small-holding radical. Shaw is a late representative of a non-Marxist political tradition that forms the basis of radical social movements in America and Europe in the nineteenth century; it finds its origins in the seventeenth-century Diggers and the eighteenth-century Jacobins.

Shaw at last took the giant step upward from renter to landowner around 1930, but "in the windup of it, big trouble come off—a shootin frolic in '32." He purchased an eighty-acre farm and was making payments on it, when a former landlord somehow acquired full title to it; "to this day I don't know how he did it." The former landlord was bitter about Shaw becoming a proprietor. "Whenever the colored man prospered too fast in this country ... they worked every figure to cut you down, cut your britches off you." Shaw was told in 1931 that the former landlord was "goin to take all you got this fall, and all old Virgil Jones got." When the landlord sent the sheriffs to foreclose on Virgil Jones' livestock, Shaw knew he was next. Thus it was his new status as a landowner that provoked the threats to himself and his property, to which he responded with force.

Shaw based his forceful defense of small property on what can only be called a labor theory of value. "I have sowed my labor into the earth and lived to reap only a part of it, not all that was mine by human right.... I stays on because its mine." Thus, he explains, "I stood up against this southern way of life. Can you call that a crime? Can *I* call it a crime?" But the defense of his property was not a solitary act; Shaw stood up to the sheriffs as a member of a group. "Durin of the pressure years, a union began to operate in this country, called it the Share-croppers Union," he says; "I was eager for it, eager." Characteristically, he joined when a white neighbor, "as big a skunk as ever sneaked in the woods," told him not to. He was also advised not to join by "some of my color who was weak, if I must say so, as goat shit."

The book's material on the Sharecroppers Union alone makes it an invaluable work. At Shaw describes it, the union held secret meetings

253

which were attended by around a dozen blacks and at which political discussions were led by an organizer Shaw refers to as "the teacher of this organization" and "the travelin man," "a colored fella—I disremember his name" who "had a different way of talking than we did"—who talked of the right to organize, of stool pigeons and Uncle Toms. The union, as Shaw saw it, "was workin to bring us out of the bad places where ... we been standin since the colored people has remembrance." The members agreed that they were "tired, tired of that way of life," and that "if we didn't do something for ourselves today, tomorrow wouldn't be no different." But "they didn't say to us how this was goin to happen," and "we didn't have time to work up a plan."

Shaw says it was only at his trial that he heard the Sharecroppers Union was associated with the Communist Party. "There's a secret in this union somewhere and I ain't never understood it ... that this union came from across the waters, and they called it a 'soviet union.'" But Shaw has no sense of having been deceived or misled by the CP policy of not revealing the party membership of organizers to members of front groups; Red-baiting is simply incomprehensible to him. It is also possible that Shaw knows more than he is letting on; could it be that a man who in the course of the book recalls the names of over 400 people would "disremember" the union organizer?

So, when a group of armed union members guarding a comrade's farm heard the cry, "yonder they come, yonder come the officers," Shaw decided that "somebody got to stand up" and that he would be the one. He emphasizes that he did not start the shooting; his tactic, learned at union meetings, was to "act humble, and be straight." But when Shaw "politely" told the sheriff, who had come to confiscate the livestock, that "he weren't goin to do it," the sheriff "got hot" and summoned reinforcements. They were told, "there stands Nate Shaw," and one shot him from behind with buckshot. Only then did he use his own gun. Four or five of his union comrades were armed nearby in a barn, including Shaw's brother-in-law, Little Waldo Ramsey; he also fired. The sound of his gunshots and the sight of the fleeing deputies are the most powerful images in Nate Shaw's memory—the time when "that .32 Smith and Wesson was barkin too much for em to stand," that moment of power and righteous retaliation for a lifetime of injustice and oppression.

The moment was brief. Shaw was taken secretly to the hospital at Tuskegee, and then hid out at a cousin's while a white mob shot up his house, hitting his daughter, and forcing his son to reveal his hiding place. When the sheriffs came to get him, another gunfight broke out with his brother-in-law, Little Waldo, who was shot three times and also captured.

In Jail, Shaw was visited by two representatives of the CP's International Labor Defense, and a white defense lawyer appeared, who said, " 'Shaw, you the best man we got, we goin to stick with you.' " Again, Shaw is unclear about the CP's relationship to his defense: the lawyer and ILD representatives "was concerned for this union, but I can't definitely say how they was connected." Shaw does not indicate that he was aware he was in the headlines of the *Daily Worker* during these weeks. After his conviction at a one-day trial, the defense group, which Shaw refers to as "my northern friends," sent him five dollars a month for the entire twelve years he was in prison, plus a big box of candy and fruitcake every Christmas. The CP takes care of its own, even though they may not know they are its own.

The title Rosengarten has chosen emphasizes the nonracist character of Shaw's politics: "All God's dangers ain't a white man" is Shaw's statement. He is careful to include poor whites along with blacks as fellow victims of the white ruling class: "the poor white man and the poor black man is sittin in the same saddle today ... the controllin power is all in the hands of the rich man." "The poor white men ... didn't have no more voice than a cat against the big man of their own color." The union sought an interracial alliance of the poor: it was "sworn to stand up for all the poor colored farmers, and the poor white farmers if they'd taken a notion to join." Apparently they did not. At the same time, Shaw argues that those who exploit black people are exclusively white: "the white man ... the bosses and the moneyed cats, as long as I ever knowed, has been takin the niggers' labor." It is because the ruling class is white that Shaw says the union sought to "push the white man back" and that blacks should not "leave the possession and use of the earth to the white man." And he recognizes the superexploitation of blacks: "a white man always wants a nigger in preference to a white man to work on his place. How come that? How come it for God's sake? ... He gets a nigger, he can do that nigger just like he wants to and that nigger better not say nothin against his rulins."

Yet Shaw feels uneasy with his call for an interracial alliance of the poor. "I know all about the rich white man," he says, "but I don't know how to take poor white people. There's some of em won't stand a nigger at all, and there's some that will go with him to an extent.... But I just can't loosen up to em; I can't lead em in the lights of nothin." Still, he reports with pleasure that a white neighbor said to him about the shootout, "'You done right, Mr Shaw, you done right,'" adding, "'Don't tell nobody that I come to see you.'"

The book is a valuable source on the structure of tenancy. Shaw describes four different systems of financing the cotton crop. Worst from the tenants' point of view, he says, was for the tenant to obtain merchandise on credit from the landlord. Better than that was for the tenant to borrow cash from the landlord, "clear cash money so I knowed exactly how much I was receivin and how much interest he was makin off me." "If the landlord advanced cash, usually the tenant was allowed to shop with the man of my choice," which was not the case if the landlord set up a line of credit with a particular merchant. Better than borrowing cash from the landlord was to borrow cash from the bank, because "when you pay back [the bank loan] and the interest on it, you was clear and loose." And the best system Shaw ever worked under was when the federal government took over financing the cotton crop during the Depression with low interest loans to tenants.

Shaw does not challenge the institution of sharecropping or the crop-lien system. He concedes the property rights of the planters. But he does raise questions about the proper division of the crop:

> It's right for me to pay you for usin what's yours—your land, stock, plow tools, fertilizer. But how much should I pay? The answer ought to be closely seeked. How much is a man due to pay out? Half the crop? A third part of the crop? And how much is he due to keep for hisself? You got a right to your part—rent, and I got a right to mine. But who's the man to decide how much? The man that owns the property or the one that worked it?

Shaw does not answer these questions; perhaps they are rhetorical.

He bitterly points out the racial injustices that accompany share-cropping. A landlord murdered a black tenant who challenged the landlord's accounting, whites were paid more than Shaw was for the same cotton, guano dealers refused to sell to him when his landlord told them not to, and white men's cows were allowed to forage in black men's corn. But despite these injustices, Shaw insists that the black farmer should not leave the rural South. Shaw understands about the black who leaves that sharecropping "was his bondage and he turnin away from it," but, by going north and looking for industrial work, "he leavin the possession and use of the earth to the white man," which Shaw thinks is a tragic mistake.

Along with the discussion of tenancy come descriptions of agricultural and craft activities that are of great historical value. There are eight pages describing how the cotton fields were plowed, planted and picked at the turn of the century; Shaw also describes how wood and iron beam plows were used, how logs were hauled with a six-steer team, how crossties were cut, how ax handles were made, how mules were hitched, and how double-barrelled muzzle-loaders were loaded.

All God's Dangers is packed with material on the black family. Shaw's was not an extended family, but a nuclear one with both parents present, along with nine children and a motherless nephew. This was a society in which women frequently died in childbirth, so there were many remarried men, and children raised by people other than their natural mothers. Shaw's own father remarried twice, giving Shaw lots of half-siblings. His sister died in childbirth, leaving two sons with their maternal grandparents and a third with Shaw, his uncle.

There seem to have been a considerable number of illegitimate children whose fathers were generally known in the community. Shaw identifies some of his neighbors as illegitimate half-siblings of his, children of his father and an "outside woman"; he reports the remarkable fact that "my own dear mother's brother married one of my outside sisters." He himself admits "maybe I've had contact with other women, but not many, not many," and he denies that he fathered any illegitimate children. The resulting kinship networks are complex. "This thing's mixed up but it ain't mixed up to where you can't look through it," he says. He himself is his "stepmother's brother's son-in-law," and his second wife Josie is his brother Peter's first cousin by marriage:

Josie's mother was a Butterfield and Peter's wife's daddy was a Butterfield. Peter's wife's daddy was Josie's mother's brother. Little Amos Butterfield, named for *his* daddy, and Mary Butterfield was brother and sister. And Mary Butterfield was a Mary Travis after she married Simon Travis. And Mary was Josie's mother.... Every time I'd go to Apafalya I'd see some of them Butterfields and some of them Travises.

This then is a world of half-siblings, step-siblings, and "outside" siblings, of complex kinship relations which, however incomprehensible they might seem to us, are fully explicable to the members of this community, or at least to Shaw.

The picture Shaw draws of his own father is unsparing. He beat his wife and children, took food from their plates, and forced them to work in the fields while he spent his days in the woods hunting; instead of sending his children to school, he put them to work for neighbors, and then spent their wages; he liked other women and shamelessly fathered "outside children." Shaw explains all this as "an old slave act ... he took what come and lived for today."

Shaw was as good a husband and father as his own father was bad. He is emphatic about the role his wife played in their household—Hannah, his "heartthrob of a girl" who was "a whole person," with whom he lived for forty years, "and that weren't enough for me." "I didn't expect her to show herself in the field," he says, and "I didn't allow her to go about washing for white folks." Her place was "at the house cookin and correctin the children or doin her other house duty." Here again is a "bourgeois" element in Shaw's position—his wife is a housewife who does not work outside the home. But there were some unusual features to this relationship: she had her own cotton patch, which he worked; after he picked and sold the cotton, he gave her the money it brought in, so that she had money of her own. Because she was literate—she could "read like a top"—and he was not, she participated in the crucial financial transactions, and Shaw reports with pride the occasion at the bank when she found a fraudulent clause in a mortgage contract that he was supposed to sign.

Why did Nate Shaw, the 84-year-old black sharecropper, tell his story to Rosengarten, the white boy from Massachusetts? Shaw gives us a hint when, discussing the 1932 shootout, he complains of his sons, "I have never had one of em even walk up to me and hold a hearty conversation in regards to this business.... Ain't a one of em ever put his arm around me and said, 'Papa, I'm proud of you for joinin the union and doin what you done.'" Regarding his own role, Rosengarten explains in his introduction, "Nate Shaw was—and is—a hero to me.... My questions unavoidably expressed this judgment." In Rosengarten, then, Shaw found the politically sympathetic young listener he could not find elsewhere. Thus the book comes to us at a great cost: the political isolation of Nate Shaw from his family and community.

On the other hand, Shaw was familiar with white northern radicals and had good reason to regard them as sympathetic comrades. As Rosengarten says, "it didn't surprise him to see us now because this was his movement ... he had been active in it before we were born." Perhaps now Nate Shaw's story will take its rightful place in his own community, thanks to Rosengarten, who has made it possible to "let the truth roll."

Journal of Social History, 1976

PART V

Heroes, Villains, and Others

31

When Old Blue Eyes was Red

I remember a Sinatra who didn't pal around with rich Republicans. During the early 1950s, at my Sunday school in St Paul, Minnesota, one of the highlights of the year was the annual screening of *The House I Live In*, a short film starring a young and skinny Sinatra. In it, he told a gang of kids that racial and religious differences "make no difference except to a Nazi or somebody who's stupid." He sang about "The people that I work with / The workers that I meet.... The right to speak my mind out / That's America to me." *The House I Live In*, made at the peak of Sinatra's popularity, won him a special Academy Award in 1945. Four years later his career was in ruins, in the wake of charges that he was tied to both the Mafia and the Communists. Forty years later his career is legend, his politics solidly conservative.

At first glance Sinatra's political odyssey from left to right seems to have followed a well-trod path. "Maturity" has been defined by figures as different as John dos Passos and Jerry Rubin as the abandonment of youthful ideals. But Sinatra's case is different. Beaten down as an activist leftist, his career destroyed by the right-wing press, he made a stunning comeback, then found himself snubbed and abused by the liberals whose views he shared. Only then did he sign up with his old right-wing enemies.

The House I Live In was a turning point. The *Cumulative Index to Publications of the Committee on Un-American Activities* (HUAC), a handy list of everyone named as a Communist in twenty years of committee hearings, indicates that in the eight years following *The House I Live In* Sinatra was named twelve times. The *New York Times Index* for 1949 contains a single stunning cross-reference: "Sinatra, Frank: *See* US—

Espionage." Sinatra reportedly denied the reports that he "followed or appeased some of the CP [Communist Party] line program over a long period of time." But once the allegations had been made, his image in the press changed dramatically. He was first linked to the Mafia in a February 1947 gossip column that reported he had been seen in Havana with mobster Lucky Luciano and other "scum" and "goons" who "find the south salubrious in the winter, or grand-jury time." The columnist's source, and the source of many subsequent Mafia–Sinatra stories, turns out to have been Harry Anslinger, a crony of J. Edgar Hoover. Anslinger served as head of the federal narcotics bureau and was out to get Sinatra because he was a "pink."

"Frank's big nosedive," as the pundits called it, began on April 8, 1947. That was the night he punched Hearst gossip columnist Lee Mortimer at Ciro's celebrated Hollywood night spot. The Hearst papers went wild, running whole pages on the incident, repeating the Mafia story and HUAC charges. "Sinatra Faces Probe on Red Ties," a headline read. Soon gossip titans Hedda Hopper, Louella Parsons and Dorothy Kilgallen were heaping abuse on him. Overnight Sinatra was transformed by the right-wing press from the crooning idol of bobby-soxers into a violent, left-wing Mafioso. Sinatra said he punched Mortimer because the columnist called him a "dago." In fact Mortimer had been calling him some other things in print. He wrote about what he called "the crooner's penchant for veering to portside" and reminded readers that Sinatra had been named in HUAC testimony as "one of Hollywood's leading travelers on the road of Red Fascism." Mortimer, nephew of the editor of the Hearst-owned New York *Mirror*, pledged that "this column will continue to fight the promotion of class struggle or foreign isms posing as entertainment"—like *The House I Live In.*

How pink had Sinatra been? HUAC's sources were pretty disreputable. The first to name him was Gerald L.K. Smith, a raucous native fascist. In 1946 he told the committee that Sinatra "has been doing some pretty clever stuff for the Reds." Sinatra was named again in HUAC testimony in 1947 by Walter S. Steele, a private Red-hunter who had once accused Campfire Girls (a scouting organization) of being "Communistic." Jack B. Tenney, a California state senator who headed a state version of HUAC, reported in 1947 that Sinatra had taken part in a dinner sponsored by American Youth for Democracy, which J. Edgar Hoover had declared a Communist front.

Between *The House I Live In* in 1945 and the big 1947 HUAC hearings, Sinatra had in fact moved much closer to organized left-wing political activity. In 1943, when riots broke out in Harlem, he went uptown to speak at two integrated high school assemblies, urging the kids to "act as neighborhood emissaries of racial goodwill toward younger pupils and among friends." Shortly after, when white students in Gary, Indiana, boycotted classes at their newly integrated high school, Sinatra spoke in the school auditorium and sang "The House I Live In." What other star at the top of the charts had thrown himself into the civil rights struggle so directly? In May 1946 Sinatra issued what *Billboard* called "an anti-Franco blast." The statement was remarkable for two reasons. First, the only people who still remembered the support that Spain's dictator received from Hitler and Mussolini were real leftists. And second, there was Sinatra's Catholic background. The comment caused the Catholic *Standard and Times* of Philadelphia to label him a "pawn of fellow-travellers."

Sinatra moved closer to the Communist Party in July 1946, when he served as vice president of the Hollywood Independent Citizens Committee of the Arts, Sciences and Professions. Known by its asthmatic acronym, HICCASP had been a broad coalition of pro-Roosevelt liberals and leftists, ranging from Thomas Mann to Rita Hayworth. Sinatra became an officer during a faction fight in which Communists pushed liberals out of the organization and steered it toward Henry Wallace's left-wing challenge to Truman in 1948. Sinatra wrote an open letter in *The New Republic* to Wallace at the beginning of 1947, calling on him to "take up the fight we like to think of as ours—the fight for tolerance, which is the basis of any fight for peace." Within three months headlines appeared linking him to the Communists. A month later he was fired from his radio show; six months after that his New York concerts flopped. Soon his personal life was falling apart as fast as his career. By December 1949 his affair with Ava Gardner had become an open scandal. Columbia Records was trying to get back the advance they had given him. In 1950 he was released from his MGM film contract, and his own agent, MCA, dropped him. He was a has-been at thirty-four.

After Sinatra's stunning 1953 comeback in *From Here to Eternity*, he remained a Democrat. He sang "The House I Live In" at the Hollywood

Palladium at a 1956 campaign salute to Adlai Stevenson. He returned to the political wars with new energy during the spring of 1960. He had two projects that season: working for the Kennedy campaign (Sinatra's version of "High Hopes" was the official Kennedy campaign song) and breaking the Hollywood blacklist that had barred left-wingers from working in the movies ever since the 1947 HUAC investigations.

The second project was announced shortly after Kennedy won the New Hampshire primary. The *New York Times* headline read, "Sinatra Defies Writer Blackist/Hires Albert Maltz for his job filming of 'The Execution of Private Slovik.'" Maltz had written *The House I Live In. The Execution of Private Slovik,* a recently published novel, told the story of the World War Two GI who became the only American since the Civil War to be executed for desertion. "This marks the first time that a top movie star has defied the rule laid down by the major movie studios" thirteen years earlier, the *New York Times* explained. Sinatra would produce, Robert Parish was to direct. Slovik would be played by a TV tough guy named Steve McQueen.

Sinatra, asked if he was fearful of the reaction to hiring a blacklisted writer, had a defiant, I-told-you-so response. He quoted his own 1947 statement criticizing HUAC's witch-hunt: "Once they get the movies throttled, how long will it be before the committee gets to work on freedom of the air? ... If you make a pitch on a nationwide radio network for a square deal for the underdog, will they call you a commie?" A square deal for the underdog seemed to be exactly what Sinatra was after—for underdog Maltz, who served time in a federal penitentiary for refusing to name names, and also for Slovik. According to director Parish, Sinatra regarded Slovik not just as a victim of an unjust system of military justice, but as "the champ underdog of all time."

"They're calling you a fucking Communist!" Harry Cohn, king of Paramount Pictures, shouted at Sinatra. The attack had come, predictably, from Sinatra's old enemies in the Hearst press. Editorial writers for the New York *Mirror* reminded readers that the guy who just hired a Red had once had a "'romance' with a dame to whom he was not then married." (Sinatra must have murmured, "Hey, that was no dame, that was Ava Gardner!")

John Wayne found Sinatra's Achilles heel. Asked for his opinion on Sinatra's hiring of Maltz, Duke said, "I don't think my opinion is too important. Why don't you ask Sinatra's crony, who's going to run our country for the next few years, what *he* thinks of it?" Sinatra responded with "A Statement of Fact," for which he bought space in the *New York Times*. In it, he declared that connecting candidate Kennedy to his decision to hire Maltz was "hitting below the belt. I make movies. I do not ask the advice of Sen. Kennedy on whom I should hire.... I have, in my opinion, hired the best man for the job." Just as the controversy seemed to be dying down, the Hearst papers ran the banner headline: "Sinatra Fires Maltz." The *New York Times* and the trades contained a new ad signed by Sinatra, headlined simply "Statement": "Mr Maltz had ... an affirmative, pro-American approach to the story. But the American public has indicated it feels the morality of hiring Albert Maltz is the more crucial matter, and I will accept this majority opinion."

In an interview shortly before his death in 1985, Maltz recalled the incident. "Sinatra threw down the gauntlet against the blacklist," he said. "He was prepared to fight. His eyes were open. The ad firing me was ridiculous. The American people had not spoken; only the Hearst press and the American Legion had. Something had come from behind that caused him to change his position."

Maltz brought out his scrapbooks. Among hundreds of faded clippings was one from Dorothy Kilgallen's gossip column. "The real credit belongs to former Ambassador Joseph P. Kennedy," she wrote. "Unquestionably anticommunist, Dad Kennedy would have invited Frank to jump off the Jack Kennedy presidential bandwagon if he hadn't unloaded Mr Maltz." Kennedy's campaign advisers worried also about Sinatra's Mafia aura and expressed the hope that the singer would keep his distance from the senator. But, the advisers said, they hoped Sinatra would help with a voter drive in Harlem, "where he is recognized as a hero of the cause of the Negro."

After the election, JFK asked Sinatra to organize and star in his inaugural gala. The singer proudly escorted Jackie, but Jack was the one he cared about. In a gesture of classic macho deference, Sinatra offered to share a prize girlfriend, Judith Campbell Exner, with the president. Kennedy liked the idea and began an affair with Exner. (Sinatra's hit that year, appropriately enough, was "All the Way.") Then Sinatra went too far; he introduced Exner to Chicago Mob leader Sam Giancana.

J. Edgar Hoover's ever-present eyes and ears quickly discovered the liaisions. Bobby Kennedy, in the middle of a campaign to crush the Mafia, put a stop to his brother's involvement with Exner. The Kennedys had been planning to stay with Sinatra in Palm Springs. He'd remodeled his house in anticipation of the presidential visit. At the last minute, JFK announced they'd stay instead with Bing Crosby—who wasn't even a Democrat. To the public, it was an inexplicable snub.

Sinatra always was, as *Village Voice* jazz critic Gary Giddins has put it, "a virtuoso at storing wounds." He got even with Bobby in the 1968 California primary by supporting Humphrey. Then he discovered the Humphrey campaign had the same reservations that the Kennedy campaign had had, and he quietly left. As youth culture flowered in 1966, Sinatra married Mia Farrow; he'd just finished an album he called *September of My Years*. He was fifty-one, she was twenty-one, five years younger than his daughter Nancy. A sixties rebel, Mia cut her hair short and wore pants, and opposed the Vietnam War. Sinatra's friends explained the attraction: "He digs her brain." Soon, however, she was denouncing him and his pals: "All they know how to do is tell dirty stories, break furniture, pinch waitresses' asses and bet on the horses," she said. She left him to join the Beatles in India, meditating with the Maharishi.

Sinatra announced his retirement in 1971. "The principal activity of his retirement years," *New York Times* music critic John Rockwell has written, "was his political shift from left to right." The key moment seems to have come when the House crime committee held a new investigation of Sinatra's Mob ties in 1972. The committee was headed by Democrats including California senator John Tunney, an old Kennedy friend for whom Sinatra had raised $160,000 with a special show. The main evidence against him was the testimony of a confessed hit man who said that a New England Mafia boss had boasted that Sinatra was "fronting" for him as part owner to two resort hotels. The committee called Sinatra. "That's all hearsay evidence, isn't it?" Sinatra asked. "Yes, it is," the committee counsel admitted.

Always a public man, Sinatra explained the shift in his political thinking in a *New York Times* Op-Ed piece he wrote just after he appeared before the committee. His old politics of standing up for the little guy had been altered. Now he embraced the right-wing populism that defined the principal oppressor of the little guy as big government. And he saw his subpoena as a prime example of government oppressing a little guy. Sinatra became a Reagan Republican. "It didn't gall him as much as he had thought it would," reported columnist Earl Wilson.

His turn to the right coincided with a deepened contempt for women and his most offensive public behavior ever. At a pre-inaugural party in 1973, he shouted at *Washington Post* columnist Maxine Cheshire, "Get away from me, you scum. Go home and take a bath. ... You're nothing but a two-dollar cunt. You know what that means, don't you? You've been laying down for two dollars all your life." He then stuffed two dollar bills in her drink, saying, "Here's two dollars, baby, that's what you're used to." He made that kind of language part of his concert routine for several months, to the evident enjoyment of his new right-wing following.

President Nixon invited him to perform in the White House in 1973—something the Democrats had never done. He sang "The House I Live In." Twenty-eight years earlier, he had sung it for students at newly integrated high schools. Now he was singing for the man who began his career as a member of HUAC from 1946 to 1950, when the committee smeared Sinatra. The president beamed with satisfaction, and Pat Nixon kept time by nodding her head. At the end of the program, for the first time in his public career, Sinatra was in tears.

The New Republic, March 31, 1986

32

Inside the Nixon Liebrary

The $21 million Nixon Library in Yorba Linda, California, which opened in July 1990, takes visitors on a twisted trip down memory lane. From Helen Gahagan Douglas, whom he defeated in the 1952 race for California Senator, to E. Howard Hunt, participant in the Watergate crimes, the effort made here to reshape popular memory is more sweeping, more relentless, more sophisticated and more expensive than that undertaken by any other president.

The dedication was a cheerful occasion. While an audience of 50,000 sweltered under the desert sun and CNN broadcast the proceedings live, former Treasury Secretary William Simon spoke of Nixon's "lifelong commitment to peace and freedom"; Ronald Reagan said "the world is a better place—a safer place—because of Richard Nixon"; and President Bush asked, "Who can forget how much he endured in his quest for peace in Vietnam?" The people watching at my house yelled something like, "How much did the Vietnamese endure?" but CNN didn't hear; anchorman Bernard Shaw called it "a grand day." It made me wish gonzo journalist Hunter Thompson had also been on the program, calling Nixon "a Born Loser ... the predatory shyster who turns into something unspeakable, full of claws and bleeding string-warts, on nights when the moon comes too close." But instead TV preacher Norman Vincent Peale wrapped things up.

Calling this a "library" is misleading; the place has no books or documents. Officials have promised to open a basement archive in 1991 to contain primarily pre- and post-presidential papers. Nixon, alone among presidents, has been denied control of his presidential papers by an act of Congress. After he resigned and was pardoned, he signed an agreement with Gerald Ford's General Services Administration allowing the destruction of some of the papers and requiring the destruction of the White House tapes. An outraged Congress passed a law taking control of the materials away from Nixon and giving it to the federal government. The disgraced but defiant ex-president then challenged the law before the Supreme Court and lost. Even today library director Hugh Hewitt says Nixon's papers were "stolen" from him.

The Nixon presidential papers and tapes now rest in Alexandria, Virginia, where the National Archives has been working at declassifying them, but Reagan-era budget cuts slowed the process. Since 1978, when the processing began, 4 million pages have been released, along with 12½ hours of Watergate tapes; that leaves 40 million pages and 4,000 hours of tape that have not yet been processed. Nixon's lawsuits have blocked the release of 150,000 pages of documents. Library officials say their basement archive will include photocopies that will constitute "a complete collection of key presidential documents"; scholars and journalists respond to that claim with understandable skepticism.

If the library is weak on archives, it is strong on video: visitors get to see Nixon's 1952 "Checkers" speech, in which the weepy vice-presidential candidate labored to exonerate himself of charges of corruption with maudlin references to his dog Checkers and his wife's "respectable Republican cloth coat." (Visitors are not told that columnist Walter Lippmann called the Checkers speech "the most demeaning experience my country has ever had to bear.") Next come the 1960 Kennedy–Nixon debates, featuring a brief glimpse of the 5 o'clock shadow that many believe lost Nixon the election. To re-create the original experience, viewers watch in a 1960 living room—an upscale one, with Reader's Digest Condensed Books on the mantel. Visitors also get to see Nixon's unforgettable 1987 eulogy for Ohio State football coach Woody Hayes (but only if they get there by 10.30 in the morning). In the opinion of museum director Hewitt, none of these videos will be as popular as the tape of Nixon's daughter Tricia's wedding, which is shown at 10.45.

The "Hall of World Leaders" is one of the best, with life-size bronze statues of de Gaulle, Adenauer, Churchill, Sadat, Golda Meir, Mao, Zhou Enlai, Khrushchev and Brezhnev posed as if they were all at the same cocktail party. By touching a video screen, the visitor can learn what the library guide calls "their thoughts on Nixon." The thoughts contain few surprises: de Gaulle, for instance, does not describe Nixon as "head of ... the racist, fascist pig power structure" (as Bobby Seale did) but rather as "one of those frank and steady personalities on whom one feels one could rely in the greatest affairs of state."

"Richard Nixon: Hiss is your life," Nixon biographer Garry Wills once wrote. Nixon, a member of the House Un-American Activities Committee in 1947, pursued Whittaker Chambers's espionage charge against Alger Hiss, a prominent New Deal figure; Hiss's conviction for perjury propelled the formerly unknown Nixon into national promi- nence. The Hiss case is featured in the library; visitors to the museum are told that Hiss's Woodstock typewriter convicted him when samples typed on it were found to match documents Chambers said Hiss had given him to transmit to the Russians. The library display includes a replica of Hiss's Woodstock, and library officials told the *Los Angeles Times* that the original Hiss typewriter is kept in a vault in the library basement. Could it be true that Nixon has the Hiss typewriter? Most of the artifacts in the library are on loan from the National Archives; I asked archives spokeswoman Susan Cooper about the typewriter in the Nixon Library vault. "It's not ours," she said, "not the National Archives'." It turns out that it isn't Hiss's either: the typewriter was returned to Hiss after his trial and is now in the attic of filmmaker John Lowenthal.

The claim that Nixon has Hiss's typewriter in a vault in the library basement adds another bizarre chapter to a forty-year saga. At the time Chambers charged Hiss with espionage, the typewriter on which Hiss was said to have typed the documents was missing; Hiss claimed it would prove him innocent. Despite a massive FBI effort to locate the typewriter, the Hiss defense found it and presented it triumphantly to the court, only to learn that it matched the Chambers documents. Ever since that time the Hiss defense has claimed that the typewriter was used to frame him, that the FBI manufactured a phony duplicate Woodstock to match the Chambers documents and left it for Hiss to find—a type of fabrication that even Hiss critic Allen Weinstein acknowledged "had become standard procedure in the repertoire of espionage agencies by the time of the Second World War." For forty years the debate has focused on the authenticity of the typewriter Hiss introduced at the trial; now it seems that in the Nixon Library vault there is a second phony Woodstock. Needless to say, the "forgery by typewriter" theory is not presented in the library display. One visitor to it commented, "Isn't that something! I remember hearing about the pumpkin deal, but I never understood what it was about."

Other exhibits include the "Domestic Gifts" section, where one can see the Colt .45 pistol Elvis Presley gave Nixon when he visited the Oval Office in December 1970. The Elvis gun is surrounded by crocheted miniature doll hats, an electric football clock and a rock in the shape of Nixon's profile. In the official White House photo of "the President and the King" on display in the museum, Nixon wears a tweed suit and Elvis sports a flowing cape and a huge gold belt buckle. The photo has sold 31,000 copies—an all-time record for the National Archives; unfortunately it's not for sale at the library gift shop. Nor does the library reproduce Elvis's letter seeking an appointment with the President, volunteering to enlist in the war against drugs: "The Drug Culture, the Hippie Elements, the SDS, Black Panthers," he wrote, "do *not* consider me as their enemy."

At the end of the exhibits comes the "Presidential Forum," where a touch-screen video monitor allows visitors to "ask" Nixon questions in what is billed as a "Face-to-Face Dialogue." He "answers" on an immense video screen. This proved to be something of a disappointment; you "ask" by choosing questions listed under topics such as Watergate, the Vietnam War and "the media." The system contains 300 answers, drawn either from past interviews with Nixon or from statements he recorded recently in a studio. The list invites visitors to ask Nixon, "What is the source of your passion for peace?" A question that is not on the list is, "Are you a crook?"

The museum's Vietnam display is its most reprehensible. It doesn't mention the fact that during the mid 1960s Nixon was the country's leading hawk, constantly attacking Johnson for not escalating the war. It barely mentions the 1970 invasion of Cambodia or the nationwide student strike that followed and the Kent State killings. It doesn't show Nixon calling campus demonstrators "bums," or the father of Allison Krause, one of the students killed at Kent State, replying on national TV, "My child was not a bum." It doesn't mention the illegal surveillance, harassment and prosecution of antiwar activists under Attorney General John Mitchell. Instead, visitors are told the antiwar movement consisted of "a violent minority" that "used force and intimidation to stifle debate; they used bombs to proclaim their message that there should be no bombing; they took lives while professing that they were trying to save lives."

The library's Watergate display, a dark, uninviting corridor filled with small print, shows that Tricky Dick is alive and well in Yorba Linda. Before the library opened, officials repeatedly told reporters three key Watergate tapes would be played in their entirety for visitors. One tape is available; its most significant portions have been deleted. It's the 18½ minute gap all over again. The "smoking gun" tape, recorded July 23, 1972, reveals that Nixon approved a plan to have the CIA tell the FBI to stop investigating Watergate. In the Nixon Library version, however, a narrator explains that what Nixon really said was, "The best thing to do is let the investigation proceed unhindered." Why that would bring Barry Goldwater and the Senate Republican leadership to advise Nixon to resign is not explained. The Watergate room leaves out a few other things. It doesn't mention Nixon's use of the FBI, CIA and White House "plumbers" to harass, spy on and punish those on the President's "enemies list." It doesn't mention the criminal convictions of Nixon's senior aides for carrying out these actions. It doesn't mention the resignation of the disgraced Vice President Spiro Agnew. Most incredible of all, it doesn't mention that Gerald Ford pardoned Nixon for his crimes. Instead, the Watergate affair is described they way Nixon has always described it: not as a systematic abuse of power but as a single act, a second-rate burglary carried out by overzealous underlings without his knowledge, followed by a partisan vendetta in which Democrats sought to reverse the "mandate of the 1972 election" by forcing him from office.

Nixon can get away with all this because it's his museum, financed completely by private donations from rich friends. His is the only privately run presidential library. The Kennedy and Johnson libraries run by the National Archives contain virtually no criticism of their subjects, but it's inconceivable that a National Archives-run Nixon Library would delete key portions of the Watergate tapes. Anyone with $21 million can build a museum and fill it with lies about what he or she has done—that's what it means to live in a free country.

Nixon has plenty of help in his campaign to rearrange his place in the cavalcade of presidents. Ronald Reagan, in an interview before the library dedication, spoke about Nixon with characteristic insight: "I think much of the criticism was based on nothing at all. I think that looking at it fairly, they should view some of the great strides that he made in international relations and so forth with our country." But it isn't just the Republicans who emphasize Nixon's "great strides"; a similar argument has been put forward by some thinkers on the left, especially Gore Vidal and Robert Scheer.

Nixon enables us to "observe our faults larger than life," Vidal writes; "but we can also, if we try, see in this huge, dusty mirror our virtues as well." Nixon's greatest virtues, of course, are his trips to Peking and Moscow, diplomacy without precedent, which "demonstrate[d] to all the world the absolute necessity of coexistence." As a result, "we are all of us in Nixon's debt" for bringing to an end "one-third of a century of dangerous nonsense." Those two trips, Vidal argues, prove "that there is not only good in him but in us as well—hope, too." Vidal happily concedes that Nixon was "corrupt some of the time, and complex and devious all of the time." But people who emphasize only these traits "make him appear uniquely sleazy—and the rest of us just grand." His predecessor LBJ "far surpassed Nixon when it came to mendacity and corruption," and the crimes and corruptions of the Reagan era outstrip anything Nixon's cronies did.

Scheer makes a similar case, relying on a Nixon expert: George McGovern, Nixon's opponent in 1972 and the principal victim of the Watergate crimes. "In dealing with the two major Communist powers, Nixon probably had a better record than any President since World War Two," McGovern said in a 1984 interview. "He put us on the course to practical working relationships with both the Russians and the Chinese." Nixon also negotiated the first strategic arms limitation treaty with the Soviet Union. After his resignation, when Reagan renewed the cold war and barked about the "evil empire," Nixon published *The Real Peace*, a defense of détente and an implicit challenge to Reagan. There's more: under Nixon the Environmental Protection Agency was established, the draft was abolished, eighteen-year-olds were given the vote and a serious reform of the welfare system was attempted.

All this is hard to swallow for those of us who have spent most of our lives as Nixon-haters. Do we have to agree with Vidal that Nixon is "an infamous man who has done great deeds for his country"? The China trip can't be separated from its context and its motivation. When Nixon went to China in 1972, the United States had been defeated in the ground war in Vietnam and was withdrawing its troops; at the same time Nixon was increasing the bombing tremendously. His motive in going to China was not to end the cold war but to prevent Chinese leaders from reacting to the intensified US bombing of North Vietnam. During his presidency, Daniel Ellsberg reminds us, Nixon was responsible for dropping 4.5 million tons of bombs on Indochina, more than twice as much firepower as was used in all World War Two on both Europe and Asia.

But did Nixon's opening to China and détente with the Soviet Union make anticommunism untenable? Did it begin the process that culminated in 1989 in the end of the cold war? Détente with the Russians was potentially more significant, but it didn't last; it didn't stop Reagan from launching what historians call the second cold war against that "evil empire," during which he persuaded Congress to pay for the biggest peacetime military buildup in our history. Nixon didn't end the cold war; Gorbachev did, and the witless Reagan will go down in history as his partner in that achievement.

There are a few other black marks on Nixon's record. He prolonged the Vietnam War for five years even though the 1973 settlement was essentially the one the Vietnamese offered in 1968. His war against Cambodia, a neutral country, was illegal and immoral, and was never declared by Congress. Others have their own favorite Nixon crime: for some it was his sponsorship of the coup against Salvador Allende in Chile, which destroyed Latin America's oldest democracy; for others it was his creation of McCarthyism—before Joe McCarthy—as a political tactic in the late 1940s; for still others it was his Supreme Court nominees—Clement Haynsworth and G. Harrold Carswell, defeated by the Senate, and finally William Rhenquist, who today serves as Chief Justice.

Thus the Nixon Library story is mostly bad news. But some of the news is good. First, Nixon had a hard time finding a place that would accept his library. Duke University and the University of California, Irvine, turned it down. The Duke faculty said it didn't want anything "designedto foster the glorification of the former President." Irvine said it would accept only if the institution was primarily a research archive.

(Journalism ethics alert: as a faculty member at Irvine, I supported the proposed restrictions.) San Clemente was another site Nixon wanted but didn't get. Yorba Linda was thus his fourth choice.

Finally, attendance at the library since opening day has been low. The day I visited, several galleries were empty. In the "Prime Time Theater," where the program was "Nixon announces he will visit China," the entire audience consisted of two people, and the large "Domestic Affairs" room had nobody in it at all. Despite massive publicity, despite the fact that Nixon put his library deep in the southern California Republican heartland, despite the fact that admission is considerably cheaper than at nearby Disneyland—$3.95 versus $25.50—people aren't showing much interest in having their historical memories reprogrammed. In this we see our virtues; we see that there is good in America after all.

The Nation, September 10, 1990

33

John Lennon versus the FBI

Is rock 'n' roll revolutionary? The question sounds foolish when Ronald Reagan has instructed James Watt on the true meaning of the Beach Boys. But rock and politics added up to a burning issue in 1971 and 1972, and the connection was taken as seriously by Richard Nixon's White House as it was by the counterculture—maybe more so. And the rock star most feared by the Nixon gang was the singer–songwriter who had first won fame as the "clever Beatle," John Lennon. As a result, Lennon became the only rock 'n' roller the government ever tried to deport because of the political power of his music. This strange story appears in the twenty-six pounds of FBI and Immigration files recently released to me under the Freedom of Information Act.

The Nixon Administration learned in February 1972 that Lennon was thinking about mounting a concert tour that would combine rock music with radical politics. Lennon's friend Jerry Rubin hoped to end the tour with a "political Woodstock" outside the Republican National Convention, where Nixon was to be renominated. This information came to the White House from a rather improbable source on concert bookings, Senator Strom Thurmond, who had written to Attorney General John Mitchell about Lennon's plans. Thurmond sent a secret memorandum, drafted by the staff of his Subcommittee on Internal Security, to both Mitchell and the White House. The memo noted that "radical New Left leaders" who were "strong advocates of the program to 'dump Nixon'" were planning "to hold rock concerts in various primary election states for the following purposes: to obtain access to college campuses; to encourage 18-year-olds to register; to press for legislation legalizing marijuana; to finance their activities; and to recruit persons to come to San Diego during the Republican National Convention in August 1972.... [Rennie] Davis and his cohorts intend to use John Lennon as a drawing card to promote their success.... If Lennon's visa is terminated it would be a strategic counter-measure."

This was precisely the sort of thing that had been contemplated by John Dean, the counsel to the President, in his famous August 1971 memo: "We can use the available political machinery to screw our political enemies." Mitchell passed Thurmond's suggestion along to the Immigration and Naturalization Service; the next month, the INS, relying on Lennon's 1968 British misdemeanor conviction for marijuana possession, ordered him deported.

Lennon's main file in the FBI Central Records System in Washington, DC, is a "100 case file." "100" is the classification number for "domestic security" investigations. Lennon's main file has 288 pages; the Reagan Justice Department has refused to release 199 of them, largely under the claim that they have been "properly classified in the interests of national defense or foreign policy." (Could this have something to do with the Lennon–McCartney song "Back in the USSR"?) The pages that have been released are riddled with deletions on the same grounds. In some cases "released" pages have been completely blacked out except for the headings. Many of the documents in Lennon's FBI file are coded teletypes, a form reserved for sensitive messages because they require complicated encrypting and decrypting. Others are "LHMs," Letterhead Memos, prepared for dissemination to other government agencies, reporting on Lennon's activities and plans. In Lennon's case confidential LHMs were distributed to the 108th Military Intelligence Group in New York, the Secret Service, Naval Intelligence, the Immigration and Naturalization Service, the State Department, the US Attorney for New York, and the CIA. Many of the reports are addressed to, or sent by, J. Edgar Hoover, who is never mentioned by name but only by the awesome title: "Director." (Hoover died in May 1972, and L. Patrick Gray became Acting Director.)

The FBI documents are written in a bizarre language: "From SAC, New York, to DIRECTOR, FBI: ReBuairtel 1/26/72, captioned Project 'Yes' IS-NL, OO:NY, enclosed for the Bureau are 10 copies of an LHM captioned as above. Copies are being designated for those offices having PCPJ in their Divisions." Fortunately, the Fund for Open Information and Accountability has published a phrase book to help readers translate such documents: *Are You Now or Have You Ever Been in the FBI Files?*, by Ann Mari Buitrago and Leon Immerman (Grove Press, 1981). "SAC" is the Special Agent in Charge of the field office; "ReBuairtel" refers to an internal Bureau communication sent by air mail. Project "Yes" was Yoko Ono's "Youth Election Strategy," the media arm of the planned 1972 tour. The FBI classified "Yes" under "Internal Security—New Left," and the originating office ("OO") was New York. PCPJ was the People's Coalition for Peace and Justice, an umbrella organization coordinating plans for demonstrations at the Republican National Convention. When the FBI described Lennon in file captions, they didn't list him as "ex-Beatle" but rather as "SM-REVACT," Hooverspeak for "Security Matter–Revolutionary Activities."

The FBI maintained files on Lennon not only at FBI HQ in the SOG ("Seat of Government"), but also in FBI field offices, especially in New York, the "OO" that had primary responsibility for the Lennon investigation. The OO file contains the most valuable documents, including virtually all such original materials as surveillance logs, interviews with informers, agents' memos on following leads, and details about how information is received and how agents are to proceed with an investigation. That file is also riddled with deletions.

The FBI has a conspiratorial conception of its enemies; it maintains massive files not just on individuals, but especially on organizations. Several hundred additional FBI Lennon pages are located in a file on a paper organization that existed for no more than a month or two: the "Election Year Strategy Information Committee," which apparently consisted of Rennie Davis at a desk in the basement of the Lennon–Ono apartment in Greenwich Village, working to set up Lennon's prospective concert tour. The bulk of the Lennon files, however, came not from the FBI but from the Immigration and Naturalization Service. The record of the deportation proceedings takes up thousands of pages, in which Lennon's brilliant lawyer Leon Wildes ran circles around the INS's struggling chief trial attorney, Vincent Schiano. The administrative memos by various Immigration Service officials, who were trying to figure out how to get Lennon deported before the Republican National Convention, take up hundreds of pages. The correspondence file grew to several thousand pages, as senators, celebrities, and Beatle fans requested information and took stands. Letters from Bob Dylan (who wrote, "[they] put an end to this mild dull taste of petty commercialism that is being passed off as artist art by the overpowering mass media. Hurray for John and Yoko!") and John Updike (who wrote, "They cannot do this great country any harm, and might do it some good") are filed next to letters from adolescents in Ohio protesting Lennon's "exportation" and "deportment."

The Nixon Administration's effort to deport Lennon made headlines during the wild political spring of 1972. In May Nixon ordered the mining of Haiphong Harbor and massive new bombing raids, setting off a week of unprecedented antiwar mobilizations and civil disobedience, more frenzied and despairing than ever before. John and Yoko spoke at a midtown Manhattan antiwar rally, then headed off to their first immigration hearing. Nixon wanted them deported, Lennon told reporters in his Liverpool accent, "because we're peaceniks." The Mayor of New York, John Lindsay, and the *New York Times* expressed their support for Lennon and Ono. Beatles fans across the nation joined a letter-writing campaign around the theme, "Let them stay in the USA." Although the Immigration Service was falling all over itself in its haste to deport the Lennons, it maintained publicly that the case was perfectly routine. The falsity of that claim did not become clear until three years later, when the Thurmond memo to Mitchell was unearthed, well after Nixon himself had been deported from Washington. The Thurmond memo helped convince a federal judge to overrule the Immigration authorities and grant Lennon permanent residency in 1975. The rest of the story, told in the FBI files, has not been known until now.

The deporation case had its roots in a concert–rally John and Yoko gave in Ann Arbor, Michigan, in December 1971—a benefit for a local activist named John Sinclair, who had served two years of a ten-year sentence for selling two joints of marijuana to an undercover cop. Lennon and his movement friends regarded the Sinclair concert as a trial run for their proposed national tour. They wanted to see how a typical rock audience would respond to a rally that combined music with radical politics. The FBI was interested in precisely the same question. Its undercover agents were salted among the fifteen thousand excited midwestern college kids who came to Crisler Arena to see John and Yoko and their friends.

The concert–rally began with poet Allen Ginsberg, who led the crowd in chanting "Om-m-m-m-m." Phil Ochs sang a song about Nixon. A local band played Elvis Presley's "Jailhouse Rock" for the man behind bars, and a version of Chuck Berry's "Nadine," with new words about Bernadine Dohrn, a member of the Weather Underground: "Ber-nadine, sister is that you? / Your picture's in the post office / But the people are protecting you." Jerry Rubin gave a speech explaining the rally's trial balloon purpose. "A lot of events like this one will take place up and down the country between now and San Diego," he said, and called for "a million of you to turn up at the Republic National Convention to humiliate and defeat Richard Nixon." Dave Dellinger, who had helped organize the 1968 Chicago antiwar demonstrations, talked about "a people's convention at San Diego next summer." Rennie Davis talked about Vietnam. Bobby Seale, then in the Black Panthers, called on the audience to "start attacking the monster of capitalism." Stevie Wonder, a surprise guest, sang and played "For Once in My Life," and delivered a brief speech attacking Nixon and Agnew.

At 3 a.m., seven hours after the concert–rally began, John Lennon appeared. Despite the lateness of the hour, no one had left. For this was a major event: Lennon's first concert appearance in the United States since the Beatles waved goodby at San Francisco's Candlestick Park five years earlier. "We came here to show and to say to all of you that apathy isn't it, that we *can* do something. Okay, so flower power didn't work. So what. We start again." Fifteen thousand people cheered. Then he sang the new song he had written for the occasion: "John Sinclair."

The undercover FBI men in the audience took it all down, scribbling even more furiously than the reporters from *Rolling Stone*, the *Village Voice*, and the *East Village Other*—and sent a 26-page report to the Director, "five (5) copies of a LHM setting forth information regarding captioned rally." The FBI at first refused to release the full report in response to my Freedom of Information Act request, citing their authority to withhold "investigatory records compiled for law enforcement purposes, the release of which would constitute an unwarranted invasion of the personal privacy of third parties." The

Assistant Attorney General for Legal Policy eventually ruled in favor of my appeal and sent the withheld portion.

The section began with a complete set of the lyrics to "John Sinclair," which the FBI had classified "Confidential," even though they were in due course printed on the sleeve of Lennon's next album, *Some Time in New York City*. It wasn't great poetry (sample: "It ain't fair, John Sinclair / In the stir for breathing air . . . Was he jailed for what he done / Or representing everyone?"), but it was no secret, either. Copies were forwarded to the FBI field offices in Boston, New York, Chicago, Milwaukee, San Francisco and Washington, DC. Perhaps this was the FBI's understanding of the itinerary Lennon and Rubin had planned for the tour. Meanwhile, back in Ann Arbor, the concert had an aftermath no one had anticipated: fifty-five hours after John and Yoko left the stage, John Sinclair was set free. A board of appellate judges released him on bond. Jerry Rubin was ecstatic, calling the release "an incredible tribute to the power of the people. . . . We won!" He called for "two, three, four, many more Ann Arbors!" No wonder the FBI was treating the lyrics to Lennon's song with such superstitious respect.

Lennon's FBI file for January and February 1972, the months preceding the deportation order, is bulging with reports on the "Election Year Strategy Information Committee," Rennie Davis's effort to set up the concert tour. Stew Albert's name appears repeatedly in the EYSIC files. Every document mentioning him explains that "Albert was arrested on April 12, 1966, at Berkeley, California," at a demonstration sponsored by the Progressive Labor Party. The next paragraph invariably explains that the PLP "was founded in 1962 by individuals expelled from the Communist Party, USA, for following the Chinese Communist line." Both those statements are true, but the implication that Albert was a member or sympathizer of the PLP is not. In fact Albert was known to the press as Jerry Rubin's "Yippie lieutenant," a bitter antagonist of the humorless PLPers. When I asked him about his 1966 Berkeley arrest, he dismissed it as "a youthful indiscretion."

The first mention of EYSIC in the FBI files is dated January 28, 1972: "The public will soon become aware of its existance [sic] and purpose—anti-Calrep activities" (i.e. demonstrations outside the California Republican convention). Several hundred pages later, a confidential LHM explains that "the organization ceased to exist approximately the first of March, 1972," one month after its founding. The INS ordered Lennon deported on March 6; thus EYSIC's dissolution did not come in response to the deportation order. Nor did the deportation order change Lennon's plans, as J. Edgar Hoover himself noted in a memo dated April 10: "Subject continues to plan activities directed towards RNC and will soon initiate series of 'rock concerts' to develop financial support." (The FBI's use of "quotes" was always curious.)

Given Lennon's refusal to change his plans, Hoover ordered his New York office to "promptly initiate discreet efforts to locate subject." The problem was that the FBI files showed his "temporary residence" to be the "St Regis Hotel, 150 Bank Street, New York City." Bank Street is in Greenwich Village; every New York cop and cab driver knows the St Regis is in midtown, at Fifty-fifth Street and Fifth Avenue. In fact, the agents who couldn't find any big hotels on Bank Street were quite close to their quarry. At the time, the Lennons were living in a two-bedroom apartment at 105 Bank Street, having checked out of the St Regis several months earlier.

The FBI worried about everything. In a coded teletype headed "urgent," the Special Agent in Charge of the New York FBI informed J. Edgar Hoover, "a source who is in a position to furnish reliable information advised that subject has been offered a teaching position with New York University during the summer ... officials presume that subject will accept." Like the Bank Street St Regis, this scrap of intelligence never quite panned out.

None of the documents that have been released was sent to or from Richard Nixon himself. But Nixon's chief of staff, H.R. Haldeman, was kept informed about the progress of the FBI's campaign to "neutralize" Lennon. The contents of an April 25, 1972, memo to Haldeman have been obliterated in their entirety, under the national security exemption. But the memo's postscript refers Haldeman to a fuller report sent by E.L. Shackelford to E.S. Miller. Those agents' names have appeared in the news in a different connection. Miller (along with Mark Felt) was found guilty of breaking and entering in the FBI investigation of the Weather Underground. He and Felt are the only FBI agents ever to be convicted of crimes committed on the job. (They were pardoned by Ronald Reagan in 1981.) Their supervisor on that case was E.L. Shackelford. Do the withheld portions of Lennon's file contain evidence that the FBI committed the same kinds of illegal acts against Lennon that the same people were convicted of having committed in the Weather Underground case?

Hoover stated in another memo that Lennon was "in US to assist in organizing disruption of RNC." That was absurd. The Lennons left London and moved to New York for a variety of reasons. For instance, they wanted to try to get custody of Yoko's American daughter by a previous marriage. But above all they came to America because it was the land of the free, the home of rock 'n' roll.

Still, it isn't hard to understand the Nixon Administration's fear of Lennon's political potential. In Ann Arbor, Lennon had shared the stage with the same people who had organized the Chicago demonstrations against the Democrats in 1968. In terms of attendance, Chicago had been a flop; only twenty thousand showed up. The following fall, a quarter of a million came to Washington for the Vietnam Mobilization, and half a million went to hear music in Woodstock that summer. Only Mayor Daley's police riot made the Chicago demonstrations a historic event. None of the big rock stars had come to Chicago. If Lennon topped the bill at a "political Woodstock" outside the 1972 Republican National Convention, Rubin and his friends reasoned, they would bring together the two strands of the sixties: counterculture and New Left, rock and radical politics. Robert Christgau, writing about Lennon in *Newsday* that summer, declared, "if rock and roll is to continue to function politically, it must continue to liberate its audience—to broaden fellow-feeling, direct energy, and focus analysis." That's exactly what Lennon and Rubin wanted to achieve. Nor were the counterculture, the New Left, and the FBI alone in believing in the political power of rock music. In 1969 *Time* magazine wrote that rock was "not just a particular form of pop, but ... one long symphony of protest ... basically moral ... the proclamation of a new set of values ... the anthem of revolution." The underground press never made a stronger claim. For once, Nixon wasn't being paranoid—or at least his deliriums were shared by others.

Lennon's lawyers successfully delayed the deportation order, and apparently advised him to cancel his rock tour plans. But the FBI still worried that he would lead demonstrations against Nixon at the convention, which had now been moved to Miami (hence his "anti-MIREP activities.") By the summer of 1972, the FBI was searching for a way to strengthen what the INS now privately admitted was a "very loose case." The FBI wrote in July that "LENNON is reportedly 'a heavy user of narcotics known as 'downers.' This information should be emphasized to local Law Enforcement Agencies ... with regards to subject being arrested if at all possible on possession of narcotics charge." If such an arrest were made, Lennon "would become more likely to be immediately deportable." FBI agents do not enforce the laws making possession of narcotics a crime. (Judging from this memo they don't even know that "downers"—barbiturates—are not narcotics.) That's why they had to get the local cops to try. And that's why this memo sounds like a proposal to set Lennon up for a drug bust to prevent him from leading antiwar demonstrations at the Republican convention.

Lennon never was busted on drug charges, and never appeared in any of the Miami news reports. But the FBI was haunted by the fear that he might have secretly demonstrated against the Republican convention. Acting Director L. Patrick Gray was informed in September by the Miami SAC that "local authorities have furnished no information to indicate the presence of the subject in Miami Beach, Florida, at any time during the summer of 1972." Nevertheless, just to make sure, the FBI decided to do an extraordinary thing. "On 8/22/72 and 8/23/72 approximately 1,200 individuals were arrested in Miami Beach by local authorities during protest demonstrations against the Republican National Convention. The records relating to these arrests were photographed by the Miami Office and the film is currently being processed by the FBI Laboratory. When the arrest records become available, they will be reviewed to determine whether subject may have been arrested during the above convention."

If John Lennon had been arrested for demonstrating against Richard Nixon, it would have been one of the biggest events in the history of counterculture politics. The FBI's belief that Lennon could have demonstrated against Nixon and then been arrested, *without anyone finding out about it*, provides a ludicrous ending to the story. Two months of work by the Miami FBI "failed to reflect that the subject was one of those arrested," L. Patrick Gray was informed. On December 8, 1972, "in view of subject's inactivity in Revolutionary Activities ... captioned case is being closed in the NY Division."

Thus the John Lennon files that have been released make the FBI look more like the Keystone Kops than the Gestapo. But the campaign to "neutralize" Lennon wasn't a joke; it was a crime. Lennon spoke out against the war at rallies and demonstrations. He associated with leading antiwar activists. But the files contain no evidence that Lennon committed any criminal acts: no bombings, no terrorism, no conspiracies. His activities were precisely the kind protected by the First Amendment. The files show that he was a victim of an Administration obsessed with its "enemies," and abusing the power of the Presidency in violation of the Constitution. And the two-thirds of Lennon's main FBI file which has been withheld in its entirety is likely to contain evidence of additional dirty tricks and interference with the Lennons' private lives.

Soon after his reelection, Nixon had bigger things to worry about than John Lennon, but the INS kept Lennon in court for three more years. By the mid seventies, rock politics proved to be more flexible, and more available to work within the system, than Lennon and his friends could have imagined in 1971 and 1972. The 1976 Democratic primary candidates relied on rock concerts for much of their fundraising. Jerry Brown had Linda Ronstadt, Jackson Browne, the Eagles and Chicago. Sargent Shriver had Neil Diamond and Tony Orlando. Birch Bayh had Stephen Stills. Hubert Humphrey had James Brown(!). Arlo Guthrie and Harry Chapin sang for Fred Harris. And Jimmy Carter had the Allman Brothers. By 1980 a new group of rock musicians were playing a new kind of political concert: the *No Nukes* film showed the Madison Square Garden concert starring Bruce Springsteen, Graham Nash, Jackson Browne, Bonnie Raitt, and others. Some of these same stars appeared at the peace demonstrations in New York's Central Park and the Rose Bowl in Los Angeles in June 1982, where hundreds of thousands of demonstrators sang John Lennon's "Imagine." The recent peace movement concert–rallies have been much tamer than what Lennon and Rubin had in mind in 1972, but they certainly helped to mobilize youthful opposition to the Reagan Administration. Perhaps the parallel between Lennon's activities and those of today's politically active rock stars may help explain the Reagan Administration's action on the Lennon FBI files.

The Reagan Administration's withholding of the Lennon FBI file is part of a larger policy hostile to public access to government information. Under the Carter Administration, documents could be classified "confidential" and exempted from release under the Freedom of Information Act only if their disclosure would cause "identifiable damage to national security." If this policy was already too vague, the recent Reagan executive order on classification made it worse. Reagan has removed the word "identifiable" from the definition. Now, an FBI classification officer can withhold documents even if the threat they pose is unidentifiable.

Among the many emotions that were released by rock music in the late sixties was a feeling for revolution. The experiences of anger and exaltation that rock music provided for countless Americans were not in themselves political experiences. Lennon knew that. He also knew that rock could become a potent political force when it was linked to real political organizing, when, for example, it brought young people together to protest the war. In 1971 and 1972 he made a commitment to test this political power. The twenty-six pounds of files reveal the government's commitment to stop him. We don't know the full extent of their effort, because so many of the files have been withheld. Was Lennon really a threat to the national security, as the Reagan Administration now claims? Or are Reagan's people trying to conceal the full story of the government's harassment of an antiwar activist?

The American Civil Liberties Union of Southern California and I hope to find out: we filed suit in federal court in 1983 to win release of the classified pages of John Lennon's FBI file.

The New Republic, May 2, 1983

Postscript: In 1988, US District Court Judge Robert K. Takasugi refused to order the FBI to release the files; in December 1989 that decision was appealed to the US Court of Appeals in Pasadena, California. In July, 1991, a three-judge appeals panel ruled unanimously that the FBI had failed to justify withholding the Lennon files. The appeals court declared that, unless the FBI could describe specifically how national security could be harmed by the release of these documents, it could be compelled under the Freedom of Information Act to release them. As of August, 1991, the FBI had not indicated whether it would pursue additional appeals.

34

Beatles Buy-out: How Nike Bought
the Beatles' "Revolution"

There is a revolution afoot, according to the Nike shoe company—a revolution in sneakers, heralded by a $7 million TV ad campaign featuring the Beatles song "Revolution." It's the first time that Capitol Records has licensed an original Beatles record for use in a TV commercial. The 30-second ads, done in a black-and-white documentary style, feature ordinary jocks intercut with sports superstars such as basketball player Michael Jordan and tennis champion John McEnroe, while John Lennon sings, "You say you want a revolution." The new sneakers cost $75 a pair.

Beatles fans are outraged. Chris Morris, the *LA Reader*'s rock critic, said: "When 'Revolution' came out in 1968 I was getting teargassed in the streets of Madison. That song is part of the soundtrack of my political life. It bugs the hell out of me that it has been turned into a shoe ad." Morris is right that the Beatles' purpose was not to sell shoes. But the story is a bit more complicated.

The 1968 song *criticized* young revolutionaries for having "minds that hate." Lennon's lyrics told the 1960s left to "count me out." They attacked kids for "carrying pictures of Chairman Mao." The New Left was shocked when the song first appeared. *Ramparts* called it a "betrayal," and the *New Left Review* denounced it as "a lamentable petty bourgeois cry of fear." "Revolution" was John Lennon's comment on May '68. It was recorded two weeks after student riots in Paris brought France to the brink of revolution. The song wasn't released until August. By that time, a thousand club-swinging New York City cops had driven Columbia University students from occupied campus buildings. In Chicago Hubert Humphrey had been "nominated in a sea of blood," as Theodore White put it. The Rolling Stones released "Street Fighting Man," in which Mick Jagger sang about the time being right for revolution; that record was banned from the airways of Chicago and Berkeley. Then the new Beatles single came out, addressing the kids in the streets: "You say you want a revolution..."

The underground press responded immediately. The Berkeley *Barb* wrote with typical excess, "'Revolution' sounds like the hawk plank adopted in the Chicago convention of the Democratic Death Party." Jon Landau, writing for Liberation New Service, agreed: "Hubert Humphrey couldn't have said it better," he wrote. Robert Christgau wrote in the *Village Voice*, "It is puritanical to expect musicians, or anyone else, to hew to the proper line. But it is reasonable to request that they not go out of their way to oppose it. Lennon has, and it takes much of the pleasure out of their music for me." *Ramparts* objected in particular to the line "you know it's gonna be all right": "It isn't," the magazine declared. "You *know* it's *not* gonna be all right." But the song was irresistible, raucous hard rock. The music contained a message of its own, a message of excitement and freedom, which worked against the "sterility and repression in the lyrics," according to Greil Marcus, at the time a writer for the San Francisco *Express-Times*. "The music doesn't say 'cool it' or 'don't fight the cops,'" Marcus wrote.

There was a second version of the song, released on the White Album two months after the single. The single version had been produced the way Paul McCartney wanted it; the album version was done John's way—slower, so that the words could be understood better. And there was one significant change in the words: after he sang, "When you talk about destruction / Don't you know that you can count me out," he added "in." "I put in both because I wasn't sure," he explained. Nike uses the first version in the ad.

Not everyone on the left attacked "Revolution." The Students for a Democratic Society newspaper at Cornell declared that Lennon rightly rejected radicals with "minds that hate," and that the increasing violence of the left needed to be criticized. Then there was the issue of the "shoo-be-do-wahs" with which Paul and George answered John's "You know it's gonna be—" on the album version. Michael Wood addressed that problem in *Commonweal*. The Beatles are not fools, he argued; they know it's absurd to say "it's gonna be all right." The "shoo-be-do-wahs" suggested "they mean that statements about whether it is or it isn't are all part of that political crap they dislike so much."

The far right also took up the question of "Revolution." William Buckley paid mocking tribute to its message in his syndicated column, and was promptly attacked by the John Birch Society. "The Beatles are simply telling the Maoists that Fabian gradualism is working, and that the Maoists might blow it all by getting the public excited before things are ready for 'revolution'—'it's gonna be all right.'" The Birch Society concluded that "'Revolution' takes the Moscow line against Trotskyites and the Progressive Labor Party, based on Lenin's *Left-Wing Extremism: an Infantile Disorder.*" (The actual title of Lenin's treatise was: *Left-Wing Communism, an Infantile Disorder.*)

Lennon and McCartney gave up ownership of their songs in the late sixties when their financial advisers told them they could reduce their tax payments (they were in Britain's 90 per cent bracket) by forming a corporation called Northern Songs that would own their copyrights, and selling stock to the public. In 1969 Sir Lew Grade's entertainment conglomerate ATV Music offered seven times the original offering price of the Northern Songs stock in a takeover bid. Lennon and McCartney were feuding at the time and unable to organize a successful counteroffer. When the Northern Songs management and shareholders accepted Sir Lew's offer in September 1969, Lennon was outraged and inconsolable. Told that his massive capital gain would allow him to make his children secure—or, in the words of the poet, "Baby you're a rich man now,"—Lennon replied, "I have no desire to create another fucking aristocracy." Grade in turn sold ATV in 1981 to an Australian tycoon with too many names: Robert Holmes à Court.

Enter Michael Jackson, whose 1982 *Thriller* album sold more than 30 million copies, making it the most successful album in the history of the world. After working with McCartney on the monster hit "Say, Say, Say," he told his lawyer, "I want to buy some copyrights, like Paul." "He only wanted songs that meant a lot to him," Robert Hillburn explained in the *Los Angeles Times,* so he bought Dion's "Runaround Sue" and "The Wanderer" but passed on Kris Kristofferson's "Help Me Make it Through the Night." But what he really wanted was the Beatles. Jackson appeared in person at the negotiations in London, wearing a colorful Sgt Pepper outfit. That "brightened everyone's mood," Hillburn reported, and Holmes à Court agreed to sell—for $47.5 million. After agreeing to license the words and music of "Revolution" to Nike, Jackson persuaded Capitol Records, owner of the rights to the Beatles' recordings, to license the original record.

The "Revolution" ad is the most outrageous example of a familiar aspect of pop culture in the later Age of Reagan. Lou Reed, a rock hero loved for his rejection of everything soft and safe in the pop world, recently licensed his signature song, "Walk on the Wild Side," for a motor scooter ad. The Shirelles' captivating "Dedicated to the One I Love" (it peaked at No. 3 in 1961) is now used to suggest that if you are dedicated, you should serve bran flakes to the one you love. Johnny Nash's stirring "I Can See Clearly Now," one of the first reggae hits (No. 1 in 1972), sells—oh no—window cleaner. "Revolution" isn't even the first Beatles song to be licensed. John Lennon's "Help," a declaration of his unhappiness as a superstar, became a Mercury ad in 1985. But a sound-alike band sang the song. And Michael Jackson does Pepsi commercials. "Mack the Knife," once sung by Lotte Lenya in *The Threepenny Opera*, lyrics by Bertolt Brecht, music by Kurt Weill, has been turned into a McDonald's commercial: "It's Mac Tonight." Frank Sinatra licensed his original recording of "The Best is Yet to Come" to Chrysler. Ringo Starr, meanwhile, is the first Beatle to appear in person in endorsing a product—a pathetic ad for a wine cooler.

A few rockers have had the integrity to refuse to license their music. Notable among them are John Cougar Mellencamp, Bob Seger, and Joan Jett. Chrissie Hynde of the Pretenders has a song on their album *Get Close* attacking Michael Jackson and others who have endorsed products, in which she asks, "How much did you get for your soul?" Bruce Springsteen has been offered the most to sell out, and he has refused. The admen, however, have taken revenge, expropriating Springsteen's style and attitude and reducing them to a formula for a variety of commercials. After The Boss turned down Lee Iacocca's offer to use "Born in the USA" to sell Plymouth Mini-Vans the company ran a rip-off TV ad with the theme "Made in America." (As Dave Marsh points out in his book on Springsteen, *Glory Days*, the car is assembled in Canada.)

What's next? "Give Peace a Chance" selling Star Wars? "Happiness is a Warm Gun" licensed to the National Rifle Association? "All You Need is Love" as the *contras'* theme song? Yoko Ono says she's confident Michael Jackson would "say 'no' to any misuse of the songs." He turned down dozens of offers before accepting Nike. And neither Ono nor McCartney objected to Jackson's licensing of "Revolution" for the Nike ad. "John's songs should not be part of a cult of glorified martyrdom," Ono argues. "They should be enjoyed by kids today. This ad is a way to communicate John's song to them, to make it part of their lives instead of a relic of the distant past." She argues also that there is nothing objectionable about Nike shoes: "Sports shoes are part of fitness consciousness that is actually better for your body than some of the things we were doing in the sixties."

Maybe there's no reason to object to turning some pop songs into commercials—they didn't say anything in particular, and were written to make money in the first place. Does anyone care that the Fifth Dimension's "Up, Up and Away" (No. 7 in 1967) has become a TWA commercial? But the "Revolution" ad is different. The song had a meaning that Nike is destroying. A spokesman for Michael Jackson says that he plans to make 40 other Beatles songs available for commercial exploitation.

Note: The author was refused permission to reprint the entire lyrics to "Revolution" on the grounds that this article would offend Nike.

The New Republic, May 11, 1987

35

Crushing a Dead Beatle:

the Case of Albert Goldman

"Lennon: cremation of; criminal ambitions of; cruelty of; defective eyesight of"—so reads a portion of the index to Albert Goldman's new book.[1] The list provides a sampling of Goldman's concerns and what is offered as "the definitive biography" of Lennon, from his birth in Liverpool through the heyday of the Beatles to his murder in New York City in 1980. Goldman claims to sketch Lennon's "complexity": Lennon claimed to be a man of peace, but he was violent at times; he said he loved his wife Yoko Ono, but he had fierce arguments with her; the Beatles on tour acted "sexless and charming," but in fact they often had sex with groupies—is this shocking to anyone?

Goldman gives readers the impression that his book is full of fresh revelations, but many of his stories have been familiar to fans for years. Incident after incident in Goldman's book will be old news to readers of the 1983 book *Loving John* by May Pang, Lennon's girlfriend during his 1974 "lost weekend" when he and Yoko separated. Pang's theme is that John loved her more than he loved Yoko and went back to Yoko only because Yoko "brainwashed" him. Goldman retells that story. More of Goldman's book comes from another 1983 book, *Dakota Days* by John Green, Yoko's tarot card reader. He claimed Lennon told him things that he told no one else, but others said that Lennon seldom spoke with him because, as Lennon declared in one of his songs, "I don't believe in tarot."

---

1. Albert Goldman, *The Lives of John Lennon* (New York: William Morrow & Co., 1988).

Much of what Goldman presents as fresh revelations comes directly from Lennon himself—from published interviews. Was Lennon at times angry, depressed, self-destructive? We don't need Goldman to provide the answer; Lennon himself described all of these in interviews, and also in his music, in songs like "Nowhere Man," "Working Class Hero," and "Help." It's not exactly news that Lennon had been a heroin addict; he spoke about it in countless interviews, and even wrote a hit song about it in 1970: "Cold Turkey."

Not all of Goldman's book consists of recycled material. The most original and disturbing section is his description of Lennon in the late seventies, when he was living as a househusband, out of the public eye. According to Goldman, Lennon in 1979 was a rock 'n' roll Howard Hughes—he suffered from malnutrition, seldom got out of bed, took a dozen baths a day, and avoided touching anyone including his four-year-old son Sean. The problem with this picture is that Howard Hughes didn't do what Lennon did: get up one morning, record a No. 1 album (*Double Fantasy*), and talk about his life in a series of interviews that were often brilliant and moving. Since Goldman's picture is so different from what the public saw of Lennon in 1980, the question becomes, what are Goldman's sources?

Virtually all of Goldman's "revelations" come from a couple of people with scores to settle or axes to grind. Fred Seaman is Goldman's most important source on John and Yoko's life in 1979–80. Seaman had been a trusted employee. Goldman doesn't tell his readers that, after Lennon's murder, Seaman set out to write his own book about them, but his publishers, Simon & Schuster, refused to release it and sued him for $500,000, declaring that they had "grave doubts about the veracity and source of the book's contents." The problem: Seaman in 1983 pleaded guilty to grand larceny. After Lennon was killed, he had systematically looted Lennon's files, taking his papers and personal journals, as well as stereo and video equipment and cash. He was also seen wearing Lennon's clothes. He received a sentence of five years' probation. When Seaman's own book was canceled, he began collaborating with Goldman. Marnie Hair, a neighbor of the Lennons in New York City, is another key Goldman source. Goldman doesn't tell his readers that she sued Yoko for $1.5 million in 1983, after her daughter was injured in an accident at Yoko's Long Island house. Hair settled for $18,000 paid by the insurance company into a trust that will become available for her daughter in the mid 1990s. It's possible that Seaman and Hair are telling the truth about John and Yoko, but neither of them can be called neutral observers.

Goldman gained fame for revealing secrets of Elvis's sex life in his previous book; readers looking for more of the same will be disappointed. He reports on what he calls "Lennon's sexual exploits," the last of which, according to Goldman, took place in 1976. Goldman "describes" Lennon's visit to Bangkok, writing about what Lennon "would have found" if he had gone looking for sex: "John might have indulged himself with a Thai boy." But, in fact, Goldman knows nothing about Lennon in Bangkok; this entire account of "Lennon's sexual exploits" is pure speculation.

Some of Goldman's earlier sexual-exploit stories are far from sordid. A fan described sex with John on the Beatles 1964 Australian tour: "I liked him so much. He wasn't macho at all.... He was a very, very funny person. We laughed all night."

Goldman says that ex-Beatle Paul McCartney was arrested for marijuana possession in Japan in 1980 because John and Yoko tipped off the Japanese customs authorities. Chet Flippo, in his new McCartney biography *Yesterday*, calls that story "a joke." The customs authorities, he points out, didn't need to be tipped off: Paul had long been banned from entering Japan because of his previous drug arrests, and "he continued to make no secret of his love of cannabis." McCartney himself doesn't believe Goldman's story, calls Goldman's book "trash," and urged fans to boycott it.

Lennon is important above all for the songs he wrote and sang—an obvious fact, but one that Goldman seems to have forgotten. What can you say about an author who thinks the Beatles first record, "Love Me Do," was a "10-inch 78," instead of a 45 r.p.m. single? Goldman dislikes most of Lennon's music: "Imagine," Lennon's best-known post-Beatles song, Goldman finds "monotonous" and "feeble." But Lennon was important for more than his music. His candor about his life, about his weaknesses and failings, made young people admire him. Goldman set himself a difficult goal: to destroy the memory of John Lennon as a man who told the truth. He hasn't succeeded.

Los Angeles Times Book Review, September 4, 1988

36

Rockin' with Ron:

Springsteen and Reagan

No one sings more passionately about the working-class victims of Reaganomics than Bruce Springsteen. So even the most cynical politicos were surprised when President Reagan dedicated himself to fulfilling Springsteen's "dream" in a recent campaign speech. George Will apparently inspired the White House with a syndicated column, titled "Yankee Doodle Springsteen," which he wrote after attending a Springsteen concert and leaving early. It held up the rock-and-roller as an example of a hard worker dedicated to traditional American values. Reagan had already lured Michael Jackson into the Rose Garden for a photo opportunity. So when Springsteen quietly declined an invitation to appear at a campaign rally with the President, Reagan did the next best thing: he claimed Springsteen for his side anyway. In a speech in Hammonton, New Jersey, on September 19, Reagan said, "America's future rests in a thousand dreams inside our hearts. It rests in the message of hope in the songs of a man so many young Americans admire: New Jersey's own Bruce Springsteen. And helping you make those dreams come true is what this job of mine is all about."

Performing in Pittsburgh two nights later, Springsteen gave a brief response: "The President was mentioning my name the other day, and I kind of got to wondering what his favorite album must have been.... I don't think he's been listening to this one." Then he played "Johnny 99," a song about an unemployed auto worker who gets drunk and shoots someone. When he is sentenced to ninety-nine years in the penitentiary, he tells the judge, "Let 'em shave off my hair and put me on that execution line." (The *Los Angeles Herald Examiner* quoted a Presidential press aide as saying that Reagan listens to Springsteen's records all the time.) At his performance the following evening, Springsteen talked about visiting Washington and walking from the Lincoln Monument to the Vietnam Veterans Memorial. He said it was a long way, adding, "And it's a long way from a government that's supposed to represent all of the people to where we are today ... and sometimes it's hard to remember that this place belongs to us, that this is our hometown." Then he sang "Our Hometown," about a father showing his young son the closed factories where he once worked.

He told the audience, "There's something really dangerous happening to us out there. We're slowly getting split up into two different Americas. Things are getting taken away from people that need them and given to people that don't need them. And there's a promise being broken." As if to answer George Will's complaint that American workers don't work as hard as Springsteen, he dedicated a song to the rank and file of Steelworkers Local 1397. After the concert he met with the local's president, Ron Weisen, who heads the rank-and-file caucus that challenged the national union bureaucracy in elections this year and will most likely do so next year.

If Reagan could use Springsteen, imagine what he might do with Elvis: taking "Don't Step on My Blue Suede Shoes" as inspiration for standing up to the Russians. Or Muddy Waters' "Got My Mojo Workin'" as an example of black capitalism. The whole thing leaves the rest of us singing "Help!"

The Nation, October 6, 1984

37

Reggae and Revolution

Bob Marley shaped reggae, the music from the slums of Jamaica whose elusive, unrushed lyrics and rhythms proclaim the possibility of revolution. Marley's songs were saturated with social realism. Their themes ranged from consolation for the suffering to fierce cries for freedom; they were incisive yet lyrical. When Marley sang "Get Up, Stand Up," hundreds of thousands of Jamaicans did, and millions of others around the world listened. Only one other musician had similar political and cultural authority: the early Bob Dylan. But Dylan—and Mick Jagger and John Lennon—moved in and out of radical politics; Marley held fast to his commitments until his death in 1981 at the age of thirty-six.

Marley's life and career, especially his formative years, are authoritatively documented in Timothy White's *Catch a Fire*.[1] As a teenager, Marley belonged to the first generation of Third World youth that grew up in the culture of the transistor radio. The Marleys had a neighbor who owned one; he hung it from a clothesline in the communal courtyard and kept it tuned to a Miami rhythm and blues station. Inspired by the hit recordings of Sam Cooke and other black artists, Marley at sixteen went into a studio and made the first recording of his own music. He got halfway home with it before realizing that no one he knew owned a phonograph.

Marley and his group, the Wailers, engaged social issues from the

---

1. Timothy White, *Catch a Fire: the Life of Bob Marley* (New York: Holt, Rinehart & Winston, 1983).

beginning. In 1964, their first smash hit, "Simmer Down," urged the island's "rude boys" (street toughs) to stop their gang wars. The song shocked respectable Jamaicans and amazed the ghetto, because the Wailers sang in the jargon and style of the underclass, at a time when pop music portrayed Jamaica as the place "down the way where the nights are gay." Outfitted in gold lamé collarless suits and pointy black shoes, the Wailers gained local fame doing romantic American rhythm and blues songs along with their own slum records. Within five years, Marley began to establish a new and indigenous music of the Caribbean islands, one that was free from the domination of the mainstream commercial sound of the United States' recording industry. He helped turn the parochial "riddims" of Jamaica's shantytowns into an expression of the suffering of poor people throughout the world, making music that could "interpret, explain, and beat back the planet's moral turpitude and racial oppression." How Marley achieved this work of cultural liberation is the subject of *Catch a Fire*.

White emphasizes Marley's adherence to Rastafarianism, a millenarian offshoot of Marcus Garvey's Back to Africa movement. Marley used the Rasta philosophy to link his identity to the history of Afro-American slavery. In the Rasta theology of liberation, a black God will redeem his people by bringing them back to him, in Africa. Garvey spoke of the Biblical "Ethiopia" as the black Zion. Rastas regard Haile Selassie (whose given name was "Ras Tafari") as the symbol of God on earth. As part of their religious rites, Rastas smoke the herb "ganja" or marijuana, citing Psalms 104: 14: "He causeth the grass to grow for the cattle, and herb for the service of man." They also refuse to cut or comb their hair; their long twined "dreadlocks" represent the flowing mane of the African lion, which is in turn a symbol of Selassie, the Lion of Judah.

In the early seventies Marley began combining his Rastafarian beliefs with radical politics. In 1972 he worked for the election of Michael Manley, socialist and trade union organizer, as Prime Minister of Jamaica, and Manley won. Marley's music also flourished during this time. In the next four years, Marley and the Wailers released four albums and became an international sensation. They toured the United States, Europe, Africa and Japan, always remaining open to diverse musical influences: "People like I," Marley said in 1975, "we love James Brown an' love your funky stuffs.... We dig inta dat American bag." In London the next year he heard the punk band The Clash, admired their angry attack on race and class oppression, and wrote a song about the affinities between punks and rastas, "Punky Reggae Party."

Marley maintained his ties to Prime Minister Manley through the 1978 election campaign, and two nights before a scheduled rally with Manley seven gunmen attacked Marley in his house with a barrage of automatic weapon fire. Marley and his wife Rita were hit but escaped serious injury. They defied their would-be assassins and appeared at the rally. Manley greeted them as 80,000 supporters cheered. Marley sang for ninety minutes, re-enacting his dance in and out of the path of death with triumphant laughter.

After the assassination attempt, Marley left Jamaica and declared his withdrawal from what he called "commercial politics." His records lost some of their compelling energy and drive during the next two years. But he returned to political music in 1979, singing about the independence movement in Zimbabwe and the attempt to kill him ("Ambush in the Night"). He declared his support for "the struggle for a truly free and independent Jamaica," White writes, separating himself from Manley and calling for "a black, Marxist government."

A year later Marley was dead of cancer at thirty-six. His body lay in state in the National Heroes Arena in Kingston, where thousands of mourners gathered. His dreadlocks, which had fallen out during radiation treatments, had been sewn into a wig and set back in place. One of his hands held a Bible; the other lay on his guitar. Both the Prime Minister and the opposition leader spoke, the Wailers played Marley's music, and his mother sang "Coming in From the Cold," an unforgettably moving song about "this oh sweet life" that Marley had written when he alone knew he was dying.

White interviewed Marley more frequently than any other writer and had the cooperation of his family and inner circle in writing this biography. Strangely, however, he devotes little space to Marley's albums. (To my mind *Natty Dread*, released in 1974, fused music with social consciousness more powerfully than any other album of the decade; the book deals with it in three lines.) And White doesn't seem to know what to say about Marley's political engagements—his support for the socialist Manley and then his move toward a revolutionary Marxism. Because of White's extensive research, this biography—especially the rich accounts of Marley's youth, daily life in the Trenchtown slums of Kingston and the rise of the Jamaican recording industry—is not only informative but also absorbing.

New York Times Book Review, August 14, 1983

38

A Soft Rain: *Dylan*

A lot of people who grew up in the 1960s and now have $35 to spend on Jonathan Cott's coffetable book *Dylan*[1] can look back on his abandonment of politics as a justification of their own. But Dylan today is a fundamentalist crank who sings about "adulterers in churches / pornography in the schools" and who recently told *Rolling Stone* that "politics is an instrument of the Devil." It's not easy to regard him as a role model. For those who care or cared about his music, Dylan is a problem; we want to know what happened to him. This book doesn't help.

Hundreds of pictures, lavishly displayed, make *Dylan* essentially a fan book, but the text is much more ambitious than the genre requires. Cott's interpretations are peculiarly pretentious, while his analysis of Dylan's origins and development avoids the hard questions.

Cott refers to the "ferment and subversiveness" of the 1960s, but he doesn't explain how Dylan's political engagements, especially with the civil rights movement, lay behind the protest songs that brought him fame. During that period the primary influence on his political ideas seems to have been his girlfriend Suze Rotolo, who worked in New York City's Congress of Racial Equality office. (She appears shivering at his side on the cover of *The Freewheelin' Bob Dylan*.) Dylan himself traveled to Greenwood, Mississippi, in 1963 to give a concert for the Student Non-violent Coordinating Committee's voter registration drive there. The book includes four pages of photographs of him in

---

1. Jonathan Cott, *Dylan* (New York: Rolling Stone Press/Doubleday, 1984).

Greenwood, printed bigger than we've ever seen them. In general, the book's format makes a virtue of photographs over text, but even here there are difficulties. Fuzzy snapshots are printed the same monstrous size as formal posed portraits, and the two are bled together; on one two-page spread, Dylan, his nose stuck into the page break, looks like a robin digging for a worm. Also, some of the captions are incorrect.

After staying up all one night talking about civil rights, Dylan wrote "Blowin' in the Wind." When civil rights leader Medgar Evers was murdered in Mississippi in 1963, Dylan wrote "Only a Pawn in Their Game"; he sang it at the 1963 march on Washington. During the Cuban missile crisis, he wrote what remains his most powerful song, "A Hard Rain's A-Gonna Fall," a series of chilling images of America. Two of those songs appeared on *The Freewheelin' Bob Dylan*, released in 1963 just after the Beatles' simple "Please Please Me" hit number one on the British charts. Dylan was only twenty-two, but he had brought his personal vision and his political commitments together with a power he would never again equal.

Another Side of Bob Dylan appeared the following year, and stunned his fans. It cast the political and the personal as antagonistic forms of liberation. "I was so much older then, I'm younger than that now," he sang, dismissing his engagement with social issues. The songs insisted that Dylan's private nightmares were more important to him than anything in the political realm. Deeply anti-authoritarian but hostile to organized politics, Dylan pointed the way to the apolitical side of the counterculture. In 1965 Dylan's *Bringing It All Back Home* merged Woodie Guthrie's music with Chuck Berry's. *Highway 61 Revisited* and *Blonde on Blonde*, released in 1965 and 1966, respectively, confirmed that he had opened rock and roll to a wider range of personal statements than anyone had imagined possible.

When Dylan stopped playing his protest songs, some of his old fans called him a sellout and a phony. The same things were said when he "betrayed" folk for rock, then rock for country. But there was a strategy behind those moves: Dylan was undercutting the role of superstar. He was trying to disappear as an identifiable persona and tell his demanding and possessive audience, "You don't own me."

Once Dylan had shattered his persona as a protest singer, he could return to political issues whenever they engaged his imagination. In 1971 he released "George Jackson," a moving portrait of the Black

Panther killed by San Quentin guards that year; Cott's book ignores the song. In 1972, John Lennon persuaded him to join in a concert tour to urge young people to vote against Nixon's reelection. The tour was to end at a "political Woodstock," a free antiwar concert and rally outside the Republican National Convention, then scheduled for San Diego. Together with Allen Ginsberg, Dylan wrote and recorded "Going to San Diego" for the tour. When Nixon found out about the plan, he ordered Lennon deported, and the tour was canceled. The song was not released until 1983, on Allen Ginsberg's album *First Blues.* Cott doesn't tell any part of that story.

Dylan performed at many of the major political concerts of the 1970s—among them, the 1971 Concert for Bangladesh and the 1974 Friends of Chile concert which raised funds for political prisoners after the coup against Salvador Allende. While they receive no commentary in the text, the concerts are documented in the book's photographs, as are Dylan's 1976 benefits for Hurricane Carter, a former boxing champion imprisoned for murdering three people in a New Jersey bar.

The Hurricane Carter benefits were more a case of Dylan's sympathy for another misunderstood superstar than a genuine political project. Dylan launched a campaign to establish Carter's innocence, starting with a good song, "Hurricane." The Night of the Hurricane benefit filled Madison Square Garden; even Representative Ed Koch came. The campaign bore fruit: the courts ordered a new trial for Carter, who went free on bail. The benefits were immensely successful, taking in some $600,000, but the *New York Times* revealed that 90 per cent of the money was spent on "expenses" for Dylan's concerts rather than on Carter's defense. The woman who chaired the defense committee charged that Carter had assaulted her in a motel room and indicated that she considered him capable of murder. At the second trial the jury affirmed the original guilty verdict, and again Carter received a life sentence for murder. Dylan had no comment and neither does Cott.

Cott lacks the critical distance that would enable him to deal with some of those issues. He did interview Dylan, who told him, "Bob Dylan has always been here. ... Before I was born, there was Bob Dylan." Taking that statement to heart, Cott has found the earlier Bob Dylans, going back to "the first known troubadour poet, the eleventh-century Guillaume IX," who, like Dylan, "revealed many faces and voices." Cott also finds something of Dylan in the thirteenth-century Carmina Burana, in the fifteenth-century French poet François Villon, the sixteenth-century Chinese philosopher Li Chih and the eighteenth-century Hasidic master Rabbi Nachman of Bratzlav. Dylan, we learn, took seriously "Walt Whitman's great and inspiring advice: ... 'Stand up for the stupid and crazy.'" (Perhaps Cott was thinking about Dylan's recent defense of right-wing Jewish groups.)

In addition to his other absurdities, Cott repeats the moth-eaten cliché that Dylan is "America's greatest poet," which Ellen Willis dispensed with in 1969. "Poetry requires economy, coherence, and discrimination," she wrote. Dylan turns out five images where one will do, his phrases are often tangled, his metaphors are silly and he tries to make everything rhyme. He's a great songwriter but a terrible poet.

Dylan's 1979 born-again album *Slow Train Coming* poses the greatest problem for Cott. He fails to see that in some ways it was another of Dylan's "betrayals" of his fans, another act of self-annihilation. It was also more than that. The problem isn't Dylan's embrace of Christianity; Biblical imagery and the theme of salvation were present in his music from the beginning. Other rock superstars have turned to Jesus: Elvis recorded four gospel albums, and Little Richard gave up his pop career to become an evangelist. While their Christian music expresses the desperate hope that Jesus will help them and that "every-thing will be all right," Dylan's *Slow Train Coming* is a slick, ugly state-ment announcing that he is saved and the rest of us will rot in hell. What happened? Borrowing Dylan's words, Cott says Dylan became a Christian because he "had offered up his innocence and had gotten repaid with scorn." His previous album, *Street Legal*, had indeed been treated scornfully: *Village Voice* critic Robert Christgau called it the work of a "boozy-voiced misogynist in his late thirties ... in love with his own self-generated misery." If only Christgau had called it "mysterious and gripping," like Cott, Dylan might never have taken shelter in the sign of the cross.

An expensive rock book doesn't have to be this dumb. Two earlier volumes in the Rolling Stone Press series, Geoffrey Stokes's *The Beatles* and Dave Marsh's *Elvis*, had stronger graphics and a genuinely serious text. Marsh, for example, argues that Elvis was a great example of the American capacity for self-invention, locked in a conflict with those

306

who dominated American culture and dismissed him as a dumb redneck. Unlike Cott, Marsh does not avoid the dark side of his subject. But Elvis and the Beatles are somehow suited to this kind of visually elegant treatment; whatever Bob Dylan has become, this $35 coffeetable book isn't his format.

The Nation, November 3, 1984

39

Tocqueville, Marx, Weber, Nixon:

Watergate in Theory

Watergate is history. The time has come to seek a theoretical perspective on those tumultuous events, to move away from yesterday's feverish absorption with "the facts" and confront the significance of Watergate for American politics and society—particularly to consider the relative merits of liberal and Marxist attempts to deal with these questions.

The dominant interpretation of Watergate has been a version of Tocquevillean pluralist theory: Watergate has significance as a despotic attack on pluralism by Nixon and his associates. This was the orientation of most House Judiciary Committee members in their hearings, as well as of most interpretations by the liberal press. From this perspective, the Nixon administration's attacks on the Democratic National Committee and the Democratic presidential contenders were a violation of the rules of pluralistic politics—that political groups accept each other as equally legitimate; that party competition, by mutual agreement, remains within clearly defined limits; that no one seeks the annihilation of his opponents. The winners are magnanimous and willing to compromise; they do not use their new power to retaliate against those who opposed them.

This was not, of course, how the Committee to Reelect the President behaved. It refused to play by the rules; it played dirty, played for keeps, played winner take all. Patrick Buchanan, Nixon's speech writer, openly affirmed the strategy of seizing power, and keeping hold of it permanently, in his testimony before the Senate Watergate

Committee.[1] Gordon Liddy told Mike Wallace that the break-in at Democratic National Committee headquarters was an "operation by one group of persons who were seeking to retain power, against another group who were seeking to acquire power. That's all it was. It's like brushing your teeth, Michael; it's basic." Nixon's only flaw, in Liddy's eyes, was that he was "insufficiently ruthless" in dealing with those who opposed him. Charles Colson said he would stomp on his own grandmother if it would help Nixon win—a sentiment clearly incompatible with the spirit of democratic pluralism. John Ehrlichman had an even more revealing exchange with Senator Talmadge:

> TALMADGE: If the president could authorize a covert break-in, do you think his power could include ... murder or other crimes?
> EHRLICHMAN: I do not know where the line is, Senator.[2]

The usually restrained R.W. Apple of the *New York Times* referred to this as advocacy of "fascist tactics."[3] This was precisely Tocqueville's concern: that there would be no check on the powers of central authority to move against citizens. The Nixon reelection campaign was dedicated to the idea that winning was the only thing that mattered. As the President said to a trusted lieutenant, " *We gotta win.*"[4] That is not a pluralist idea. Nixon and his staff apparently developed this unprincipled commitment to victory-at-any-price in the wake of the razor-thin victory of 1968. Never again, they vowed, would they exercise genteel restraint in the face of such a risk.

Tocqueville was particularly concerned about political corruption in democracies.

> It is useless to say that dishonest passions are found among all ranks, that one may find despicable men at the head of aristocratic nations as well as democracies.... There is, in the corruption of those who reach power by

---

1. US Congress, Senate, *Report of the Select Committee on Presidential Campaign Activities* (Washington, DC: Government Printing Office, 1974), Testimony of Patrick Buchanan.

2. *The Watergate Hearings: Break-in and Cover-up* (New York: Viking/Bantam, a New York Times Book, 1973), p. 521.

3. *Watergate Hearings*, p. 53.

4. *The White House Transcripts* (New York: Viking [hardcover], Bantam [paper], a New York Times Book, 1974), transcript of June 23, 1972.

chance, something coarse and vulgar which makes it contagious to the crowd. But in the depravity of great noblemen there is often a certain aristocratic refinement and an air of grandeur which prevents it from being communicated. It is difficult for the people to discover the baseness hidden under elegant manners, refined tastes, and graceful phrases. But stealing from the public purse or selling the favors of the state for money—these are matters any wretch can understand and hope to emulate in turn.[5]

Selling favors of the state was precisely the kind of corruption that led to Agnew's fall, but it was not what Watergate was about. Nixon probably was financially corrupt, and it is possible that public outrage over this issue was the major cause of his downfall. But the crucial issue of a pluralist politics has to do not with money but with power. Tocquevillean liberals fear that centralized power will destroy individual rights. Only voluntary associations could serve as a check on such despotism, defending individuals against the tyrannical tendencies of the state. "If each citizen of a democracy did not learn to combine with his fellow citizens to defend their freedom ... tyranny would unavoidably increase," Tocqueville wrote.[6] This argument overlooks the possibility that some citizens might combine, not to defend freedom but to attack it, and that some voluntary associations might not play by the pluralist rules—as CREEP, for instance, did not. Americans join not only the League of Women Voters and the PTA but also the Birch Society and the Ku Klux Klan. Liberals hope that such groups will balance one another out, at least so long as the government itself does not tip the balance.

Nixon sensed that the case against him was based on a concept of pluralism, and defended himself by calling for a reassertion of pluralist virtue in words that Tocqueville himself might have uttered:

Ultimately the answer ... lies in a commitment by all of us to show a renewed respect for the mutual restraints that are the mark of a free and civilized society ... respect for the system by which our conflicts are peacefully resolved and our liberties maintained.[7]

---

5. Alexis de Tocqueville, *Democracy in America*, J.P. Mayer, ed. (New York: Doubleday, 1966), p. 513.
6. Tocqueville, pp. 220–21.
7. Nixon's TV address of August 15, 1973.

Nixon was not the only Watergate figure to explain and justify his actions in Tocquevillean terms. "The American revolution was not a class revolution, but a successful separation of a colony from an empire. Class warfare, therefore, is of foreign origin." This eminently Tocquevillean statement comes from, of all people, E. Howard Hunt.[8] For him, the implication is that class warfare of the kind exhibited by, say, George McGovern, is unAmerican, outside the American consensus, and thus a legitimate target for ruthless tactics. There is an irony in this use of Tocqueville's notion of consensus to justify despotic treatment of political opponents.

Why was Nixon forced out? This is a crucial question for any theoretical account of Watergate, and there is a Tocquevillean answer to it. Nixon was forced out because America is a society of consensus —a society that recognizes limits in what those in power can do to their opponents. The Republican Party is part of this consensus; its members do not challenge the fundamental rule of pluralistic politics that neither major party seek the annihilation of the other. This is what Theodore White was referring to in arguing that Nixon broke faith with the American people—and even with fellow Republicans. It was his own party's refusal to defend him that led to Nixon's downfall. For CREEP was set up beyond the pale of pluralist consensus, which is to say, outside the Republican Party. It was Barry Goldwater, and Hugh Scott, and Orange County's Representative Charles Wiggins who sealed Nixon's doom. All this suggests that the public debate over Nixon, the terms in which he was accused and in which he defended himself, were basically Tocquevillean. It suggests that behind Woodward and Bernstein's investigations, behind Leon Jaworski's indictments, behind Eric Sevareid's pear-shaped phrases lie the ideas of Alexis de Tocqueville.

But if Watergate was a despotic attack on pluralism, it was not the kind of threat Tocqueville imagined would confront democracy in America. It was neither a case of the tyranny of the majority, the lack of protection for minority rights (after all, the Democrats were the majority party); nor was it an example of the benevolent despotism that Tocqueville believed found fertile soil in the egotism and isolation of

---

8. Cited by Gore Vidal in the *New York Review of Books*, December 13, 1973, p. 6.

mass society (there was nothing particularly benevolent about the Nixon social policies of "benign neglect"). While it is possible to find in Tocquevillean theory an analysis of the significance of Watergate—indeed, it is the dominant conception of Watergate—Tocqueville himself did not foresee the possibility that this kind of despotic attack on pluralism would be a significant threat to democracy in America.

An alternative liberal conception of Watergate is the Weberian notion that it was a consequence of the growth of bureaucratic power to the point where it threatened democracy. From this perspective, argued by Arthur Schlesinger Jr, and Archibald Cox, Watergate was a conflict between the administrative officials of the executive branch, with their characteristic attachment to secrecy, and the elected officials of the legislature, more committed to democratic values.[9] This was a classic confrontation in which "democracy inevitably comes into conflict with bureaucratic tendencies." For Max Weber, "bureaucracy is a precision instrument which can put itself at the disposal of quite varied interests in domination. The mechanism is easily made to work for anybody who knows how to gain control of it"—even Richard Nixon.[10] Watergate has been interpreted as the culmination of a long process of the centralization of power in the executive branch, a centralization that began as a response to foreign policy needs. Arthur Schelsinger has written that, as the presidential bureaucracy "overwhelmed the traditional separation of powers in foreign affairs, it began to aspire toward an equivalent centralization of power in the domestic polity."[11] The Watergate crisis was resolved by a reassertion of power by the elected officials of the legislative branch.

An alternative Weberian conception of Watergate is that it was a conflict, not between bureaucracy and democracy, but between two different conceptions of legitimate authority—between the rational authority of a set of legal rules, and the charismatic authority of the president. This conception is richer than the first but in some ways

---

9. Archibald Cox, "Ends," *New York Times Magazine*, May 19, 1974, p. 28.

10. Hans Gerth and C. Wright Mills, eds., *From Max Weber: Essays in Sociology* (New York: Oxford University Press, 1958), "Bureaucracy," pp. 226, 229.

11. Arthur M. Schlesinger Jr, *The Imperial Presidency* (Boston: Houghton Mifflin, 1972), p. 205. I am indebted to Keith Nelson for calling this to my attention.

more problematic. Politics for Weber is first of all a question of the "inner justifications" people give to their acts of domination and obedience—the meanings people attribute to their relations with the powers that be. Thus Weber would have us ask, what were the inner justifications with which the Watergate principals acted? (They claimed in their own defense that "everybody did it," a bastardized version of the "authority of the eternal yesterday.") From this perspective, the Watergate principals rejected the notion that their highest obligation was to a rationally created system of legal rules (the Bill of Rights). They did not believe that they had an ultimate duty to legal statute, that obedience to the rules is required in discharging statutory obligations. Instead, Nixon's staff people saw themselves as acting on the basis of an absolutely personal devotion to Nixon's individual leadership; for them, Nixon possessed an extraordinary and personal value, the kind of appeal Weber called "charismatic." Instead of believing in the rules, they believed in him.

While George Gallup never hesitated to ask Americas, "How much charisma does Nixon have: a good deal, some, or none?" today the notion that Richard Nixon possessed a unique gift of grace seems ludicrous—this man who was called "Tricky Dick," or of whom it was said, "Would you buy a used car from him?" In retrospect he does not seem to have been capable of the kind of prophetic revelation and heroism that in Weber's terms inspire an absolutely personal sense of devotion. Nixon himself found it necessary to issue a disclaimer against charismatic justifications of Watergate. He denounced "a few over-zealous persons who mistakenly thought their cause justified violations of the law," and he refused to accept the "blame" for their excess of enthusiasm.[12] Haldeman coldly denied that Nixon had been a charismatic figure for him: "I do not love Richard Nixon," he said. But by early 1975 few were about to admit that they had loved Nixon, and Haldeman had never been the kind of person of whom it could be said that he was in close touch with his emotional life, much less given to effusive TV statements while his conviction was under appeal. In any case, devotion to charismatic criminals is not grounds for overturning trial verdicts in the American legal system.

---

12. Nixon's TV address of April 30, 1973.

Nixon seemed to doubt his own charismatic appeal, to have a gnawing suspicion that he was not what Weber described as "an innerly called leader of men." Would such a person tell the nation, "I'm not a crook"? But for Weber, charisma is not restricted to rare appearances of saints and prophets. Charisma is the basis of political party life in modern democracies; it is the bread and butter of electoral competition. Thus it seems completely appropriate in Weberian terms to regard Nixon as a leader exercising charismatic authority. In the Weberian conception, White House assistants committed the Watergate crimes for *him*, because keeping him in office was their most important task. Weber would have to say that Nixon's staff valued him not so much for any rationally constructed political program as for his own status as a uniquely valuable individual. Here the contrast with a Marxist position is striking. In modern politics, for Weber, the message is not what counts. It is heroes, not party programs, that win the enthusiasm and devotion of followers, of the staff as well as the masses.

Weber makes a distinction between two ways of making politics one's vocation. One can live "off" politics, or one can live "for" politics—a distinction worth pursuing in relation to Watergate. Watergate was not a matter of living "off" politics. Haldeman, Ehrlichman, Liddy and Hunt didn't do it for the money, but rather because Nixon was their life. Nixon himself labored mightily to acquire the sense that he too lived "for" rather than "off" politics, to persuade himself that he was one of those leaders with what Weber called "an inner balance" and a firm knowledge that their "life has meaning in the service of a cause."[13] Thus Nixon told the country that his leadership had brought not just the end of a war but a generation of peace. Yet living "off" politics—corruption in the common Tocquevillean sense— turns out always to have lurked beneath the surface of Nixon's vocation—for example, his tax deductions, his home improvements. What Tocqueville denounced as "corruption," Weber describes neutrally as one way of making politics one's vocation.

Why did Nixon fall? What forces brought him down? Weberian references to Nixon's "loss of legitimacy" coming in the wake of a "failure of charisma" offer no real analysis. Weber's writings lack any elaboration of the process by which charismatic figures lose legitimacy.

---

13. *From Max Weber*, "Politics as a Vocation," p. 84.

(His work on "routinization" deals only with the cases in which charisma succeeds.) Similarly, Weber did little work on the social origins of charismatic authority. The conditions favoring its demise, like the conditions favoring its appearance, remain largely unexplored in his work.

We can understand the outcome of the Watergate affair as the triumph of a rational–legal system of authority over charismatic claims to legitimacy. For Weber, however, such a development was by no means necessarily a desirable one. Weber welcomed charismatic "interruptions" of legal rationality as the only force that could keep modern society from becoming an iron cage of bureaucratic stagnation. He seems to have assumed that charismatic leadership is, in principle, fully compatible with an otherwise instrumentally rational political system. But according to his definition of charisma, the successful authority figure is "entitled to unrestricted obedience from his followers," who by definition see no conflicting obligations to a system of laws. Indeed, for Weber, political commitment and action are fundamentally emotional and irrational responses to the claims of heroic individuals. Politics in democratic states, he wrote, consists of "a sort of charismatic rule concealed behind a legitimacy which is formally and rationally derived from the will of the governed ... but in fact, the leader rules by virtue of the devotion of his followers." This leadership does not base its appeal on a rational political program. Weber writes scornfully of the "merely abstract program of a party consisting of mediocrities" (and what party doesn't?); adherence to a program, he feels, provides little inner satisfaction compared to devotion to great leaders. He rejects the description of democratic politics as rational consideration of alternative polices—the classical Tocquevillean conception—and argues instead that it has become a "dictatorship resting on the exploitation of mass emotionality."[14] This he does not see as a threat to democratic government, or a problem for liberal states; this is the essence of liberal democracy. Weber thus lacks a conception of a possible conflict between charismatic and rational–legal forms of authority.

---

14. Max Weber, *Economy and Society*, Guenther Roth and Klaus Wittich, eds. (New York: Bedminster Press, 1968), vol. I, p. 268; *From Max Weber*, "Politics as a Vocation," pp. 103, 107.

Weber also lacks a conception of "illegitimate domination" that could accompany his theory of legitimate authority and would be useful in understanding Watergate. This was an explicit rejection on Weber's part, not an oversight. To develop a concept of illegitimate domination he regarded as an unscientific undertaking, a value judgment that belonged properly in the realm of politics rather than science. A judgment that Nixon's administration engaged in illegitimate activities might be necessary, but it belongs in the political arena and not the scientific. For Weber a stable political administration was by definition legitimate, and a genuinely unstable one would apparently not last long enough to require analysis.[15]

Weber believed that the greatest threat to human freedom lay in the steady growth of bureaucratic structures, which brought with them a social ossification and a life-denying stagnation. Charismatic leadership alone could break this deadening routine by its dynamism and creativity. He apparently did not foresee that such a process could bring to power leaders whose "dynamism" and "creativity" would threaten freedom in a fundamental way.

Watergate seems to pose problems for Marxist analysis. Some Marxists contented themselves with the observation that Watergate was not a class conflict; others argued that Nixon's "real crimes" were not against Larry O'Brien (the Democratic National Committee chairman, whose office was a target of the Watergate burglars), but against the people of Vietnam, and to a much lesser extent, against American radicals, black and white. Noam Chomsky called Watergate a "tea party" in comparison to what Nixon was doing in Vietnam.[16] The implication here was that Marxists should not be overly concerned with Watergate; that it was only an exaggerated case of politics as spectacle functioning to conceal the "real" historical developments with which Marxists ought to be concerned; that all there is to be revealed about Watergate is politics as usual in bourgeois society—corporate domination of the

---

15. Wolfgang J. Mommsen, *The Age of Bureaucracy: Perspectives on the Political Sociology of Max Weber* (Oxford: Oxford University Press, 1974), chapter 4, especially pp. 84–5.

16. See, for example, Noam Chomsky, "Watergate: a Skeptical View," *New York Review*, September 20, 1973, p. 3.

candidates and dirty tricks against the people. Had there ever been a candidate who refused corporate contributions? Had not John F. Kennedy gained the presidency through a suspicious counting of votes in Chicago?

But if presidents from Roosevelt through Kennedy and Johnson accepted corporate contributions, played dirty tricks, and covered up with public lies, they did not get driven from office for it. The argument that Watergate was "business as usual" cannot explain why *this* piece of political business should provoke the greatest political crisis in modern American history. Watergate was an unprecedented disruption of politics as usual, a genuine crisis rather than simply a media spectacle. Even though we need to be reminded that Nixon committed more serious crimes elsewhere, such a unique political development deserves Marxists' attention. Indeed, the question is precisely why these lesser crimes led to a president being forced out of office for the first time in history, when far more serious ones did not.

One possible Marxist approach to Watergate is the argument that the McGovern campaign represented a genuine threat to the hegemony of the corporate elite, something close to a popular radical movement that could bring a fundamental transformation in the structure of power in America. It was therefore necessary for the corporate elite to discard the veil of legality, the pretense to pluralism that prevails in normal times; in the words of one Marxist, Watergate reveals that "the American ruling class can no longer exercise its power without resorting to the increasingly systematic use of methods which are illegitimate and illegal by this class's own standards."[17] Though Nixon and his staff seem to have held precisely this view of McGovern, there are serious problems with such an analysis. First, McGovern was never close to winning, and thus there was hardly a need to "strip away the veil of legality" at this historical moment. There was no threat that the power of the corporate elite would be diminished or abolished; Watergate was at best a bizarre overreaction, a major miscalculation by the President and his staff, not an objective necessity required by deepening contradictions. Second, McGovern was no threat to the capitalist class even had he won. His was not a socialist party, not an

---

17. Bruce Brown, "Watergate: Business as Usual," *Liberation*, July–August 1974, p. 17.

anticapitalist party, not a working-class party, hardly even a party; he did not lead a national organization capable of pushing a program through Congress. It was essentially a single-issue campaign that was not incompatible with corporate interests, especially since many corporate leaders themselves no longer supported the war in Vietnam.

What was Watergate? From a Marxist perspective, it can be seen as a split in the ruling class, a split of the kind Marx described in the *18th Brumaire of Louis Bonaparte*, between capitalist groups with different economic interests that had been developing since World War Two.[18] In the *New York Review* and *Ramparts*, Kirkpatrick Sale and Carl Oglesby have called this the "Yankee–Cowboy" theory of Watergate, a conflict between the eastern old money elite and the new money of the "Southern Rim."[19] Nixon represented the "new money" group in challenging the dominant position of the "old"; the challenge succeeded temporarily but was followed in the Watergate affair by the reassertion of the eastern group.

The Yankee–Cowboy theory describes the same regional class coalition as do the theories of the "emerging Republican majority" and "the southern strategy." In the view of Sale and Oglesby, the Yankee group consists of the eastern establishment, of second- and third-generation elite families, of Wall Street and the Ivy League, with interests primarily in international finance and manufacturing. This old money, represented above all by Nelson Rockefeller, was challenged by men of new money from the Sun Belt, above all by Goldwater, and later by Nixon. The Southern Rim is anchored at one end in Orange County, California, land of the Birch Society, and particularly in Newport Beach, home of Nixon's personal lawyer Herbert Kalmbach, of his partners Frank DeMarco, who prepared the fraudulent deed for the donation of Nixon papers to the people of the US, and Arthur Blech, the President's notorious tax accountant. The Sun Belt of the new money goes south down the San Diego Freeway,

---

18. Karl Marx, *The 18th Brumaire of Louis Bonaparte*. I refer here to Marx's discussion of the way different legitimist factions represented different capitalist economic interests. His analysis of Bonapartism does not seem appropriate for Nixon and Watergate.

19. Kirkpatrick Sale, "The World Behind Watergate," *New York Review*, May 3, 1973; Carl Oglesby, "In Defense of Paranoia," *Ramparts*, November 1974.

past San Clemente, the Versailles of the Rimsters, further south, past La Costa Country Club, where Nixon's staff retreated to plan the Watergate coverup; then east by Lear jet into Goldwater's Arizona, to Texas, home of John Connolly and H.L. Hunt, and finally to Florida, to Senator Gurney, to Bebe Rebozo, to the Cuban emigrés who did the dirty work for the Nixon reelection campaign. "It is no accident," as the Marxists say, that one end of the Southern Rim is anchored in San Clemente, the other in Key Biscayne.

But this is not just a geographical theory of American politics, not just an argument that too much sun makes capitalists into right-wing extremists. In the Sun Belt, it is argued, there has arisen a new breed of capitalists in the post-World War Two period, men who based their recent rise to wealth on government contracts in military and aero-space industries, on the oil depletion allowance, and on farm price supports. Their interests tend to be in domestic enterprises rather than foreign. The newness, the rawness of their wealth has made them typical self-made men, reactionary "individualists" with all the self-assurance, greed, and simple patriotism of the heroic first generation of robber barons. Reiterating the development of their predecessors two generations ago, they are relatively unrestrained in pursuit of profits and political power; they are militantly anti-union, antiblack, and anti-communist, with a lack of interest in high culture and little concern for "social problems" as perceived by the foundations of Rockefeller, Ford, and Carnegie. Their political ethics match their business and social ethics; they tend to be ruthless, to avoid the "civilized" restraints practiced by their eastern rivals.

This "new money" group seized control of the Republican Party in 1964 when Goldwater defeated Rockefeller to win the nomination. Nixon represents them, he is their man—not just because he too is from Orange County, but because he found his financial backers, his personal staff, and his political ideology among them. What we see in Watergate is a display of the political attitudes and practices character-istic of this group—a willingness to use ruthless tactics considered illegitimate by their eastern rivals for power. According to the Yankee–Cowboy theory, the conflict between the two groups was not only about the Cowboys' attempt to exclude the Yankees from power, but also over policy matters. The Cowboys are foreign policy hawks and the Yankees more conciliatory. The Cowboys seek high military budgets as the principal means by which the state can augment their capital, while the Yankees' interest is in a relaxation of international tensions and active government support for increased foreign trade.

Some of the eastern rivals of the Cowboy new money were members of the Democratic Party, which has always found leaders from among the more liberal members of the elite—the Roosevelts, the Harrimans, the Stevensons. What was the crime for which Nixon was forced out of office? One Marxist answer is that he treated the liberals as if they were radicals. He aimed the same weapons at the liberal members of the Democratic Party elite that previous Democratic administrations had aimed at radicals in the antiwar and black power movements: bugging, sabotage, infiltration, acts of provocation. This was the crime to which liberals objected—treating them as if they were beyond the pale, like radicals. As long as Nixon confined his "fascist tactics" to radicals, he was not investigated, much less driven from office.[20]

It is useful to recall that the attacks on liberals in the campaign were only one part of a general push toward the right for which Nixon was gearing up at the end of his first term. This was Nixon's response to a domestic crisis of authority fostered largely by opposition to the war in Southeast Asia, and to an international weakening of American corporate power in relation to Japanese and European rivals. Nixon mounted a general attack on the liberal welfare state that centered on revenue sharing to reduce federal social programs, and on turning the Supreme Court from an activist agency of change into a bulwark of the status quo. The push toward the right included an attack on working-class organizations, centering around wage controls, plus Republican support for the Teamsters in their struggle against the Farmworkers— pitting the most reactionary against the most progressive union. The turn to the right also included an attack on the radical left unprecedented since the days of Joseph McCarthy. This was accompanied by vicious attacks on the leading liberal ideological organs, particularly by Agnew's diatribes against network television news, the *New York Times* and the Washington *Post*. All this was justified by a strident assertion of nationalist ideology around the notion of the "Bicentennial Era," which was to correspond to Nixon's second term of office.

---

20. Geoffrey Barraclough, "The End of an Era," *New York Review*, June 27, 1974, p. 19.

Nixon's strategy was thus a comprehensive and far-reaching attempt to shift the country to the right. His staff was explicit about this. John Mitchell said in 1972, "This country is going to go so far to the right you won't recognize it," and the *New York Times* itself anxiously announced in January 1973 that with Nixon's second term, "a tide of reaction ... is sweeping across America."[21] It was in this context of a highly self-conscious attack on the liberal policies advocated by the eastern corporate elite that Watergate became an issue, and it was made an issue by precisely those elite groups Nixon sought to drive from power—network television news, the *New York Times* and the *Post*, the liberal members of Congress.

Marxists must also ask, how was it possible that such a deep split between two groups within the ruling class was permitted to come out into the open? Why weren't these differences ironed out in private, at the Burning Tree Country Club? First, because Nixon wasn't interested in compromise, he was interested in defeating the eastern old-money elite; he thought he had the power to do it. But then it must be asked, why was the eastern group willing to take such drastic and unprecedented measures against him? Here it seems that the absence of any radical threat in the country convinced many that the society could take a large dose of political disruption at the top. There was no significant radical movement left on the campuses or in the ghettos arguing that the political system was illegitimate; and, because the 1972 election had been so overwhelmingly one-sided, there would not be any Democrats who would argue that dirty tricks determined the outcome and therefore that McGovern deserved to be president.

Thus, from a Marxist perspective, Watergate was not simply unpluralist behavior; it was unpluralist behavior with a specific class content and a specific ideological orientation. Watergate was the battleground of a national struggle for power between two groups within the corporate elite that had different politics. The Nixon campaign consisted of a reactionary attack by the more right-wing element in the capitalist class against the older and more liberal, and the subsequent crisis and investigations were a successful counter-attack.

But there are serious problems with the Yankee–Cowboy theory of

---

21. *New York Times*, January 15, 1973, p. 28.

Watergate. First of all, the economic interests of the two groups have not been shown to be clearly distinct. It does seem that the Cowboys are more immediately dependent on government contracts, but the Yankees too have their share of federal help. And Cowboy capital is often linked to Yankee capital through interlocking boards of directors, holding companies, and stock ownership.

Second, the political differences between Yankees and Cowboys are not fully explained by their different economic interests. The "dovishness" of the Yankees is at most a matter of degree rather than a difference in kind. The hawkish American intervention in Vietnam was the creation of the Yankee circle around Kennedy and Johnson; Yankee–Cowboy theorists would presumably describe counterinsurgency and limited war as policies whose purpose was to defend the global interests of international Yankee capital. It was not until late in the conflict that the Yankees backed off from the war they had created, while the Cowboys continued to defend the old Yankee position. Indeed, Goldwater has said of Rockefeller's foreign policy views, "he'd make me look like a dove."[22] Nixon's foreign policy, created by Rockefeller representative Henry Kissinger, was pure Yankee—disengagement from Vietnam, détente, and trade with Russia and China. From the perspective of the Yankee–Cowboy theory, Nixon's role was not so much the Cowboy antagonist of Yankee interests, but the Cowboy who gained his place in history by turning US foreign policy down the road of new Yankee interests in détente and trade. Even the apparently more liberal social concerns of the Yankees are open to question. Rockefeller's actions at Attica are difficult to explain from the viewpoint of Yankee–Cowboy theory; his policy there was more brutal than anything Ronald Reagan ever did as governor. Can it really be argued that the Yankees are more "civilized" in their domestic social policies?

A final problem with the Yankee–Cowboy theory of Watergate is that the linkages between the two economic groups and the political structures through which the Watergate crisis developed are not clear. Rockefeller never pushed for exposure of Nixon's Watergate activities or for impeachment. McGovern got virtually no support from the

---

22. Associated Press dispatch, June 16, 1975.

Yankee press in arguing that Watergate was a presidential crime for which Nixon should be excluded from office. The Senate and House committees were not dominated by Yankees; Sam Ervin and Peter Rodino would never pass for Cabots or Lodges.

These three problems with the Yankee–Cowboy theory of Watergate—a lack of evidence of distinct economic interests, an unclear relation between the politics and the economic interests of the groups, and an absence of linkages to the politics of the Watergate crisis itself—have led some Marxists to argue that Watergate was a conflict between ruling groups that do not represent consistently well-defined sectors of the economy. This kind of analysis stresses the relative autonomy of political developments and the shifting nature of political coalitions in American society.

For the "Kapitalistate" group around James O'Connor, Watergate was a Habermasian crisis of legitimation for the entire ruling class.[23] Watergate constantly threatened to turn into an indictment of American "democracy" as a whole, as evidence kept appearing and suggested that Nixon didn't do anything his predecessors hadn't done. Confronted with this problem, Congress and the liberal press defined the issues in such a way as to focus on the personal corruption of Nixon and his associates, rather than on American war crimes, systematic denial of civil rights to radicals, or corporate domination of the two-party system. The public impeachment hearings in July 1974 served as the vehicle for relegitimation as committee members and commentators pitted the Constitution against a corrupt president. Finally Gerald Ford proclaimed that the entire episode demonstrated that "our system works," Theodore White enshrined this success in his book, and Dustin Hoffman and Robert Redford played Bernstein and Woodward in the Hollywood version of *All the President's Men*.

In general, Marxists have been considerably more successful at describing the social and political forces that form the background to Watergate than at describing the crisis itself. The major weakness of

---

23. "Watergate, or the 18th Brumaire of Richard Nixon," by the San Francisco Bay Area Kapitalistate Group, in *Kapitalistate: Working Papers on the Capitalist State* (no. 3) Spring, 1975, pp. 3–25. This in turn draws on James O'Connor, *Fiscal Crisis of the State* (New York and London: St Martin's Press, 1974), and Jurgen Habermas, *Legitimation Crisis* (Boston: Beacon Press, 1975).

the various Marxist approaches is that they penetrate too quickly the ideological surface of political events—in this case, the terms in which the crisis was fought out and eventually resolved. Liberals, under an attack from the right unprecedented since the days of Joseph McCarthy, chose to fight back on the terrain of pluralist rules of the game and the rational authority of law by reasserting constitutional freedoms. This has significant consequences for American politics in general and radical politics in particular.

One would think that "relegitimation" would conclude with a celebration of American political virtue once the corrupt president had been expelled. But in fact the opposite has occurred; 1975–76 saw revelation after revelation of abuses of power by the Federal government. Nixon's resignation did not close the books but on the contrary led to closer scrutiny of government attacks on the political freedom of radicals during the previous twenty-five years. Watergate was followed by revelations of massive illegal FBI and CIA surveillance of Americans that began under FDR and took a great leap forward on the orders of Lyndon Johnson; of American efforts to "destabilize" Chile, Kennedy's secret war against Cuba, and so on. And it was congressional liberals and the Yankee press who did the investigating and made the revelations. In so doing, it is they who provided evidence for the case Marxists themselves were making during the Watergate crisis: Nixon's acts were not unique but were part of a pattern of repression that includes the nation's most celebrated liberal presidents. In this respect, what has occurred is not a relegitimation of politics as usual but, on the contrary, a legitimizing of crucial elements of the radical critique of 1960s liberalism, previously viewed as a paranoid fantasy. Those who savor paradox and irony will find this development particularly tasty.

Dissent, Spring 1976

40

Tom Hayden's New Workout

Tom Hayden, searching for "a new political center for the Democratic Party," closed down his ten-year-old Campaign for Economic Democracy (CED) in fall, 1986, and established a new organization, Campaign California. The group was to be "less critical of business," Hayden has said, and "more supportive of the private entrepreneur as a source of economic growth, jobs and innovation." That emphasis was to appeal to a constituency Hayden calls frumpies, "formerly radical, upwardly mobile young professionals."

At its height, in the late 1970s and early 1980s, CED had thirty chapters and 8,000 members; it was California's largest single organized force on the left. Hayden came up with the idea for the group in 1975, arguing that Watergate and the US defeat in Vietnam had created an opening in electoral politics that the left should explore. His campaign for the Senate the following year was a test of that theory. Against John Tunney in the California Democratic primary, Hayden made "economic democracy" the campaign's standard. He received nearly 40 per cent of the total, an astonishing 1.2 million votes for the former antiwar activist. CED was founded in early 1977 to continue the same strategy. The group planned to challenge corporate power by electing local officials. Its statement of purpose declared, "Economic democracy means that ownership and control will be spread among a wide variety of public bodies: city, state and Federal governments, churches, trade unions, cooperatives and community groups, small business people, workers and consumers." The organization attacked corporations for endangering the environment with toxic emissions; it organized renters to fight landlords, argued that research and development of solar energy were being thwarted by the energy multi-nationals, and made pro-choice politics a top priority.

CED's electoral strategy met with success; the group elected more than fifty of its members to city and county offices, including Hayden himself, who was elected to the State Assembly in 1982. Other CED candidates won elections in Berkeley, Oakland, Los Angeles, Davis, Santa Cruz, Santa Monica and three California counties. CED-backed referendums on rent control won in four California cities. Hayden established close ties to California Governor Jerry Brown, and CED members held one-quarter of the delegate seats on the Democratic State Central Committee. In 1984 CED registered 110,000 new Democrats.

Among its other accomplishments, the organization owned the most successful business in the history of the left: Jane Fonda's Workout. Jack Nicholl, Campaign California's director, explained: "CED never could raise enough money, and was always going to Jane. In 1979 she said, 'Why don't I start a little business; you can own it and make the money.'" The Workout began as an exercise studio in Los Angeles. Then came the book, the record, the video. The original "Jane Fonda's Workout" was the best-selling videocassette of all time; more than 1 million have been sold. The original Workout book sold more than 2 million copies. The profits from Workout videos, books and records all went to CED. By 1982 the group had earned enough from the Workout to establish an endowment to fund its operations for the fore-seeable future. Since then, according to Nicholl, the business's profits have gone to Fonda alone. It is rumored that the Workout earned $18 million for CED. The group refuses to make public the actual figure, but Nicholl has said, "We didn't get half that much." One of CED's chief activities has been the affirmative investment of its Workout endowment. Nicholl says the income from those investments will be $850,000 in 1986; the organization raises another $800,000 each year through door-to-door canvassing.

Why did Hayden abandon the banner of economic democracy? CED's electoral success was its downfall as a grass-roots organization, he argued; half its activists ended up working in local government in the early 1980s—some as elected officials, others on their staffs or on rent control boards or city planning commissions. Derek Shearer, co-author, with Martin Carnoy, of *Economic Democracy*, worked on the program for Hayden's Senate race. He has a different analysis: "CED was not sustained and nurtured because Tom's needs as an elected official had a higher priority than developing the grass-roots organization. Tom didn't want the grass-roots out of sync with his strategy in the legislature." Hayden has admitted in retrospect that "1982 was the end." That was the year he won his Assembly seat, and George Deukmejian replaced Jerry Brown in the governor's office. Some CED activists disagreed with Hayden's priorities and took on other commitments; others burned out. Hayden couldn't attract younger, post-sixties people to the group. The thirty chapters, which had recruited and trained activists in electoral politics, became moribund. Thus, closing down the organization was simply facing reality.

Hayden continues to call himself a progressive; he told me that he wants to "build a progressive politics in California that can deliver California in 1988 to the Democratic nominee so we can win the presidency." He added that "those of us who are in progressive politics want to be part of a majority party, instead of a wing of a minority party that's out of power." His strategy in the 1986 election focused on a statewide antitoxics initiative, Proposition 65, to bar companies from releasing carcinogenic chemicals into drinking water. The "Get tough on toxics" campaign, which Hayden chaired, explicitly went after the oil and chemical corporations. "Big chemical companies and major industrial polluters are trying desperately to stop Proposition 65," its television advertisements warned. Those corporations spent more than $5 million to defeat the proposition, against the campaign's $1.7 million. Although virtually all the major newspapers in the state opposed the measure, the initiative won handsomely, with 63 per cent of the vote.

Despite the shift in his organization, Hayden says he continues to believe in the agenda he put forward in *The Nation* in 1981: energy conservation, taxing the corporate rich, a "Spartan" national security, overcoming economic discrimination, democratic control of investments from pension funds, and "a new partnership in making economic decisions among corporations, labor, government, and public-interest groups." What's different is Hayden's emphasis on encouraging entrepreneurial activity. "When America was a growing economic power, it was appropriate to be a consumer advocate, a labor advocate, a minority advocate, trying to redistribute the wealth generated by the private economy. But now the US is in a relative economic decline in a highly competitive new arena called the Pacific Rim.... The Democrats have to become much more involved in fostering an entrepreneurial strategy." For that reason he favors restoring tax breaks for entrepreneurs. Hayden adds that such a strategy has to be "tied to environmental protection and employee rights," but he doesn't say how those conflicting interests will be harmonized. The entrepreneurial emphasis is part of Hayden's political strategy for the Democrats. "There's a class of younger people out there who are successful in business, or who want to be, but who don't want to give up the values they had in the 1960s," he says. "They feel rebuffed by the Democratic Party, but they feel very uncomfortable with the Republicans, especially with their social morality and their military policies." Gary Hart was the candidate who appealed most to this group, and Hayden was a Hart supporter in the 1988 primaries. Yet union members, minorities and women who work outside the home, among others, have very different interests and needs; why they would ally with Hayden's frumpies is hard to see.

The name "Campaign California" is part of Hayden's new strategy. It was selected after extensive testing of focus groups. Hayden hopes "yuppies, new-collar workers, baby boomers, sixties people"—the target constituency of his new organization—will associate the name with the Eagles song that begins "Welcome to the Hotel California." He may have forgotten that the song concludes, "You can check out any time you like, but you can never leave." Hayden defends the name change. " 'Campaign California' doesn't mean anything in particular, but going door to door we found that 'economic democracy' didn't mean anything either. We fell into the oldest trap of the left, associating ourselves with vaguely European phrases and ideas. Our experience was that people could be brought into the organization around rent control, toxics cleanup, child care, pro-choice—issues that embody the idea that people, not economic elites, should have more control over their lives. But people don't understand the generality without the specifics. 'Economic democracy' was incomprehensible except to intellectuals."

"Tom Hayden gives opportunism a bad name." That line has been attributed to Gore Vidal, but the sentiment is held by many on the left, and it is not new. His critics point to some recent cases: shortly after the Russians shot down Korean Air Lines Flight 007 in 1984, Hayden spoke at a protest rally in Los Angeles. He attacked the Reagan Administration for not being "anti-Communist" enough and called for a boycott of Stolichnaya vodka. "Anyone drinking Russian vodka after this atrocity is washing down the blood of innocent people," Hayden told the crowd, which consisted mostly of Korean-Americans and members of the anti-Soviet Baltic American Freedom League. Members of the audience weren't convinced of his sincerity. They chanted back, "Once a commie, always a commie!" In 1986 Hayden said nothing had changed his mind about the KAL incident. He rejected Seymour Hersh's evidence that Reagan lied about the Soviet Union's motives, commenting, "I find people who are unable to criticize the Soviet Union to be fundamentally incapacitated."

Hayden reached the heights of opportunism, his critics argue, in July of 1982, when he visited Israel during the invasion of Lebanon. Hayden and Fonda declared their support for the invasion and visited wounded Israeli troops in Lebanon. Hayden was running for State Assembly at the time; Jewish voters formed a key group in his district; a Jews-against-Hayden organization had been put together; and his opponents charged that he was sympathetic to the Palestine Liberation Organization. Even Hayden's critics agree that unqualified support for Israel is a prerequisite for Democratic candidates, especially in a strongly Jewish district like Hayden's. "The Israel issue provides an easy way for the left to beat up on Tom Hayden," says Sam Hurst, who was Hayden's press secretary in the 1976 Senate campaign and CED's staff director from 1977 to 1980. "But the left shouldn't ask an Irish Catholic running in a heavily Jewish district to lead the Jews toward a progressive policy on Israel. It's absurd." Derek Shearer disagrees, "In public Tom can't say critical things about Israel, but going to Israel while they are invading Lebanon is different. He didn't have to do that."

While people on the left criticize Hayden for shifting to the right, the right attacks him for his radical past. That constituted the central battle of his 1982 campaign. Hayden's opponent in the primary bought a full-page advertisement in the *Los Angeles Times* and reprinted passages from Hayden's 1970 book, *Trial*: "We want to abolish a private property system which ... benefits only a few while colliding violently with the aspirations of people all over the world." Hayden responded to his right-wing critics with a 24-page glossy booklet, *Growing Up With America: the Life Story of Tom Hayden.* It offered a version of his life sharply at odds with what most people on the left remember. The booklet described Hayden's "roots in Middle America," his ties to Martin Luther King Jr, his arrest as a "young civil rights worker" in Georgia in 1961, his role in ending "riots in Newark" and in bringing home US prisoners of war from Vietnam, and his ties with Jimmy Carter and Jerry Brown. The centerfold was a four-color photo of Tom fishing with Henry Fonda; the booklet concluded with a quote from Jane: "Great as he is in bringing citizens together, he's also great at keeping a family together."

Hayden's election didn't end the right-wing attacks. In summer 1986 veterans' groups gathered 258,000 signatures on petitions demanding that he be ousted from his seat in the Assembly, on the ground that his four trips to Hanoi during the Vietnam War consti- tuted treason. Hayden "was not a simple, spit-on-the-flag, burn-your- draft-card protester," declared Republican Assemblyman Gil Fergusen, a 63-year-old retired Marine lieutenant colonel. "Tom Hayden was a traitor." California Representative Robert Dorman joined the attack, calling Hayden "a traitor, a liar and a coward." The Assembly vote took place while the Veterans of Foreign Wars and the American Legion were holding their state conventions, and the two groups turned out two hundred anti-Hayden demonstrators at the State Capitol.

Hayden defended himself in an emotional speech to the Assembly. "I am a patriotic American," he said. Legionnaires who had packed the galleries roared their disagreement. "I'm not the kind of patriot who believes 'My country, right or wrong,' but I'm the kind of patriot who believes, 'My country, let's right its wrongs.'" He told the Assembly that, on his trips to North Vietnam during the war, he "was in contact with ... State Department representatives [and] with members of our intelligence community" to win the release of prisoners of war. That came as a surprise to many on the left. He admitted that he had "made mistakes" as an antiwar leader: "I'll always regret ... the way in which my anger drove me to extreme positions." He assured the Assembly that he was "not the same angry young man I was twenty years ago." The Assembly voted along partisan lines, 41 to 36, not to expel him; he was reelected November 4, 1986, with 59 per cent of the vote after a campaign that cost him less than $100,000.

For the left, the costs of having Hayden as an elected official are greater than the benefits, according to Shearer. "If there had been an organized left movement that was democratic, it wouldn't necessarily have said Tom should be the candidate," he said. "It might have said the candidate should be a feminist or an environmentalist or a labor person. Another candidate would vote the same as Hayden in the Assembly and could be even more effective because he or she wouldn't be attacked for Vietnam the way Hayden has been. But no discussion like that took place. CED people were told, 'Tom wants to run.'" As Hurst said, pointing out that electing Hayden to the Assembly cost $1.7 million, "Tom's campaign was like using cannons to ring door-bells." Stanley Sheinbaum, a Californian active in progressive politics, agreed that the left lost more than it gained when Hayden won his office: "California lost its best organizer when Tom went to the Assembly." Since becoming an elected official, Hayden has to "watch what he says and what he writes," according to Shearer. "Everything has to be guarded." Hayden doesn't dare alienate Democrats in the Assembly; as was demonstrated in July 1986, he needs virtually every one of their votes to protect him from being expelled.

Hayden has replied that he's still organizing and still independent, pointing to the statewide antitoxics initiative. "The Democrats in the Legislature are too influenced by industry to be able to take a strong position against toxics. My choice was to go over their heads, behind their backs, directly to their voters." His defenders argue that his Assembly seat gives him a platform and a legitimacy in pushing a progressive agenda that he would otherwise lack. "Now he's identified as the Democratic Assemblyman from Santa Monica. If he didn't have that, where would he be?" asked Stephen Rivers, a spokesman for Fonda, who was Hayden's press secretary in 1979. "He'd still be the 'former antiwar activist.'"

Hayden has been trapped in a contradiction, according to Hurst. "On the one hand Tom has an analysis that says liberalism is bank-rupt. On the other hand he has a strategy that calls for an alliance with liberals. He has to work every day with liberals. The Democratic Party doesn't like Tom Hayden. It doesn't want Tom. For them he's too principled, too capable, too talented. But it has to deal with him because he has his own base and is powerful. Tom's torment is that he's not a liberal Democrat. He has a terrible time trying to be one. As a result he's floundering politically."

At issue is the future of the Democratic Party. Economic democracy constituted an alternative agenda aimed at restoring the Democrats' identification with the people. Political consultant Bill Zimmerman managed Hayden's Senate campaign. He directed Harold Washington's 1983 mayoral race in Chicago and Gary Hart's 1984 presidential nomination bid, among other campaigns. "This is precisely the time when economic democracy becomes a salable concept," he says. "For the first time in generations we have a common perception that the economy is screwed up: our standard of living is going down, our children won't have the same advantages we did. As a result, there is enormous dissatisfaction and confusion. The problem is to organize that feeling, structure it and point it in the direction of a solution." Even if Tom Hayden has given up that project, it ought to remain at the top of the progressive agenda.

The Nation, November 29, 1986

41

The Other Nancy Davis:

Not Necessarily the First Lady

Nancy and Ronald Reagan met, they have repeatedly said, when she was blacklisted by mistake in the early 1950s after having been confused with another actress who had the same name, Nancy Davis. The other Nancy Davis, they said, really was a Communist. Reagan, then president of the Screen Actors' Guild, helped the first Nancy prove she wasn't the Communist Nancy Davis, and she was able to work again. Along the way they fell in love, and the rest is history. In 1987, the other Nancy Davis was working at a snack bar in Ventura, California. "She's been lying about me for years," she said of the First Lady. "I never was a Communist. I told Reagan back in the fifties that if she didn't stop saying I was a Communist, I'd sue her."

Ronald Reagan wrote in his autobiography, *Where's the Rest of Me?*, that because his wife-to-be was assumed to be the other Nancy Davis, "her name kept showing up on rosters of Communist front organizations, affixed to petitions of the same coloration, and her mail frequently included notices of meetings she had no desire to attend, and accounts of these meetings as covered by the *Daily Worker.*" The events he described took place in 1953, according to Anne Edwards's recently published *Early Reagan*, based in part on SAG archives. Nancy Davis Reagan was asked by Columbia Pictures to explain why her maiden name appeared on the amicus curiae brief supporting the Hollywood Ten. Ron, who was by then her husband, contacted B.B. Kahane, Columbia vice president in charge of security, indignantly explaining that there were two Nancy Davises and that the other one was the Communist.

Nancy herself demanded an apology, and got one from Kahane:

"Of course, we could have taken it for granted that the wife of Ronald Reagan could not possibly be of questionable loyalty and could have disregarded that report." You could call that innocence by association. Kahane continued: "But as the citation was merely the signing of the amicus curiae brief and many persons signed this brief who we have been convinced are not now and never were Communists or sympathizers, we informed you of the citation believing that a satisfactory explanation would be forthcoming."

That was a lot nicer than the letter Kahane had written to Rita Hayworth's attorney, Martin Gang, the previous year, when Kahane sought to clear her name from the blacklist. Hayworth, unlike Nancy Reagan, was asked to submit a sworn statement that "should set forth the fact (if, as I assume, it is a fact) that she is not now and never has been a member of the Communist Party. It should also contain a positive, forthright affirmation of her loyalty to the United States and I hope, a strong condemnation of Communistic subversive groups and ideologies."

Kahane's letter to Nancy contained one striking admission: the studio recognized that not all supporters of the Hollywood Ten were Communists or "sympathizers." Obviously, this included the Nancy Davis who had signed the brief. Nevertheless, Nancy Davis Reagan has repeatedly described the other Nancy Davis as a Communist. "It's not true," said the other Nancy Davis, who skated in several Sonja Henie movies. "I didn't have anything to do with the Communists. I never signed anything about the Hollywood Ten. After I threatened to sue her, she stopped saying those things for a while. Then in the eighties it's begun again.

"It is true that we were confused with each other. I'd get her paychecks and she'd get mine. Hers were bigger. We'd exchange them. And once I got an invitation to a fancy event at the Beverly Hills Hotel; it said, 'Bring Mr Reagan.' I brought Tony Reagan; he was a casting director at Paramount." The other Nancy was summoned to a meeting with SAG president Reagan to discuss the "two Nancys" problem. "He told me I had to change my name," she recalled. "He suggested I use 'Nancy Lee Davis.' I told him I wouldn't; I was the first Nancy Davis in the guild, so under the rules she had to change her name. But he was the boss, and he insisted. I realized he could cause me a lot of trouble. So I changed my name."

After Nancy Davis Reagan was cleared to work in 1953, she appeared in a supporting role in *Donovan's Brain*. In the film, an evil tycoon dies and his brain is kept alive by a scientist, played by Lew Ayres; the brain takes the scientist over and makes him do terrible things. (The film was recently brought to life with William Casey as the dead tycoon and Reagan himself in the Lew Ayres role.)

What about Nancy and Ronald Reagan's story that they met and fell in love when he cleared Nancy of charges that she was associated with Communists? It couldn't have happened the way they said it did because, according to Anne Edwards, Nancy Davis Reagan was not linked to the Hollywood Ten by Columbia Pictures until 1953, when she was already married to the future President. In fact they had met in 1949, when, according to Edwards, Nancy had told producer Dore Schary's wife, Miriam, she wanted to meet Reagan, and the Scharys invited both to a small dinner party. The Scharys' daughter, author Jill Robinson, recalled the evening: Reagan described the evils of Communism and Nancy "kept smiling at him in agreement." Soon after, Reagan's brother Neil told a friend, "It looks as if this one has her hooks in him."

Thus there were two Nancy Davises in Hollywood in the early 1950s. One called the other a Communist. That was not true. The first one ended up in the White House, and the other one ended up in Ventura, California, flipping burgers in a snack bar. That's show business in America.

The Nation, October 3, 1987

POSTSCRIPT

42

Footnote—Or Perish

A footnote appears, at first sight, a trivial thing, and easily understood. But in the pages of the new *Social Sciences Citation Index*, these scholarly creations step forth as independent beings, endowed with a life of their own. The *Citation Index* is the most recent, and most titanic, achievement of the burgeoning information storage and retrieval industry. It is dedicated to the proposition that the best way to find out what an article is about is not to look at its title, but at its footnotes. As the publicity brochure explains, "no human indexer has to decide what is the subject of an article. The author of a new article indexes his own work through his references." The *Citation Index* thus "breaks the subject index barrier." An author who footnotes sources you consider to be important ought to be consulted, and an article that fails to footnote the important sources is probably not worth reading. With this notion in mind, the *Citation Index* has taken on the herculean task of indexing the footnotes in 3,000 social science journals in twenty-six languages. You look up an author, and the *Citation Index* refers you to all the articles, published in a given period, which have cited various works of his.

The *Citation Index* lists something like 175,000 citations of 125,000 articles by 100,000 social scientists, and it does this every four months. In a year, it indexes around half a million footnotes from 80,000 articles. Of the 3,000 journals whose footnotes are indexed, 1,000 receive "full coverage"—every footnote to a different source is punched into a database, fed into the computer, and published in the next issue of the *Citation Index*. The other 2,000 journals receive "selective coverage" of the appropriately social-scientific articles they publish. In a four-month period, the average social scientist (of the 100,000 who are footnoted) has 1.2 articles cited, and he is cited on the average 1.7 times. In fact, a small number of scholars are cited hundreds of times a year, while the majority are cited once per issue.

The purpose of the *Citation Index*, according to its advocates, is not only to serve as a reference tool, but also to "identify" the scholars "who have had a major impact on their fields," those "who have truly influenced the course of science."[1] "True influence" and "impact" are measured by frequency of citation; the more often you are footnoted, the greater your intellectual contribution, the more valuable your scholarly work. To the extent that the *Citation Index* becomes an accepted measure of scholarly importance, it will play a role in promotion and tenure of college and university staff, alongside the more traditional methods of evaluation. As one citation authority has written, "it was a logical step" to use the *Citation Index* to "measure current performance of scholars." If a young social scientist is footnoted often, his work will be judged important and valuable by his superiors, and he will be promoted; if no one footnotes somebody's work, that will be an argument for firing him. To paraphrase Thomas Hobbes: to be cited regularly, is felicity; to be cited most, bliss; and not to be cited at all, death.

All this may seem fanciful; it is not. The prestigious journal *Science* has run a series of articles arguing that the "quality of scientific output" of an author can be accurately measured by the number of citations he receives, that the number of citations provides the best available measure of the "value" of an author's work, that the "best" contributions are among those cited most, and the "least important" attract few, if any, citations, and that an author's "outstanding" work is the one that is cited most often.[2] An article in the British journal *Nature* claims that "valid correlations can be obtained between individual performance and citation counts"; ominously, this finding was reported in the *IEEE Transactions on Military Electronics.*[3] Such a claim

---

1. Eugene Garfield, "Citation Indexing for Studying Science," *Nature* 227 (1970), pp. 669–71.

2. Jonathan R. Cole and Stephen Cole, "The Ortega Hypothesis," *Science* 178 (1972), pp. 369–70; J. Margolis, "Citation Indexing and Evaluation of Scientific Papers," *Science* 156 (1967), p. 1213.

3. Garfield, *Nature.*

may send a chill down the spines of assistant professors; what is this "performance" that military electronics experts have tied to our footnotes?

The potential of citation indexing for measuring academic status can be seen in a pre-*Citation Index* study of the *American Sociological Review*, comparing individuals' citation frequencies for 1958–62 with those for 1967–68 in the same journal.[4] The five most often cited sociologists between 1958 and 1962 were, in order, Durkheim, Parsons, Shils, Sorokin, and Lazarsfeld; in 1967–68, the top five were Lipset, Parsons, Merton, Etzioni, and Goode. Of the ten most often cited sociologists in 1958–62, only four remained in the top ten six years later.

The fastest rising sociologist for this period was Seymour Martin Lipset, who rose from eleventh to first. Among those who dropped off the list of the top twenty-two were not only Shils and Sorokin, but Max Weber himself. Durkheim also took a big fall, from first to fifteenth. Predictably, Parsons was the only one to remain at the top of the list for both periods. Fully fifteen of the twenty-two most often cited sociologists in 1967–68 were not on the list for 1958–62.

The name Karl Marx does not appear among the twenty-two most frequently cited scholars for either period; one would have to conclude that his work had little "impact" on sociology, that it lacked "quality," and that it is not among the "best contributions" to the field.

The frequency of publication of the *Citation Index*—three times a year—offers the potential of regularly updated measures of intellectual status. The computer could easily list authors in order of the number of their citations every four months; the sister publication *Science Citation Index* already lists the top fifty scientists each year in order of citation frequency. It is possible to rank-order all 100,000 social scientists three times a year. For an individual to move from, say, the 85,274th most often cited social scientist in May, to the 67,319th in December, would be an indication of intellectual growth and increasing status, a reason to go out to dinner, if not to ask for a promotion.

---

4. M.J. Oromaner, "Contemporary American and British Sociology," *British Journal of Sociology* (1970), p. 329.

Of course almost everyone is cited once or twice, so it is only at the top that real distinctions could be made. This makes often cited social scientists something like professional athletes—citations are like home runs, citation rates like batting averages. Presumably there is a Babe Ruth of lifetime citations (Talcott Parsons?), and the academic world is waiting for the Hank Aaron who will challenge him (Seymour Martin Lipset?). The *Citation Index* can be used to identify fast-rising rookies, players at the peak of their careers, and over-the-hill performers, along with those who peaked too soon. The year-by-year pattern of citations provides a concrete quantitative measure of an individual's intellectual development: Professor X started his rise in 1963, hit his peak in 1970 with his most often cited work, and has been resting on his laurels ever since, having the same old articles cited, and slowly sliding downhill in the rankings. Intellectual styles are reflected in the patterns of citations: some authors are cited at a slow and steady pace, while others alternate flashy peaks with long troughs of inactivity (teaching? administration? mental depression?).

The *Citation Index*'s computer data bank is updated weekly. Dissemination of weekly changes in citation frequency rates and rankings could provide an extremely sensitive measure of intellectual status. One imagines the eventual establishment of a social science ticker tape, which would spread citation rates to the offices of deans and department chairmen instantaneously. (A burst of noise from the ticker; the dean rushes over and reads off the sputtering tape, "Dan Bell up 6.")

The *Citation Index* can be used not only to see who has the most footnotes of all, but to compare the citation rates of authors of related works to see who has had the greater "impact," whose "contribution" to a particular area has been more "significant." For instance, if we consider theorists of comparative modernization, we find that Samuel P. Huntington's *Political Order in Changing Societies* was cited in 16 different articles in four months of 1973, Barrington Moore Jr's *Social Origins of Dictatorship and Democracy* got 10, and Cyril Black's *Dynamics of Modernization* got only 4. (Black need not despair; he might demand that his publisher advertise more, or bring out a cheaper paperback edition, to get more books in the hands of potential footnoters; simply insisting that his own graduate students footnote him more often could raise his citation rate considerably.)

Publishers of the *Citation Index* have suggested a further use for their product: citation frequencies should be the basis of awarding prizes, grants, and fellowships. The *Citation Index* will be useful for "efficient management" of "increasingly scarce intellectual and financial resources."[5] To further such use in the sciences, the *Science Citation Index* plans to rank the 20,000 most cited papers each year, and has listed the fifty most often cited authors in rank order each year.

If citation indexing becomes a basis for promotion and tenure, for grants and fellowships, the implications for one's own footnotes are clear. In the marketplace of ideas, the footnote is the unit of currency; to footnote an author is to cast a vote for his tenure or grant. One should therefore be judicious in his footnoting: footnote friends and don't footnote enemies. The most likely consequence will be an inflation of citations; as the importance of being footnoted becomes increasingly clear, each author will footnote more people—to gain their friendship and their footnotes in return. The average number of citations per author will creep up, and the standards will have to be revised to reflect the new footnoting practices.

One must remember that the median citation rate is around one footnote per scholar every four months. If one friend cites you in an indexed journal, you are listed in the *Citation Index*, and you avoid falling into that terrible class of the never-cited. Thus one should definitely footnote his friends (once in an article is all that counts), and do what is possible to see that that they footnote you in return (send them offprints, suggest relevant references to your work, etc.).

The easiest way to avoid the dustbin of the uncited is to cite oneself. From the viewpoint of the citation indexers, this is perfectly kosher; for all the computer knows, another person with your name is citing you. (Indeed, if there is another social scientist among the listed 100,000 with your last name and initials, the *Citation Index* considers the two of you to be a single person, and intermingles your footnotes indiscriminately.) Every article of yours ought to cite your other published works—once is enough for each. However, it is undesirable if the only citations to your work come from yourself. This is not a substitute for friends' citations, it is merely a way of boosting your rate. To paraphrase Rabbi Hillel: if I do not cite myself, who will? If I cite myself

5. Garfield, *Nature.*

alone, what am I? And if not in this article, when? (To the question, "If I cite myself alone, what am I?" a sociologist of science has answered, "parochial, eccentric, mediocre.")

All of these procedures have been practiced with a vengeance by Eugene Garfield, founder and president of the *Citation Index*'s parent firm (and also its publisher: the Institute for Scientific Information, in Philadelphia).

The *Citation Index* lists 21 articles written by Garfield, which were referred to a total of 19 times in the indexed journals in four months of 1973. This puts Garfield high in the citation frequency rankings—higher than Robert Merton or Daniel Bell, for instance. Close inspection of his citations reveals the following: of Garfield's 21 articles, 13 are cited only by himself; of the 19 references to Garfield's *Corpus*, 15 come from himself. That's a self-citation rate of 79 per cent. And, of his 21 articles, 9 were published in *Current Contents*, of which Garfield himself is founder, publisher, and editor. Perhaps, as president of the firm that publishes the *Index*, Garfield is entitled to take these liberties.

The *Citation Index* is intended not only to provide a quantitative basis for firing or promoting you, but also to refer people to your work. This has further implications for the structure of one's own footnotes. Potential readers, using the *Citation Index*, are led to your published work by your footnotes; thus the more footnotes you have, the more people using the *Citation Index* are likely to come up with a reference to your article. The key is not just adding more footnotes to your articles, but adding wide-ranging footnotes that may be only tenuously related to your topic. Even if a footnote is not altogether appropriate, someone may still be led to read your article as a result of finding its footnotes in the *Citation Index*.

These implications for altering one's own footnoting practices have further implications for journal editors and referees. Increasingly they will become the arbiters of what is a legitimate footnote and what is simply an attempt to advance a friend's work, improve one's own citation rate, or draw the attention of users of the *Citation Index*. It will be up to journal editors to permit, or to eliminate, such footnotes. (Those submitting articles might seek to avoid criticism of their footnotes with a few judicious citations of works by the editors of the journal in question.)

Citation indexing has more far-reaching implications for journal editors. The five-year cumulation of the sister publication *Science Citation Index* listed not just authors, but also journals in order of frequency of citation. Not surprisingly, 1 per cent of the scientific journals received 24 per cent of all the references, and 6 per cent of the journals received half the citations. Half of all articles footnoted at least one of the twenty-five most frequently cited journals at least once.[6]

The same conclusion has been drawn about journals as about individual scholars: in the words of the leading advocate of citation indexing, "citation frequency reflects a journal's value."[7] He suggests that frequency of citation should be the basis of library subscriptions; citation frequency "provides a solid basis for cost-benefit analysis in the management of subscription budgets." To assist librarians in this task, the creators of the *Citation Index* also publish *Journal Citation Reports*, listing citations by journal instead of author. If a journal isn't footnoted often, it's not "useful to the scientific community"; it's not worth reading, and thus not worth a library subscription—which will make certain that even fewer read the more obscure articles.

Editors thus need to be concerned about the citation rate of their own journals, and ought to seek to avoid the downward spiral of a decreasing citation rate bringing about a decline among library subscriptions. The simplest method by which editors can keep their journal's citation rates high is to make sure each article in their journal footnotes other articles in earlier issues of the same journal. Editors would thus want to suggest the addition of appropriate footnotes in articles accepted for publication, or perhaps reject articles whose footnotes do not contribute to the citation rate, and thus survival, of the journal.

The *Citation Index*'s creators also believe the index can help editors select articles for publication by providing standards to determine what constitutes up-to-date footnotes. Sociologists of science who study citation patterns have concluded that it is more scientific to footnote recent works than older ones. It is a characteristic of science, we are told, that "new contributions will supersede old ones," and this

---

6. Eugene Garfield, "Citation Analysis as a Tool in Journal Evaluation," *Science* 178 (1972), pp. 474–5.

7. Garfield, *Science*.

"should be observable in the distribution of footnote citations." We can tell that physics is more scientific than sociology because 50 per cent of cited physics articles in a recent journal-year were less than three years old, while 50 per cent of sociology footnotes were more than six years old. What is true of fields is also true of individual articles.[8] The *Citation Index* can provide averages to suggest what the acceptable "half-life" of references ought to be in a genuinely "scientific" work; presumably, editors of social science journals should look suspiciously on articles submitted for publication whose footnotes are primarily to works more than seven or eight years old.

The publishers of the *Citation Index* believe it can indicate "how each brick in the edifice of science is linked to all the others"; it will rewrite the intellectual history of social science, and the rewriting will be done by a computer.

> In the near future a historian or sociometrist will be able to sit before a computer console and specify some starting point—a person, a word, a citation.... The computer will respond by drawing or displaying a historical road map which will show ... a graphical approximation of the history of that subject.[9]

The computer will do this by tracing citations back into the past. Talcott Parsons footnotes Durkheim and Weber; therefore he was influenced by Durkheim and Weber. Parsons does not footnote Marx; therefore Marx's work did not influence Parsons. The computer console thus will dispense with such arguments as Alvin Gouldner's, that Parsons can only be understood as an attempt to come up with a conservative alternative to Marxism during a time of capitalist crisis.

The publishers of the *Citation Index* offer a wide range of other "information services." The "Automatic Subject Citation Alert" is an "individualized, computer-produced, weekly alerting service" which will send you the latest footnotes every week from 3,200 journals on a topic of your choice. You could, for instance, receive weekly listings of

---

8. Duncan McRae Jr. "Growth and Decay Curves in Scientific Citations," *American Sociological Review* 34 (1969), pp. 631, 634.

9. Garfield, *Nature*. See also N.C. Janke and Kenneth O. May, "Abuses of Citation Indexing." *Science* 156 (1967), pp. 890–92.

all articles in the 3,200 indexed journals which footnoted you. For those scholars at the low end of the citation frequency lists, this experience could be depressing: to be informed every week, month after month, that no one cited you this week.

Current Contents is in some ways the boldest of all the related publications; it is a weekly journal which consists solely of reproductions of the tables of contents of "the important journals." For this intellectual breakthrough, it received the first "Information Hall of Fame Award."

But there is one group of social science writers and editors that need not concern themselves with any of the foregoing: those whose published work appears beyond the pale of the indexed journals. No computer database contains the references in their work. In fact, the editors of the *Citation Index* made some curious choices about which journals to index and which to exclude. Among the 3,200 indexed journals, selective coverage is given to such unlikely titles as *Mosquito News, Soap/Cosmetics, Digestion*, and to the *Tasmanian Journal of Agriculture*, but there is no coverage at all of journals like the *Review of Radical Political Economy, Radical America, Socialist Review, Telos, Insurgent Sociologist* or *Monthly Review*, to name a few. If a footnote to your work appears in *Commentary* or *The Public Interest*, you get counted; if it appears in *New Politics*, or *New Left Review*, or *Dissent*, you don't. Could it be that there is some logic behind these choices of the editors? Those who want their work to be indexed ought to ponder this question with particular care.

Dissent, Fall 1974

Index

INDEX

civil rights movement 217–23
    and radical history 179, 191–2
    and SDS 239
    Sinatra and 263–5
The Clash 301
Class Conflict, Slavery, and the Constitution
    (Lynd) 195–6
Cloak and Gown (Winks) 119–24
Closing of the American Mind (Bloom) 99,
    102
Cockburn, Alexander 169–70
Cockburn, Patrick 169–70
Cohn, Avern, Judge 136, 138–9
Cohn, Harry 266
COINTELPRO 236–7
"Cold Turkey" (Lennon) 295
Cold War and radical history 185–6
Cold War ideology 71–8
Cole, William 144–5
Collapse of the Weimar Republic
    (Abraham) 63–70, 106–7
Collier, Peter 102
Colson, Charles, would stomp
    grandmother for Nixon 309
Columbia University 120, 159–60,
    163
"Coming in from the Cold" (Marley)
    301
Commentary 56, 189
Communist Party 168–71, 231, 254–5
    and Boorstin 55–9
    British, and historians 114–15
    and history-writing 183
    Nancy Reagan accused of links with
        333–5
    Frank Sinatra accused of links with
        263–9
Confessions (Rousseau) 6
confrontation tactics 154, 220
Congress on Racial Equality (CORE)
    231, 301
Congressional Black Caucus 59
Connolly, John 318
consensus history 209–10
conservative academics 112–18, 166–8
    and Accuracy in Academia 109–12
    Continuity and 115–16
    foundation grants to 99–103
    humanities agenda of 116

journals of 115–16
National Assocation of Scholars
    166–8
New Criterion and 112–14
    and radical history 112–14, 175–216
Reagan Administration support for
    116
Continuity 115–16
Contours of American History (Williams)
    176, 182
contra aid, opposed by Organization of
    American Historians 118
Cooke, Sam 299
Cooper, Susan 272
CORE (Congress on Racial Equality)
    231, 301
Cornell University 18, 154, 181
Corngold, Stanley 14
corporate liberalism thesis 186–8
corporations, ties to universities 87–93
Corsini, Gianfranco 169
Coser, Lewis 152
Cott, Jonathan 301–7
counterculture 224, 241–2, 244–5,
    278–88
Countryman, Matthew 165
Cousins, Norman 231
Cox, Archibald 312
Cox, Harold 220
CREEP (Committee to Reelect the
    President) 310–11
Crenshaw, Kimberlé 131, 133–4
Critical Legal Studies 133–4
Criticism and Social Change (Lentricchia)
    6
Crosby, Bing 268
Csorba, Les 104–11
Culler, Jonathan 17 n2
Curti, Merle 179, 184–5

Daily Worker 56, 255
Daley, Richard 226, 245
Dallin, Alexander 79–80
Darnton, Robert 113
Dartmouth College 144–5, 159
Dartmouth Review 146
Davies, Norman 79–86
Davis, Nancy 333–5
Davis, Natalie 63, 117–18, 207

and Nazi collaborators 71–2, 74
profit-making by 87–93
recipient of Olin grant 100, 102
Russian Research Center 71–2, 74, 77
strike (1969) 224
Harvard Watch 91
Hatfield, Mark 59
Hawkins, Augustus F. 27
Hayden, Tom
California Assembly campaign 329–32
Campaign California formed 325–32
Campaign for Economic Democracy closed 325–7
and Democratic National Convention, 1968 Chicago 236, 245
1976 Senate campaign 325
1981 agenda 327–8
North Vietnam trip 195, 236
patriotism of 330
and Port Huron Statement 232–3
and SDS 152, 233
Hayes, Carlton J.H. 123
Hayes, Woody 271
Haynsworth, Clement 276
Hayworth, Rita 265, 334
Healy, Richard 170
Heidegger, Martin 10
"Help Me Make It Through the Night" (Kristofferson) 291
"Help" (Beatles) 295
Henwood, Doug 50
Hersh, Seymour 329
Hertz, Neil 3, 9
Hesseltine, William 184–5
Het Vlaamsche Land 10
Hewitt, Hugh 271
Hexter, J.H. 114
Hicks, Granville 55
high school students, protests by 156–7
Higham, John 177 n2
Highlander Folk School 219
Highway 61 Revisited (Dylan) 304
Hilberg, Raoul 7
Hilburn, Robert 291–2
Hill, Christopher 115
Hilton, Rodney 115

Himmelfarb, Gertrude 113–14
Hirzy, William 61
Hiss, Alger 272–3
historians
and CIA 119–20, 123–4
and freedom of speech, in Norman Davies case 79–86
and McCarthyism 55–7, 62, 179–83, 182–3, 190–91
and politics
in Abraham case 63–70
in Boorstin case 55–62
radical 175–216
see also radical history
as recruiters for CIA 119–20, 123–4
history
black 217–23, 247–59
and causation, in Abraham case 69
College Board examination in 114
de Man's critique of 6–7, 9
from the bottom up 192–3, 203–4
and objectivity, in Norman Davies case 80
profession
critique of, by radical historians 204
changes in, during 1960s 175–216
Nixon's version 270–77
and "truth," in Abraham case 63–70
women's 23–9, 33, 177, 204–7, 209
see also radical history
Hitler, Adolf 4, 17, 73
Hobbes, Thomas 340
Hobsbawm, Eric 114–15, 117, 213–14
Hoffman, Abbie 153, 245
Hofstadter, Richard 179, 185, 200, 209–11
Hofstra University 107
Holdheim, Wolfgang 21
Holley, Charles 147
Hoover, Herbert 48–9
Hoover, J. Edgar
and Martin Luther King Jr 221
and John Lennon 278–88
and SDS 236–7
and Frank Sinatra 264–5
see also FBI
Hopper, Hedda 264
Horowitz, David 102

THE HAYMARKET SERIES

Already Published

BLACK MACHO AND THE MYTH OF THE SUPERWOMAN *by Michele Wallace*

INVISIBILITY BLUES: From Pop to Theory *by Michele Wallace*

THE LEFT AND THE DEMOCRATS *The Year Left 1*

TOWARDS A RAINBOW SOCIALISM *The Year Left 2*

RESHAPING THE US LEFT: Popular Struggles in the 1980s *The Year Left 3*

FIRE IN THE HEARTH: The Radical Politics of Place in America *The Year Left 4*

Forthcoming

GENDER AND CLASS *by Johanna Brenner*

ENCOUNTERS WITH THE SPHINX: Journeys of a Radical in Changing Times *by Alexander Cockburn*

THE MERCURY THEATER: Orson Welles and the Popular Front *by Michael Denning*

THE POLITICS OF SOLIDARITY: Central America and the US Left *by Van Gosse*

JAMAICA 1945–1984 *by Winston James*

BLACK AMERICAN POLITICS: From the Washington Marches to Jesse Jackson (Second Edition) *by Manning Marable*

THE OTHER SIDE: Los Angeles from Both Sides of the Border *by Ruben Martinez*

THE *SOCIALIST REVIEW* READER